THE DIRECTOR

INS

& 1

KII

ST

NCY

LAW IN POLICING: LEGAL REGULATION AND POLICE PRACTICES

CLARENDON STUDIES IN CRIMINOLOGY

Published under the auspices of the Institute of Criminology, University of Cambridge, the Mannheim Centre, London School of Economics, and the Centre for Criminological Research, University of Oxford.

GENERAL EDITOR: ROGER HOOD (University of Oxford)

EDITORS: ANTHONY BOTTOMS and TREVOR BENNETT
(University of Cambridge)

DAVID DOWNES and PAUL ROCK
(London School of Economics)

LUCIA ZEDNER and RICHARD YOUNG
(University of Oxford)

Recent titles in this series:

Prisons and the Problem of Order

SPARKS, BOTTOMS, and HAY

The Local Governance of Crime

CRAWFORD

Policing the Risk Society

ERICSON and HAGGERTY

Crime in Ireland 1945–95: Here be Dragons

BREWER, LOCKHART and RODGERS

Sexed Work: Gender, Race and Resistance in a Brooklyn Drug Market

MAHER

Forthcoming titles:

Victims of White Collar Crime: The Social and Media Construction of Business Fraud

LEVI and PITHOUSE

Procedural Fairness at the Police Station

CHOONGH

Law in Policing: Legal Regulation and Police Practices

David Dixon

CLARENDON PRESS · OXFORD

1997

Oxford University Press, Great Clarendon Street, Oxford OX2 6DP

Oxford New York

Athens Auckland Bangkok Bogota Bombay
Buenos Aires Calcutta Cape Town Dar es Salaam
Delhi Florence Hong Kong Istanbul Karachi
Kuala Lumpur Madras Madrid Melbourne
Mexico City Nairobi Paris Singapore
Taipei Tokyo Toronto
and associated companies in
Berlin Ibadan

Oxford is a trade mark of Oxford University Press

Published in the United States
by Oxford University Press Inc., New York

British Library Cataloguing in Publication Data
Data available

Library of Congress Cataloging in Publication Data
Dixon, David.
Law in policing: legal regulation and police practices / David Dixon.
p. cm.—(Clarendon studies in criminology)
Includes index.
1. Police—Great Britain. 2. Police questioning—Great Britain.
3. Police questioning—Australia. I. Title. II. Series.
KD4839.D59 1997 344.42'052—dc21 97–226
ISBN 0–19–826476–3 (h/b)

1 3 5 7 9 10 8 6 4 2

Typeset by Hope Services (Abingdon) Ltd.
Printed in Great Britain by
Bookcraft Ltd., Midsomer Norton, Somerset

For Crewe and Louis

General Editor's Introduction

Clarendon Studies in Criminology, the successor to *Cambridge Studies in Criminology*, which was founded by Leon Radzinowicz and J.W.C. Turner more than fifty years ago, aims to provide a forum for outstanding work in criminology, criminal justice, penology and the wider field of deviant behaviour. It is edited under the auspices of three criminological centres: the Cambridge Institute of Criminology, the Mannheim Centre for Criminology and Criminal Justice at the London School of Economics, and the Oxford Centre for Criminological Research.

David Dixon's contributions to the debate on the extent to which legal regulation of police powers affect police practices are already well known through his highly regarded articles. In this valuable book *Law in Policing* he critically examines the issues from a wide variety of perspectives: theoretical, comparative, historical and empirical. His central argument is that 'legal regulation and policing practices are inextricably intertwined: their relationship is interactive, one cannot be understood without the other'. This is well illustrated by his analysis of how policing developed differently in England and New South Wales from the same common law base to produce different legal powers and police practices which no single theoretical model—whether 'legalistic-bureaucratic', 'cultural' or 'structural'—can explain. Indeed, his interesting socio-legal study of custodial interrogation in New South Wales shows the danger of generalising about the relationship between rules and behaviour, which, he convincingly argues, depends on the cultural and socio-political context within which it develops.

Drawing upon this comparative and empirical approach, Dixon subjects the research, interpretations and policy implications of the major British studies of the subject, particularly the work of what he calls the 'Warwick school' as embodied in McConville, Sanders and Leng's influential *The Case for the Prosecution*, to a sustained but well-balanced critical analysis.

His survey of the ineffectiveness of attempts to change police practices through additional legal regulations relating to arrest and interrogation is revealing, as is his admirable discussion of the notion of consent within a relationship where there is inequality of status, knowledge and power. Of particular interest is his first-rate analysis of the right to silence debate: its genesis, its mistaken assumptions, and distortions of evidence. This should be read by everyone concerned with this issue.

David Dixon believes that his evidence might moderate the opposition of some British scholars to police self-regulation and self-governance which he sees as a vital accompaniment to effective legal and political procedures for external accountability. By moving the debate on the relationship between consent, legal regulation, and the pursuit of fair yet effective policing on to a more constructive plane, this work will undoubtedly stimulate a wide debate. *Law and Policing* will be essential reading for anyone studying criminal justice. It should also be on the shelves of lawyers, police officers, and anyone involved in law-making in this difficult field.

The editors are confident that this will prove to be an influential text and are pleased to welcome it to the growing corpus of work on policing in the *Clarendon Series*.

Roger Hood
Oxford, March 1997

Preface and Acknowledgments

IN an authoritative review of British policing studies, Robert Reiner criticized the narrow focus of much research:

> In their commendable rush to publish, in order to influence policy and practice as much as to keep sponsors off their backs, researchers are more concerned to relate their results to the concerns of practitioners than to relate them to earlier research, to policing in other times, other places, and by other means than formal state police (1992b: 490).

Despite the emergence of some important theoretical work (reviewed in Dixon 1997), Reiner's dissatisfaction with the general state of the field is well-founded. This book responds to his criticism by discussing aspects of the relationship between law and policing in a theoretical, comparative, and historical way. It seeks to broaden the debate about policing by examining strengths and weaknesses in competing conceptions and by suggesting how policing studies can benefit from theoretical development. This is approached through a critical exposition and development of theoretical perspectives in policing studies. In addition to using North American literature, the book provides a significant comparative element by drawing on my research on Australian policing: this gives a particularly useful point of comparison, given the common origins of (and continuing connections between) English and Australian policing. Despite its potential abuse (Holdaway 1989: 58), comparative work provides a sense of perspective, a standpoint from which to look differently at the (sometimes all too) familiar. The book has a strong historical emphasis, reflecting my belief that historical perspective is crucial to an understanding of law and police practices (Dixon 1996b). My purpose here is to put the relationship between law and policing (with particular attention to the crucial practice of custodial interrogation) into some of the broader contexts which Reiner suggests. This does not exclude consideration of policy: on the contrary, I would argue that theoretical understanding is vital for good policy-making. I have benefited considerably here from Australian criminology, in which a distinguishing feature of the best work is an unselfconscious ability to combine theory, empirical research, and policy analysis. It uses (rather than merely recites) theory, avoids abstracted empiricism, and deals with policy without being slavishly bound to the agenda of funding agencies.

The spark for the project was provided by another complaint about theoretical and conceptual inadequacy. Richard Kinsey and Robert Baldwin pointed to a fundamental weakness in the British debate about policing reform in the early 1980s: it

completely ignored one of the key questions, namely the role of legal rules in regulating police behaviour. . . . Nobody thought to ask whether, how or why the police would get around the rules. No research was done on the extent to which the police were hindered by a lack of powers, on the reasons why officers fail to adhere to rules, on alternative ways of regulating police behaviour . . . or on the ways that rules operate under different policing strategies (1985: 89).

Their criticism was directed specifically at the Report of the Royal Commission on Criminal Procedure (RCCP 1981b). More than a decade and another Royal Commission later, the level of official debate has actually fallen: while the earlier Commission at least packaged its recommendations in some principles for criminal justice, the Royal Commission on Criminal Justice shunned principle and theory as unnecessary and responded to the spirit of the times by presenting a thoroughly 'businesslike' Report (RCCJ 1993). Rather than on principle or theory, it seems we must, like John Mortimer's Judge Ollie Oliphant, rely on 'good old English common sense'. In Australia, the situation is slightly different: there have been some exemplary official reports (ALRC 1975; NSW LRC 1990; CJC 1994), but these are all too often ignored by politicians driven by a cynical populism of law and order.

Despite the considerable volume of research on British policing in recent years, Kinsey and Baldwin's criticism of the failure to examine fundamental issues is still valid. There is one major exception: McConville, Sanders, and Leng (and their colleagues in various publications) have used their empirical work on aspects of policing to develop a significant account of law in policing. By locating their work in a broader theoretical context, this book deals with issues which are at the heart of contemporary debates about policing. This analysis and critique leads to the formulation of an account of how law relates to police practices: this is developed through specific conceptual, historical, and comparative analyses.

The structure of the book is as follows. Chapter 1 provides a detailed critical reading of three theoretical conceptions of law in policing which I term legalistic-bureaucratic, culturalist, and structural. The opportunity is taken here for extended discussion and comparison of a variety of work which is much cited, but rarely analysed in depth. Chapter 2 examines the concept of 'police powers'. Using historical material from England and Australia, it discusses where police powers came from, what they are, and what we can expect them to produce in terms of crime control. The way in which empirical work can generate conceptual reconsideration is demonstrated in Chapter 3. Research on the Police and Criminal Evidence Act 1984 (see below) made clear how 'consent' could often be used to evade legal regulation. This chapter suggests that this is not an isolated phenomenon, but is a product of a contrast between two modes of policing, 'policing by law' and 'policing by consent'. It considers the implications for contemporary developments in policing, particularly the increasingly significant field of 'private policing'. Chapters 4 and 5 focus on the key policing practice of custodial interrogation in, respectively, England and Wales, and Australia. They contrast national developments in police cultures, legal provisions, and judicial practices, providing case studies for evaluating theories of law-policing relationships. Consideration of custodial interrogation leads, in Chapter 6, to the long controversy about the right of silence (and to its severe restriction in England and Wales by the Criminal Justice and Public Order Act 1994). A feature of criminal justice to which attention should be drawn is our lack of knowledge. This is particularly relevant to historical gaps, as Chapters 2, 4, and 5 point out, but it applies throughout. This is not just the standard call for more research: my point is that knowledge is always going to be partial, in both senses of the word. The discussion in Chapter 6 of the right of silence illustrates this, focusing on the role of legal advisers at police stations. Extensive research evidence suggests that concern about (ab)use of the right of silence was not justified. But this was to miss the point: the 'right of silence' had become a symbolic issue. Sections of the police and government were committed to securing legislative change. This chapter emphasizes the irrational and symbolic nature of much debate on this topic. It closes with comments about the theoretical implications of the problems encountered in defining and counting instances of suspects using the 'right to silence' and on the possible effects of the 1994 Act. Chapter 7 revisits theoretical perspectives in a discussion of how the practices and forms of law and policing intersect, discussing the limits and possibilities of controlling policing by law. It connects with broader debates about the rule of law and techniques of controlling power in a variety of Australian, British, and American literatures, including public law, policing studies, and work on regulation and compliance. In doing so, it seeks to emphasize the need to go beyond 'police studies' in order to understand policing.

This book draws heavily on empirical research in England and Australia. What is usually referred to below as 'the PACE project' was carried out by Keith Bottomley, Clive Coleman, and me, with research assistance from Martin Gill and David Wall. In examining the effects of the Police and Criminal Evidence Act 1984 on a police force in the north of England, it included analysis of custody and other records, formal interviews with 160 officers, and some 870 hours of field observations (Bottomley et al. 1991). It was funded by the Economic and Social Research Council (grant E 1125 0001). Complementing this was 'Solicitors, Suspects, Runners, Police' which was funded by the Hull Law School and carried out by me with research assistance from David Wall. This project involved lengthy semi-structured interviews with thirty-five legal advisers who regularly provided services in the stations studied in the PACE project. My research in Australia was primarily supported by a post-doctoral fellowship in the Faculty of Law at the University of New South Wales. I spent six months in two Sydney patrols, observing general duties and detective officers and conducting tape-recorded interviews using a semi-structured questionnaire. Unless indicated otherwise, quotations from police officers and legal advisers are taken from these projects. Subsequent research on policing in New South Wales has been supported by the Law Foundation of NSW and the UNSW Law Faculty. Some material is also drawn from my current research on audiovisual recording of police questioning which is funded by the Australian Research Council.

I have run up many debts in writing this book. Many thanks to Richard Hart for, once again, encouraging and publishing my work. Thanks also to Elissa Soave and Kate Elliott at Oxford University Press. My grateful acknowledgements are due to those who have supplied research funding. The book draws on some previously published material, and I am grateful to publishers for permission to do so: Chapter 2 revises a paper published by the University of Wales

Press (in Noaks *et al.* (eds.) 1995); Chapter 3 is a heavily revised version of a paper published in the *Journal of Law & Society* by Blackwell; some of the arguments in Chapter 4 were first presented in an article in *Social & Legal Studies*, published by SAGE; Chapter 6 draws in part on 'Legal Advice, Common Sense and the Right to Silence', published in *Public Law* by Sweet & Maxwell. Contributing to reviews of police powers by, both, the NSW Law Reform Commission and the Queensland Criminal Justice Commission provided opportunities to learn about Australian policing and encouraged me to focus on what can and cannot be changed in policing, as did writing two research reports for the Royal Commission into the NSW Police Service. I am grateful to those responsible for these inquiries, particularly Susan Johnson at the CJC. Police officers both in our 'Northern Force' and in Sydney were helpful and hospitable. Ed Cape, Rod Morgan, and Andrew Sanders commented critically and very constructively on an early draft: I am particularly grateful to Andrew for his support for this project. John Braithwaite's advice helped greatly with the argument in Chapter 7. I was greatly assisted by access to pre-publication drafts of David Brown's Home Office survey of PACE research and D. J. Smith's paper 'Case Construction and the Goals of Criminal Process'. As an institution committed to research excellence, the University of New South Wales has provided an ideal setting for my work. I have been indeed lucky to be able to rely on the advice of my colleagues, especially Mark Aronsen, Dave Brown, Janet Chan, Jill Hunter, and Martin Krygier. Like anyone interested in historical perspectives on Australian policing, I owe a considerable debt to Mark Finnane. Thanks also to Martin Gill, Naomi Sharp, Gail Travis, David Wall, and Cathie Warburton for research assistance. I am particularly grateful, once again, to Clive Coleman and Keith Bottomley, two exemplary criminologists from whom I have learned much more than criminology. Thanks, specifically, to them for allowing me to use in Chapter 3 material from a jointly written paper (Dixon *et al.* 1990b). Many thanks to Jenny Bargen, Mary Dixon, Elaine Fishwick, David Greenhill, Alexis Hailstones, Michael Hogan, and Christie Kable for their friendship and assistance. Lisa Maher's encouragement, example, and theoretical acuity have been vital in completing this project; but that represents only a small fraction of my debt to her, which starts with a new life in Australia. This book is dedicated to our sons, Crewe and Louis: having one parent writing a book may be bad luck, but having both parents writing books at the same time, for the same publisher, with the same submission date, is something else.

DAVID DIXON
Sydney, October 1996

Contents

Abbreviations

AC	Appeal Cases
ACPO	Association of Chief Police Officers
A Crim. R	Australian Criminal Reports
All ER	All England Law Reports
ALJR	Australian Law Journal Reports
ALR	Australian Law Reports
ALRC	Australian Law Reform Commission
B & C	Barnewall & Cresswell's King's Bench Reports
CA	Court of Appeal
Ch.	Chancery Reports
CID	Criminal Investigation Department
CJC	Criminal Justice Commission (Queensland)
CLR	Commonwealth Law Reports
Cox CC	Cox's Criminal Cases
CR	Canadian Reports
CRNZ	Criminal Reports of New Zealand
Cr. App. R	Criminal Appeal Reports
Crim. LJ	Criminal Law Journal
Crim. LR	Criminal Law Review
DNA	Deoxyribonucleic Acid
ESRC	Economic and Social Research Council
EHRR	European Human Rights Reports
Doug.	Douglas' King's Bench Law Reports
FLR	Federal Law Reports
HL	House of Lords
HO	Home Office
HRA	Historical Records of Australia
IRLR	Industrial Relations Law Reports
JC	Justiciary Cases
KB	King's Bench Reports
LAPD	Los Angeles Police Department
LRCC	Law Reform Commission of Canada
NSW	New South Wales
NSW CCA	New South Wales Court of Criminal Appeal
NSW LRC	New South Wales Law Reform Commission

NSWLR	New South Wales Law Reports
NZLR	New Zealand Law Reports
PACE	Police and Criminal Evidence Act 1984
PSI	Policy Studies Institute
QB	Queens' Bench Reports
RBT	Random breath testing
RCCJ	Royal Commission on Criminal Justice 1991–3
RCCP	Royal Commission on Criminal Procedure 1979–81
RCP	Royal Commission on the Police 1960–2
RCPPP	Royal Commission on Police Powers and Procedure 1928–9
SASR	South Australian State Reports
S Ct.	Supreme Court Reporter
SR(NSW)	State Reports (New South Wales)
St. Tr.	State Trials
TIC	Taken into consideration
UNSW	The University of New South Wales
US	United States Supreme Court Reports
VR	Victorian Reports
WLR	Weekly Law Reports

1

Theories of Law in Policing

the whole subject of the triangle of criminal, copper and the courts is so intricate, practically and philosophically, that it can't possibly be explained in a short answer (MacInnes 1974: 98).

In literature and debates on policing, it is possible to distinguish three significant conceptions of the relationship between policing and legal rules: legalistic-bureaucratic; culturalist; and structural. This Chapter provides a critical analysis of them. They are not formal conceptual models: works to which reference is made seldom fit neatly within these categorizations, and the examples are not intended to provide an exhaustive taxonomy. Rather, the intention is to draw attention to a variety of emphases in policing studies. This Chapter will outline these conceptions, paying particular attention to a variety of structural accounts. The concluding chapter will return to these themes in an attempt to synthesize and develop elements of them.

i. Legalistic-bureaucratic

At the heart of the legalistic-bureaucratic conception are beliefs that law is the major determinant of police activity and that police institutions conform to an efficient bureaucratic model, in which senior officers are able to direct the activities of their subordinates by means of training, policy statements, and internal regulation.

Legalism suggests that, in order to understand policing, we need only or primarily to look at the laws governing it. Such a conception occurs in several, related accounts. It is the 'common sense' of traditional legal and constitutional material on the police, in which accounts of what the police ought to do are presented as if they were descriptions of practice: in the cruder formulations, what the law says is what the police do. Legalism has often characterized the self-presentation of police organizations: a central tenet of the police claim to legitimacy is their subordination to law. Policing is about the application of an objective set of laws, which are given coherence by the rule of law: it is portrayed as the expression of a reified 'higher authority dictating appropriate police action' (Grimshaw and Jefferson 1987: 7; see, e.g., Hall 1953).

For policy-makers and legislators, legalistic accounts imply a particular response to perceived problems which is more generally characteristic of legalism: they 'are typically seen as arising from ambiguities or "gaps" in the rules, calling for clearer interpretations or further legislative or quasi-legislative action' (Lacey 1992: 362). If law dominates policing, legal reform should provide the remedy for its problems: legal change should effect change in policing practice (see e.g. Brittan 1985). In consequence, attempts have been (and continue to be) made to influence police conduct and structure police discretion through clarification and codification of police powers and criminal procedure. It is assumed that 'it is in some way possible to divorce the legal rules governing police powers from organizational facts: that if one gives clear and balanced powers and duties that this is an end of the matter' (Kinsey and Baldwin 1982: 308). As Brogden, Jefferson, and Walklate point out, conceiving the organization as 'a "machine" with "faulty" rules' suggests a remedy: '[c]hange the rules and behaviour will change. It is a very traditional and sociologically impoverished notion of organizations and how they work' (1988: 164). None the less, it is this conception which has been largely taken for granted by Royal Commissions, legislators, and superior court judges in many jurisdictions.

The sources of this variety of legalism are several. One is the traditional, simplistic account of the rule of law in which executive discretion found no place, other than as deviance. Even when theoretical work on public law belatedly got under way, attention paid to policing was rare (LaFave 1965: 495). This was particularly so in Britain, where the first significant work did not appear until the 1980s (Lustgarten 1986; contrast Davis 1971, 1975 and see Ch. 7, below). For legislators and policy-makers, the attraction of legalism is its promise that their interventions will be effective and efficient. The appeal to the police of legalism is the political autonomy which it justifies. If the police are accountable to the law, then, it is argued, other modes of accountability are deemed superfluous or inappropriate. If problems in policing arise, it is the law which has become unrealistic and inadequate. From this perspective, policing is essentially a straightforward matter: the law and common sense were all that were required. Such arguments became familiar in Britain in the 1970s and 1980s.

While it has also served as a mode of resisting external accountability in the United States (LaFave 1965: 62), legalism had particular political leverage there. In its challenge to the corruption and brutality of city policing in the early decades of the century, reform policing developed a legalistic conception of professionalism. For many years, the true nature of American policing was camouflaged by legal duties of full enforcement—the myth that police could and did enforce the law to the full without the mediation of discretionary decision-making (Goldstein 1960; Kelling 1992; LaFave 1965: 76 – 9; Brown 1981: 40; Williams 1984: ch. 2). It was assumed that a decision not to enforce a law 'was an indication of inefficiency, incompetence, or corruption' (Remington 1965: xvii). Such a conception simplified both the external image maintenance of the police and training, which is 'an easier task in a department committed to the facade of full enforcement than in one in which it is assumed that police officers must share some responsibility for making decisions with important social implications' (LaFave 1965: 494). Closely linked was another myth—that policing was essentially about crime fighting via law enforcement. The installation of this as 'common sense' was a major achievement of professional policing in the early and mid-twentieth century (Bittner 1990: chs. 4 and 5; Ericson 1982; Marenin 1985; Reiner 1992a: 138 – 46).

Modern academic work on policing begins with the 'discoveries' that police work is, by nature, highly discretionary and that most of it does not involve law enforcement (e.g., Reiss 1971; Wilson 1968: 294). This paradigmatic shift in police research was begun by the American Bar Foundation's project on criminal justice (LaFave 1965: 61; Miller 1969: 352; Ohlin and Remington (eds.) 1993; Tiffany *et al.* 1967). While it may have been a naïve, atheoretical attempt at 'empirical vacuum-cleaning' (McIntyre 1967: viii), it provided the basis for a new understanding of policing (Kelling 1992; Walker 1992, 1993: 5–12). Thereafter, to treat discretion as (at best) a necessary evil was seen as naïve and misleading. To treat policing as being essentially about enforcing the criminal law was to misrepresent by omitting a large proportion of it.

It might be thought that evidence of the rule-dominated nature of policing is provided by the voluminous books of rules and regulations which most police forces have produced (Finnane 1994: ch. 8). Bittner remarked that American police organizations were 'permanently flooded with petty military and bureaucratic regulations' (1990: 223). This was not simply official excess: 'the requirement for administrative due process in police discipline', attempts to avoid civil liability by having 'guidelines prohibiting the act in question', and agency accreditation requirements have all encouraged the production of formal policies and rules (Cordner 1989: 18; cf. Sitkin and Bies (eds.) 1994). In addition, rule-making was promoted as the best way of controlling police discretion by legal academics, notably K. C. Davis (1971; see Ch. 7, below).

But this 'flood' itself belies legalistic-bureaucratic claims: 'the rules and regulations which typify police departments are so numerous and patently unenforceable that no one will (or could) obey' them all (Van Maanen 1974: 100). The Boston Police Department's *Rules and Regulations Manual* is frank:

It is a common notion . . . that rules and regulations, procedures, policies, and such are of little or no value to actual police operations and really exist so that the Department has a tool with which to punish police officers who 'rock the boat'. This is difficult to dispute because rules are so often misused in exactly that fashion (quoted, Krantz *et al.* 1979: 53).

A NSW officer's response to an inquiry about the influence of Commissioner's Instructions was illustrative: 'they're not really accessible . . . Where would you find them in this police station? Probably locked up in the boss's cabinet. And they're so full of legal jargon, no-one actually sits down and reads them.' Until recently, amongst the rules and regulations for the New South Wales Police, this was included:

Hair will be neatly cut and conform to the following requirements. . . . Not to extend at the back below a line 1.5 centimetres above the shirt collar. . . . Side-burns, if worn, not to extend below lines level with the points where ear lobes join the face, to be evenly tapered, not thick and bushy and must not increase in width throughout their length.

Such precision rubs shoulders with much broader rules: for example, officers 'who habitually quarrel with comrades will be liable to dismissal'.[1] Such rules aspire to a world in which everything can 'be

---

[1] NSW Police Instructions (1989), 2.38 and 2.48. Young provides a good example of regulatory precision—rules specifying the type of wreath or spray appropriate for funerals of various levels of staff, including prescribed wording for the accompanying card (1993: 232). See Wansbaugh's comment (1976:7) on such regulations.

controlled, ordered, disciplined, checked, scrutinized' (Young 1993: 177).

However, reality is rather different. On his appointment as NSW Police Commissioner in 1991, Tony Lauer referred to 'the difficulty of relying on "two huge volumes" when no-one, including himself, knew exactly what was in them'.[2] Bradley, Walker, and Wilkie suggest that such rule-books 'should be seen as blueprints, guides to a possible reality, an abstract and partial account of how things could or should be, rather than an account of how things are' (1986: 121). While Bradley *et al.* see them as 'conceptions', a Metropolitan Police Sergeant described his force's General Orders as containing '140 years of fuckups. Every time something goes wrong, they make a rule about it' (quoted, Manning 1977: 165; on 'reactive rules', see Bottomley *et al.* 1991: 194–5; Walker 1988: 368). Such rules then provide a managerial resource: as an Australian officer commented, '[t]hey say to be a good police officer, you need to use common sense. But when the shit hits the fan, they say you should have used the rule book' (quoted, McConkey *et al.* 1996: 41). Rule books have been a major characteristic and tool of police departments as 'punishment centred bureaucracies' (Gouldner 1954: chs. 11 and 12). Any observer of policing is soon aware of how limited is the effect of standing orders and force instructions on police. As part of more general changes in policing, several forces are responding by scrapping their voluminous rule books in favour of brief statements of values and objectives.[3]

Legalism is closely linked to the conception of police organizations as effective bureaucracies. For example, a crucial assumption of policy- and law-making has been that, once rules have been clearly formulated, the police will act in accordance with them. As Grimshaw and Jefferson suggest, quasi-academic variants of this 'machine model' can be found in texts on police management the source of which is organizational theory, rather than empirical studies of policework (1987: 6–7). Indeed, the operation of police management generally escaped critical academic analysis until Grimshaw and Jefferson's study (which presents a very different picture of the process of policy formulation and implementation within the police) and Bradley *et al.*'s *Managing the Police* (1986), which exposes the

---

[2] *Sunday Telegraph* (Sydney), 17 Mar. 1991, 3.

[3] See Tendler 1988; Wright and Burke 1995. Hilliard (1988: 1489) notes the replacement of 13,000 pages of standing orders to West Midlands Police by 'a 300 page volume and a yellow card giving 10 criteria for the efficient performance of police duty'.

myth of the machine model and the deficiencies of the managerial theories upon which it relies.

Like legalism, the self-presentation of police as effective bureaucracies has been an important mode of legitimation and a defence against external control (Manning 1977: 103–4). Manning stresses the gap between claim and reality: the 'police are symbolized externally as a paramilitary bureaucracy, but lack of internal control, of close supervision of lower participants, and their freedom of action make it more a symbol than a reality' (1977: 109 and see *ibid.*: ch. 7 for his critique of presenting police organizations as professional bureaucracies). It is almost a cliché to cite Wilson's observation that 'the police department has the special property . . . that within it discretion increases as one moves down the hierarchy' (1968: 7). A police force which operates 'as a tightly organized, self-regulating body, with a highly efficient hierarchical command structure, exercising direct operational control' exists only in the nightmares of conspiracy theorists and the 'public dreams and wishful thinking' of some senior police managers (Baldwin and Kinsey 1985: 99).

A bureaucratic approach can also be identified in another, much more sophisticated, group of police studies—the new 'police science' in which academic and professional researchers carry out policy-oriented projects, particularly using experimental methodologies. A classic example is Sherman's research on domestic violence. Its fundamental assumptions have been that policies (e.g., mandatory arrest) can be operationally tested by requiring officers to act according to them and that, once the best policy has been identified, it can be put into practice by regulation and instruction (Sherman 1992a, 1992b). Enlisting sociology in the service of crime control in this way has provoked a fractious dispute (Manning 1993; Sherman 1993, 1995).

The concept of professionalism implicit in legalistic-bureaucratic accounts has been criticized by those who suggest that 'professionalism' provides a 'powerful symbolic canopy' under which police can extend their political autonomy and influence and broaden their discretion (Holdaway 1983: 163; see also Ericson 1981b: 222–7). As Manning suggests, the 'rhetoric of professionalism is the most important strategy employed by the police to defend their mandate and thereby to build self-esteem, organizational autonomy, and occupational solidarity or cohesiveness'.[4] The claim to autonomy

---

[4] 1977: 127. This is true of contemporary 'new professionalism' (see Ch. 4, below) as much as it is of older 'law enforcement' professionalism.

based on expertise is a pervasive problem in modern policing which continues to be dominated by a belief that significant knowledge about policing is held exclusively by police, a resistance to external involvement in police policy, and, frequently, a belief that police are solely qualified to decide what powers they need. This spills over into the current enthusiasm for community policing and problem-oriented policing: in both cases, a central characteristic is police hegemony which is expressed in continuing police 'ownership' of policing (Brogden and Shearing 1993: 170) and an insistence that they must have the leading and defining role in organizing community responses to crime.

This 'new policing' includes a new approach to the law–policing relationship: it is argued that true professionalism requires wide discretion rather than rule-based direction (NSW Police 1988; Sparrow *et al.* 1990). Drawing managerialist lessons from corporate practice, '[p]olice executives are . . . relying less on rules and constant supervision and more on selection, training and the articulation of values to create a culture that can properly guide officer conduct' (Moore and Stephen 1991: 5; see also Cordner 1989; Dixon 1995b). These are ripples of a much deeper change in theories and rationales of policing. The new policing associated with problem-solving and community-oriented strategies (Moore 1992) distances itself from older traditions of professional policing the priorities of which were autonomy and crime control (Walker 1993b: 44–5). But it also distances itself from law: 'enthusiasm for these reforms grows precisely because of the perceived failures of the rule of law' (Mastrofski and Uchida 1993: 353; Mastrofski and Greene 1993). Just as law enforcement is no more than one part of the police function, so law loses its place as the prime legitimator of policing. In a complex and related development, US policing has increasingly been assessed in terms of efficiency in tackling illegal drugs and drug-related crime (Skolnick 1994). Supported by assertions that problems of police illegality were in the past, ends could justify means. The beating of Rodney King and its aftermath provided sharp reminders of the cost of that approach (Walker 1993b: 34; Skolnick and Fyfe 1993).

Legalistic-bureaucratic accounts take the efficacy of law for granted: it is assumed that any significant variation in the impact of rules (so long as they are competently drafted) is due to external factors (e.g. inadequate preparation by proponents or resistance to rules from their target) rather than from their nature. It hardly needs to be pointed out that this is jurisprudentially naïve. In the context of the policing literature, a significant critique of this approach was provided by the Policy Studies Institute (PSI) study of the Metropolitan Police (Smith and Gray 1985). The PSI suggested that legal rules have a variable influence on police behaviour depending on whether they are treated as 'working rules' (internalized and effective in guiding behaviour), 'inhibitory rules' (non-internalized rules which are taken into account in decision-making), or 'presentational rules' (non-internalized and ineffective, except in their use as justification and legitimation of activities determined by working rules: Smith and Gray 1985: 440–2; cf. Banton 1964).

The PSI's classification has been much-quoted, but it has deficiencies. By focusing on the effect of specific rules, it understates the need to consider the cumulative effect of groups of rules. In addition, rules are not self-executing: an apparently 'presentational' rule may be made to work in an inhibitory way by means of 'organisational and institutional changes' (Baldwin and Kinsey 1985: 91). It has also been pointed out that the classification needs to be extended to include other types. For example, there are 'reactive rules' (created by police hierarchies in response to specific incidents) and 'routinized rules' (which may initially have been effective, but which have become ritualized: see Bottomley *et al.* 1991: 193–4; Manning 1977: 164–79). In general, there is a need to appreciate processes of change and variation in the effects of rules. These additions really disclose the theoretical limitations of this functional approach to rules: new types of rules can (and presumably will) be added as further research is conducted. However, the PSI's account does not 'help much in assessing the conditions under which various forms of legal rules have a genuine regulatory function' (Baldwin 1989: 165). The PSI's report was commissioned by the Metropolitan Police, and this presumably influenced the way in which it was presented. The theoretical sources, contexts, and implications are underplayed: the PSI's report was notable for its failure to refer to other work in the field (Holdaway 1989: 67). However, more recent work by D. J. Smith shows how the PSI's research can lend itself to conceptual development beyond an accumulation of divergent instances and variations (Smith 1995; see sect. iii, below).

ii. Culturalist

A familiar approach in sociological studies of policing is the study, usually by observational methods, of police culture. Inspired by Banton's work (1964), it dominated studies of British policing through the 1960s and 1970s.[5] Similarly, an impressive body of work accumulated in the United States, exemplified by Skolnick's *Justice without Trial* (1975) and Rubinstein's *City Police* (1973). The focus is usually on general duties patrol officers: indeed Reiner comments that, in Britain, 'studies of police culture have been coterminous with patrol culture' (1992b: 465). The same is generally true in the United States, although Skolnick's study, which is usually taken as the classic of this kind, also studied a specialized detective unit (see also Manning 1980).

Such studies emphasize the strength and influence of police culture. It is this which connects work which draws upon a wide variety of theories beyond the interactionism with which it is usually associated (Holdaway 1989: 67–8). In a comprehensive survey, Reiner defines the 'core characteristics' of police culture as 'values, norms, perspectives and craft rules' (1992a: 109) which include a sense of mission, a commitment to crime-fighting action, cynicism, pessimism, suspiciousness, group solidarity coupled with social isolation, conservatism, and pragmatism (1992a: 109–29). The culture is presented as devaluing rules and as assuming that effective police work cannot be done according to legal procedures. Consequently, law is primarily considered from this perspective either as a 'resource' (see below) or 'in terms of how it engenders deviancy' (Kemp, Norris, and Fielding 1992: 87). It is often regarded as being, at best, marginally relevant and, at worst, a serious impediment to the business of policing:

often an officer views the judge's decision as justice subverted, because for him [*sic*] a case is not isolated. Rather it is part of an order of behaviour and events that he, the officer, is expected to control in a specified way. . . . Police subculture consists in part of developing standards of doing justice (Reiss 1971: 139–40).

An officer 'knows' that a suspect is factually guilty—it is why she or he was arrested and charged—and the insistence that there is another standard, 'legal guilt', which must be achieved by running

[5] On the influence of Banton's work, see Reiner 1992b: 439–43, 464–8; 1994: 711–13; Reiner and Morgan (eds). 1995.

the gauntlet of legal technicalities, the burden of proof, and exclusionary rules (cf. Packer 1968) is seen as excessive. Backed by the evidence that Supreme Court decisions such as *Miranda* had little direct effect on police behaviour,[6] culturalists claim that procedural rules are ineffective in controlling police behaviour. Bittner, for example, jumps from the finding that discretion cannot be eliminated to the conclusion that it cannot even be curtailed or structured (Bittner 1990: 92–3; cf. Doyle 1992: 52). This is an example of a more general tendency for culturalists to translate uncritically the common sense of police culture gathered from observations of street policing into academic formulations of the irrelation between law and policing. Further, both this common sense and its academic expression are influenced by fictional representations: between Chandler's Captain Gregorius ('There ain't a police force in the country could do its job with a law book': 1959: 40) to Eastwood's Harry Callahan ('the law's crazy': cf. Smith 1993: 90–107), the unruly police officer became a cliché.

In Manning's ironic approach, it is the contradictory demands of productivity in crime-fighting and adherence to rules which produce the cultural solutions of bending and breaking the law by employing informal working rules which guide practical policework (1977: 162 and ch. 6 *passim*). Somewhat similarly, Skolnick identifies strain as the key to an understanding of policing; in his argument, it is between law and 'norms located within the police organization . . . the process of interaction between the two accounts ultimately for how police behave' (1975: 219). His stated purpose was

not to reveal that the police violate rules and regulations. That much is assumed. The interest here is analytic description, the understanding of conditions under which rules may be violated with greater or lesser intensity . . . [T]here are systemic pressures upon police to break certain kinds of rules in the interest of conforming to other standards (1975: 22, 109).

Drawing on the sociology of work, Skolnick saw 'the policeman as a craftsman rather than as a legal actor, as a skilled worker rather than as a civil servant obliged to subscribe to the rule of law' (1975: 231). This theoretical foundation is usually under-emphasized in assessments of Skolnick's work. He writes not just of the familiar strain between law and order: in addition, he identifies tension between, on

---

[6] 384 US 436 (1966). See Leo 1996c; Walker 1993: 44–51 and p. 306 n. 45 below for studies of *Miranda*'s effects.

one side, the 'ideology of democratic bureaucracy' and 'the democratic ideology of work', and, on the other, legalistic policing and 'the legal philosophy of a democracy' (1975: 6, 235). He emphasizes the premium placed on initiative and efficiency in the former as running contrary to legal pressures. In this way, Skolnick's work is much more ambitious than an account merely of police culture (1975: 6, 235; see also Wilson 1968: 283).

By virtue of their argument about normative conflict of strain, these classic American studies did not ignore the law (at least in the sense of legal ideals). Indeed, Skolnick considered his to be a study in the sociology of law (1975: 15, note 35). By contrast, other studies tended to overlook the law, largely in consequence of the objectives and methodology of such research. As defined by Banton, their primary concern was 'to clarify what the ordinary policeman did most of his time and how he did it'. When such work began, 'these data were nowhere available'. The aim, therefore, was a 'more systematic examination of the commonplace events of everyday behaviour' (Banton 1964: x). Their finding, that law enforcement played a small part in everyday police work, had a profound effect on understanding of policing. When laws were enforced, these usually involved minor charges to which defendants pleaded guilty: the influence of exclusionary rules and higher court decisions on such practices was minimal (Bittner 1990: 116–19; Reiss 1970: 20; Tiffany et al. 1967: xvii; Skolnick 1975: 13).

The assumption of the legalistic-bureaucratic model that law enforcement is the sole function of policing is replaced by a realization that the priority of police work is service-provision and order-maintenance, and that these are usually achieved by methods other than law enforcement (Reiner 1992a: 139–46; Ericson 1982: 3–11). Several authors made the point strongly: 'when one looks at what policemen actually do, one finds that criminal law enforcement is something that most of them do with the frequency located somewhere between virtually never and very rarely' (Bittner 1990: 240). Reiss found that '[n]o tour of duty is typical except in the sense that the modal tour of duty does not involve an arrest' (1970: 19), while Ericson sardonically commented that 'the bulk of the patrol officer's time was spent doing nothing other than consuming the petrochemical energy required to run an automobile and the psychic energy required to deal with the boredom of it all' (1982: 206).

In emphasizing that police work entailed order-maintenance and social-service, culturalists tended to overstate the distinction between these and law enforcement, and to suggest that incidents had a pre-given character as crime, order, or service. Subsequent researchers have demonstrated that the nature of police response to many incidents depends upon (and can vary according to) officers' interpretation and definition of events and participants, and their evaluation of consequences of different courses of action (Kemp *et al.* 1992: ch. 5; cf. Ericson 1982: 113; Lustgarten 1986: 10–11). It may also depend upon policy, as in attempts by police departments to redefine domestic violence as appropriately dealt with by law-enforcement rather than order-maintenance techniques.[7]

This emphasis on the interpretive and definitional nature of police work fits well with perhaps the most important culturalist insight. Law was presented, not as the template of policing, but as a resource which is employed in order to achieve goals established by police culture: 'To the patrolman [*sic*], the law is one resource among many that he may use to deal with disorder, but it is not the only one or even the most important. . . . Thus, he approaches incidents that threaten order not in terms of enforcing the law but in terms of "handling the situation" ' (Wilson 1968: 31). To tell an officer simply to 'enforce the law' is not enough because 'the law is a constraint that tells him what he must not do but that is peculiarly unhelpful in telling him what he should do. . . . [T]he law provides one resource, the possibility of arrest, and a set of constraints, but it does not supply to the patrolman a set of legal rules to be applied'.[8] From this perspective, full enforcement of law is a chimera. This is a matter, not simply of limited resources and the necessity of discretion, but, much more significantly, of the nature of the laws most relevant to street policing:

Most criminal laws define acts . . . people may disagree as to whether the act should be illegal . . . but there is little disagreement as to what the behaviour in question consists of. Laws regarding disorderly conduct and the like assert, usually by implication, that there is a condition ('public order') that can be diminished by various actions. The difficulty, of course, is that public order

---

[7] See, e.g., Hanmer *et al.* (eds.) 1989; Kemp *et al.* 1992: chs. 5 and 6; Sherman 1992b. Mandatory arrest policies are one among several factors which suggest that 'police work has, in fact, become more crime oriented in recent years, calling into question one of the orthodoxies of earlier studies' (Reiner 1992b: 460).

[8] Wilson 1968: 31, original emphases removed. See also Bittner 1990: ch. 2; Chatterton 1976; 105–22; Skolnick 1975: 108.

is nowhere defined and can never be unambiguously defined because what constitutes order is a matter of opinion and convention, not a state of nature (Wilson 1968: 22–3; see also *ibid.*, 294, note 10; Reiner 1992a: 212).

A great advantage of street or public-order offences to police is that an officer's evidence is usually sufficient to ground a charge. By contrast, more substantive charges entail the collection and presentation of evidence, more paperwork, and 'a great deal of organisational time and energy from both the police and other agents of the criminal justice system' (Kemp *et al.* 1992: 117). Unless police have reason to upgrade response to an incident, resource charges are economical. As Kemp *et al.* emphasize, this police appropriation of an incident may not be in the best interests of the victim who 'is, effectively, made absent from the processing of her own dispute' (1992: 117; cf. Christie 1977).

Wilson's and Bittner's early work provides the classic examples of such analysis, while Chatterton (1976) was responsible for translating the idea to the English context. But it is in Ericson's study of police patrol work, in which McBarnet's influence (see sect. iii(c) below) is clear, that the idea of law as a resource gets its most eloquent and extended discussion (see Ericson 1982: 13, 24, and *passim*; see also Miyazawa 1992). Ericson confirms the usual observation that most patrol policing does not involve law enforcement, that the officer's mandate is the reproduction of social order, and that law enforcement is a means of achieving that end, not an end in itself (1982: 24, 170–1, 197). In accounting for how and when police use the resource of law, Ericson relies on culturalism: the 'motive for patrol officers' actions comes from particular interests defined within their occupational culture. This includes an array of "recipe" rules.'[9]

Despite these significant insights, the culturalist approach 'substantially neglects the significance of legal rules in shaping police work' (Kemp *et al.* 1992: 87). As Skolnick suggested, when 'it becomes clear that laws are not nearly so certain as was assumed, and that organizational and situational requirements often affect the actor's interpretation of laws, the sociologist may tend to forget about the rules and to interpret behaviour almost purely as a

---

[9] 1982: 14. However, he does acknowledge instances where law is determinant, e.g. arrest of people with warrants outstanding (*ibid.* 170–1). For Ericson's autocritique of the conception of culture used here, see Shearing and Ericson 1991, and below, in this sect.

response to situational factors' (1975: 27). The law in many culturalist accounts is an insubstantial presence, 'law in the books' which
must be contrasted with the reality of policing practice, 'law in
action' (Fielding 1989: 77). For example, while Skolnick did not
neglect the law, his account tended to be idealistic: heavily influenced
by Fuller and American constitutionalism, he invokes law as an enterprise with its own dynamic and character, rather than as a material
force providing specific constraints and resources (1975: 22, 36). Law
is founded in consensus: 'the *raison d'être*' of police and criminal law
is 'the underlying collectively held moral sentiments which justify
penal sanctions' (1975: 45). Familiar dichotomies appear: 'the central
task of the administration of justice is to balance the conflicting principles of order and liberty' (1975: 71).[10] By failing to theorize law adequately, such assumptions survived as the (more often unstated)
common sense of culturalist accounts.

Holdaway has criticized suggestions that culturalists ignore the
law: this is 'to miss the point that is being made. Law and policy are
not obliterated within the occupational culture but re-worked,
refracted in one direction or another as they do or do not resonate
with the themes of the occupational culture' (1989: 65). Law is among
the materials from which the culture is 're-created and sustained'
(1989: 66). However, this leaves culture as the determinant, with law
in a clearly subordinate position. Researchers moving beyond the culturalist tradition have been more willing to equalize the relationship,
or to reverse it, seeing law as a frame, structure, or discourse within
which culture operates. A prominent English culturalist, Nigel
Fielding, has acknowledged the deficiencies of the approach: the
'development of our understanding . . . now calls for a different focus
using different methods to pursue the determinants of on-the-street
policing within the organization and in the relation of police to other
social and state institutions' (1989: 77). This was carried through in
his study (with Kemp and Norris) of police dispute-handling in which
'the negotiation process into which police officers are drawn when
called upon to resolve a dispute . . . is as much about "law in action"
as police organisation and subculture' (Kemp *et al.* 1992: 118). This
reconsideration of culturalism involving serious attention to law is
largely a product of structuralist critiques which are discussed below.

Quasi-participant observation provided culturalism with both its

---

[10] See Ch. 7 below for a critique of this balance metaphor.

strength and weakness (Brogden *et al.* 1988: ch. 3). While insights into otherwise inaccessible activities and ways of thinking were provided, their contexts were often not fully appreciated. As Punch suggested, 'researchers tend to become mesmerized by the police world and to attribute behaviour uniquely to its culture whereas fruitful similarities and contrasts, abound with workers in other types of organisational settings' (1985: 187). Bittner insisted that research should start with the 'reality conditions and practical circumstances' of policing: as for the law and the police mandate, we should 'keep them in mind as something to be worked back to, rather than as a point of departure' (1990: 93). This journey was rarely completed. Interactionism did not provide the theoretical or methodological resources needed to link what researchers saw with deeper structures: 'whilst the daily happenings, on the streets and in the locker room, are examined in all their apparently kaleidoscopic variations, the law, the formal organization, its policies and senior officers are all assumptive categories: essentially unexamined' (Grimshaw and Jefferson 1987: 8). Culturalism could not fully explain what it saw (*ibid.* 290) and what it did see was only part of the picture: significant areas of police work were simply not open to observational study. In part, this was a matter of access—senior officers who happily allowed researchers to 'ride along' with patrol officers would resist study of specialist squads or themselves. But there was also the methodological problem: observational study of senior officers doing their usual bureaucratic tasks sitting at a desk is neither productive nor enjoyable.[11] The limits of observing general duties patrolwork have also to be acknowledged: only the most naïve researcher would claim to have seen and heard all (Brogden *et al.* 1988: 45–6) and Young offers a depressing corrective to police researchers who optimistically believe that they have achieved 'rapport' with their subjects (1991: 20–1; see also Van Maanen 1978).

Too much discussion of police culture has the celebratory but critical tone of a Wambaugh novel (e.g. 1976). Culturalists' accounts are by nature fascinating. It is not surprising to find the best of them, Rubinstein's *City Police*, packaged as a 'true crime' airport paperback.[12] While they have to be appreciated as a response to what had

[11] Malcolm Young, uniquely, was able to avoid these problems by being a genuinely participant observer in the work of police management: see Young 1991 and, especially, 1993. Other researchers have had to use other methodologies (e.g. Reiner 1991).

[12] And described by the 'blurb' on the cover as '[a]n incredible insight into a cop's world. Tough, brutal . . . and the action can be deadly!', with *Playboy* as the source of the critic's comment.

gone before and as a product of limited theories and methodologies, Grimshaw and Jefferson's assessment is harsh but fair: they 'provide an accurate descriptive empirical catalogue of happenings and influences without in any way being able to explain what makes it all possible. Worse still, if empirical influences are mistaken for structural determinations, the chance of an adequate understanding gets lost for fair' (1987: 290).

The most significant theoretical deficiency of culturalist accounts has been the lack of serious attention to the central concept of culture: the 'assumption that there is something called "police culture" is at best naïve, and results in crude generalizations in the quest for common characteristics so as to make the results virtually meaningless' (Hobbs 1991: 606). Early critiques pointed to the existence of more than one culture within policing (Reuss-Ianni and Ianni 1983). Their focus was on a perceived split between 'street cops and management cops', which overstated both this division (Grimshaw and Jefferson 1987: 18–19; contrast Young 1993) and the homogeneity of 'street cop culture'. More recent work has identified three subcultures: 'command, middle management, and lower participants' (Chan 1996: 111, citing Manning). As Banton pointed out, 'anyone acquainted with the police' is well aware of the divisions and tensions within their number . . . [T]he police are divided internally into all sorts of factions, interest groups and sections' (1964: 263). In addition to distinctions produced by functional specialization (Hobbs 1991: 606), 'police organizations represent a hodgepodge of cliques, cabals, and conspiracies' (Van Maanen 1978: 322, note 12). Law contributes to these divisions. Police forces are (as officers so often insist in explaining their world to outsiders) disciplined organizations. The mass of rules (see sect. i above) cannot be fully enforced: it provides a reservoir of power which facilitates the unpredictable, even capricious, nature of the disciplinary system (as Van Maanen 1978: 322; Ericson 1981b: 24–7; 1981b; Dixon 1992: 528).

Culturalists' accounts can suppress the individuality and, consequently, the agency of officers. Vincent makes this point well:

They are not simply automatons who react similarly and thoughtlessly to the formative influence of a deterministic occupational environment; on the contrary, they act on and affect the social environment in which they work out their destiny. They will share many attitudes and behavioral tendencies, but at the same time they differ markedly on a wide variety of matters (1990: 8).

A more sophisticated account of culture has to allow for the agency of individuals who shape, as well as are shaped by, their social world.

Contrary to assumptions that police culture is universal and permanent, it is clear that the cultures of various police organizations vary and have changed. First, national and regional variations have to be appreciated. The challenge is to combine an appreciation of diversity with a perception of common elements which goes further than Trotsky's observation that there is 'but one international and that is the police' (quoted, Van Maanen 1974: 84). National differences are sometimes directly related to contrasting legal systems. For example, the police culture studied by Skolnick and other American writers has to be understood in the context of the Supreme Court's development of suspects' rights in the 1960s. There was some law which needed to be avoided, unlike the contemporary situation in Australia and England, where much law on police procedure was opaque and insubstantial. While encouraging comparative studies, Holdaway (1989) correctly warns against uncritical transportation of concepts from the United States which is 'taken as a sort of paradigm case for future trends and tendencies in the Western world, especially in Britain' (Hall *et al.* 1978: 21)—and, it must be added, in Australia, where media and (all too often) political discourse relating to crime and law enforcement is obsessed with American comparisons. Significant differences within police cultures can also be identified at a local level. Foster shows how officers at two London police stations exhibited 'very different attitudes, styles and approaches to their work' which were products of the socially contrasting areas which they policed (1989: 128).

Secondly, police culture has a timeless quality in some culturalist accounts. However, it is becoming clear that changes over time occur (Holdaway 1989: 65; Caiden 1977: x). A critical history of US police reform begins by challenging the 'myth of the unchanging police. . . . In both popular discourse and academic scholarship one continually encounters references to the "tradition-bound" police who are resistant to change. Nothing could be further from the truth' (Walker 1977: ix). In England, Brogden's oral history (1991) of policing interwar Liverpool finds little evidence of 'canteen culture . . . just tedium, isolation, discipline and chill' (Cain 1993: 321). It has been argued that legal regulation has contributed to shifts in culture since the mid-1980s in England and Wales (Dixon 1992: 528–9; Rose 1996: ch. 6). As for Australia, only someone with a short memory could argue that

Australian police cultures have been completely unaffected by the anti-corruption and organizational reforms which began in the mid-1980s (Chan 1997). It is perhaps necessary to stress that police cultures may not change 'for the better'. The transformations of the Los Angeles Police Department from 'one of the most corrupt and lawless departments . . . in the 1930s' to 'the epitome of police professionalism' in the early 1960s (Brown 1988: xiii; cf. Caiden 1977: ch. 11; Kelling 1992; Van Maanen 1978: 324) to paramilitary 'efficiency' in the 1990s (which still awaits its historian, but cf. Davis 1990: 250–322) does not fit any simple paradigm of 'progress'.

Finally, what is 'cultural' about 'police culture' is taken for granted: it is a category too often founded in common sense and unreflexive reliance on occupational sociology and role theory. As Thompson comments, 'culture' tends 'to nudge us towards over-consensual and holistic notions . . . [it] is a clumpish term, which by gathering up so many activities and attributes into one common bundle may actually confuse or disguise discriminations that should be made between them. We need to take this bundle apart, and examine the components with more care' (1993: 13; cf. Chan 1996: 110–12). It is usually used quite uncritically, with no reference to contemporary theoretical debates about and revisions of 'culture'. Indeed, its use has become a cliché which provides pat explanations (see e.g., Fitzgerald 1989: ch. 7). Alvesson is blunt: culture 'is a word for the lazy' (1993: 3).

The works of Goldsmith, Shearing and Ericson, and Chan demonstrate, in different ways, the potential for developing studies of police culture. Goldsmith (1990) criticizes the negativity of most accounts of police culture: he argues for 'taking police culture seriously' and seeing its positive potential. This is developed in an account which draws on studies of administrative and legal regulation which criticize traditional deterrence models and argue for more positive uses of regulation (see also Ch. 7, below). The lack of proper attention to law leads to a failure to identify law (and laws of a particular type) as being among the structuring conditions for the growth of police cultures (cf. Lustgarten 1986: 180–1).

While the standard accounts treat police culture as a set of informal rules, Shearing and Ericson (1991) present culture as a sensibility constructed through stories: action is not rule-directed, but rather is the product of an 'instinct' or 'common sense' which is a cultural construction. Their reformulation of police culture has the mark of a classic. They latch on to the stories which all police researchers have heard, laughed at, been bored by, and repeated, but have usually regarded as essentially trivial.[13] Instead, Shearing and Ericson present these stories as the key to understanding police culture. It is through telling and hearing them that officers know how to act. Importantly, this account provides for agency: officers are not 'cultural dopes', but make choices in performing police work. Among the strengths of this approach is seeing culture continually as being produced and reproduced, rather than as a permanent set of values or norms imposed upon officers. Shearing (1995) makes clear the implications for police reform: in his view, most efforts at bringing about cultural change have been ineffective because their subject has been misunderstood. This account of culture is an excellent example of the use (as opposed to mere recitation) of theory. Many criminologists who have been intimidated or alienated by poststructural theory will see here the value of theorizing in this way. However, some qualifications may be raised.

Shearing and Ericson's account provides a convincing way of understanding police activity on the street. The construction and deployment of suspicion, in particular, is much better understood through this type of analysis than simplistic assumptions about cultural norms. This has important implications for the legal regulation of street policing, which has often failed because its nature was misunderstood by rule-makers (Dixon *et al.* 1989). However, the rejection of a normative conception of culture is taken too far. Contrary to Shearing and Ericson's argument (1991: 482; cf. Pennings and Gresov 1986: 323), there *are* cultural rules for which the evidence is not merely (and tautologically) the activity which they are supposed to explain (see e.g. Manning 1980: 104–6). In my experience of fieldwork in policing, there are informal rules which are expressed and experienced as prohibitions and directives, and which are not merely retrospective justifications for action. Obvious examples are rules of collective solidarity (e.g. back up your colleagues and don't snitch or dob) and rules of behaviour (e.g. don't let a challenge to your authority pass without response). There may well be stories which convey the same message: stories and norms may be complementary. In challenging the orthodoxy, Shearing and Ericson go too far: there would

---

[13] But please note the discussion of 'war-stories' and anecdotes in Van Maanen 1974: 90; 1979: 316 n. 9; and Young 1993: 6–7, 283. For a broader account of such narratives, see Ewick and Silbey 1996.

appear to be good explanatory reasons for (and no theoretical reasons against) developing a broad conception of culture which includes both elements.

For example, Janet Chan has done this in her combination of insights from Sackmann's organizational theory with Bourdieu's analysis of habitus and field (Chan 1996; 1997). This approach, which sees police culture as constituted by interaction between the legal and political contexts of policing and police organizational knowledge, provides a sophisticated and comprehensive understanding of police culture. Chan's framework

recognises the interpretive and creative aspects of culture, allows for the existence of multiple cultures, and takes into account the political context and cognitive structures of police work. . . . Thus police cultural practice results from the interaction between the socio-political context of police work and various dimensions of police organizational knowledge (1996: 110).

Her interpretation of habitus and field allows Chan to provide an account of police culture which is able to accommodate and relate cultural knowledge and its socio-political context. Her analysis of specific components of culture contributes to the debates about change and reform in policing: she shows that more careful analysis of what is and is not malleable in police culture is vital for debates about the limits and possibilities of change in policing.

Goldsmith, Shearing and Ericson, and Chan are not a homogeneous group. What these authors do have in common is ability to go beyond 'police studies' into contemporary social theory. Their work shows clearly how policing research benefits by engagement with theory developed in other contexts.

iii. Structural

(a) *Kinsey and Baldwin*

In this section a variety of structural approaches to law in policing will be reviewed, starting with Richard Kinsey and Robert Baldwin, whose work provides an account of policing structured by legal and situational factors. While their critique of McBarnet's theory of law–policing relations will be considered below, attention here focuses on their distinctive situational account. They 'prescribe . . . a difficult middle road that concedes a limited but important role to legal rules in regulating police activity' (Kinsey and Baldwin 1982:

315). Both the limits and the possibilities of rules are their concern. Like the PSI, they recognize that rules can take different forms, and so it is vital to choose an appropriate type: far from being 'a homogeneous group of norms', rules have to be distinguished 'according to such factors as status, sanctions, degree of specificity, procedure and enforcement practice' (Baldwin 1989: 166). The corollary was that police researchers had to broaden their focus from the profane reality of the patrol car and the police canteen in order to take account of their locations. These include the structuring effect of rules: Kinsey refers disparagingly to 'a naïve sociological realism' in which there is a tendency 'to ignore the efficacy of rules almost entirely. . . . Put crudely, the police are typified as doing what they will; they will be supported by the judiciary who will connive at or otherwise legitimate their activities, and legal controls are merely "symbolic" or "ideological" ' (1982: 478).

Legalistic-bureaucratic accounts fair no better. Baldwin and Kinsey (who identify legalism as a particularly strong influence in the production of the Criminal Justice (Scotland) Act 1980 which, *inter alia*, made crucial changes in police powers to detain for questioning) strongly criticize the failure to take account of the broader context of fundamental changes in policing organization and practice towards 'reactive and pre-emptive policing'. For example, they point to the need to understand rules on custodial interrogation by appreciating the shifts in criminal justice which created its pre-eminence among investigative strategies (Kinsey and Baldwin 1982: 304). Other aspects of policing which have to be taken into account include the 'changing patterns of policing in the post-war period in terms of developments in the technological and organisational base of police work' (Baldwin and Kinsey 1980: 249). Our research in Northern England emphasized the significance of training, force commitment to implementation, and supervisory officers' ability to enforce rules (making the visibility of officers' activities a crucial factor). Baldwin and Kinsey's argument connected with debates in the 1980s about local political accountability of police: 'where legal certainty runs out the need for alternative control over the police begins. . . . A realist analysis must . . . examine the use made of complementary control systems which exist as alternatives to law'. Pre-eminent among these were 'external control and accountability' (1985: 92; see Ch. 7, below).

Baldwin and Kinsey indicate the need to differentiate among policing practices in terms of their amenability to legal regulation.

Equally, rules have to be distinguished 'according to such factors as status, sanctions, degree of specificity, procedure and enforcement practice' (Baldwin 1989: 166; Baldwin and Kinsey 1985: 91). Research experience has shown that it was correct, for example, to warn that rules on stop and search were unlikely to be successful (Baldwin 1985: 20; Baldwin and Kinsey 1985: 96). Studies of PACE have shown the contrasts between the regulation of activities within and outside police stations (Dixon *et al.* 1989; Chs. 3 and 4, below).

They go further, pointing out that the effect of rules will be significantly influenced by their context: being 'realistic about legal rules and policing . . . means looking to particular aspects of police activity and judging their amenability to legal controls' (Baldwin and Kinsey 1985: 92). They argue that the role of rules cannot 'be considered in isolation and it must take into account not only the way policing is organised in a geographic area but also the feasibility of different styles of policing within particular localities and even alongside particular economic strategies' (Kinsey and Baldwin 1982: 315; cf. Chan's use of Bourdieu's concept of 'field' in this context: Chan 1996, 1997).

Geographic location is important: legal rules and attempts to change policing have to take account of the variations, not just at the most general level between country and city, but between regions and areas (1982: 308–9; cf. Cain 1973; Young 1993). This has been notably demonstrated by Brogden's histories of policing in Liverpool which have demonstrated how both a particular mode of legal regulation ('permissive and inquisitorial street powers') and a particular relationship between the police and the local state were products of developments within the political economy of that city (Brogden and Brogden 1984: 46; cf. Brogden 1982, 1991). Research on the effects of PACE has found some stark contrasts (sometimes between geographically similar areas) in uses of various powers to detain for lengthy periods, investigative methods, custody officers' practices, and requests for legal advice (Dixon 1992: 526–7; Ch. 4, below).

It is also emphasized that the impact of rules is dependent on the broad political environment (Baldwin and Kinsey 1982). This is similar to Grimshaw and Jefferson's 'environmental model' (1987: 9–11) which they identify with studies which 'conceive the behaviour of the [police] organization—its structure, policies and working practices— as the product of a series of negotiations with what Reiss and Bordua call its "environing system" ' (1987: 9). For example, Banton's comparison of Scottish and American policing connected socio-political culture and policing style (1964). Most significant of such studies is J. Q. Wilson's attempt to demonstrate that there is 'an observable relationship between the working "style" of officers, departmental policies and organizational codes, and the prevailing political culture' (Grimshaw and Jefferson 1987: 10; see also Wilson 1968; Krantz *et al.* 1979: 9; Walker 1996b). The emphasis on 'watchman', 'legalistic', or 'service' style was substantially influenced by the social and political context of the eight police departments which he studied. This perspective can also be associated with the emergence of studies of police work which combine high-quality observational and interview data with an understanding of political and administrative theory which has been largely absent from previous accounts (Brown 1988; Muir 1977).

It is worth noting Walker's caution that there is no simple relationship between political environment and police reform (or lack of it): '[s]ome of the most significant advances in the control of police discretion . . . occurred in an allegedly conservative period' (1993a: 14). Nevertheless, it is hard to ignore the significance of policing's environment in Australia, where the police forces of Queensland and New South Wales were instrumentally and culturally inseparable from corrupt political regimes (Fitzgerald 1989). These forces are (according to optimistic accounts) in the process of fundamental change as a result of the downfall of those old regimes or are (according to pessimistic accounts) largely immune to change because of the longevity of the old regimes. The reality is somewhere in between: change is occurring but reform efforts are impeded both by political caution and by the uncharted depths of the relations between police, politicians, and legal and illegal business. The socio-political aspects of policing's legal environment may also be significant. In England and Wales, pessimistic predictions about effects of PACE have turned out to be somewhat mistaken, in part because of the political effects of the miscarriage of justice cases. However, in the mid-1990s, the Conservative Government's reversion to neanderthal law-and-order politics and the negative effect of the Report of the Royal Commission on Criminal Justice (RCCJ 1993) have allowed the police to weather the storm of the miscarriage cases, and to emerge with increasingly confident revival of complaints about criminal justice's bias towards 'criminals' (see Ch. 4, below).

It is appropriate here to indicate that Baldwin and Kinsey's work is significant in connecting law in policing with broader debates about regulation which will be considered further in Chapter 7, below (cf. Baldwin 1989; 1990; 1995; Baldwin and McCrudden (eds.) 1987). Policing research too often presents policing as if it is isolated from changes in public administration (Baldwin 1989: 157; Reiner 1992b: 490). Baldwin in particular valuably links changes in policing to broader trends in regulatory activity. He notes, for example, 'the increasing attractiveness of rules that give the appearance of conformity to the rule of law but which offer limited and sometimes illusory opportunities of redress' (1989: 160) and 'a retreat from primary legislation in favour of government by informal rules' such as circulars and codes of practice (Baldwin and Houghton 1986: 239). Again emphasizing the significance of situational factors, Baldwin argues that, in the illustrative context of health and safety at work, 'the role of rules and the nature of the optimal rule differ according to a number of variables, notably the favoured enforcement strategy, the type of regulatee and the type of hazard' (Baldwin 1990: 328).

Baldwin and Kinsey proposed a 'realistic' account of rules, arguing that 'realism demands that police powers be designed with an element of stretch built in' (Baldwin 1985: 21). The subjects of rules will always try to escape their grasp, so working rules and the law are always going to be different (Baldwin 1985: 20–1). 'The problem is that if the law is to "inhibit" police officers then it must always diverge to some extent from the rules that officers would write for themselves' (Baldwin and Kinsey 1985: 91). If, metaphorically, they are given authority to drive at 30 mph, they will drive at 35. 'To increase the limit to 35 mph will not close the gap', but will simply lead to 40 mph driving (Baldwin 1985: 21). Such accounts can slip too easily into what Reiner calls 'a law of inevitable increment: whatever powers the police have they will exceed by a given margin' (Reiner 1992a: 217). Reiner goes on to provide a good critique of such formulations:

police abuse is not the product of some overweening constabulary malevolence constantly bursting the seams of whatever rules for regulating conduct are laid down. It is based on pressure to achieve specific results. . . . If the police can achieve their proper objects within the law then one strain making for deviation disappears (Reiner 1992a: 217–18).

Baldwin suggested that an (inevitably unsuccessful) attempt to ease this strain had been made, in England and Wales, by legalizing worst police practice: 'draconian powers have been drafted so as to cover worst cases' (Baldwin 1985: 18).[14] He preferred the pre-1984 informal situation in which detention for questioning was permissible so long as the length of the period was reasonable (Baldwin 1981: 275). This position depends on a somewhat rosy view of policing practice before legislation and a gloomy prediction of post-PACE judicial practice. The latter was hardly surprising, given the English judiciary's contemporary performance in cases like *Sang* and *Holgate-Mohammed* v. *Duke*,[15] Baldwin and Kinsey's experience of legal reform in Scotland (Baldwin 1985: 26–7; 1989: 163–4) and the limited exclusionary provisions in the early versions of the PACE Bills. It will be suggested in Chapter 4 that, for a variety of reasons, this pessimism was overstated: events since 1986 made the courts more 'activist' in their interpretation of PACE than was generally anticipated.

More generally, it may be that it is better to attempt a clear definition of police powers and suspects' rights through legal regulation (McBarnet 1981b). As Reiner suggests, '[t]his does not mean that unacceptable practices should be legitimated. But it does suggest that the police must have adequate powers to perform the core tasks which are expected of them' (1992a: 218). But this, once again, depends on situational factors: several Australian jurisdictions have legislated on detention for questioning in a way which has led to just the result predicted by Baldwin and Kinsey for Britain (see Ch. 5, below).

(b) *Jefferson and Grimshaw*

An ambitious attempt at a structural theory of law–policing relations comes in the work of Tony Jefferson and his colleagues (Jefferson and Grimshaw 1984; Grimshaw and Jefferson 1987; Brogden *et al.* 1988: 34–5, 94–7, ch. 7). This begins with a major study of police accountability, in which Jefferson and Grimshaw identify the doctrine of constabulary independence as the key to an understanding of English policing (1984; see also Grimshaw and Jefferson 1987: 290 and Ch. 2, below). Somewhat ironically, their account of constabulary independence recuperates a traditional legal view which has been

---

[14] Here, Baldwin and Kinsey laid much of the ground work for McConville, Sanders, and Leng (1991a), discussed below.

[15] [1980] AC 402; [1984] AC 437; see Ch. 4, below, for details.

severely criticized by leading public lawyers (Lustgarten 1986; Marshall 1965). According to Jefferson and his colleagues, constabulary independence negates attempts to control policing. Within the legal vacuum which it creates, police culture grows, structuring the choices which discretion makes necessary. 'The independent office of constable effectively grants the constable discretion over legal decision-making. Where the law is unclear or ambiguous, officers . . . fall back on . . . their own occupationally structured, learned, subcultural "common sense" ' (Brogden *et al*. 1988: 82; see also Grimshaw and Jefferson 1987: 97). From the perspective of police management, the gap between law and practice should be bridged by the formulation and implementation of policy. However, attempts by management to intervene by means of policy directives are inevitably negatived by the autonomy which constabulary independence provides: 'effective operational policy (authoritative statements signifying settled practices of law enforcement) cannot exist. The universality of constabulary independence makes operational policy effectively redundant' (Grimshaw and Jefferson 1987: 291; see also Brogden *et al*. 1988: 168–9). These attempts to demonstrate the ineffectiveness of policy are not fully convincing, requiring the adoption of a somewhat idiosyncratic definition of 'policy' (Grimshaw and Jefferson 1987: ch. 6; contrast Lustgarten 1986: 18).

In this account, law (in the form of constabulary independence) is the source of the problem: but it also provides the solution. For Jefferson and his colleagues, it is the power of law which can cut through the defensive barrier of constabulary independence:

the key lies with the formal rules, on the grounds that it is the permissiveness of the external structure (the uncontrolled discretion), and the concomitant internal permissiveness (an inevitable consequence of a system of legal accountability which renders operational policy redundant) which creates the space for the occupational culture to flourish (Brogden *et al*. 1988: 170; see also Grimshaw and Jefferson 1987: 97).

Legal regulation is, therefore, a first step towards their aim of creating an accountable police service: '[t]he argument for prioritizing rule change . . . is that the current permissive structures—external and internal—enable the cop culture to flourish. It follows that rule tightening would disable' (Brogden *et al*. 1988: 170). Legal regulation by itself is insufficient: it must be accompanied by the promotion of 'principles of justice to guide the exercise of discretion' (Grimshaw and Jefferson 1987: 284). This connects with their conception of socialist justice developed elsewhere.[16]

Grimshaw and Jefferson demonstrate a refreshing willingness to consider law as something other than the vague reification found in some other accounts. They combine a broad theory of law as a social practice (derived principally from Hirst (1979) and similar to that implicit in McBarnet's work: see below) with an acute perception of the variety of police powers and criminal offences. In this account 'law' is not all of a kind, but can be more or less influential, more or less constraining: this is 'a composite and differentiated conception', in which they examine 'law as a contemporary process rather than searching for a unitary essence' (Grimshaw and Jefferson 1987: 271). It is argued that specific knowledge of powers and offences needs to replace the prevalent idealistic notions. By implication, concern about specifics of the powers and offences provided becomes worthwhile (Grimshaw and Jefferson 1987: 15–18, 45–6, 91–2).

In their major work, Grimshaw and Jefferson (1987) subject empirical material on 'policy and practice in forms of beat policing' to a sustained evaluation of theories of policing. They develop their own structural account, an ambitious adaptation (and critique) of Althusserian structuralism (drawing also on Gramsci and Foucault). In this account, law is central to an understanding of policing: 'law provides the central discursive framework for police activity; it defines the principal elements of the police task, distinguishes the police from other state institutions and produces the forms of police accountability . . . [T]he discourse of law is the starting-point for making sense of policework' (Grimshaw and Jefferson 1987: 274, see also 290). Law is theorized as the determining but not necessarily dominant structure in policing—'the relationship between the structures is structured by law . . . without that in any way implying that law will be the dominant structure of organized policework in particular instances' (Grimshaw and Jefferson 1987: 24–5, see also 290). Currently, structuralist theory of this kind is distinctly unfashionable. None the less, it does have explanatory power when applied to their empirical material, notably in their account of how the 'absence of legal work' conditions the activities of resident beat officers (Grimshaw and Jefferson 1987: 179–80, 290). Whatever one thinks of structuralism, Grimshaw and Jefferson's study is a notable attempt

[16] See Jefferson and Grimshaw 1982; 1984. It has, of course, been argued that 'principles' are as much part of law as are rules: see Dworkin 1977 and below.

to theorize policing, to drag its study out from the 'police studies' backwater into the mainstream of social theory. Similarly, their insistence on the need to develop principles of justice resonate powerfully with more recent attempts to provide a new political philosophy for criminology (e.g. Braithwaite 1992). Grimshaw and Jefferson's work is both difficult and challenging: the lack of attention which it has received in police studies is regrettable, but not surprising.

(c) *McBarnet*

In contrast, much more attention has been paid to the work of Doreen McBarnet, and it is with a critical examination of her work that much of the rest of this Chapter will be concerned. While McBarnet's work is often cited, it has not received the detailed critical treatment which it deserves. McBarnet's work takes as problematic what legalistic-bureaucratic and culturalist conceptions both assume: it examines critically the nature of the law itself. This has been extremely influential in the United Kingdom and Australia (although much less so in the United States, where some difficulty was apparently experienced in distinguishing between rhetoric and theoretical critique; e.g. Skolnick 1982). In Canada, Richard Ericson has shared and expanded McBarnet's perspective in his impressive series of studies (Ericson 1981a; 1981b; 1982; Ericson and Baranek 1983). Via Ericson, it has also illuminated Miyazawa's study of policing in Japan (1992).

In *Conviction: Law, the State, and the Construction of Justice* (1983) and a series of associated essays (1976; 1978a; 1978b; 1979; 1981a; 1981b; 1982), McBarnet fundamentally challenged culturalist accounts of the relationship between law and policing. The contexts of her work are significant: these were the law-and-order politics of Britain in the 1970s and early 1980s and, secondly, the challenge of structuralism to interactionism in criminology and the sociology of law. McBarnet argued powerfully that the dominant accounts of criminal justice were constructed around false dichotomies—law in the books and law in action, due process and crime control, law and order (see also Hunt 1993: ch. 4). Such dichotomies reflected ideology rather than reality, and their use in academic accounts was a product of the political and methodological narrowness of culturalist/interactionist studies. These accounts corresponded, ironically, with those of police lobbies and civil libertarians (although their prescriptions for reform differed somewhat).

For McBarnet, the relevant contrast is between the rhetoric of legality (in which due process and other rights are venerated) on one side, and the reality of legal rules and procedures (which routinely deny them) on the other. This gap is not contingent. Rather it is crucial to the operation of criminal justice in maintaining law's ideological power while serving other instrumental ends. In perhaps her most well-known aphorism, McBarnet insisted that if 'we bring due process down from the dizzy heights of abstraction and subject it to empirical scrutiny, the conclusion must be that due process is *for* crime control' (1979: 39, original emphasis). The political implications of this are clear: criminal procedure should be located within an account of the state as a whole. McBarnet argued that attention should be switched from the bottom to the top, from 'the petty administrators of the law . . . to the people with the power to make it—the judicial and political elite of the state' (1976: 199). The methodological imperative was to shift away from observation of street-cops to a study of how their practices were permitted and created by the law, and thence to a critical study of legality itself: '[t]o question whether the law incorporates its own rhetoric is to ask whether deviation from standards of justice and legality are not merely the product of informalities and unintended consequences at the level of petty officials, but institutionalised in the formal law of the state' (1983: 8). The result of doing this was to show that the activities which culturalists categorized as 'deviant' were in fact legal: they were authorized either by statute or, more significantly, by judicial practice.

Since *Conviction*, McBarnet's research has shifted away from the police to other areas of regulatory activity. However, her insights continue to be of relevance. Writing with Whelan, she has emphasized the problem of ' "creative compliance"—using the law to escape legal control without actually violating legal rules. This perspective focuses on the active response of those subject the law, not just in political lobbying but in post hoc manipulation to turn it . . . to the service of their own interests and to avoid unwanted control' (1991: 848). In this work, she makes explicit a theory of law which was developed in her studies of policing. For McBarnet, law provides a flexible and permissive structure within which police work can be conducted. Her work 'points to an indeterminacy in rules, broad or narrow, and to the scope within law to legitimise contradictory decisions' (McBarnet and Whelan 1991: 852). Such observations are now common in modern legal theory, from Hart's insistence on the open texture of rules (1961)[17] to (as McBarnet and Whelan point out) the insistence on indeterminacy by critical legal studies writers (1991: 853). However, McBarnet's formulation is notable for its development through empirical study. It treated law

> not merely as substance, a body of requirements and prohibitions served up on a platter to be accepted or rejected. . . . Rather it approached law, after legislation, as a 'raw material to be worked on' . . . as something which might be used, manipulated, crafted to suit one's own interests. The approach focused less on the content of law . . . and more on exploring its methods, structures and ideologies, its 'facilitative form', and how it could be actively used (McBarnet 1992: 248).

Taking account of the active response of those subject to legislation challenges presentations in which police are the passive subjects (or, as some police see it, victims) of statutory change. The significant response here is not evasion of legal control (although this occurs, e.g. in use of 'consent': see Ch. 3, below), but in *use* of law. In our research on policing in Northern England, several officers told us that they had 'learnt to make PACE work for us' (Dixon *et al.* 1990a: 137; cf. McConville *et al.* 1991a: 43–4). This meant, for example, using PACE's record-making requirements to insulate actions from criticism. If an otherwise thorough and apparently authoritative custody record does not show a detective's visit to a suspect's cell, it will be very difficult to establish that improper questioning or bargaining took place. Similarly, McConville *et al.* have shown how reliance on custody records can give a misleading picture of custody officers' practice in informing suspects of their rights (1991a: ch. 3). Provisions for electronic recording of questioning may have a similar effect: McConville has argued that when 'informal' exchanges are followed by a formal videotaped interrogation, 'the position of a complaining suspect will be weakened rather than strengthened because of its apparent ability to capture reality' (1992: 961; cf. Dixon and Travis 1997). Law can also be used for other purposes: Egger and Findlay demonstrate how New South Wales Police exploited the flexibility of public-order offences in order to mount a political campaign against the State's Attorney-General (1988). This echoes the culturalist view of criminal law as a resource in dealing with situa-

---

[17] Hart is rarely cited by policing scholars even when their formulations bear an obvious if perhaps indirect debt: see e.g. Bittner, 1990: 92.

tions encountered by patrolling officers; but here the focus is wider, showing how law provides a resource for the accomplishment of many goals. Far from being restrictive, it is a positive, enabling resource.

While acknowledging the advances made by McBarnet's work, some criticism may be made of it. In turn, her responses to some critics can be considered. Despite her insistence on 'the need to probe the substance and form of law itself' (1983: ix), McBarnet's theory of law is never fully articulated, and remains a underdeveloped combination of structuralism and radical realism. Conceptual distinctions are not clearly made between 'the rhetoric of law, the form of law, the content of law, and the practices of its participants' (Hutton 1987: 113). Reference is sometimes made to 'form' when it seems that rhetoric or principle is really at issue. While this is partly a result of the complexity of empirical reality, it causes some problems in McBarnet's account.

Other (generally sympathetic) critics have tried to reinstate conceptual distinctions between types of rule-following and rule-breaking. Nelken criticizes her 'for ignoring the difference between those rules which offer illusory safeguards because they are unenforceable, those which could protect but are in fact unenforced, and those which . . . do exercise some inhibitory influence' (1987: 151). Essentially the same point is made by McConville and Baldwin, when they argue:

Whilst it is true to say that the law often fails to incorporate its own rhetoric, it is also true to say that it does sometimes give rights, and in this latter situation it is meaningful to speak of breaches. . . . [T]he important point to determine is whether those rights are breached or unenforced because (i) there is no effective mechanism to ensure compliance, or (ii) the courts choose not to enforce them (1981: 200).

The outcome is

not a simple picture of formal law taking away with one hand what it has given with the other. . . . If we are to understand the criminal justice system, these distinctions must be appreciated even if we are led to conclude that, for one reason or another, it is almost meaningless to speak of suspects' rights in the actual operation of the law (McConville and Baldwin 1981: 201–2).

The importance of such distinctions is illustrated by the reception of McBarnet's work in the United States, where interpretation of the Constitution by the Supreme Court has provided substantial due-process rights, but where the problem has been their unenforce-ability in the face of routine non-compliance or evasion by police and other agencies (see Skolnick 1982: 1332–3).

An illustrative example from England and Wales is the Criminal Law Act 1977, section 62, which notionally entitled a suspect in cus-tody to have someone informed of the arrest and of the place of detention. This 'right of intimation' was hedged by qualifications of reasonableness and the possibility of 'necessary' delay, in an appar-ently deliberate and successful attempt to produce 'a paper rather than a real reform' (King 1981: 146). As such, it provided a good example for McBarnet's argument. PACE, section 56, replaced this provision with a right of intimation: this is qualified by exceptions which are closely specified and which can be relied upon only with the written authorization of a superintendent. Custody officers have specific, sanction-backed responsibility for offering intimation. The result in our research force was that offering intimation became part of standard procedure—although delivering it could be delayed, whether by necessity or design (Bottomley *et al.* 1991: ch. 6). However, the right to legal advice, which is symbolically and instru-mentally much more significant to police, has been less easily accom-modated (see Ch. 6, below). So, procedural rules are not all the same: their content, their significance to police, and their likely enforce-ability are important variables.

Despite the strength of such criticisms of McBarnet, they seem to underestimate the extent to which she relies on an implicit alterna-tive legal theory, at the centre of which is an expanded notion of law which includes procedures and practices as well as rules. In this sense, the distinctions noted above lose some significance if breaches are, by redefinition, made part of legal practice. Nonetheless, McBarnet maintains a distinction between law (in this broad sense) and rhetoric. She has been criticized for this by Nelken, who would fol-low Dworkin in arguing that 'rhetoric' is part of a broader non-pos-itivist concept of law:

Her contrast between the world of 'rhetoric' (where procedural safeguards do exist) and the law itself . . . runs the risk of reproducing, at a higher level, the artificial distinction between 'law in books' and 'law in action' which she is at such pains to reject. The view that 'rhetoric' lies outside the law rests on an unexamined positivist separation between the rules of law and the broader principles which animate it . . . 'rhetoric' serves as the source of prin-ciples which can generate or limit legal rule-making even though it does not and cannot function in the same way as rules (1987: 151; cf. Hogg 1991a: 23–5).

McConville, Sanders, and Leng take this further, arguing that the dichotomy of crime control and due process permeates throughout criminal justice: it is to be found not just in the law but also in the rhetoric and fundamental principles (1991a: ch. 9). Their development of McBarnet is explored further below.

McBarnet's theory of the unity of law and practice is largely a product of her experience of trying to understand law 'in its own terms' and having to make sense of its impenetrability and uncertainty: 'it became clear that it was not my lack of legal learning that made the law so elusive: that was the nature of law, a will-o'-the-wisp pausing but for a moment before the next decision, and then only "clear" for the particular circumstances of that particular case' (1983: 164–5). As this suggests, it is the form of case law which McBarnet considers crucial:

Since every case is, or can be made out to be unique, this means that what the law is in relation to that case, whether it will continue an established line of reasoning or establish a new refinement, cannot be definitely known in advance. The case by case method means that you literally never really know what the law is (1982: 412–13).

Case law allows the judges to retain their power, even when legislatures seek to define the law:

general powers or rights . . . cannot cover all specific cases. This is not only because life does not fit so easily into neat legal categories, but because the trade of advocates in making cases is to make quite sure it does not. The applicability of the letter of the law to the case in hand is put in question by selecting, framing and presenting the facts to ensure that the facsimile of life so created slips between the pigeonholes . . . of the law (1981b: 452).

Case law is particularly responsible for maintaining the gap between ideology and law/legal practice. In the occasional 'great case', judges may seek to concretize principle; but this is soon worn away by the steady drip of exceptions and specific application in subsequent cases. McBarnet's example is the Scottish case, *Chalmers*.[18] She argues that

---

[18] [1954] JC 66. Cf. the discussion of *Alladice* ((1988) 87 Cr. App. R 380) and *Williams* ((1986) 66 ALR 385) in Chs. 4 and 5 respectively below. This analysis could also be applied to the fate of the US Supreme Court's decisions in *Miranda*, n. 6 above, and *Mapp* v. *Ohio* 367 US 643 (1961).

its stand against detention for questioning 'was so "clarified" by succeeding cases that it might never have happened' (1982b: 411). The
principle is trumpeted, but the practice subverts it: 'the form of case
law itself provides one mechanism by which the law can maintain at
a plausible level the ideology of justice, while simultaneously and
routinely subverting it' (1982: 412).

McBarnet's account is not just that (in jurisprudential terms) of a
rule-sceptic, but also of a fact-sceptic. She stresses that the facts of a
case are constructed and reconstructed out of competing, malleable
accounts presented by parties with very different resources of power.
Criminal justice purports to deal with facts and 'truth', but is better
seen as a process in which knowledge 'has to be worked out, constructed, rationalised, negotiated', from the beginning, at the discov-
ery of a crime, through the processes of police investigation
(particularly interrogation), to trial and judgment (Sanders *et al.*
1989: 139; see also McConville and Baldwin 1981: 98, 190–2; Dixon
1991a; McConville *et al.* 1991a).

McBarnet's echoing of some elements of American legal realism is
apparently unconscious. In this respect, her work suffers from the
general lack of communication between legal theory and criminology
which results in considerable duplication of effort. Her account is
open to criticisms of realism which have long been familiar in legal
theory: law is not just what judges say or officials do. The point was
made clearly in a critique by Baldwin (1981, expanded in Kinsey and
Baldwin 1982), who insists on the need to retain a distinction between
law and practice. He challenges McBarnet's account of how courts
whittle away at principle: while cases may make exceptions (e.g. brief
detention of motorists without reasonable suspicion for alcohol testing), this does not mean that the principal rule (no detention without
arrest) is abandoned.

The difficulty with this response is that exceptions may not, in fact,
be exceptional. They tend to accumulate, leaving the general rule an
empty shell:

The very fact that case law refinements are posed as exceptions serves of
itself to reiterate the general principle even if the concrete cases have
become so numerous and sophisticated that the exceptions have in effect
become the rule. . . . The power of the case law form lies in the fact
that it can simultaneously incorporate as the law both civil rights and the
extensions of police powers that undermine and deny them (McBarnet 1982:
414).

A good example here is *Holgate-Mohammed* v. *Duke*, where the 'rule' in English common law prohibiting detention for questioning was finally abandoned, after having been chipped away through the cases and developments in practice.[19] Similarly, the disjuncture between 'freedom of speech' and public-order law has been indicated as a good example of McBarnet's argument (Galligan 1987: 194). In police law, the exceptions have often been more significant than the supposedly fundamental rule or principle.[20]

A second objection to McBarnet's account of legal reasoning is to insist on the distinction between fact and law. If courts interpret (and even blatantly misinterpret) facts, this is not the same as changing the law: '[s]o long as tied to individual facts, a decision does not change the wider rules of law' (Kinsey and Baldwin 1982: 313). For example, if a court concludes that a person was 'consenting' to be with police (see Ch. 4, below), this has no effect on the law relating to detention for questioning:

That courts have allowed police officers, by way of bluff or other methods, to detain persons in a coercive manner may be a true description of fact, but to state that they may do this by law is to confuse law and practice. . . . [T]o argue that rules are not enforced is by no means to show that such rules do not exist in law (Baldwin 1981: 275).

From a jurisprudential point of view, there is an important difference between judges widening or narrowing the law and those particular cases where they make findings of fact that in police terms produce convenient legal results (Kinsey and Baldwin 1982: 312).

This critique was dismissed by McBarnet as being trapped inside the very legalism which she was challenging: the distinction between fact and law was an artificial device, 'a demonstration of one of the many techniques by which legal reasoning can endorse police powers that undercut the rhetoric of civil rights at the same time as vociferously upholding them' (1982: 413). To some extent, the difference between McBarnet and Kinsey and Baldwin is one of perspective, sociological *v.* jurisprudential, or outside *v.* inside law. The sociological view seems more attractive, not least because it has more relevance to the experience of people dealt with by the criminal justice system.

---

[19] N. 15 above. This case is discussed in Ch. 4, below.

[20] In public law more generally, traditional texts in administrative law have been virtual caricatures: a rule or principle is established, and then the author provides dozens of pages of exceptions and 'specific applications'. See, e.g., Wade 1988.

Doctrinal distinctions between fact and law are unlikely to seem very significant to the defendant on the receiving end of some 'creative' legal reasoning.

None the less, this is a debate not just about theory but about policy: both 'sides' were concerned about contemporary developments in criminal justice politics. This requires returning to the issue of law's 'resourcefulness' which was discussed above. Kinsey and Baldwin insist that their approach has practical political significance in establishing that police activities are not self-validating, that the law is not just what the police do. The law is a constraint on police, even though a flexible one:

> there is a world of difference between giving officers discretions that are in fact allowed by courts to cover a wide range of circumstances and giving them discretions that are unlimited or unreviewable at law. The fact that courts often allow police to 'bend the rules' does not indicate that the police at present do assume a legal right to extend their powers (Baldwin 1981: 275).

The abandonment of the concept of police illegality could never really be more than a rhetorical flourish. Wide as the law is, officers do break it: this 'remains true even though most police illegality is insulated from scrutiny and remains unsanctioned. . . . Concentrating on the elasticity of the law should not blind us to the fact that malleability is finite' (McConville *et al.* 1991a: 175; on police illegalities, see *ibid*: 176–7).

If McBarnet's account is more convincing when the focus is on the suspect/defendant, then Kinsey and Baldwin's regains ground when it is on the police. At least in England in the late-1980s and 1990s, officers did not talk or act as if the law was no constraint upon them: it was one of numerous constraints about which they complained. (The same is not necessarily true in other times and places: see Ch. 5, below). As the comments above on culturalism suggested, police cultures are not immune from law, but are shaped by both its influence and their reaction against that influence. The law may be bent or stretched: this is not the same as disregarding it. Law also has effects on the way in which police managers 'design policing tactics, train officers, and exercise discipline' (Baldwin 1981: 275).

The political dangers of conceding that the police define their own powers is stressed by Kinsey and Baldwin: '[p]olitically it is important to assert the legal limitation of powers, even if rules are routinely by-passed in particular trials: to do so is to preserve the language of civil rights when dealing with the rules of criminal procedure' (1982: 313). Preserving a critical distance between law and practice provides 'a medium through which policing methods can be debated' and political interventions effected (1982: 314). McBarnet's response is to suggest that this gap has harmful political effects, masking the reality: it would be better to 'close the gap between what people believe their rights are and what the law actually provides. It makes the law more open to reaction, whether approving or horrified' (1981b: 451).The context of this exchange was the debate about the proposals which eventually became PACE. In retrospect, it may be that McBarnet and Kinsey and Baldwin (like most other critics) misjudged the likely effects of the legislation, both by being excessively cynical about the limits on the new powers and by not appreciating broader changes in contemporary policing. These issues are discussed further in Chapter 4, below.

Moving to another field of criticism, a central problem in McBarnet's work is the essentialism which characterizes some of the epigrammatic statements for which her work is best known. Take, for example, the claim quoted above that 'due process is *for* crime control'. This is presented, not just as a conclusion about the Scottish criminal justice system in the 1970s (the subject of her empirical work), but as a statement about the essence of criminal justice in (at least) Britain and the United States. The criteria for this broader relevance are not made explicit: it is not clear whether, for example, the basis is mode of production or the legal form, which may be characteristic of more than one mode of production. In both cases, the geographical claims of the theory would be widened. Similarly, there is no temporal reference for the account, and little sense of historical change.

Such essentialism obscures differences between, and change within, criminal justice systems which are significant at the level of analysis of the bulk of McBarnet's work. As noted above, the relationship between law and policing in England and Wales has been changed substantially by a number of factors, including PACE. In Canada, assessing the impact of the Charter of Rights effects is controversial, but it is seems clear that it has been significant (e.g. Penner 1996). By contrast, Chapter 5 will suggest that New South Wales currently has a law–policing relationship very similar to that described by McBarnet. My research found among police officers a general satisfaction with the powers available, which was expressed in a way which made clear that legal controls are generally so wide or flexible as to interfere minimally with everyday police work based on 'common sense' and cultural standards of 'reasonableness'.

Australian law on pre-charge detention provides an excellent example of McBarnet's argument. However, this situation is not permanent. The Federal law on custodial interrogation has been reformed, providing powers to detain for investigation for not more than twelve hours.[21] Similar changes have been proposed in New South Wales (NSW LRC 1990) and Queensland (CJC 1994) and there is considerable political dispute about the issue, centring on whether detention length should be limited by specific maxima or by a police assessment of what is reasonable. This is an area of political contestation rather than fixed positions.[22] Also, the politics involved are constituted differently from in England and Wales: as noted above, NSW is dominated by the simplistic politics of law and order. The opposition to this is, all too often, an invocation of 'common law rights' which has little contact with reality or relevance (see comments in NSW LRC 1990: 18–21, 86–7). To dispel any suggestion that this account implies that change is always progressive,[23] the example of Victoria should be cited. There, controls on detention for questioning were introduced, only to be substantially weakened as a result of protests from police (NSW LRC 1990: 90–1). Similarly, it is instructive to compare the Scottish and Anglo–Welsh experiences. The former was much less successful than the latter (with large numbers of suspects being treated as volunteers outside the time limits set by the Criminal Justice (Scotland) Act 1980) because inadequate steps were taken to ensure that change was effectively implemented (Currie and Carnie 1986; see Ch. 3, below).

There is a significant ambivalence in McBarnet's work. At one level, she argues that, for example: '[l]asting reforms cannot be possible without some deeper change in the form of law itself' (1983: 161). This emphasis on problems of structure seems to leave little room for interest in conventional law-reform strategies. Moreover, it might seem that there is little point in resisting the formal extension of police powers, if police already use such powers informally. Here she seems to slip into something of which she accuses others: 'the old errors of functionalism, taking the aims of the system as given, focus-

[21] Crimes (Investigation of Commonwealth Offences) Amendment Act 1991.
[22] For full discussion, see Ch. 5, below.
[23] Cf. the comments on Devlin 1960 in Ch. 4, below.

ing on the functions of existing situations rather than their historical purposes, on logical inevitability rather than social determinants' (1978a: 29). But, at the same time, she engages in discussion about change of a less fundamental nature, and the essentialism of her approach at times runs contrary to her willingness to concede that legal change may be beneficial.

In this respect, McBarnet's work reflects the substantial political dilemmas of theory in the late 1970s, which had to work through the old counterpositions of short- or long-term change, reform or revolution, pragmatism or the progressive. In retrospect, such dichotomies are just as unhelpful as those which McBarnet's work criticized so roundly (Ericson 1981b: 224). Miscarriage of justice cases of the last decade in Britain and Australia illustrate the potential for individual instances to become the vehicle for wider change. These illustrate the need to combine detailed analysis and short-term political campaigning with a deeper analysis of the structuring conditions in which miscarriages of justice occur (e.g. Carrington *et al.* (eds.) 1991; Dixon 1992).

McBarnet accepts that legal change is not necessarily ineffective: 'to say that people do not necessarily obey the law is not to say they never do. The law can constrain, especially when it is public and subject to controls' (1983: 7; see also Ericson 1981b: 216–17). Elsewhere, she stresses the significance of the 'elements of accountability and sanctions introduced by formal rules' (1979: 27). As noted above in the discussion of culturalist theory, legal change may penetrate deeper than its direct effects may suggest: if 'abstract rules are redefined and used according to practical purposes, then practical purposes, the "needs" of crime control, may also be redefined according to the demands of formal rules' (1979: 27).

An example which McBarnet cites is the reported effect of 'due process' decisions in some areas of the United States in encouraging police to rely less on interrogation in crime investigation (1979: 27). While the extent of such change may be a matter of dispute,[24] this is one of the observed products of legal regulation in England and Wales (Dixon *et al.* 1990a; Ch. 4 below). McBarnet acknowledges the crucial point that the effect of law in such circumstances cannot be read off from some deterministic calculus: '[i]t is endemic in judicial discretion that cases can be used in court . . . to sanction the police.

---

[24] See Walker 1993a and Ch. 4, sect. vii, below.

Indeed it is endemic in common law that it changes, swings from crime control to legality—and back again. The swings are patterned, of course, and historically located' (1983: 40; see also 1979: 40). So, for instance, concern about policing and revelations of police mal-practice were at least partly responsible for a series of cases in the later 1980s and early 1990s in which PACE was interpreted strictly against the police (see Ch. 4, below). Characteristically, the effect of this has been limited by a failure to develop firm guidelines for the use of judicial discretion and by the ability of courts to interpret facts against apparently undeserving appellants.[25] Developments such as these are, therefore, conjunctural rather than contingent, revealing the deeper 'patterning' of the criminal justice system, its priorities, and its commitment to achieving convictions.

Discussion here has focused on some problems in McBarnet's account. This should not divert attention from the broader signifi-cance of her work in shifting attention away from the police to polic-ing in its legal and political contexts.

(d) The Warwick School

An influential contribution to the debate on law in policing in Britain has been made by a group which I will term (conveniently if some-what loosely) the Warwick School.[26] The major contributions have been McConville, Sanders, and Leng's *The Case for the Prosecution* (1991a) and Sanders and Young's *Criminal Justice* (1994a). However, these central texts have been accompanied by an impressive range of major articles (e.g. Sanders and Young 1994b), reports and research studies (notably Sanders *et al.* 1989; Leng 1993; McConville and Hodgson 1993), and books on closely connected matters (McConville *et al.* 1994; McConville and Shepherd 1992). Inevitably, unifying a body of work such as this under the label of a 'school' risks artifi-ciality: there are differences of emphasis both within the group and sometimes within the same authors' publications.[27] None the less, it

---

[25] See the discussion of *Alladice*, n. 18 above, in Ch. 4, below.

[26] Mike McConville has been a focus of the group at Warwick, where Roger Leng also now works. Andrew Sanders, originally at Birmingham, is currently at Bristol. Elsewhere (Dixon 1992, 1995c), I applied the label 'new left pessimists', which was intended ironically to indicate the link between their work and the earlier left pes-simism identified and criticized by E. P. Thompson (1980: 164–80).

[27] This unsurprising feature of collaborative work can also be found in the research with which I have been associated (e.g. Bottomley *et al.* 1991; Dixon 1992).

is worth pulling the fundamental connecting themes from the group's work (with particular reference to *The Case for the Prosecution*), both to emphasize the breadth and significance of the Warwick School's contribution to criminology and to focus on some particularly important issues which their work identifies.

In Chapter 4, section vii, below, the Warwick School's interpretation of the Police and Criminal Evidence Act's impact will be considered. Based on their analysis of law's role in criminal justice, this leads to a rejection of reformist strategies in criminal justice. These offer:

the false promises of liberalism legalism: namely that the law offers significant protection of the person of the individual; that the law assists citizens in making decisions free of restraint, coercion and undue influence; that the behaviour of official actors is normatively ordered according to legal rules and legally recognized principles; that adversarial confrontation is the hallmark of criminal justice; and that all significant decisions are made according to revealed criteria in public settings (McConville *et al.* 1991a: 191).

The tone is one of deep pessimism about and rejection of reform strategies. In this section, attention is on the theoretical foundations of the School's empirical work and their political analysis.

The Warwick School's general theoretical approach is to integrate structuralist and interactionist insights into a version of social constructionism (McConville *et al.* 1991a: 11). At times, their structuralism tends to slip into the somewhat crude functionalism which has often featured in criminological analyses of relations between the economy and the neo-conservative state: 'Crime Control ideology . . . is a product of capitalism's requirement of a strong state' (1991a: 182; see also Sanders and Young 1994b: 129). The fundamental changes that they advocate ('overturning police culture, . . . redefining the police mandate and . . . instituting new forms of accountability': 1991a: 205–6) are regarded as unattainable: '[f]or the state, existing modes of law enforcement *work*. And this is so even when they sometimes fail or encounter resistance: indeed, occasional failure and the possibility of resistance is a *requirement* for an effective *legal* system' (1991a: 208, original emphases). Such functionalism is not only theoretically unsustainable: it also implies a political pessimism and abstention which is belied by the authors' involvement in reform activity (Smith 1995).

However, if one shifts from these rather rhetorical summary

formulations to the bulk of the work, the account becomes more subtle. McConville *et al.* draw on interactionist accounts of police culture, but insist that the structural location of cultures must be specified. Police culture is revived as the determinant of policing. They argue that legal reform has failed to penetrate a police culture which dominates policing: 'where legal rules cut across well-established cultural norms . . . they are unlikely to have instrumental effect' (McConville *et al.* 1991a: 200) because 'police behaviour is structured by police working rules more than by legal rules' (Sanders and Young 1994b: 129). Sanders and Young argue that the 'police choose to deviate from the rhetoric [of law] because the working rules they wish to follow are incompatible with any form of legalistic structuring of their work' (1994b: 138).

A problem with this formulation is that it seems sociologically unconvincing to treat police practices in case construction and what the police 'want' as if they were natural phenomena divorced from the law itself, or as if they were determined straightforwardly by prevailing economic and political forces. As noted above, a deficiency of cultural analysis has been failure to appreciate the complex relations between law and police culture: this tends to be reproduced at a higher level in the work by members of the Warwick School. Their own work shows the need for a more complex formulation. For example, Sanders and Young note that police use of interrogation is linked to the need to prove certain mental elements of offences (1994b: 139–40). The historical relationship between police practice and substantive criminal law in this area requires more specific study, but it seems likely that what would be found is a complex interactive relation between practice and law which assertions of police culture's dominance serve only to obscure.

A significant and characteristic emphasis of the Warwick School is on process: they 'understand criminal justice not as a *system*, which implies a relatively static unity with fixed boundaries, but as a *process*' (McConville *et al.* 1991a: 1, original emphases). While connecting themselves to structural traditions, their account evokes poststructuralist themes, both in their rejection of the concept of 'system' (cf. Hogg 1983 for an important statement of this argument) and in their identification of processes of social construction. However, their lack of engagement with post-structuralism reflects the critical, political edge to their analysis.

Beyond references to Cicourel and Ericson, McConville *et al.* provide no theoretical context for their constructionism. This is perhaps understandable: constructionist accounts of crime have been strongly criticized, notably by the new realists (e.g. Young 1994a: 111–13) and others.[28] In theoretical debates, the interactionism of early constructionist accounts has been overtaken by post-structuralism. In both criminology (Rafter 1990: 380) and social science more generally (e.g. Sarbin and Kitsuse 1994: 4; Holstein and Miller (eds.) 1993), attempts to incorporate post-structuralism into constructionism succeed largely in demonstrating the latter's increasing theoretical incoherence beyond opposition to positivism.[29]

Despite the background of these theoretical disputes, the Warwick School's work shows the viability and potential strength of a constructionist account of criminal justice. This is perhaps particularly so in decision-making processes in adversary systems which turn on whose account is sufficiently persuasive. While positivism receives the standard denunciation (McConville *et al.* 1991a: 9), this no longer entails the rejection of quantitative methods: these are used in a typically pragmatic (cf. Cohen 1988: 21) and somewhat unsophisticated way (Dixon 1995c: 222).

McConville *et al.* demonstrate clearly how cases are socially constructed:

It must be emphasized that at each point of the criminal justice process 'what happened' is the subject of interpretation, addition, substraction, selection and reformulation. This process is a *continuous* process, so that the meaning and status of 'a case' are to be understood in terms of the particular time and context in which it is viewed, a meaning and status that it may not have possessed earlier or continue to possess thereafter. The construction of a case . . . infuses every action and activity of official actors from the initial selection of the suspect to final case disposition. Case construction implicates the actors in a discourse with legal rules and guidelines and involves them in using rules, manipulating rules and interpreting rules. . . . Evidence is not something 'discovered' or 'unearthed', but is produced by all the parties (victims, witnesses, suspect, lawyers and police) involved in the investigation of the case (1991a: 12, 36, original emphasis).

---

[28] In a survey broadly sympathetic to left realism, Cohen dismisses the 'social constructionist paradigm' as 'now kept alive only by liberal sociologists working in the tradition of labeling theory' (1988: 21).

[29] It perhaps also suggests the capacity of American social science to soak up fundamental challenges and to trivialize them as additional 'perspectives', another chapter to be added to the student textbook.

Social construction involves actors in creating their social world: the focus of this perspective is on process, negotiation, and interaction. As theory and methodology, it has no preconceptions about whose interests will prevail: it is 'neutral in terms of social effects' (McConville and Sanders 1995: 191) and has 'no perjorative [*sic*] overtones. Construction does not require or imply that cases are necessarily unworthy, unmeritorious or against the interest of the object of the construction'. It is, they emphasize, 'a feature of *any* criminal justice process' (McConville *et al.* 1991: 11, original emphasis). The realist critique of constructionism—the moral and epistemological problems of extreme relativism about crime—loses force when the subject is the construction of a case.[30] Acknowledging the reality of crime (in terms of its occurrence and impact on victims and communities) is not inconsistent with a strong claim about the process by which an incident is transformed into a case. While the Warwick School's particular interpretation of this process may be questioned (see Ch. 4, sect. vii, below), their general analysis of the process of case construction is very useful. In addition, they eloquently acknowledge that the research process also involves social construction: '[r]esearch, like the world of its subjects, is a process of construction. . . . The fact that researchers do not and cannot have unmediated access to the "truth" is not a strength or a weakness of the research and is not a deficiency in our method: it is an epistemological reality' (1991a: 13).[31]

The theoretical bite of the Warwick School's approach comes when it is argued that social construction takes place within structural contexts, and it is these which determine outcomes. In the case of criminal justice, the key structural factor is the dominance of the police as 'the key actors' in an adversary system which 'makes case construction a particularly partial and partisan process (1991a: 36, 11). There is nothing particularly original here: the importance of the work is its clear articulation of a theoretical approach used by earlier researchers, notably Richard Ericson (1981b; 1982), in similar fields.

[30] Contrast D. J. Smith's criticism (1995) of this aspect of *The Case for the Prosecution* (1991a).

[31] This was ignored by some critics, who rushed to point out that the Warwick School select facts and construct cases just as the police do. The suggestion that '[s]ocio-legal researchers . . . should let the evidence speak' and allow readers 'to make [their] own judgements on the basis of the case material' (Davis 1992: 323–4) threatens to degenerate into a naïve empiricism. It should hardly need to be pointed out that evidence never has its own voice, but is always selected and spoken by authors.

The Warwick School relies on Packer's due process/crime control dichotomy. For example, Sanders and Young's *Criminal Justice* seeks to define 'where on the spectrum between crime control and due process the English system of justice is today to be located' (1994a: 20; see also 1994b: 130), and the book shows the pedagogical utility of this approach, in which the preference for due process is clear (contrast Smith 1995). However, McConville *et al.* offer a significant development of Packer's analysis of the due process/crime control dichotomy by criticizing McBarnet for seeing 'the rhetoric of law as unproblematic' (1991a: 178) and thereby assuming that due process is the superior value in legal ideology. This ideological view of legal ideology ignores the hold of crime control values in dominant ideologies such as the 'rule of law':

whilst McBarnet assumes that the fundamental principles of criminal justice constitute, or derive from, Due Process ideology, it is more plausible to see fundamental principles as constituting, or deriving from, both Due Process and Crime Control ideologies. . . . [B]oth form part of the fabric of law in all its manifestations—principles, rules and practice (1991a: 179, 180; see also Sanders and Young 1994b: 131).

This is an important insight which directs critical attention towards legal principles and provides an escape from assumptions about fundamental commitments to due process which ignore evidence of crime control at this level or which treat them as an intrusion or mere ideological deviance. McConville *et al.*, understandably, do no more here than point the way to a fundamental deconstruction of legal values and the legal paradigm. In one sense, their formulation accords with Packer's original formulation of these models: he acknowledged the common ground of values underlying them (1968: 154–7) and did not intend a descriptive dichotomy between law (whether principles or rules) and practice. However, in directing attention back to Packer, McConville *et al.* opened the way for a significant critique of their own work and of customary interpretations of Packer's work.

As D. J. Smith argues, authors in the Warwick School do not apply their insight that legal rhetoric incorporates both due process and crime control in their substantive analysis: there, the rhetoric refers to due-process principles. If crime control was included in the rhetoric, then the authors' contrast between rhetoric and practice would collapse (Smith 1995; see e.g. McConville *et al.* 1991a: 176;

Sanders and Young 1994b: 138). At the heart of the problem is the way in which Packer's dichotomy is routinely presented as simply a more sophisticated version of the dichotomies between law'n'order and civil liberties, or police powers and suspects' rights.[32] D. J. Smith attempts to rescue Packer from this misuse: he argues that Packer's concept of crime control is comprehensible only in terms of Packer's account of the fundamental nature and purpose of criminal justice, the prevention of crime. This involves returning Packer's dichotomy to its context. 'Part 1: Rationale' in *The Limits of the Criminal Sanction* analyses justifications for punishment.[33] In this account;

punishment can only be justified if both utilitarian and retributive conditions are met. Punishment is imposed only on a person who is found to have culpably committed an offence, but it is also at the same time designed to prevent the commission of offences, and could not possibly be justified otherwise. A central theme of Packer's book, therefore, is that crime control is inescapably an objective of criminal justice (Smith 1995: 15).

Due process is not crudely to be balanced *against* crime control: rather, due process is seen as intertwined with and contributing to crime control (in a more subtle way than that suggested by McBarnet). The ideological effect of criminal justice (expressed by Packer in terms of deterrence and value-reinforcement) requires that punishment should be seen to be legitimate and deserved: proof of guilt must include intention and capacity through a process which respects individual rights. In this liberal account, law's purpose is the protection of individual freedom. Law does so by preventing crime, but it can undermine freedom if this goal is taken too far, so the limitation of due process is integral to the ideological role of criminal justice (Smith 1995:16; cf. Packer 1968: 65–6).

From this perspective, due process is a crucial but secondary imperative: it sets limits on the ways in which crime control can be achieved. 'Due Process is not a goal in itself. It would make no sense to say that the criminal justice system has the function of delivering Due Process. Due Process only acquires a meaning in the context of

---

[32] That it lends itself to such use can be related to the context of its production—the controversies about crime and the Warren Court's rulings on criminal procedure in the 1960s (Packer 1968: 4–5). In addition, despite Packer's expressions of intent (1968: 152–4), his 'models' include elements of both description and prescription.

[33] It is indicative of how Packer has usually been read that the library copy which I use is pristine in part 1, while part 2 (especially Ch. 8, 'Two Models of the Criminal Process') is annotated, underlined, and dog-eared.

the pursuit of other goals, such as Crime Control' (Smith 1995: 18). As Sanders and Young point out, the only way that miscarriages of justice could be eliminated would be not to prosecute anybody. This 'cannot be countenanced', so a rhetorical weighing is carried out: ten (but not 100 or 1000) guilty people should escape rather than one innocent person be convicted (1994a: 3). Consequently, to argue that the police fail to achieve due-process standards is not *per se* a cause for condemnation: the Warwick School's analyses of their empirical material, which 'test the actions of the police against ideals and rules of due process and find them wanting', are fatally flawed (Smith 1995: 2). Due process becomes relevant only in the context of the goal of crime control, and cannot supplant it: 'institutions within the criminal justice system, such as the police, cannot be understood or explained on the assumption that their sole and central objective is, or might be, to pursue Due Process values' (Smith 1995: 21).

A problem of this critique (and of Packer's account) is its insistence on the secondary status of due process. Such an approach would undermine Ashworth's attempt (1994) to construct a theory of criminal justice based on rights, for to do so would be to deal with means rather than ends. Alternatively, it could be argued that the real foundation of criminal justice is neither criminal justice's ends nor its means, but the complex of relations between state and citizen. Due process (by, for example, protecting a suspect's rights) can then be regarded as just as fundamental as crime control. Criminal justice is a way in which the state carries out its role of protecting citizens by providing security through crime control: the way in which this is done *can* be related to a separate goal, that of maintaining and enhancing citizens' rights. Of course, such a formulation is simplistic and raises its own problems by its implicit reference to social-contract theory and its one-dimensionally positive account of the state. However, for present purposes, it is enough to show the need to avoid essentialist accounts of criminal justice founded on either due process or crime control. Equally, it suggests that there is a constant, inevitable tension between due process and crime control which cannot be reduced to the simplistic accounts of conflict or searches for 'balance' (see Ch. 7, below). Such tension demands 'examination of specific laws and legal processes' rather than analysis only of abstractions and rhetoric (Hogg 1991a: 22).

Another major criticism levelled by Smith at the Warwick School concerns conceptions of the police function. According to Smith, *The*

Case for the Prosecution treats policing too legalistically, assuming that 'police actions can be understood in the light of the objectives and concerns of the system of criminal process' (1995: 22). Drawing on Bittner's classic account, Smith argues that policing has a much wider function of social ordering, in which legal powers and procedures provide the means but do not set the objective (e.g. arresting someone to restore public order without expecting that the person will be charged). The importance of not identifying policing functions and objectives with the law must be acknowledged more generally, and will be discussed in the context of the limits of legal regulation in Chapter 7 below.

From this critique of the Warwick School's work, a broader lesson can be drawn which has relevance to all the theoretical accounts of law in policing which have been surveyed above. In different ways, they all attempt to go beyond the empiricism which has been common in policing studies. The drift to theorizing is to be welcomed and encouraged: in particular, it is clear that the traditional theoretical resources of policing studies need to be augmented by drawing on other theoretical perspectives from other disciplines, from historical research, and from comparative studies. The sociological perspectives provided by the classic studies of the 1960s and 1970s are inadequate to provide a focus on contemporary policing. In consequence, studies of policing are being reinvigorated by engagement with newer sociological and social theory. As well as those noted above, examples include Keith's work on racism and policing (1993), Braithwaite's interpretation (1992) of republican theory to help define 'good policing', Ericson and Haggerty's (1997) reformulation of policing as risk-management practices, Finnane's Foucaultian police histories (1994), and Loader's use of Habermas in his study of youth and police accountability (1996). Against the trend of specialization in a sub-discipline, it is increasingly recognized that the study of policing needs to be tied into broader theoretical developments (Dixon 1997).

2
Police Powers: Law in the Books and Elsewhere

If it is law, it will be found in our books. If it is not to be found there, it is not law.[1]

If you know what you are doing, if you know the law well enough . . . you can make it do wonderful and marvellous things.[2]

This Chapter is concerned with the nature of police powers in England and Australia. The focus is not on specific powers (although some are discussed as examples) but rather on 'police powers' as a concept. Issues discussed include the origins and development of police powers, the relationship between powers and duties, the role of powers in policing practices, the legal concept of police powers, and the utility of changing police powers in response to concerns about crime and disorder. The argument running through what follows is that police powers cannot usefully be considered in legalistic isolation. What a power means is usually defined (at least in part) by how it is used. In this sense, police powers and policing practices cannot be clearly distinguished.

i. Histories of Policing

There is difficulty in separating the history of police powers from the broader history of the police, especially when (as in Australia) historians have only recently begun to concern themselves seriously with police history. Sections i to iv discuss police powers, and focus on their relationship to the reorganization of policing in England and Australia, in the first half of the nineteenth century.

---

[1] Camden LJ in *Entick* v. *Carrington* (1765) 19 St. Tr. 1030.
[2] From an interview with a NSW police officer.

On a thumb-nail, the traditional account of English police history is as follows. The village constable was the product of a tradition of self-governing, responsible, local communities in the early middle ages. In the early-modern period, the institution of constable declined into the caricatures provided by Shakespeare—Dogberry in *Much Ado About Nothing* and Elbow in *Measure for Measure*. By the eighteenth century, England was an almost unpoliced society. After years of combating dogged, irrational resistance, enlightened reformers led by Robert Peel succeeded in introducing a professional police force to London in 1829 which rekindled the office of constable and the relationship between police and community. There was no deep divide between police and people; rather, the police were merely 'citizens in uniform'. In such accounts, the introduction of the 'New Police' is 'regarded as the social equivalent of the steam engine in the process of industrialization: the "heroic" invention which transformed the situation from one of persistent disorder to one of relative tranquillity' (Stevenson 1979: 321). Peel's Metropolitan Police set the example which provincial England, Australia, and much of the common law world followed, while the rest of the world looked on in envy.

Social historians have exposed this account as being largely ideology and teleology, misleading in most significant respects (for reviews of this extensive literature, which is by no means homogeneous, see Brogden *et al.* 1988: chs. 2 and 3; Emsley 1991; Reiner 1992: part 1; Robinson 1979). From their perspectives, the story is to be told in a different way. The village constable was the product, not of arcadian self-government, but of the intersection of contrasting forms of political organization—the local Anglo-Saxon state and the increasingly centralized Norman state. This tension was felt subsequently, for example in the seventeenth century, as constables mediated between the norms of village communities and the central state's attempts to impose new standards of moral and social discipline (Wrightson 1980).

The constable's role was not policing in its modern sense; rather it involved much more general social ordering. This was reflected in the broad use of the term 'police' when it first entered the language in the eighteenth century: when people used the word, 'they were referring to the general regulation or government, the morals or economy, of a city or country. The French word derived from the Greek polis, the root base of the words "politics", "polity", "policy" ' (Palmer

1988: 69). So 'policing' originally referred to the general functions of civil government: the constable in, for example, the seventeenth century village engaged in a wide range of administrative duties (Kent 1986). Later, 'the word "police" began to be used, in its continental sense, to refer to the specific functions of crime prevention and order maintenance' (Johnston 1992: 4; see also, on 'that strange word "police"', Radzinowicz 1956: 1–8). None the less, the 'new police' inherited or were subsequently allocated many administrative functions (Steedman 1984; Emsley 1991: 75–8). Some of these were related, directly or indirectly, to law enforcement and crime prevention: what Chadwick called 'collateral services' could encourage public co-operation with police, while inspecting lodging houses was a way of controlling potentially criminal vagrants (Emsley 1991: 77–8). However, other administrative duties[3] were allocated to police simply because they constituted a reservoir of state bureaucracy which was available to carry out tasks in lieu of another agency to which they could be assigned. Their Australian colleagues followed suit: in 'the absence of developed regional authorities, councils and public servants, police had to perform numerous tasks. Their range is extraordinary' (Garton 1991: 21; cf. Moore 1991: 116). Examples range from the duties of inspecting and licensing butchers' shops in the Sydney Police Act 1833 to modern police officers conducting driving tests in Australian country areas. A significant strand of nineteenth- and twentieth-century police history has been the ambivalence of police about these administrative duties: on one hand, they distract from 'real police work'; on the other, they may justify the allocation of resources and other bureaucratic benefits and may soften the police image. More recently, police have returned to a broader conception of policing: in some versions of 'community' or 'problem-oriented' policing, police seek to organize and co-ordinate public services such as crime prevention, housing, and welfare (Moore 1992).

The role and activities of the constables of the 'old' (pre-nineteenth century) police must be assessed in their own terms (which changed over the centuries), not against standards and job-descriptions of modern policing (Kent 1986: 6; Philips 1980: 161). For example, social historians have shown how the apparently irrational and illogical aspects of eighteenth-century criminal procedure have to be decoded according to their, not our, logic and rationality (Hay 1975). The

---

[3] Emsley's examples include collecting market tolls, inspecting cattle, and acting as assistant excise officers and assistant highway surveyors (1991: 79).

distinction between the civil and criminal aspects of a wrongful act were insignificant before 1800 (Lenman and Parker 1980: 12). Early modern constables are no more accurately portrayed as Dogberry or Elbow than early twentieth-century American police are portrayed as the Keystone Kops (Sharpe 1983: 2).

Far from there being a clear distinction between the old and the new police, there was considerable continuity. The old were more organized and efficient, and the new less disciplined and effective than was traditionally suggested: '[t]he development of paid policing and police forces was happening long before the setting up of the Metropolitan Police in 1829, while professionalization, central direction and standardization remained weak long after that date' (Styles 1987: 18). Meanwhile, 'the "new" police often turn out on closer examination to be akin to the old, in personnel, efficiency and tactics' (Gatrell 1990: 260 ; cf. Philips 1980: 160). The significance of the reorganization of English and Australian policing in the second and third quarters of the nineteenth century is that it was the central state's attempt to monopolize policing activity by its concentration in a 'professional', organized body: 'in the long view 1829 may be of interest mainly for the trend it revealed towards an ever increasing subjection of law-enforcement in all its aspects to central direction' (Gatrell 1990: 260). More generally, it was part of the long-running process in which the state took over the processing of disputes which would previously have been settled privately. This state monopolization of policing increasingly appears to be a historically discrete development. Before the new police, much police work was done by private individuals and organizations. The second half of this century has seen the re-emergence of a private security 'industry', increasing pressures of privatization on police forces, and recognition of the significance of policing by the public in all its varieties (Johnston 1992; Shearing 1992; Shearing and Stenning (eds.) 1987).

The ideology of constables as 'citizens in uniform' has been important both as a legitimating device and as an impediment to proper consideration of the nature of police powers. In 1929, the Royal Commission on Police Powers and Procedure claimed:

The Police . . . have never been recognised, either in law or in tradition, as a force distinct from the general body of citizens. . . . [T]he principle remains that a Policeman . . . is only 'a person paid to perform, as a matter of duty, acts which if he were so minded he might have done voluntarily'. Indeed, a policeman possesses few powers not enjoyed by the ordinary citizen, and public opinion, expressed in Parliament and elsewhere, has shown great jealousy of any attempts to give increased authority to the Police (RCPPP 1929: 6).

This account was approved by the Royal Commission on the Police in its 1962 Report, which endorsed 'the principle that police powers are mostly grounded in the common law and differ little from those of ordinary citizens' (1962: 11). Such blinkered and inaccurate views contributed substantially to the lack of attention to the reality—a linear growth of special police powers—and were founded in the assiduously cultivated myth of the 'special relationship' between police and people in England and Wales (Weinberger 1991). Concealing this reality allowed the need to regulate the exercise of police powers to be overlooked (Reiner and Leigh 1994: 70).

Far from achieving early acceptance, the new police operated as a disciplinary force in a deeply divided society. Consent to policing is not merely an ideological fiction: but equally, it is not a natural condition. Rather, the construction of consent to policing was a long-term, intensive, often deliberate, and never fully successful project of negotiation between police and people (for a summary of relevant research, see Dixon 1991c: 261–6). Such negotiations are carried out in part at a general level (e.g., the construction in post-war films and television series of a 'police image'). But they are also specific and must be related to the particular circumstances of policed communities: this is shown brilliantly in studies by Brogden of Liverpool (1981, 1991), by Hogg and Golder of Sydney's Newtown (1987), and by Cohen of Islington (1979). This should warn against simplistic analysis of Australian policing as if it was just an extension of a homogenized new police. The very particular relationships between Australian police forces and publics still await proper historical treatment, although a start has been made (Finnane 1994; Finnane (ed.) 1987; see also Byrne 1993: ch. 6; Haldane 1995).

While traditional police histories treated London's Metropolitan Police as the path-breakers, recent historians have pointed out that other reorganized forces came earlier, notably in 1822 with the establishment of the Royal Irish Constabulary (Palmer 1988). The particular significance of the RIC is that it provided a paramilitary model of policing which was at least as influential in the production of colonial police forces as the English model.[4] Both forces

[4] See Anderson and Killingray 1991; Hawkins 1991; King 1956; Palmer 1988: 543; note however Brogden's argument (1987a; 1987b) that this contrast understates the paramilitary ability and influence of the Metropolitan Police.

provided models and personnel for early Australian police
(Haldane 1995: 27).

ii. Original Police Powers?

The revision of police history noted above has principally been concerned with issues of organization, constitutional position, and
police–public relations. Relatively little attention has been paid to the
nature of police powers. Indeed, in this respect there is little to distinguish old and new histories. Generally, both speak as if the old
police (constables who were elected from within a community to
serve for a year, although deputies were often employed) were
restricted to common law powers: 'precisely because in legal theory
he was a sort of delegate of the community, the constable exercised
common law powers only' (Lustgarten 1986: 28). These were passed
on to the new police (in England and Australia) and subsequently
were strengthened by the addition of statutory powers. The history
of police powers is ripe for a thorough reassessment. Here, it is possible only to suggest how such a project could begin.

The methodology of much writing about early policing is historically deficient because most authors tend to think about policing in
modern rather than contemporary terms: they try to find evidence in
the historical records of how the old police carried out functions
characteristic of modern police. They distort history by using modern concepts of law and authority. Despite the emergence of published guides such as Lambard's *The Duties of Constables* (1599), the
extent of the early constables' authority was neither widely known
nor clear. In the seventeenth century, the 'law was a maze to the
unwary officer . . . many constables were "doubtful of what power
they have," for the simple reason that "the law is very dark" '
(Wrightson 1980: 28, quoting Worsley from 1655). The constable's
authority stemmed more from practice than from powers which were
legally defined by Parliament or the courts.

The modern concept of police powers was produced from the
redefinition of state–society relations in seventeenth- and eighteenth-
century England. It is in the eighteenth century that crucial developments in police powers emerge. These included the Constables
Protection Act 1750, granting legal immunity to constables who
acted under a magistrate's warrant: the late provision of this vital

protection illustrates well that challenges to a constable's legal authority were the product of late-modern socio-political change. In 1765, *Entick* v. *Carrington*[5] defined the modern concept of police powers premised upon the relations between the citizen and the liberal state. The central principles established in *Entick* v. *Carrington* were:

every official interference with individual liberty and security is unlawful unless justified by some existing and specific statutory or common law rule; any search of private property will similarly be a trespass and illegal unless some recognised lawful authority for it can be produced; in general, coercion should only be brought to bear on individuals and their property at the instance of regular judicial officers acting in accordance with established and known rules of law, and not by executive officers acting at their discretion; and finally it is the law, whether common law or statute, and not a plea of public interest or an allegation of state necessity that will justify acts normally illegal (Polyviou 1982: 9).

From 1765, it was not enough that police action was carried out at the direction of government, whether central (ministers) or local (justices of the peace). As Lord Chief Justice Camden stated in *Entick* v. *Carrington*, '[i]f it is law, it will be found in our books. If it is not to be found there, it is not law.'[6]

Consequently, the process of providing police powers, of putting them into the law's books, got under way. For example, the early constable's legal powers of arrest were the same as the ordinary citizen's: reasonable suspicion was not enough and a felony had actually to have been committed. However, the assumption that early constables did not arrest on suspicion (e.g. Denning 1949: 19) is another example of transposing modern ideas onto inappropriate historical contexts. They did, and it was challenges to the practice of arrest on suspicion which led to its legal formalization and development in *Samuel* v. *Payne*[7] and *Beckwith* v. *Philby*.[8] These cases established that people reasonably suspected of felonies could be arrested by constables, while the ordinary citizen's arrest power continued to depend on the actual commission of an offence. It was only at this relatively late date that this distinction, which is usually cited as the exemplar of the constable's common law powers, was made.

---

[5] N. 1 above.   [6] *Ibid.*   [7] (1780) 1 Doug. 349.
[8] (1827) 6 B & C 635.

iii. Police Powers after Reorganization

The introduction of the new police in England was initially accompanied by the creation of few powers. The Act for Improving the Police in and near the Metropolis which established London's Metropolitan Police in 1829 contained only two powers. Section 9 provided for police to grant bail, while section 7 authorized a constable

> to apprehend all loose, idle, and disorderly persons whom he shall find disturbing the Public Peace, or whom he shall have just Cause to suspect of any evil Designs, and all Persons whom he shall find between Sunset and the Hour of Eight in the Forenoon lying in any Highway, Yard, or other Place, or loitering therein, and not giving a satisfactory Account of themselves.

It has been suggested that 'the question of whether or not the new forces would require statutory powers or whether the traditional common law power would suffice' was generally ignored in the debates about policing in the first quarter of the nineteenth century (Brogden 1982: 125). In part, this was due to political considerations: the opposition to reorganization of policing might well have recovered its former strength if the new police had been provided with an array of powers. Issues of accountability and control were more significant than powers.

A related factor was that the primary mandate of the new police, as expressed in their initial instructions, was the prevention of crime: '[t]o this great end every effort of the police is to be directed. The security of person and property and the preservation of a police establishment will thus be better effected than by the detection and punishment of the offender after he has succeeded in committing crime'.[9] In turn, this was a partly rhetorical gloss on the intention that the new police should be concerned primarily with public disorder. The Metropolitan Police gradually shifted from being a preventative force to one strongly committed to crime investigation (Weinberger 1991).

However, this standard account of the powers initially provided for the new police overlooks a crucial factor—the extensive statutory powers which were already available. From the early middle ages, statutes had reacted to fears of deviance, crime, and disorder. 'Forasmuch as from Day to Day, Robberies, Murthers, Burnings and

---

[9] 1829 Metropolitan Police Instructions, quoted, Critchley 1978: 52–3.

Thefts be more often committed than they have been heretofore', began the Statute of Winchester in 1285. While the language is archaic, these sentiments resonate with modern 'moral panics'.

Pre-eminent among such legislation were the Vagrancy Acts which were passed from the mid-fourteenth century. If policing is properly understood as being about order maintenance and the control of socially marginal groups as much as it is about law enforcement, the importance of the Vagrancy Acts becomes clear. From the middle ages, a long series of additions provided powers for the control of social deviance. The objectives of such control shifted from the protection of trade to the disciplining of labour, and then to the suppression of incipient criminality (Chambliss 1964; but see also Adler 1989a; 1989b: Chambliss 1989). The Metropolitan Police Act 1829 did not need to include extensive powers because this had, in part, been done five years earlier when the Vagrancy Act 1824 reformed provisions for 'the Suppression of Vagrancy and for the Punishment of idle and disorderly Persons, and Rogues and Vagabonds'. This Act provided wide-ranging proscriptions of deviance. Failing to support or deserting one's family, prostitution, begging, fortune-telling, 'wandering abroad . . . not having any visible Means of Subsistence', displaying obscene pictures, indecent exposure, public gambling, and possessing implements with intent to commit a felony were just some of the prohibited activities. The power of arrest was available to any citizen, but was obviously most useful to police. In addition, section 4 included a provision which was to become notorious (Demuth 1978): 'every suspected person or reputed Thief, frequenting . . . any Street . . . or any Place of public Resort . . . with intent to commit Felony' could be arrested and punished as a rogue and vagabond.

These pre-existing powers of the new police in London were soon considerably extended by the Metropolitan Police Act 1839: this reflected an early decline of upper- and middle-class opposition to the new police, as it became clear that the police protected rather than threatened their interests. The 1839 Act provided power to arrest and to enter and search property in numerous instances. It also gave the Metropolitan Police Commissioner authority to issue regulations for the use of public streets. Many detailed offences were created, including sliding upon 'Ice or Snow in any Street to the common Danger of the Passengers'[10] and, much more importantly, the use of 'threatening,

[10] S. 53(17).

abusive, or insulting words or Behaviour . . . whereby a Breach of the Peace may be occasioned',[11] the origin of later public-order summary offences. Power of arrest without warrant was provided to constables for all these offences, and in any case when an offender's name and address were not known.[12] A constable was also empowered to arrest without warrant

> all loose, idle, and disorderly Persons whom he shall find disturbing the pub-
> lic Peace, or whom he shall have good cause to suspect of having committed
> or being about to commit any Felony, Misdemeanor, or Breach of the Peace,
> and all Persons whom he shall find between Sunset and the Hour of Eight in
> the Morning lying or loitering in any Highway, Yard or other Place, and not
> giving a satisfactory Account of themselves.[13]

In addition, a power was created to stop and search vehicles and 'any Person who may be reasonably suspected of having or conveying in any Manner any thing stolen or unlawfully obtained'.[14] Already, the Metropolitan Police had much more than common law powers. Police outside London were provided with local powers, which were consolidated in the Town Police Clauses Act 1847. This growth would continue in a process of *ad hoc* growth discussed below in section vi.

iv. Early Provisions for Police and Police Powers in Australia

Bland claims that the powers of Australian police were modelled on those in England and Wales (e.g. Chappell and Wilson 1969: ch. 1; Milte and Weber 1977: ch. 1) are misleading. Several points illustrate this. First, early Australian police were appointed as constables and had the constable's common law powers; but as noted above, these were not as clear as is often suggested. Secondly, Australian police powers drew on English law, but soon developed specific characteristics. The first legislation to provide a statutory basis for Australian policing, the Sydney Police Act 1833, is routinely said to have been modelled on the Metropolitan Police Act 1829. While this was true in terms of the constitutional and bureaucratic structure of the new police organization, the Sydney Police Act 1833 also included a mass of detailed and specific rules for 'the greater regularity and convenience' of the town and a comprehensive battery of offences, many

---

[11] S. 53(13).   [12] Ss. 53 and 63.   [13] S. 64.   [14] S. 66.

of them accompanied by a power to arrest without warrant. This was soon followed by the Vagrancy Act 1835, modelled on the English Act of 1824 (Finnane 1994: 95–6). Thirdly, the social context of police in the new colony was quite different from that of their counterparts in England or Ireland.[15] The first civil police in Australia, a night watch established in 1789,[16] were themselves convicts. From the beginning, police powers (provided in Governor's Orders) were controversial. Marines (who had apparently been responsible for many of the property offences which the watch had been established to suppress) objected to being detained by a watch made up of convicts. What was recognized at the time as a power to detain on suspicion for questioning was amended so that soldiers could be stopped only if they were 'found in a riot, or committing any unlawful act'.[17]

Apart from enduring problems of personnel, early Australian constables were policing a special kind of society and were provided with very extensive powers of discipline and surveillance. For example, a reconstituted night watch was instructed in 1796 to enforce Sunday observance, 'to apprehend all night-walkers, all disorderly and suspicious persons' and to 'interrogate all . . . found idling about in their division, not being inhabitants thereof, and oblige them to give an account of themselves'.[18]

In 1811, Governor Macquarie reorganized the Sydney police and issued detailed regulations which criminalized 'a vast range of public conduct' (Brennan 1983: 44). This was legislation for a penal colony, a society which was deeply divided between free and convict, between civil and military, and in which fear of disorder merged with fear of insurrection. Surveillance was exemplified by the instruction to the Chief Constable to 'watch narrowly all prisoners and Suspected Persons, and make enquiry as to their different Modes of employing their own hours' and 'in general do his utmost endeavour to preserve Publick [sic] Decorum, and to report every Breach thereof'.[19] He was to record the name and place of residence of all convicts in Sydney and to order constables 'to visit the Houses of such prisoners at certain Times during the Night'.[20] The magistrate designated Superintendant [sic] of Police was directed to 'keep a

---

[15] See Neal 1991: 143. For an analysis of the specificity of Australian policing, see Moore 1991.

[16] i.e. within two years of white settlement.

[17] Government and General Order, 9 Nov. 1789, in HRA 1914: 139.

[18] *Ibid.* 701.   [19] Police Regs. 1811, s. 5(5) and (6) in HRA 1916: 409.

[20] S. 5(8), in *ibid.* 410.

Register, in which he shall Enter the Names and places of Abode of every Housekeeper in the Town of Sydney, or within One Mile thereof, and of every person comprising their respective families, and the situations which such persons fill therein'.[21] Convicts and house-holders were obliged to provide police with the information to be held in these registers.[22] The 'Idle, Disorderly or Suspicious' (including convicts, whom police were instructed to 'strictly stop') found in the streets after 9 pm were to be arrested.[23] Convicts and 'labouring persons' were prohibited from being 'abroad or away from their houses' between 9 pm and dawn without 'reasonable Cause'.[24] The Chief Constable was directed to arrest 'all Persons whom he shall see drunken, idle, or disorderly in the Streets, at any Time, and all persons who have no apparent Means of obtaining a livelihood'.[25] Those 'breaking or profaning the Sabbath day' were to be also arrested.[26]

The police were under the direction and control of a Magistrate whose duties included not just 'the general Care, Superintendence and inspection of every thing and person connected with the police of the Town of Sydney', but also the trial and punishment of offenders. Convicts found guilty of 'Wilful Neglect of Work, of being abroad during the Night after the limited hours, or of being intoxicated in the publick Streets at any time' could be sentenced to fifty lashes and hard labour for thirty days.[27] The same punishments faced anyone who fell within the compendious description of 'idle and disorderly' persons: this included:

all poor persons not using proper means to get employment, or spending their money in Ale-houses or places of bad repute, or not applying a proper proportion to the maintenance of their families, or threatening to desert their families, or wilfully absenting themselves from their Work, or publickly breaking or profaning the Sabbath Day, or attempting to Commit any Felony or Misdemeanour, or to break any house, or shall refuse to assist any Constable in the execution of his Duty, or being out after hours at night without reasonable Cause, or being drunken or riotous in the streets during any time.[28]

---

[21] S. 6(13), in *ibid*. 411.   [22] S. 6(10), in *ibid*. 412.
[23] Ss. 1(3) and 4(4), in *ibid*. 406, 408.   [24] S. 6(1), in *ibid*. 412.
[25] S. 5(4), in *ibid*. 409.   [26] S. 5(7), in *ibid*. 409.
[27] S. 6(6), in *ibid*. 410.   [28] S. 6(9), in *ibid*. 411.

That no specific powers were provided for the enforcement of such prohibitions seems hardly significant: it was clearly expected that the police would arrest suspected offenders.[29]

Police also had extensive authority to enter and search property: they had 'a discretionary power of calling at houses where prisoners reside, or at any other Suspicious Houses, at any Time during the Night, to see if such prisoners or other Suspicious Characters are within, and if not, they shall examine the Master or Mistress of the house thereupon'.[30] Licensed premises, which had to be closed by 9 pm, could be entered thereafter if 'any riot or disturbance' was heard within.[31] Houses suspected of being of 'ill-fame' or at which alcohol was sold illegally could also be entered. People found 'Tippling or Drunken, or misconducting themselves therein' could be arrested.[32] Police were instructed to be 'diligent in pursuing, searching for, and apprehending all Felons, Burglars, Housebreakers, Riotous and disorderly Persons'.[33] The breadth and detail of these prohibitions and powers reflected the special position of the early Australian police and the nature of the society in which they worked.

Fourthly, New South Wales was not only a penal colony, it was also a new society in a very material sense: in Sydney, a new city was being constructed (King 1956: 218). This emphasizes the need to see policing and police powers in their specific contexts, rather than as some generic activity or institution. As well as reorganizing the structure of the police and adding new provisions for 'the maintenance of the public peace and good order', the Sydney Police Act 1833 provided a code of rules for urban life, covering such matters as the permissible location of certain social and economic activities, 'the removal and prevention of nuisances and obstructions',[34] permissible uses of public and private places and resources, town planning, and public safety. Rules, accompanied by offences for breach, were created for a range of matters such as cleanliness and use of water supplies; the regulation of carters, porters, and boatmen; public preparation; sale and transportation of goods; disposal of refuse; traffic; keeping of animals; naming of streets; covering of coal-holes and

---

[29] The power to impose corporal punishment was disapproved by the Government in England: see Earl Bathurst to Governor Macquarie, 23 Nov. 1812, in *ibid*. 666–9, at 666. Macquarie replied, insisting on the need for such punishments: see Governor Macquarie to Earl Bathurst, 28 June 1813, in *ibid*. 707–30, at 720.

[30] S. 4(5), in *ibid*. 408.   [31] S. 4(10), in *ibid*. 408.

[32] S. 4(11), in *ibid*. 409.   [33] S. 4(12) in *ibid*. 409.   [34] S. 1.

cellars; provision of guttering. The Town Surveyor was responsible for supervision of many of these matters. Almost all were backed by offences of failure to comply.

A battery of specific offences was created. Section 25 alone prohibited the use of public places for, *inter alia*, beating carpets; flying kites; 'breaking, exercising or trying horses'; disposing of 'any ashes, rubbish, offal, dung, soil, dead animal, blood, or other filth or annoyance, or any matter or thing'; butchering animals; and using vehicles or animals on 'foot ways'. Offences which were more serious or required immediate action in an emergent urban community were accompanied by specific police powers, usually of arrest without warrant. Constables were given this power to deal with a disparate range of offences. These included bathing in the harbour between 6 am and 8 pm, damaging roadways by hauling building materials, breaking or extinguishing street lights, and throwing dead animals into the harbour.[35]

The priorities of a growing urban community were expressed in the special provisions regarding disposal of 'night soil'. A person who emptied privies or drove a 'night soil' cart between 5 am and 10 pm or who allowed its contents to spill could be arrested by 'any person or persons whomsoever'.[36] The seriousness of the problem was expressed not only by the available punishment for emptying privies and transporting nightsoil outside permitted hours (a fine and thirty days' imprisonment) but also by the instruction to constables that they were 'strictly charged' by the Act to arrest such offenders.[37] Similarly, traffic was already a perceived problem: 'many accidents happen and great mischiefs are frequently done in the streets and public places . . . by the negligence or wilful misbehaviour of persons driving therein'. Powers were provided for constables and private citizens to arrest without warrant drivers of carts and other vehicles who, for example, did not keep to the left of the road or who 'by negligence or misbehaviour prevent, hinder or interrupt the free passage of any carriage or person'.[38]

The objects of social cleansing were human as well as material. Some types of people were made subject to police powers which were concerned with disturbances of public order and the supposed potential for other criminality. In a section drawing on the English Vagrancy Act 1824, police were authorized to arrest 'all loose, idle,

---

[35] Respectively, ss. 21, 27, 36, and 37.   [36] Ss. 33 and 34.   [37] S. 34.
[38] S. 50.

drunken or disorderly persons' who were found between sunset and 8 am 'lying or loitering in any street, highway, yard, or other place . . . and not giving a satisfactory account of themselves'.[39] In a society such as early New South Wales, a person's status was vital. Some people were penalized for being in the wrong place at the wrong time: sailors found in public places (including pubs) between 9 pm and sunrise could be arrested unless they carried a pass from their ship's captain.[40] Similarly, convicts assigned to private service could be arrested and 'shall be deemed guilty of disorderly conduct' if found in a public place without a pass between sun-set and sun-rise.[41]

It is essential not to read such legislation as an inappropriate but expedient combination of police and other public matters: this is to impose a modern distinction. Instead, policing in the early colonial period has to be understood as a general enterprise of social ordering from which the responsibilities of a professional police only gradually emerged as a distinct area. The result was that specific police powers were scattered through the 1833 Act according to a logic which appears only in retrospect to be deficient. The role of the police in 'disseminating discipline' (Websdale 1991) was, in Foucault's terminology, a new form of 'governmentality' (Barry *et al.* (eds.) 1996; Burchell *et al.* (eds.) 1991).

The subordination of police to judicial authority was an important feature of the early legislation, and another example of Anglo-Irish influence. Police were appointed by and under the direction of two Justices of the Peace who were the Police Magistrates. It was the latter's duty 'to suppress all tumults, riots, affrays, or breaches of the peace, all public nuisances, vagrancies, and offences against the law; and to uphold all regulations . . . for the management and discipline of convicts'[42] and to 'cause to be dispersed' people playing public games in breach of Sunday observance rules.[43] They appointed police constables, who were sworn to 'obey all such lawful commands as they may from time to time receive from any of the said Justices for conducting themselves in the execution of their office'.[44] The extensive arrest powers noted above were for the purpose of bringing suspects before a Justice 'to be dealt with according to law'. Justices could provide warrants for police to inspect and give directions for the cleaning of butchers' premises. They also approved applicants for carters' licences which police issued.[45] Magisterial involvement and

---

[39] S. 6.   [40] S. 44.   [41] S. 55.   [42] S. 4.   [43] S. 11.   [44] S. 4.
[45] Respectively, ss. 26 and 54.

control were central to early nineteenth-century conceptions of policing (Golder 1991; Palmer 1994): as Chapters 4 and 5 will suggest, this was soon to change, at least in practice.

From its origins in Sydney, Australian policing gradually developed and spread. Forces modelled on Sydney's were established in emergent towns in New South Wales, while a number of specialized forces were also set up: '[b]y the 1840s there were six separate forces in New South Wales. In addition to the Sydney City Police, a harbour-based Water Police authority and the rural constabulary, there were three rural forces: the Mounted, the Native and the Border Police' (Moore 1991: 110). A similar process developed elsewhere:

By the 1850s . . ., Australia's various colonies all had a number of police forces. The two largest colonies of Victoria and New South Wales had some ten police forces between them in addition to the many constables working solely on behalf of local magistrates. Forces were created not as a result of any grand plan but as a need arose and was recognised (Moore 1991: 112).

Gradually, these were consolidated into unitary state forces: a centralized force emerged in New South Wales in the 1860s (Moore 1991: 116; Walker 1984: 25; for a summary of other state developments, see Chappell and Wilson 1969: ch. 1; Finnane 1994). However, the basic structure of police powers remained the same. The pattern of *ad hoc* growth which was found in England and Wales continued to characterize Australian policing (Finnane 1987: 90).

v. 'Police Powers'

The focus now shifts from historical to conceptual discussion. Police powers are not coterminous with the police. In some instances, they long predated organized police forces. In certain circumstances, they are available for use by people who are not police officers, both private citizens and state officials. Meanwhile, many police duties, responsibilities, and activities are not facilitated by the provision of specific powers. The focus here is on the coercive powers which are available to police officers, and their use thereof.

As a legal concept, 'police powers' are simply exemptions from criminal or civil liability for what otherwise would be unlawful acts. For example, a search of a person constitutes an assault unless a power is provided.

It is in this sense, then, that search and seizure laws confer powers. More particularly, they confer exceptional powers, powers to do what an individual is, in ordinary circumstances, forbidden to do. . . . Rules defining police powers have a specific function . . . they set out exceptions to the ordinary prohibitions against intrusions upon an individual's person, private domain and possessions. While this function is a critical one it is also in a sense quite modest. Our legal tradition does not purport to devise permissible enforcement strategies or define situations in which intrusions should be performed. Rather it establishes when intrusions may be performed, by requiring that when law enforcement officers determine to pursue an investigation through an intrusive action, they justify the intrusion, obtain the proper authorization and perform it within the limits set down in the law (LRCC 1983: 10, 122).

If police officers do not have authority, their actions can be lawfully resisted just as if they were private citizens infringing another's interests. The result can be seen in cases in which people have been acquitted of assaulting police officers who have been found not to be acting within their duty in searching, detaining, or touching.[46] There is nothing special about the powers of the police from this perspective. Police powers are not conceptually distinct from, for example, a citizen's right to make arrests or the powers of a wide range of public officials (immigration officers, welfare officers, revenue officers, public utility officials) to enter property or to arrest in certain circumstances.

If a police power exists and is exercised, it 'transforms legal relations between state and individual. A peace officer who arrests an individual puts that individual in lawful custody, from which escape is an offence, and deprives the citizen of a right to resist what would, without the authority to arrest, amount to an unlawful assault' (LRCC 1985: 2). However, it is important to note that this transformative process is not all negative: arresting a citizen may activate certain rights (e.g. to publicly-funded legal advice) which a person who merely 'assists officers with their enquiries' may not possess (see Ch. 3, below).

A doctrinal corollary of this approach to police powers is that they should be clearly defined and specific, so that police and citizen alike know what is and what is not authorized. This is a traditional

---

[46] E.g. *Pedro* v. *Diss* [1981] 2 All ER 59. Judicial discomfort with such results is evident in attempts to avoid the conclusion that the officer was not acting in the course of duty: see e.g. *Donnelly* v. *Jackman* (1970) 54 Cr. App. R 229.

account of the rule of law, usually associated with A. V. Dicey (1927; see Ch. 7, below). As will be shown below, the considerable distance between concept and legal reality limits the validity of this approach.

The police do not need to have legal powers for everything that they do. Like other citizens, they may do anything that the law does not forbid. Indeed, most police work entails duties which do not involve the use of coercive powers: 'the police (contrary to popular mythology) do not mainly operate as crime-fighters or law-enforcers, but rather as providers of a range of services to members of the public, the variety of which beggars description. . . . [C]rime fighting has never been, is not, and could not be the prime activity of the police.'[47]

Powers are only necessary when a person's identifiable interest is infringed. The common law's definition of such interests is limited. For example, a man whose telephone was being tapped sought an injunction against London's Metropolitan Police. This was refused on the ground that the telephone tapping did not involve any trespass or other unlawful act: the court could identify only the Post Office's property interest and not the man's interest in privacy, communication, or the message communicated. It was for Parliament to legislate for the controls on telephone tapping which were needed to needed to satisfy obligations under the European Convention on Human Rights.[48]

The limitations of a narrow legal conception of police powers are clear. Practices of arrest and search by organized police forces involve much more than mere exemptions from legal liability.

The . . . proposition that the police should not be subject to any special restrictions that don't apply to other people . . . is absurd, because the power (both legal and physical) that the police have makes them especially danger-ous *as well as* useful. Acting within the state apparatus, officials can do things to citizens which are quite different in character from the sort of things cit-izens can do to one another (Waldron 1990: 41, original emphasis: the ques-tion of resolving this 'absurdity' is considered below).

---

[47] Reiner 1992a: 139, 212, and see 139–46 for a good summary of the police role which avoids simple dichotomies of 'force' and 'service'.

[48] *Malone v. Metropolitan Police Commissioner* [1979] Ch. 344. For a critique, see Harlow and Rawlings 1984: 16–18. As *R v. Khan* ([1996] Crim. LR 733) suggests, even if an investigative activity infringes a proprietorial interest (as when a listening device was attached to the external wall of a suspect's house), a trial judge has a discretion under PACE, s. 78 to exclude resulting evidence which was unlikely to be exercised when, as in *Khan*, the defendant was recorded admitting involvement in heroin impor-tation.

In consequence, any useful discussion of police powers must break out of the limits set by legalistic definitions (see sect. vii).

Waldron's indication of the ambivalent nature of police powers reflects a discomfort which police officers often display in using the term 'police powers'. Several police officers have bridled when asked about aspects of their 'powers'. Similarly, the Queensland Police Service, in its submission to the Criminal Justice Commission's review of police powers, preferred to speak of 'policing authorities' rather than powers (Queensland Police Service 1991: 1). Such use of euphemisms is not uncommon in policing: they are used to present what is thought to be a more favourable aspect.[49] In the present case, the sensitivity is misplaced: the use of the word 'powers' in the context of policing should have no pejorative implication, and 'powers' is a standard usage in legal discussion of public bodies.

The *Malone* case illustrates well another sometimes problematic consequence of conceptualizing police powers as exemptions from prohibitions. In legal systems such as Australia and the United Kingdom which lack constitutional measures such as a Bill of Rights, the relevant prohibitions are those specified in tort and, particularly, the criminal law: Malone's investigators did not need to consider the possibility that their actions might be unlawful by virtue of transgressing a constitutionally protected right to privacy.[50] They were simply doing something which was not unlawful. By focusing on prohibitions, this legal tradition sees the non-prohibited as a legal vacuum. Activities within it are private rather than public, as the discussion of 'consent' (in Ch. 3, below) illustrates. The creation of a new offence simply reduces the area of the vacuum. Limitations on this legalistic way of conceptualizing police powers and criminal law are apparent: the legal vacuum has social and political substance. When people object that a proposed extension of police powers or criminal law would infringe their 'rights', this is not a mistake, an expression of legal unsophistication. These kinds of rights are much less clear than those specified in constitutional documents, but they are none the less significant (not least because the latter are often products of the former). At issue here are understandings of the limits of acceptable state intervention which are historical products of

[49] As in the current English police fashion of describing charge rooms and cells as 'the custody suite'.

[50] Although they should have considered the European Convention on Human Rights: see *Malone* v. *UK* (1985) 7 EHRR 14.

social and political disputes and negotiations. When Malone complained that his right of privacy was infringed by telephone tapping, the implicit reference was to a social and political understanding of the citizen's relationship with the state. This originated in the liberal democratic settlement which emerged from the social, political, and legal conflicts of the seventeenth and eighteenth centuries. The potency of this concept of rights did not lie in its legal or even historical accuracy. For example, it relied on an account of the 'freeborn' Anglo-Saxon Englishman [sic] and his subjugation to the 'Norman Yoke' which was largely mythical, but which was highly significant in the democratic movements of the eighteenth and nineteenth centuries (Hill 1954; 1996; Thompson 1963: ch. 3).

vi. Types of Police Powers

This section presents an overview drawing on studies of police powers in England and Wales, Canada, and Australia. While comparative material is useful, it is again important to note differences in national (and state) developments. Senior Australian and Canadian courts have been less willing than those in England and Wales to extend police powers (LRCC 1983: 47). Similarly, there are important differences in the extent to which criminal procedure has been legislated and codified.

(a) Statute

As sections iii and iv above showed, a major source of police powers is legislation prohibiting an activity. While the primary focus of such legislation is the substantive criminal law, its corollary is an extension of police powers. This may result either explicitly when a statute provides a special power facilitating enforcement of a prohibition or, more commonly, implicitly when a statute, for example, designates an activity as an arrestable offence. Again, this designation may be explicit or implicit, for example by setting a penalty which is above the level at which certain police powers become available.

The distinction between offence and power is sometimes overlooked (or is practically irrelevant). A good example here is the controversy in New South Wales in the late 1970s and 1980s about public order laws. At issue were offences (notably, offensive language and conduct). However, the debate was conducted largely in terms of powers: police argued that their powers had been reduced when an offence had been statutorily amended and that they should be restored.[51] Similarly, the 1988 legislation (which 'restored' police powers supposedly removed in 1979) 'contained only a single new provision that deals with police powers, allowing police to seize liquor from minors in a public place and administer a caution. . . . The new Act did, however, expressly re-criminalize offensive language, further restrict soliciting for the purposes of prostitution, and increase the penalties for most offences' (Brown *et al.* 1996: 917). The implications of this example are:

First, substance and process are so inextricably bound up, that to 'increase police powers' may actually mean 'to create substantive offences which make it easier for police to charge people'. . . . Second, the enormous discretion which is vested in police to operate this system on the streets is bounded as much, or as little, by the prevailing ethos as by the 'requirements of law'. The 1979 and 1988 legislative shifts only marginally impinged on formal police powers. Of considerably more importance were the signals given to police and magistrates by those changes.[52]

The linking of offences and powers has been influenced by the way in which statutes are written. As the examples cited in sections iii and iv demonstrate, the favoured style of legislative drafting in the nineteenth century was to define offences very specifically and minutely, rather than the broader generic drafting now adopted. Powers were attached to (or implied from) prohibitions. Similarly, when a perceived need for a power arose, it would be tagged on to other legislation. As in the case of Canadian search powers, the result was 'an assortment of powers' which was

the product of a growth that has occurred in piecemeal fashion over the past 300 years. The tendency of legislators has been to enact a search power and append it to a particularized enactment when and where the need for one has been evident. Consequently, search and seizure powers have been regarded individually, as incidents of larger enactments, rather than collectively, as incidents of a category of powers. . . . [P]rocedural rules governing search have not so much developed as accumulated (LRCC 1983: 8).

[51] This legislation did include some powers, but these were not at issue in the controversy.
[52] Brown *et al.* 1996: 917; see also Egger and Findlay 1988. In the early 1990s, two older officers still spoke bitterly about the 1979 legislation which 'allowed . . . hoodlums to run wild' and 'gave the streets back to the hoodlum element', and was the responsibility of an Attorney-General who was a 'self-proclaimed communist or socialist'.

This approach was a corollary of the definition of powers as exemptions which has been discussed above. As Leigh suggests:

English law insisted strongly that invasions of liberty . . . had necessarily to be grounded in positive law. . . . Government did not seek to create a comprehensive framework of police powers; instead, powers were granted on an ad hoc basis, sometimes grudgingly, sometimes as with the old Vagrancy Acts, entirely too readily, but generally with some reference to some demonstrable need. Unfortunately, and perhaps inevitably, the particular settlement arrived at became both cumbersome and in many respects illiberal (Leigh 1985: 33, 35).

This incremental accretion of powers via prohibitions resulted in confusion and anomaly until significant codification of major police powers was provided in the Police and Criminal Evidence Act 1984.

(b) Common Law and Judicial Interpretation of Codes and Statutes

English judges have often prided themselves as protectors of citizens' rights. This image is easier to maintain if attention is directed towards great eighteenth-century cases, such as *Entick* v. *Carrington* (see sect. ii, above). Their more recent record indicates a selectivity in their concern for citizens' rights. Courts became increasingly willing to extend police powers in the 1960s and 1970s, notably in search and seizure and pre-charge detention for investigation (see Ch. 4, below). Canadian courts felt pressure to expand police powers in the same way. As in England, courts typically dealt with cases *ad hoc*. Discussion of the nature of powers and of the proper relationship between powers and duties was generally lacking. The result was 'a body of contradictory case authority for which the underlying principles remain unclear' (LRCC 1985: 37).

While principles and policies were never properly articulated, this tendency 'to construe the rules liberally in order to allow some scope to police inquiries' constituted a move 'tentatively towards an ancillary powers doctrine which would enable the police to perform such reasonable acts as are necessary for the due execution of their duties' (Leigh 1975: 31, 33).[53] A notable example was the judicial approval of police action in the 1984–5 miners' strike: a duty to prevent a breach of the peace founded a power to stop pickets leaving a motor-

---

[53] For a critique of this doctrine in the context of detention for questioning, see Ch. 4 below.

way several miles away from a colliery.[54] Similarly, Canadian courts have sometimes recognized ancillary powers, 'the notion that the duties conferred upon peace officers imply the powers necessary and incidental to their performance' (LRCC 1983: 14–15; 1985: 37, 9). A concern here was to align more closely police powers and police duties: an action might be considered as a police power (i.e. protected from the consequences of unlawfulness) if it was carried out justifiably in the course of police duties (LRCC 1985: 3). This potentially broadened police powers very considerably: '[t]he obvious problem with the doctrine is that general police duties are extremely wide, and a test of whether or not an action is a "justifiable interference" with liberty or property is not sufficiently precise to be any real safeguard to fundamental rights and freedoms' (LRCC 1985: 39).

It is possible to distinguish between power ancillary to another power and power ancillary to a duty. This contrast may be drawn, for example, between allowing police during a search to seize articles which had not been specified in an authorizing warrant and allowing police to cordon off a street or to detain witnesses or groups of people, for example in crowd control or as part of a major crime investigation. The latter type of action is so rarely challenged that its legal basis is not an issue of dispute in practice: its existence is assumed from necessity and practice.[55] This raises an issue which will be considered further in section viii, below: the interrelation of law and policing practices

(c) Codified Powers

While codification of criminal law has a long history, codification, or even extensive consolidation, of criminal procedure has received much less attention until recently. Since the 1970s, there has been increasing interest in the reform of criminal procedure in common law countries, notably in the work of the Canadian Law Reform Commission, the Royal Commissions on Criminal Procedure and on Criminal Justice in England and Wales, the Thompson Committee on Criminal Procedure in Scotland, the New Zealand Law Commission and Public and Administrative Law Reform Committee, the

---

[54] *Moss* v. *McLachlan* [1985] IRLR 76.
[55] The difficulties of providing an appropriate statutory power apparently discouraged the British Government from following the Royal Commission on Criminal Procedure's recommendations on this: see RCCP 1981b: paras. 3.91–93.

Australian and New South Wales Law Reform Commissions, and the Criminal Justice Commission in Queensland.

A notable feature of this trend has simply been the recognition that police powers are extensive, significant, and more than merely those of a citizen in uniform. A corollary, in some of these, has been a concern to develop principles upon which to base criminal procedure.[56] This is a deliberate shift away from the traditions of *ad hoc* change. These principles are, invariably, a more or less sophisticated version of the problematic metaphor 'balance' between police powers and suspects' rights (Ashworth 1994; see Ch. 7, below). The major legislative product of this trend in England and Wales is the Police and Criminal Evidence Act 1984. As Chapter 4 below will indicate, this legislation has, amongst other things, demonstrated that police powers and suspects' rights can be increased together, and that such change need not necessarily be at the expense of one or the other. However, the inadequacies of PACE which have emerged since 1986 show how fundamental restructuring of criminal procedure must be if it is to be successful. In Australia, codification of criminal procedure is complicated by a federal system in which most criminal law and procedure is the preserve of the states. This has led to a process of collaboration in the production of a more model criminal code (Brown *et al.* 1996: 24–5). Similarly, the Commonwealth has produced evidence legislation which has been almost directly copied into New South Wales law (Aronson and Hunter 1995; Dennis 1996). As regards police powers, there has been less overt collaboration: however, the Commonwealth's legislation (notably the Crimes (Investigation of Commonwealth Offences) Amendment Act 1991) has provided a powerful model against which legislative proposals and changes can be measured.

(d) 'Exceptional' Powers

A category which would conventionally be included here is 'exceptional' or 'emergency' powers, i.e. those introduced to deal with a special situation in a way which does not accord with usual standards regarding suspects' rights. The Prevention of Terrorism Acts in England and Wales (which have been renewed repeatedly since the 1970s) are the usual example. Australia provides some notable exam-

[56] See, in particular, RCCP 1981b: chs. 1 and 2; LRCC 1988. The Royal Commission on Criminal Justice provides an unfortunate exception: for a sustained critique of its evasion of principle, cf. Ashworth 1994.

ples of exceptional powers: these include old legislation such as the Bushranging Act 1834, and extant provisions in modern statutes, such as consorting and garotting provisions in the NSW Crimes Act 1900,[57] as well as public order laws.

However, it seems preferable to resist the dichotomous classification of normal and exceptional powers. It relies on a rosy view of 'normal' powers, usually associated with the account of common law powers which was criticized in section iii above. It understates the strength of 'normal' powers provided by statute (see sects. iii and iv). Many 'normal' (or 'normalized') powers are the result of short-term moral panics; but they stay in the statute book long after the panic has subsided. Garotting, the Victorian equivalent of 'mugging', is an example (Davis 1980) as, much more significantly, is the Prevention of Terrorism Act (Hillyard 1987, 1993). 'Exceptional' powers may be introduced and then extended far beyond the original threat: the restriction of the right to silence first in Northern Ireland, then in England and Wales provides a good example (see Ch. 6 below). It is better to conceive of police powers as being on a continuum, rather than as being neatly divided into 'normal' and 'exceptional'.

vii. Powers: The Law-Practice Dichotomy

To this point, the analysis has been largely formalistic in implicitly defining police powers as specific authorities provided by statute or common law. However, a discussion of police powers as provided by case law inevitably stretches this formalistic definition and demands consideration of the relationship between law and policing practice. Powers cannot be considered in isolation from other features of criminal justice systems. For example, police powers of custodial interrogation are particularly significant in adversary systems 'in which the surest way to "victory" is aborting formal combat—the trial—by obtaining the other side's surrender—a guilty plea or at least a confession' (Lustgarten 1986: 9). Powers which are conducive to producing confessions are also increased in importance when proof of

---

[57] Respectively, ss. 546a and 37. The former is an offence of habitually consorting with persons known to have been convicted of indictable offences. In 1995, a NSW Police report recommended the revival and active use of this notable Australian contribution to criminal law: see 'Issue paper 1: Investigative Practices', 92–104, in NSW Police 1995.

intention is stressed in substantive criminal law. Juries may infer intention from actions; but the best evidence of it will always be a reliable confession. These factors provide the context for the emphasis which police have placed on interrogation and the significance to them of appropriate powers to detain for questioning. Similarly, if police are responsible for prosecutions (or have great influence on public prosecutors), then the power to arrest and charge assumes greater significance than when an effective screening of prosecutions is provided by a powerful and independent public prosecutor (Lustgarten 1986: 4–7).

Judges can develop (or limit) police powers only when disputes about an existing police practice reach their courts. In this sense, a judicial decision is reactive rather than creative: it transforms practice into authority (or stamps practice as being illegitimate). So, as suggested in section ii, what came to be dignified as 'common law police powers' were in some important respects simply established practices which lacked formal judicial recognition.

For example, the power to search arrested people is often assumed to be traceable to the earliest days of common law jurisprudence. . . . In fact the practice of such searches clearly predated the existence of any specific authority for them . . . these searches seem to have been simply assumed over the course of time to be proper and valid. This is due in large part to the historical tolerance of intrusive and indeed violent acts towards persons accused of crimes (LRCC 1983: 48).

Similarly, the Royal Commission on Police Powers and Procedure found in 1929 that there was no clear authority for police in England and Wales to search an arrested person's premises. However, 'the practice seems to have had the tacit approval of the Courts for so long that, in the opinion of the Home Office, it has become part of the common law' (RCPPP 1929: 14). This opinion was crucial: police forces would seek guidance on such matters and the Home Office's opinion would be decisive. In this sense, the executive was responsible for shaping the law at least as much as the judges. Dignifying such practices by describing them as common law had clear legitimating effects.

Police powers can be increased by judicial inaction as well as action. If judges consistently refuse to exclude evidence obtained in some unlawful way, then that practice has a judicial imprimatur which is hard to distinguish from authorization. (While it is true to say that the practice is not fully legalized in the sense that it may found a civil claim, this possibility is usually not significant.) A central example (discussed in detail in Chs. 4 and 5) of this in both England and Wales and Australia is custodial interrogation. In both jurisdictions, the police practice of detaining and questioning suspects before charge was able to become entrenched in the middle of this century because courts did not enforce statutes and Judges' Rules which prohibited such detention for questioning by refusing to accept the evidential products of it. If judges (and other actors, notably defence lawyers) condone legal fictions about police practices, they are substantially, if not formally, legalized. A major issue here is the way in which restrictions on police powers may be avoided by obtaining a suspect's 'consent' to police activity. Analyses of this issue often conclude that a clear distinction between consent and coercion cannot be made when policing activities are involved, and that consequently 'consensual' activities should be brought within a framework of legal regulation (see LRCC 1983: 160 and Ch. 3 below).

An account such as this must not slip into a mirror image of whig history, in which there is a relentless expansion of police powers as police push at or evade their legal limits: as will be suggested below, this would be to misrepresent both police attitudes to law and the effect of legal change. The argument advanced here is that a clear line cannot be drawn between law and practice in the police powers which have developed in jurisdictions based on or emergent from the common law. As McBarnet (1983) has argued, the appropriate distinction is not between law and practice, but rather between the law and practice on one side and legal rhetoric and ideology on the other. The vehicle for this combination of law and practice has been the case law form, with its flexibility and adaptability (on McBarnet's discussion of this, see Ch. 1, above). Police powers cannot be considered apart from the broader criminal justice system in which they are located.

viii.   The Office of Constable

Police powers are sometimes distinguished from those of other state officials by the nature of the 'office of constable': the 'essential feature which distinguishes Police organizations from most other organized bodies is that the Policeman's powers are not delegated to him by superior authority' (RCPPP 1929: 15). Powers are said to be given to an officer as a constable, not as a member of a police force: 'in essence a police force is neither more nor less than a number of individual constables, whose status derives from the common law, organized together in the interests of efficiency' (Hailsham 1981: 107). The doctrine of the constable's office has been the subject of (and been confused by) considerable controversy in British debates about police accountability (see e.g. Brogden 1982; Jefferson and Grimshaw 1984; Lustgarten 1986).

While it is true that officers must make their own decisions about, for example, whether they have reasonable suspicion necessary to exercise a power, and in this sense cannot be ordered to exercise powers, this is not distinct from a general administrative law requirement that officials should exercise discretion given to them by law and must not act under dictation. There is nothing special about police or police powers in this regard. Concentration on this legal requirement largely serves to ignore the reality of police organization and command, which does assign officers to tasks, including the exercising of powers (Hogg and Hawker 1983). An administrative law requirement that a public official should make her or his own decision and not act under dictation is not inconsistent with the operation of a bureaucratic structure of this kind. It certainly does not provide the basis for the assertion of some unique constabulary independence. As Lustgarten suggests, the exceptional cases of officers persevering with prosecutions against orders in fact prove the rule rather than subvert it: subsequent prosecutions are brought by the officer as an individual, not as a member of a police force (1986: 11–13, 171).

Why has the office of constable been a source of such confusion? In a valuable critique, Hogg and Hawker 'elucidate the contours of this lack of clarity . . . and the purposes served by it' (1983: 163). They suggest that it 'has certain beneficial effects for governments and police in that it has created a space for manoeuvre on specific occasions without requiring concessions on principle. . . . The police are permitted to argue that what they do is outside politics and governments are able to relinquish responsibility for law enforcement policy' (1983: 165). The instability of such arrangements has been illustrated by the constitutional confusion evident on occasions when relations between police and government have broken down.[58]

[58] For examples, see Hogg and Hawker 1983, Moore and Wettenhall (eds.) 1994, and the *Second Report of the Joint Select Committee upon Police Administration* (NSW Parliament, May 1993).

ix. What are Police Powers for?

A legalistic answer to this question would be specific and simplistic. For example, it is said that the power of arrest begins the process of bringing suspected offenders before the courts to be tried (Devlin 1960). The reality of arrest in policing practice is rather different. As the American Bar Foundation's survey and subsequent research have shown, arrest serves a number of other functions: people are 'taken into custody to conduct further investigations; for harassment, as a means of controlling a problem; to preserve testimony; and for safekeeping' (Goldstein 1993: 35; cf. *ibid*. 34–6, 47–52). Arrest also allows officers to establish authority, collect information,[59] and ensure self-protection[60] (Dixon *et al*. 1989: 189–90; Milner 1974: 32–4; Wilson 1968: ch. 2). In the 'war on drugs' in the United States, a notable use of arrest as a means of control and harassment is 'the practice of conducting street "sweeps," making hundreds of arrests that are not subsequently prosecuted' (Goldstein 1993: 51; cf. Maher 1997: ch. 2). In addition, arrest can be preventative. This is legally recognized in the power to arrest to prevent a breach of the peace and under statutory powers (such as suspected persons or loitering offences). In such circumstances, arrest is an expression of power, a demonstration of police control over a situation. Arrest can serve as punishment. It is now well recognized in criminal justice studies that the experience of arrest, detention, and trial can be just as punitive as any formal punishment which a court imposes (Feeley 1979).

This perspective provides a way of understanding disputes about powers associated with public-order offences. Those who argue that, for example, offensive language should not be an arrestable offence (as it is in New South Wales) on the ground that a summons will usually be appropriate overlook the ways in which police use such a charge, especially in their control of Aboriginal people. Often, this is not (or not simply) to respond to an offence. Rather, an offensive-language charge is a method of control, a justification for removing a person from a public place. This is particularly the case when, as

---

[59] The frequent use by English officers of the word 'checking' as a synonym for stopping, questioning, and possibly searching is a good indication of the exercise's nature.

[60] As Milner points out, legal restrictions on search powers are unlikely to be effective if, e.g., an officer suspects (although lacking 'reasonable grounds') that a suspect is armed (1974: 33–4).

so often happens, the victim of the offensive language is a police officer (Egger and Findlay 1988). Public-order law provides clear examples of the breadth of police discretion, but similar analysis can be made of much policing activity:

'enforcing the law', in the sense of arresting someone, may be only one of several resources available to policemen [*sic*] for handling incidents. From this point of view an arrest is not adequately explained by the evidence presented by the arresting officer to justify his use of the resource, i.e. his use of his powers of arrest. For on other occasions when this power might have been invoked, an alternative resource may have been used to deal with the incident (Chatterton 1976: 105).

Chatterton goes on to insist that we should suspend 'the conventional idea that laws are things to be enforced, and [think] of them instead as resources to be used to achieve the ends of those who are entitled or able to use them' (1976: 114; cf. Bittner 1990 and Ch. 1, above). These ends include resolving trouble, restoring public order, getting a suspect into custody so that other possible charges can be investigated, and punishing the blameworthy. As a NSW officer commented, '[i]f you know what you are doing, if you know the law well enough . . . you can make it do wonderful and marvellous things'. So, arrest powers are not just the legal method of setting the criminal process in motion: the choice of their use is also to be seen as a tool of social discipline.

    It is important to stress that this perspective requires abandoning the mythology in which crime-fighting is the sole police function (see sect. x):

The core mandate of policing, historically and in terms of concrete demands placed upon the police, is the more diffuse one of order maintenance. Only if this is recognised can the problems of police powers and accountability really be confronted in all their complexity, and perhaps intractability. The vaguely defined 'public order' offences . . . (which are such a scandalous embarrassment from either a crime control or due process approach) speak to the heart of the police function (Reiner 1992: 212; cf. Smith 1986: 87).

It is only in this context that, for example, pressure from Queensland police for a 'move-on' power can be properly addressed (Queensland Police Service 1991; CJC 1993). To concentrate on the penalty for a failure to move on draws attention away from the central issue of how police contribute to social ordering, the diversity of behaviour which a society can tolerably encompass, and the relations between police and the socially marginal groups which are directly affected by order maintenance policing.

Similar issues arise in the case of powers to stop and search. Historically, stop and search has been used not just to investigate those suspected (reasonably or not) of having committed offences, but as a more general technique of social surveillance and discipline—checking on people whose appearance is incongruous because, for example, they appear to be in an inappropriate place at an inappropriate time (young people in a commercial area at night; a black person in a white neighbourhood). The use of such powers is justified as contributing to crime detection (even if only some 12 per cent of officially recorded stops lead to arrests: Home Office 1996: table 1), to information gathering (particularly in the case of stops for suspected illegal drugs), and to crime prevention (deterrent stop and search is an important, if often unrecognized, part of a beat officer's activities). But these are only part of a more general use of a power for purposes of social surveillance and discipline.[61]

The case of stop and search is an excellent example of how excessive use of a police power can be dysfunctional or counterproductive. A major precondition of the 1981 Brixton riots was the intensive use of stop and search powers which worsened relations between police and young black people. The result was rioting and the commission of many serious offences (Scarman 1981). Similar results have been produced by other instances of intensively using stop and search or 'field interrogation' in an aggressive patrol strategy. Studies in the United States and in England suggest that the level of some crimes may be reduced, but 'the price in alienation of some sections of the public (primarily young males, especially blacks) is very high' (Reiner 1992a: 154). The lesson to be learnt is that any potential benefits which police powers may provide can be dissipated if they are used inappropriately. This is particularly significant, given police reliance on information from the public in crime detection: this issue will be raised again in the context of police effectiveness in the next section.

Scarman's discussion of stop and search powers in his Brixton report insisted that police powers cannot be considered in isolation from their use or from the broader context of police duties and responsibilities. In an analysis which has been influential, Scarman argued that the primary police duty is the maintenance of social

[61] For a discussion of these issues related to stop and search in England and Wales, see Dixon *et al.* 1989 and Ch. 3, below.

order. Enforcing the law is a secondary duty. It may be a means of achieving the former, but on occasions 'law enforcement puts at risk public tranquillity . . . [and] can cause acute friction and division in a community' (1981: paragraph 4.57). When a conflict between the duties arises, the maintenance of order must take priority. This is achieved by the use of the discretion which 'lies at the heart of the policing function' (1981: paragraph 4.58). The important link which Scarman makes is to stress that the balance between law enforcement and order maintenance will only be achieved when another, that between police independence and accountability, is successfully made. This balance in turn depends upon the police securing the consent of the communities in which they work (1981: paragraphs 4.59–60). Scarman's Report showed clearly the indissoluble links between police powers, discretion, and accountability (even if his social democratic proposals for remedial action were flawed: see Hall 1982).

While stop and search attracted most attention in debates about policing in the early 1980s, the central issue (in both in England and Wales and Australia) in the late 1990s is custodial interrogation. From a legalistic perspective, the central purpose of police powers to detain for questioning is the collection of evidence for potential use in court. A more socially realistic perspective suggests that the division between investigative and judicial functions is too neat. Criminal justice systems which depend on very high rates of guilty pleas for their effective functioning have transferred the crucial site of determination from the court to the police station. When cases may be effectively determined by a confession, then a power to detain and question is more, in practice if not in law, than an investigative power.

It may seem 'common sense' that providing new police powers by legal change means extending police power. This may not be the case, and (as noted above) one effect of legislating on police powers may be to control police power. This paradoxical result may be produced when police have developed informal practices such as relying on 'consent' in order to search or detain for questioning, or when more clearly coercive unlawful practices are not challenged in court, or when legal powers are used inappropriately (e.g. when stop and search is carried out without reasonable suspicion). If a legislature provides formal legal powers, these may authorize less than what was previously common practice. The contrasting effects of attempts in

PACE to regulate detention for questioning and stop and search illustrate again the inseparability of law and practice (Bottomley *et al.* 1991).

x. Police Powers and Police Effectiveness

[A] constant call from police circles is for more powers to be able to deal with crime suspects. The assumption is that if more powers were available, the police would be able to detect more crime, successfully prosecute more offenders and thus significantly reduce crime levels. The implicit claim is that there exists a causal link between the powers provided and 'success' in the 'war against crime'. Apart from the fact that in many instances the police already exercise the powers that they are seeking (and in asking for changes to the law they are, in effect, asking for their present practices to be given legal status), short of granting quite draconian powers, what evidence there is raises very considerable doubts about the validity of the assumptions made by the police and others in arguing for more powers (Sallmann and Willis 1984: 217)

How is police effectiveness influenced by a change in police powers? It is important to examine this question because an answer to it is usually taken for granted in calls for the extension of police powers. When a problem of crime is perceived, the remedy most commonly advanced is an extension of police powers to deal with it. As Sallmann and Willis suggest, some advocates of this remedy do not fully consider either the powers already available to police or the likely effect on the perceived problem of extending powers, or indeed whether measures other than police powers might be more effective. This suggests the crucial symbolic significance of police powers. As Reiner argues:

Until relatively recently discussions about criminal justice policy, and the police specifically, have been locked into the law and order myth that given adequate resources and powers the police could tackle the problem of rising crime. The only opposition to the law and order lobby was on the civil libertarian grounds that police effectiveness must not be bought at too high a price in the undermining of civil rights. However, a recent wave of . . . research in the United States and Britain has begun to question the assumption that increased police power and resources can control crime (Reiner 1992a: 146–7).

The relationship between police powers and police effectiveness has received much less detailed attention than have the relationships between police resources and policies and police effectiveness. It is helpful to note some of the lessons and conclusions which can be drawn from debates about the latter, because they are in many respects comparable to our current concerns. First, crime rates cannot be used as a simple indicator of police success: 'one of the classic pitfalls of police performance analysis is the tendency to use crime statistics to measure effectiveness' (Grabosky 1988: 3). At base, they are no more than a record of the documented activities of police officers: their relationship with 'actual crime' is mediated through a series of policies and recording practices which fundamentally affect the result. Carefully analysed, they can still be useful sources of data (Bottomley and Coleman 1981; Coleman and Moynihan 1996). What is clear is that a falling (or rising) crime rate cannot simply be read as denoting police success (or failure). The creation of a new police power (either directly or via a new offence) may lead to an increase in the crime rate (i.e. if police are able to deal with more suspects or if an activity is newly criminalized). Matters are rarely as straightforward as this; but the fundamental point is that increasing police powers may increase (officially recorded) crime.

Secondly, 'a significant proportion of police resources is devoted to tasks quite unrelated to the prevention of crime and the apprehension of offenders' (Grabosky 1988: 1). Meanwhile, most criminal activity is unaffected by the police either because it is not reported or is, to all intents and purposes, undetectable (Bayley 1994: ch. 1; Hough and Clarke 1980: 7–8; Skolnick 1994: 296–8). At levels of resources and power which can currently be contemplated, the police are too far removed from criminal activities for them to have a decisive impact. The classic example here is the Kansas City Preventive Patrol Experiment, in which very different styles of policing were found to have no significantly differential effect on crime or on fear of crime or on attitudes towards police: indeed, it seems that they were hardly noticed by many residents.[62] Together, these factors mean that a change in police powers is unlikely to have a direct or substantial effect on crime.

[62] See Kelling *et al.* 1974 and, for a review of later research, Reiner 1992a: 147–9. L. W. Sherman (1993) has strongly criticized the Kansas City research, associating it with a ' "politically correct" orthodoxy' which is 'against police even *trying* to control crime' (1993: 174, original emphasis). From a British or Australian perspective, Sherman's critique appears, at best, dated, in its ignorance of the realist influence in contemporary criminology (Young 1994a) and caricatured in its misreading of Packer (cf. Smith 1995).

Thirdly, fear of crime is a factor which should be taken into account in evaluating police effectiveness. For many people, fear of crime is at least as great a problem as the real likelihood of victimization. Police forces are important producers of knowledge, information, and opinion about crime: the 'popular image of the police battling with an almost intractable crime problem is arguably the main source of people's fear of crime—a fear justified neither by the risks nor by the nature of the vast bulk of crime' (Hough and Clarke 1980: 9; cf. Weatherburn *et al.* 1996). When police officers complain that they cannot do their job properly because of a lack of powers, this is likely to increase public fear of crime. Consequently, considerable responsibility should be exercised in making such claims. There have been some unfortunate examples of irresponsibility, such as the advertisement placed in Sydney's *Daily Telegraph* in 1979 by the NSW Police Association as part of its campaign over public order legislation:

You can still walk on the streets of NSW, but we can no longer *guarantee* your safety from harassment. . . . What concerns Police is that you have families who use our streets and we can no longer guarantee them protection from harassment by the hoodlum element. But there is an even more alarming factor—there is a real danger that Police could eventually lose control of the streets. . . . Is it possible that the Offences in Public Places Act (1979) could be the seed from which a growth pattern of New York style street crime will be the future harvest? (quoted, Brown *et al.* 1996: 916).

As a compendium of moral panic clichés and exaggerations, this would be hard to match.

Finally, a lack of powers does not emerge from relevant research as a significant factor influencing the effectiveness of the police. Research commissioned for the Royal Commission on Criminal Procedure concluded that there 'are no obvious powers which police might be given that would greatly enhance their effectiveness in the detection of crime' (Steer 1980: 125; cf. Cameron 1990: 512). The detection and clear-up of most crime depends, not on police powers, but on the provision of information by the public:

the prime determinant of success is information immediately provided by members of the public (usually the victim) to patrol officers or detectives. . . . If adequate information is provided to pinpoint the culprit fairly accurately, the crime will be resolved, if not it is almost certain not to be. This is the conclusion of all the relevant studies (Reiner 1992a: 151).

If the flow of such information is so crucial, it may be more useful to concentrate efforts on improving police-community relations than on increasing powers: indeed, if an increase in powers contributes to alienation between police and public, the result may well be counter-productive.

Calls for increasing police powers usually include as a corollary reducing suspects' rights. These rights, it is claimed, obstruct effective police work. Three points should be made here. First, suspects rarely exercise the rights which are supposed to be so obstructive. The prime example here is the 'right to silence', the target of concerted attacks from police since the 1960s (see Ch. 6 below). Secondly, the legal status of these rights is often doubtful. The lack of legal substance for a suspect's 'right' of access to legal advice in Australia (and in England and Wales before 1986) provides a good example. If 'rights' are neither protected by the courts nor made real by the provision of services such as publicly-funded duty solicitors in police stations, then they are of little value or meaning (Brown 1984). Thirdly, the assumption that rights obstruct policing depends on a model of criminal justice as balanced between police powers and suspects' rights: increase one, and the other must decrease. Research on the effects of the Police and Criminal Evidence Act 1984 shows how unhelpful such dichotomous thinking can be (see Chs. 4 and 7, below).

In an authoritative review of the research literature, Robert Reiner concludes that it is 'not plausible that changes in police powers would significantly increase police effectiveness in crime control. . . . There is no evidence that rules of criminal procedure allow a significant proportion of suspects to avoid conviction' (Reiner 1992a: 213). Such findings are a better basis for public policy than the rhetoric and misinformation which generally characterize debates about police powers. In any case, to focus on a supposed lack of power (or any single factor) is misleading because neither policing in general nor law enforcement in particular is a unitary activity. In order to understand the field, the focus must be much tighter, concentrating for example on factors such as varying detectability of types of crime, the likelihood of one detection leading to other crimes being cleared up (as offences 'taken into consideration' or 'written off'), the influence of relationships between suspect and victim, and between police and public (Bottomley and Coleman 1980: 85–98; 1981). In sum, policing is a much more complex activity than nostrums about the need for more powers would suggest. Claims for more powers need to be analysed specifically: what principles and rights are involved and how should they be weighted? what is the problem to be addressed? how would increasing police powers help to solve it? what are the alternatives? what would be the costs of increasing powers, and might these be greater than the benefits?

It should perhaps be emphasized that this argument does not suggest that police are irrelevant to crime control or that they should not aim to control crime (contrast Sherman 1993). Rather, the research evidence suggests that in certain circumstances 'the police *can* effect marked reductions in crime, but usually only in cooperation with other agencies and only if they adopt strategies which are in stark contrast to those dictated by the "professional law enforcement" model' (Homel 1994: 32; cf. Moore 1992). The 'rational deterrent' model of policing implicit in 'common sense' discussions of police effectiveness has been properly criticized.[63] Its concept of effective policing is unproblematic, but 'such clarity of vision is a form of myopia' (Hough and Clarke 1980: 2). Similarly, much discussion of police powers relies on what was described in Chapter 1 as a legalistic-bureaucratic model of policing. In relation to police powers, this model has been shown to be inaccurate by the considerable number of empirical studies of policing which have been produced in the United States since the 1960s and the United Kingdom since the 1970s (for a review, see Reiner 1992a). Crucially, the assumption that changing a police power will have a direct, intended effect on policing practices must be abandoned. Such legal changes are communicated and mediated through layers of organization and culture.

An extension of police powers is one of the clearest way in which politicians can signify that they take public concerns seriously. When the demand is to 'do something about the crime problem', a change in police powers is an attractive option: it is likely to be popular, highly visible, and cheap. In such a context, more searching questions about the utility or likely effect of a change tend to be overlooked. Pressure for changes in police powers often comes from the police themselves. The 'perennial clamour by law enforcement officials for increased powers' can be traced back to the earliest days of organized police forces in Australia (Haldane 1995: 15). Current concerns have to be seen in the light of their long history (Finnane 1987; 1989;

---

[63] But cf. Homel 1994 for a careful critique of wholesale rejection of deterrence.

1989a; 1994). In recent decades, senior officers have become increasingly frequent and influential contributors to public debates about policing and a wide range of social matters. Clearly, police have status as experts in areas of their specialization. However, it is equally clear that claims for increased powers are made by police, not just as disinterested experts, but as politically aware bureaucrats. Claims for increased police powers are often linked to other bureaucratic interests, notably increased resources and establishments. Once again, claims for more police powers may have a very significant symbolic dimension, drawing attention to perceived crime threats or needs of police, or indeed drawing attention away from other public concerns such as police corruption or indiscipline.

This suggests that there is difficulty even at a superficial level in knowing what a change in police powers achieves. Some examples demonstrate that the measurement of effects is likely to be a highly complex matter. A simple case is a police power to conduct random breath testing (RBT) for alcohol on drivers. Measures of effectiveness would include trends in convictions and road deaths. In New South Wales, the introduction of RBT was followed by a dramatic, sustained decrease in fatal car crashes (Homel 1994: 23). However, a direct relation between the power (to carry out random breath-tests) and the result (declining alcohol-related road deaths) is confounded by other immeasurable factors, such as the effect of road safety advertising and, more generally, changing social attitudes towards drinking and driving. Homel points out that Tasmania introduced RBT at the same time as New South Wales, but did not have similar success. The significant difference was not in policing: on the contrary, Tasmania 'achieved even higher levels of testing. . . . The major difference between the two states was the use in New South Wales of extensive and sophisticated television, radio and newspaper publicity, in contrast to the almost total lack of such publicity in Tasmania' (Homel 1994: 24).

Other examples are less straightforward. Police powers and their use in dealing with domestic violence illustrate the point. In a number of jurisdictions (notably in the United States), police have been directed to use arrest powers in dealing with incidents of domestic violence. (Although new arrest powers are not usually introduced, the effect is comparable to such a legal change.) The impact of such policies has attracted a great deal of research, probably more than on any comparable shift in police power and practice (Sherman 1992a).

Early claims that such a policy reduced domestic violence (Sherman and Berk 1984) led to their widespread adoption in numerous jurisdictions in the United States and elsewhere.[64] However, it is now becoming clear that the effects are much less certain and desirable than the initial studies suggested. Far from reducing domestic violence, mandatory arrest policies have increased arrests in half of the cities where the original research has been replicated. It is suggested that arrest has different effects on different kinds of people (see Sherman 1992b: 203–12 for a summary of this research). Apart from the problems identified in replication studies, the domestic violence experiments have attracted a wide range of other criticisms: indeed, they are the subject of a major controversy in contemporary criminology. The simple and attractive early message—arrest deters domestic violence—has been overtaken by contrary empirical evidence, general and specific methodological concerns, and theoretical and political critiques (e.g. Bowman 1992; Manning 1993; McCord 1992; Stanko 1995; cf. the response by Sherman 1995).

   A final example is the effect of the Police and Criminal Evidence Act 1984 on the investigation of crime in England and Wales. As Chapter 4 will show, irreconcilable predictions were made about the likely effects of this legislation, and empirical studies of its effects have reflected these expectations (Dixon 1992). Brown's study of the impact of the Police and Criminal Evidence Act on investigations of domestic burglary provides useful insight into these problems of evaluation. It was commissioned in response to 'a fall in the number and percentage of crimes cleared up by the police' in 1986 (the first year that the legislation was in force) which 'some took . . . to indicate that PACE had indeed given the balance of advantage to the suspect' (Brown 1991: vi). After 1986, the statistics returned to their previous pattern and it appears that the 1986 dip was 'a temporary aberration' which was largely due to officers' unfamiliarity and caution in operating new procedures (Brown 1991: vi, 85). However, this does not mean that the Police and Criminal Evidence Act did not change policing, but rather that its impact cannot be adequately grasped at the level of generalities. Brown examined the way that the Police and Criminal Evidence Act affected burglary investigations at three stations which contrasted sharply in their investigative methods: one 'cleared a high proportion of burglaries through interviewing

----

[64] See, e.g. *New South Wales Police Policy and Procedures in Domestic Violence* (NSW Police 1988); Home Office Circular 60/1990 *Domestic Violence.*

convicted offenders in prison about other offences'; at the second, suspects were frequently interviewed at the station for offences that might be taken into consideration (TICs) along with the main charge; while at the third 'the policy tended to be to charge offenders and lay little emphasis on interviewing about further offences' (Brown 1991: vii). The research found that these contrasting practices significantly affected the impact of the Police and Criminal Evidence Act which varied from station to station, but that there was 'no evidence that PACE led to any consistent reduction in police effectiveness against burglary' (Brown 1991: xi). It also emphasized other differences between the stations, notably 'in the standard of evidence considered necessary to justify an arrest and subsequent detention at the police station' (Brown 1991: xii). Brown makes clear the difficulty in disentangling the effects of the Police and Criminal Evidence Act (which itself is complex and multi-faceted) from other contemporary changes, many of which are immeasurable, some of which may be imperceptible. These range from changes of personnel at the research sites to other legislative changes (notably, the introduction of the Crown Prosecution Service), to broader social and political changes (Brown 1991: 8).

Such vital considerations tend to be overlooked when legislative changes are discussed. In such debates, there is a good deal of loose talk about legislative 'intention'. Indeed, legislation is sometimes anthropomorphized, as when people talk about the Police and Criminal Evidence Act 'trying' or 'intending' to achieve some objective (Dixon 1992: 523–6; see, e.g., Bottomley *et al.* 1991: 165, 170, 171, 178). While this is, of course, largely a matter of shorthand, it threatens to over-simplify matters. To ask whether the Police and Criminal Evidence Act achieved its objectives is a misleading question: such complex, multi-determined legislation can only in a very qualified sense be said to have 'intentions' (Dixon 1992).

These examples suggest the need for great care and specificity in making claims about the effects of proposed or actual legislative changes in police powers. Sweeping generalizations and unfounded assumptions need to be replaced by thorough, well-grounded research. The outcome need not be an accumulation of specific case-studies without more general relevance. Brown provides an exemplar of how broader lessons may be drawn from closely-focused studies (Brown 1991: ch. 8)

xi. Conclusion

It is hoped that this Chapter makes clear the need for considerable re-evaluation of the topics which have been considered. While the history of police powers awaits the depth of historical revision to which other aspects of policing have been subjected, it is clear that received wisdom about constables' original common law powers needs to be revised by greater attention to the historical contexts, notably the seventeenth- and eighteenth-century ideological shifts. Provision of wide-ranging statutory powers is no modern development, but can be traced back to early vagrancy legislation. Social and national contexts are also vital: the nature of early Australian society transformed the imported traditions of Anglo–Irish policing. A proper understanding of police powers requires attention to be paid to the interactive relationship between law and practice. Rhetorical generalizations need to be abandoned in favour of specific, informed analysis of what particular police powers are, how they are employed, and what their use can achieve.

3
Policing by Law and Policing by Consent

If you ask people for consent, they seem to think that they have the right to say no.[1]

i. Legal regulation and consent

As suggested in Chapter 2, the adoption of techniques of legal regulation has become increasingly common in attempts to change and control policing in a number of jurisdictions (including Australia, Canada, the United States, New Zealand, Scotland, England and Wales). The general aim is the extension (or formalization), clarification, and specification of police powers and of suspects' rights. My concern here is with a major issue which the strategy of legal regulation has not yet adequately faced—the problem of consent. Police officers may be able to achieve their objectives (e.g., to interrogate or to search) not by using a legal power, but by securing the 'consent' of the suspect or other subject of their attention. If 'consent' is obtained, *prima facie* the legal relationship between the actors is not that between a state official and a private citizen, but rather that between two private citizens. This practice has long been used by police officers, not just to supplement what are regarded as inadequate or unclear powers, but as a way of doing police work more generally.

As legal regulation comes to delimit police powers, 'consent' becomes increasingly significant. Some of the consequences of 'consensual' encounters are that statutory requirements for the exercise of powers do not apply (so that, for example, a suspect can be searched without reasonable grounds for suspicion), record-making is unnecessary (rendering supervision more difficult), and the rights of the

---

[1] An English officer explaining practices in house searches.

suspect do not have the protections which are the corollaries of the exercise of legal power. There is a long, largely unwritten, history of Australian police relying on 'consent' rather than legal powers. Similarly in, for example, Scotland and the United States, police have responded to the tightening of legal regulation by using 'consent' (Curran and Carnie 1986; LaFave 1965: 351–2; Skolnick and Fyfe 1993: 100). It was predicted that this would be the police's response to the Police and Criminal Evidence Act (Baldwin 1985, 1989). PACE included some specific provisions which regulate activity carried out with 'consent'. The discussion below will focus on PACE, with comparative material from Australia, and will consider the ways in which 'consent' has created problems for the legal regulation of stop and search, search of premises, and arrest, detention, and questioning, and will also note some of the attempts to deal with these difficulties. The aim is not just to list various incidents of 'consent', but to illustrate a way of thinking about and doing police work which constitutes a social practice, policing by 'consent', which is distinct from the usual conception of 'policing by law'. The Chapter will conclude with some observations about the history and prospects of these sometimes competing and sometimes complementary practices.

The focus here is on the relationship between consent and police investigative powers. However, the effects of granting (or claiming) 'consent' are of interest and concern in a wide variety of other legal settings. The later stages of criminal process depend heavily upon the willingness of suspects and defendants to cooperate by pleading guilty or accepting cautions (Mack and Anleu 1995; Sanders and Young 1994a: chs. 5–7; 1994b: 134). In substantive criminal law, consent plays a controversial role in the definition of certain offences, notably sexual and other assault (Law Commission 1995). Elsewhere, it is raised by questions of capacity, especially in medical law concerning consent to treatment. As Lee comments, 'the concept of consent features throughout the law' (1987: 199; for a detailed survey, see Young 1986).

Up to this point, 'consent' has been put between quotation marks in order to acknowledge problems with bland uses of the term: it is clear that what is classified, in practice, as consent covers a range of states, which include approving agreement, unwilling acquiescence, submission, and a co-operation or compliance ignorant of the possibility of acting differently. There is a mass of philosophical literature on what constitutes consent (and correlative concepts such as coercion). I do not intend to explore that literature here: it is enough for present purposes to suggest, not a definition, but an indication of two significant components of consent which must be considered in any discussion of the concept. These are (i) knowledge: i.e. information and understanding about what is requested; and (ii) power: i.e. an ability to make choices on the basis of knowledge, to use the available knowledge.

Given the nature of the relationship between police and citizen (whether suspect or not), an equality of power is extremely unlikely. 'Full consent' is, therefore, in practice unattainable. As Vega has argued in another context, the concept of the fully consenting individual is a product of the liberal concept of the autonomous subject, 'the naturally free, abstract individual' (1987: 77). This causes great problems in most legal considerations of consent: they assume rationality and free will as the natural state, and then try to take account of incursions into that state. The law relies on dichotomies—voluntary/involuntary, responsible/irresponsible, consenting/non-consenting—and takes the first part of each pair as the natural state. This leads to concentration on active, external forces which can be positively identified. A good example is a statutory definition from the Tasmanian Criminal Code of 1924:

A consent freely given by a rational and sober person so situated as to be able to form a rational opinion upon the matter to which he consents. A consent is said to be freely given when it is not procured by force, fraud or threats of whatsoever nature (quoted, Young: 1986: 14).[2]

Consent is, in practice, often limited, not by external factors, but by the subject's social and psychological position, lack of knowledge, and lack of power. For example, it is widely accepted that true consent cannot be obtained by a wrongful claim to authority, as when officers are allowed to search premises after claiming untruthfully that they had a warrant which would authorize search if permission was not granted (Wertheimer 1987: 114).[3] The law can deal with such objective circumstances (if they come for adjudication, which usually they will not). However, it has difficulty with the much more common and important instance of the search which is allowed without

---

[2] See also Scott LJ's comments on free will in *Bowater* v. *Rowley Regis Corporation* [1944] KB 476, at 479.

[3] On misrepresentations which lead to 'voluntary' confessions, see *Hawkins* (1994) 122 ALR 27 and *Mason* [1987] 3 All ER 481.

any positive misrepresentation by the police, but which the householder assumes to be legally authorized.[4] When such subjective factors are recognized, legal consideration tends to degenerate into the
inconclusive citation of individual factual instances, leading to the
enunciation of unhelpful 'principles' such as: the 'word "consent" has
different meanings in different branches of the law' (Young 1986:
219).

Problems of dealing with 'consent' are not resolved by ditching the
term in favour of another (acquiescence or whatever) or by regarding it as 'an ideological farce and merely constitutive of moments of
coercion'. Rather, consent should be seen as an area of negotiation
over shifting elements of knowledge and power: it 'cannot be considered independent of coercion . . . nor as identical to it' (Vega 1987:
86). The practical implications of this include the need to see police
work 'by consent' as being neither inherently preferable, nor necessarily undesirable, but rather as requiring attention and, when appropriate, regulation just as much as the use of police powers.

ii. Consent to Stop and Search

The problems of using law to regulate consensual stop and search or
(a close neighbour) 'field interrogation' by consent are illustrated by
Tiffany et al.'s explanation for the lack of specific discussion of the
topic in the American Bar Foundation's survey:

> it is not meaningful in practice to attempt to distinguish between field inter-
> rogation with consent and that which takes place without consent. In high-
> crime areas, particularly, persons who stop and answer police questions do
> so for a variety of reasons, including a willingness to cooperate with police,
> a fear of police, a belief that a refusal to cooperate will result in arrest, or a
> combination of all three. It would be extremely difficult to determine what
> motivated an individual citizen to stop and answer police questions in a par-
> ticular situation. Also, it is unlikely that authorizing the police to stop and
> question those who consent would prove realistic in practice.[5]

Some of the most important provisions in PACE construct a legal
framework for stop and search. These were both controversial and
significant because of the clear evidence that abuse and over-use of
stop and search were a major factor in worsening relations between

---

[4] See sect. iii, below and *Scheckloth* v. *Bustamonte* 412 US 218 (1972).
[5] 1967: 17. On legal regulation of stop and search in the US, see LaFave 1993:
231–40.

police and sections of the public, notably young black people. PACE provides legal powers to stop and search for various articles: reasonable grounds for suspicion are required.[6] Code of Practice A (which applies both to PACE powers and to those provided in other statutes, e.g. the Misuse of Drugs Act) provides guidance on what can and what cannot amount to reasonable grounds.[7] The Code requires officers to complete a record giving details of, *inter alia*, themselves, the suspect, and the grounds for and purposes of the stop and search. These provisions were justified as providing the police with necessary but strictly regulated and supervised powers (RCCP 1981: paragraphs 3.20–28).

The conclusion of our research (see Dixon *et al.* 1989; Bottomley *et al.* 1991: ch. 2) was that PACE operates here largely as what the Policy Studies Institute called 'presentational rules' which

> put a gloss on policing behaviour so as to make it acceptable to the wider public. . . . Presentational rules . . . exist to give an acceptable appearance to the way that police work is carried out. It is important to realise that it is not only or mainly the police who seek to put this gloss on the reality of policing behaviour and interactions between the police and the public. Most of the presentational rules derive from the law and are part of a (successful) attempt by the wider society to deceive itself about the realities of policing (Smith and Gray 1985: 441–2; see Ch. 1, above).

Indeed, (pre-PACE) stop and search was the PSI's own example of such rules (Smith and Gray 1985; see also Smith 1986).

The apparently crucial changes in stop/search powers had little impact on the practice of many officers. In our interview study, 71 per cent of those with pre-1986 operational experience told us that PACE had not affected the way in which they carried out stop/searches (cf. Skogan 1990: 42). Our research force has some 2,000 officers. In 1987, they recorded 722 stop/searches. In the same year, the total of 124,102 officers in England and Wales recorded 118,300 stop/searches (Bottomley *et al.* 1991: ch. 2). Of course, by no means all of these officers were operational: none the less, this amounted to fewer than one recorded stop/search each annually. This sat uneasily with our observations of street policing and, indeed, with reports from officers that they would expect to carry out four

---

[6] Additional powers to stop and search in anticipation of serious violence or to prevent acts of terrorism were provided by the Criminal Justice and Public Order Act 1994. For statistical details of their use, see Home Office 1996: 8–9.

[7] This was considerably revised in the 1991 Code, sects. 1.5–7.

or five stop/searches when patrolling on a late shift. People walking late at night (particularly young people carrying bags) would be routinely stopped, asked who they were and where they were going, and often searched. This is not surprising, given the usefulness to the police of stop/search as a source of arrests (despite the low 'success' rate[8]) and especially given its attractiveness to uniformed officers as one of the few methods by which they can engage in proactive crime work (Dixon *et al.* 1989). By 1995, the number of searches recorded nationally had increased more than five-fold.[9] While there has been some critical comment about this (e.g. Statewatch 1996), the relative lack of public disquiet about what was, apparently, a great change in policing may indicate that at least part of what changed was the recording, rather than the practice of stop and search. Even this substantial recorded increase accounts for only a fraction of the stop/search activity which occurs (Skogan 1990: ch. 3). This indicates, as Young suggests, the presence of 'a dark figure of policing'.[10]

The major device which bridges the gap between the records and the reality is 'consent'. Suspects 'consent' to being stopped and searched: consequently, no power is employed and (subject to regulations to be noted below) no record need be made. In our research force, three-quarters of interviewed officers had done a consent stop/search since the introduction of PACE, while only a quarter said that they had used statutory powers. Many distinguished between types of encounters. Some officers considered that a stop/search meant a thorough search of the suspect's pockets and clothes: they classified simply looking in a bag as a (non-PACE) 'stop/check' for which legal authority was not provided and was, in any case, unnecessary, because 'consent' would be obtained. Several officers told us that they did not even bother to carry stop/search forms when they were on patrol. They, and many others, said that they would try to get consent from a suspect: if this was not forthcoming, they would arrest him or her. As elsewhere, the very process of trying to obtain consent allows officers to test their suspicion about a person. As the

[8] In 1995, 12% of recorded PACE stops and searches led to arrest (Home Office 1996: 2).

[9] See Home Office 1996: table 1. There was great regional variation: while 2 forces did 200 or fewer, 13 did 1,000 or more (*ibid.* 4; see also Statewatch 1996).

[10] 1994b: 1. Local crime surveys provide a way of delineating this dark figure which, as Young argues, is not equally distributed, but rather is affected by the variables of age, race, gender, and area (*ibid.*; see also Coleman and Moynihan 1996; Jefferson *et al.* 1992).

hoary truism insists, only the guilty have reason to refuse it. One officer explained: '[i]f they are decent law-abiding citizens they wouldn't
mind being stopped because they'd appreciate the police being
about.'

Similar practices and attitudes were found to be evident in New
South Wales. Stopping, questioning, and searching are central to
everyday street policing. When officers were asked what they would
do if a person whom they stopped on the street refused to give his or
her name and address[11] or to be searched,[12] the responses were consistent. People seldom refused: if they did so, they would be talked,
bluffed or coerced into giving the information and allowing the
search. One officer explained how he reacted to a refusal:

As the law says, there's not much you can do. But what you actually do is a
bit different. . . . Ninety per cent of it is common sense and dazzle them with
bullshit. You know, 'There's been a bust up the road. . . . We just want to
clear you from getting in the shit.' More times than not they will come
around and just let you search them.

He explained that, if consent is refused, 'the main thing I do is just
lob them back into the station and have a chat to them here.'[13]

'Consent' frequently consists of acquiescence based on ignorance:
many people assume that the officer who says '[w]hat have you got
in your pockets?' or '[l]et's have a look in your bag' has a power to
search. The words are expressed as an instruction, not as a request.
In the English research, we asked officers how often people whom
they stopped and searched knew their rights: 79 per cent said rarely
or never. Such lack of knowledge must mean that their 'consent' has
little substance. Familiar strategies are used to deal with those who
do raise questions about the authority to search. As an English
sergeant put it, '[a] lot of people are not quite certain that they have
the right to say no. And then we, sort of, bamboozle them into allowing us to search.' 'Bamboozling' is done by appealing to the willingness of the innocent to be searched, by threatening arrest, or by
claiming the authority of fictional powers (typically, what officers
would call the 'Ways and Means Act' or, a popular local variant, the

[11] There is no power to require this in NSW, other than from motorists, although
a Street Safety [sic] Bill providing such a power is in preparation at the time of writing. On police requests for such powers, see CJC 1993b: ch. 14.

[12] There is a broad stop/search power in the NSW Crimes Act 1900, s. 357E.

[13] It should be noted that there is no power to detain for questioning: see Ch. 5
below.

'Barbed Wire Act'). The obtaining of 'consent' is related dialectically to the complexity and ambiguity of law providing police powers. Police often prefer to work with 'consent' and are able to do so because of legal uncertainty. In routine work:

the police do not approach their task in the guise of legal officials, rather they prefer to resort to informal methods, even in instances where they may have powers to act. A significant result of this informality is the blurring of exactly which powers and duties the police have in such situations. Since the police do not communicate about their powers and purposes, members of the public can regard what they do only in terms of an arbitrary power which it is safer to assume is legal than not. . . . What appears as informality on the police's part also contains a mystificatory element which multiplies the potential power of the police (Grimshaw and Jefferson 1987: 96).

This is certainly the way in which some people are handled: however, it is too legalistic as an account of how many interact with officers on the street. The reality for them may be, not acquiescence based on ignorance of rights, but submission rooted in an appreciation of the contextual irrelevance of rights. As Brown points out, many young people know that

their relations with police on the streets are not governed predominantly by some set of 'rights', 'rules' or police instructions, but largely by their own attitude and demeanour, by the manner of their response to police questioning. Some of these 'ignorant' kids know only too well that invocations of 'rights' are . . . interpreted . . . as disrespect, as lack of deference, as being a 'smart-arse'. . . . In short, the problem is not that of people not being aware of or not asserting their 'rights' but rather that non-cooperation is viewed by police as a challenge to their authority (1984: 187; see also Abramovitch et al. 1995; Collison 1995: 64; Hogg 1991b; Ericson 1982: 148).

'Rights' are seen by officers as properly belonging to some people, but not to those with whom they usually come in contact. An English officer made the point in explaining what he would do if someone refused to show what was in a bag: '[i]f it is someone of reasonable intelligence, I'd leave it at that. If it was a scruff, I'd probably have a look myself.'

For 'scruffs' to assert their rights is 'buggering about' (see below) and itself suspicious: reference to rights may be regarded as a challenge to police authority and/or an indication of previous contact with police, and therefore as worth further investigation (cf. Ericson 1982: 148–9). These points are illustrated by the following account (from a NSW police statement) of an encounter between officers and a male juvenile. His 'suspicious activity' was to watch an unmarked police car which drove past him. The officers (P) turned back and approached him (S):

P: What's your name?
S: I don't have to tell yous[14] nothing, my lawyer said to tell you nothing. . . .
P: How come you were so interested in what we were doing?
S: I'm not telling you anything. . . . I know my rights. . . .
P: Look mate don't play silly buggers alright, all we want to do is search you for some ID. You seemed pretty agitated when you saw us back there. . . .
S: I know me rights you can't do this. . . .
P: All right mate, do you know what section 357 E of the crimes act [sic] is? Well you've given reasonable cause to believe you are in possession of something you shouldn't be and that gives us the power to stop search and detain you. . . .
S: Yous are going to get shit for this, I'm telling my lawyer, yous are going to get a false arrest against yous. . . .
P: Look mate you don't seem to know your rights like you keep telling us. You've resisted and hindered us in our duty so I'm taking you to Kings Cross [a police station] where we can sort this out.

As this exchange illustrates, the police are assisted here by the breadth of discretionary powers and of some criminal offences. As McBarnet argues (1983; see also Ch. 1, above), it is the law itself, not its abuse or its breach, which is inconsistent with principles of legality. This is well illustrated by provisions for street policing such as, in England and Wales, the Public Order Act 1986, section 5 and, in New South Wales, the Summary Offences Act 1988, section 4.[15] Account must be taken of the substantive reality of the police function in order maintenance on the street and of material relations between police and policed (see below in this section). A strategy of rights and legal regulation which overlooks them will be misleading and ineffective.

In the circumstances, it would reasonable to ask why *any* PACE stop/searches get recorded. First, some are recorded for operational purposes, notably drugs intelligence. Secondly, records are more likely to be completed if a probationary constable carries out the stop

---

[14] By 'accurately' recording the suspect's mode of speech, officers seek to indicate social status and moral character.
[15] Another excellent example of McBarnet's argument is the consorting provision in Crimes Act 1900, s. 546A: see Ch. 2, note 57, above.

and search, if a supervisory officer is present, or if senior officers have commented on the lack of recorded stop/searches. (This accounts for some fluctuations in recorded PACE stop/searches.) The steady increase in reports is due to the 'normalization' of PACE: many younger officers without pre-PACE experience see its requirements as just part of the job. Thirdly, if a prohibited article is found and an arrest is made, officers may 'cover their back' by completing a record. Fourthly, a record would be completed if 'comeback' were a possibility: if, for example, a middle-class person who was aware of his or her rights happened to be stopped. As an officer put it: if suspects 'know more about PACE, you would probably revert to the standard opening speech procedure'. For several obvious reasons, this is unlikely. As suggested above, refusal of consent is a rare experience for officers. One commented: 'I have never had any problems with anyone refusing to be searched . . . so I have never had to fall back on proving my reasonable suspicion.' As these points suggest, stop/searches usually come to be recorded because of contingent factors, rather than statutory criteria. It is important to note that many of these operate retrospectively: an officer begins operating with 'consent' and may only later reinterpret the encounter as being a PACE stop/search. Indeed, several officers defined a PACE stop/search as being one in which the suspect does not consent.[16] 'Consent' is also often a retrospective legitimation of a stop/search which, for whatever reason, requires justification rather than a meaningful description of the interaction between police and the person searched.

The authorities have, to some extent, been aware of the problems of consent stop/searches. The Code of Practice is supplemented by Home Office circulars and Force Orders. The circular issued at the implementation of PACE stated that in 'any situation where a constable exercises a power of search . . ., the cooperation of the suspect should not be taken as implying consent, and the exercise of the power should be noted in the appropriate record'.[17] An additional circular (which did not get beyond draft stage) sought to 'amplify' this guidance:

In any situation where a constable exercises a power of search . . ., a record should be made even though the person may consent to the search. Where a constable does not have the power to search a person but nevertheless has

---

[16] Some of the implications of this for seeing stop/search as an interactive process are examined in Dixon et al. 1989.

[17] HO 88/1985, app. A.

legitimate reasons to invite cooperation, and the person consents to being searched (knowing that he is free to refuse to co-operate), it is not necessary to make a record.

These provisions confuse matters by referring in a loose manner to the 'exercise' of a statutory power. Here, the consent or otherwise of the suspect is apparently taken to be legally irrelevant to whether a power is exercised. In the table below, if a stop and search takes place in the circumstances of cell 4, the situation is regarded as being analogous to cell 3: both are PACE stop/searches, and so should be carried out according to the Code of Practice and appropriately recorded.

How the presence or absence of consent and legal power affects the legal status of stop and search

	NO POWER AVAILABLE	POWER AVAILABLE
CONSENT ABSENT	1 No power—stop/ search unlawful	3 PACE stop/search
CONSENT PRESENT	2 No power— 'voluntary' stop/ search only	4 ?

However, if a suspect consents to being searched, even where a power is available to the officer, it can be argued that the power is not exercised: the presence of consent and the exercise of statutory power are mutually exclusive. According to the practice of many research force officers (see above in this section), a stop and search in the circumstances of cell 3 would clearly represent the exercise of a statutory power, while one in the circumstances of cell 4 would not: cell 4 would be analogous to cell 2 rather than to cell 3, and PACE procedures would not be necessary.

Our research force made several attempts to clarify this matter. In an amendment to standing orders in 1993, officers were instructed that a record should be completed when a statutory power is exercised, and also when 'although consent is given a statutory power to search exists and it would have been necessary to exercise it . . . if consent had been withheld'. A consent search when no power exists need not be recorded on a PACE form, although a 'note book entry . . . should be made'. Here, the crucial criterion is existence of a power, rather than either its exercise or consent: again, an attempt is made to assimilate cell 4 with cell 3. One problem with this approach

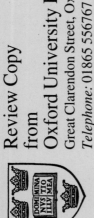

Review Copy
from
Oxford University Press
Great Clarendon Street, Oxford OX2 6DP
Telephone: 01865 556767

LAW IN POLICING
Legal Regulation and Police Practices
David Dixon

0 19 8264763
Price: £40.00
Publication Date: 10th July 1997

The source of the book should be given as

Clarendon Press, Oxford

(Clarendon Press is the academic imprint of the Oxford University Press)

The publisher requests that no review should appear before the publication date and would be grateful for a clipping of your review. Further information on the book or its author will gladly be given by the Publicity Department.

is that it potentially distorts the statistics collected from records, suggesting that statutory powers are being used more often than is in fact the case. This may be thought a minor problem, given the general unreliability of statistics as an indicator of stop/search activity. It may be an occasion when it is better to try to get some control by imposing recording requirements, whether they are strictly appropriate or not.

It might well be argued that a legalistic attempt to make sense of such regulations misses the point. Indeed, an earlier similar version of the research force order quoted above went on inconsistently to follow the Home Office approach and to require that a 'search record must be completed in all cases when . . . a statutory power to search has been exercised . . . irrespective of whether or not the person consented to the search'. As noted above, such rules have some presentational value. They may also serve reactive purposes, being produced in response to a specific incident and then providing a potential resource for disciplining officers in case of recurrence (Bottomley *et al.* 1991: 194). Officers usually pay little attention to internal rules of this kind, particularly when they are complicated and confusing as in this case. Our research force trainers found these provisions too complex to communicate, so typically told probationers to record all stop/searches (while acknowledging privately that they knew that many probationers would not do so in practice). Indeed, we found very few officers who understood or even were aware of the Home Office or the research force provisions. The use of stop and search powers (and the recording thereof) was governed largely by the informal norms which police culture and the policing mandate generate.[18] The benefits of informality to police are clear: as one officer put it: '[b]y filling that form in, you've got to justify that you had reasonable suspicion.' This was, of course, exactly what the PACE provisions require. Informality is typically justified or legitimated as being better for police–public relations.

A covering letter issued with a Home Office draft of the 1991 Code stated that a ' "voluntary search", which takes place with consent and where the powers contained in the Act are not exercised, remains outside the scope of the code'. It was expected that elaboration would be provided by Home Office circular. However, none emerged. Consent searches were not affected by the revisions of the Code

[18] But please note the critique of this view of police culture in Shearing and Ericson 1991; see Ch. 1, above.

which took effect in 1995. Stop and search in general was almost ignored by the Royal Commission on Criminal Justice (cf. RCCJ 1993: 10) despite significant evidence of its significance for police investigations and police attitudes towards legal regulation (McConville *et al.* 1991a: 22, 182–3, 194–6). However, the 1991 revisions of Code A did touch on 'consent' searches at a number of points. A note which has not attracted the attention which it deserves states that '[j]uveniles, persons suffering from a mental handicap or mental disorder and others who appear not to be capable of giving an informed consent should not be subject to a voluntary search'.[19] While still prey to officers' distinction between checks and searches (see above), this provision is presumably responsible for some of the increase in recorded stop/searches. As regards adult, 'non-vulnerable' suspects, the Code approves the use of consent searches in notes which appeal to community relations and civic responsibilities:

This code does not affect the ability of an officer to speak to or question a person . . . without detaining him or exercising any element of compulsion. It is not the purpose of the code to prohibit such encounters between the police and the community with the co-operation of the person concerned and neither does it affect the principle that all citizens have a duty to help police officers to prevent crime and discover offenders. . . .

Nothing in this code affects . . . the ability of an officer to search a person in the street on a voluntary basis. In these circumstances, an officer should always make it clear that he is seeking the co-operation of the person concerned.[20]

This was an attempt to strengthen a provision in the original Home Office circular:

While it is legitimate to invite co-operation from the public in circumstances where there is no power to require it, the subject of a voluntary search must properly understand the position and not be left with the impression that a power is being exercised. Voluntary search must not be used as a device for circumventing the (PACE) safeguards.[21]

Implicit here is a distinction between passive co-operation and an active, informed voluntariness. In the draft circular quoted above, non-completion of a record requires the suspect to have consented 'knowing that he is free to refuse to co-operate'. The 1993 research

---

[19] Note 1E, which also appears in the 1995 Code.
[20] Notes 1B and 1D(b).   [21] HO 88/1985, app. A.

force order instructs officers carrying out voluntary searches that they
'*must* ensure persons so consenting are fully aware that there is no
statutory power to search. A note book entry to that effect should be
made' (original emphasis). The feasibility of such requirements may
well be questioned: they would require officers to make suspects
understand the limits of their power in a way which might be difficult and certainly would subvert their dominance of the situation and
the imposition of unqualified, unchallengeable authority which is
the officers' priority. In practice, it seems likely that the effect of the
revised Code A has been to contribute to the steady increase in the
recording of stop/searches, but not to any substantial change in practice.

In some situations, the Code itself provides for the use of 'consent'
to by-pass legal safeguards: it notes that 'the routine searching of persons entering sports grounds or other premises' is not affected by
PACE.[22] These (very common) mass searches are justified as consensual or as a contractual condition of entry in the same way that, e.g.,
some people have their bags searched before they board a plane (cf.
Sarre 1994). Consent has little substance if the alternative is exclusion
from the relevant activity.[23] In the case of football matches, people
are searched under these provisions not only at the stadium turnstile,
but also a considerable distance away. The Code provides that (when
power rather than consent is used) a written record need not be made
if 'it is not practicable to do so, on account of the numbers to be
searched or for some other operational reason, e.g. in situations
involving public disorder'.[24] This relieves the recording requirement,
but not that of reasonable grounds for suspicion: in practice, these
will usually be lacking. The simple reality is that law has little to do
with the policing of incidents such as 'disorder occurring in seaside
towns during Bank Holiday weekends or the search of football sup-
porters entering or leaving a ground'.[25]

The point must be emphasized that current practice in street policing is not to be understood simply as 'deviance': rather it is a normative product of the historical mandate of the police to control the
streets and to reproduce social order. The central task of street police

---

[22] 1991 and 1995 Codes, Note 1D(a).
[23] Cf. the US Supreme Court's treatment of a Florida sheriff's department 'program
of boarding buses at scheduled stops and asking passengers for permission to search
their luggage' (Skolnick 1994: 282) in *Florida* v. *Bostick* 111 S Ct. 2382 (1991).
[24] S. 4.1.   [25] Examples given in the original Code, s. 4.1.

work is not law enforcement, but order maintenance: an essential part of the police's historical mandate has been the control of street economies, recreations, and people (see Reiner 1992a: 139–46, 212: Brogden *et al*. 1988: 93–9). This means employing wide discretionary powers against categories of the population which police culture distinguishes from 'respectable people'—the 'toe-rags', the 'rubbish', the 'shit', the 'scruffs', or, in NSW, the 'hoodlums', 'hoons', and 'scrotes'.[26] Concepts such as rights and informed consent fit very uneasily with police images of such 'police property' (Lee 1981) as being stupid, low-status, marginal, troublesome. Legislation like PACE (ironically, from a police perspective, a product of the 'respectable', but socially naïve people who are protected from the rubbish by the police) is widely regarded as being simply inappropriate as a means of carrying out this task: as one officer put it starkly, 'PACE was meant to protect decent people, but we don't deal with decent people.'

iii. Consenting to the Search of Premises

Both the attractions to police officers of searching premises by consent[27] and the difficulties of regulating the practice have been recognized in a variety of jurisdictions.[28] 'The advantages of resorting to consent as the basis of authorization for a search or seizure are many—a diminished likelihood of review, a possible psychological edge over the person searched, the less burdensome procedural requirements, and the absence of confinement to the usual "grounds

---

[26] The etymology of this term provides a good example of cultural transmission and relations between practice and fiction: NSW police adopted 'scrote' from the English TV series 'The Bill', in which fictional police borrowed the term (possibly via the screen-writer's contact with real police) from Wambaugh's fictions (1976:2) based on his experience in the LAPD. As Walker suggests, 'life imitating art imitating life is precisely the kind of complex reflexivity we should expect when certain institutional tasks and predicaments are viewed as paradigmatic of wider social issues' (1996a: 56).

[27] Search may not be the only reason for police to enter by consent: they may, for example, enter to speak to witnesses or suspects. Consent may be complex if occupiers disagree: the Crimes Act 1900 (NSW), s. 357F, provides that an invitation to enter or remain in a dwelling cannot be overruled by another occupant if an officer believes that the person making the invitation is or (is likely to be) a victim of domestic violence. Search consent by third parties—e.g. landlords, relatives, hotel desk clerks—has attracted judicial attention in Canada and the US: see Barton 1993b. On such consents under PACE, see Code C, s. 4.1 and note 4A.

[28] See e.g. Barton 1993a; Ericson 1981a: 148–56; Miller *et al*. 1991: 295–317; Sutton 1986: 415–17; Tiffany *et al*. 1967: ch. 10; Van Duizend *et al*. 1985: 68–70.

of belief" ' (LRCC 1983: 159). Search of premises was an area in which problems relating to consent had been recognized before PACE, and consequently with which provisions in the original Code of Practice B tried to deal. It was widely acknowledged that both law and practice in this area were unsatisfactory (RCCP 1981b: paragraph 3.37). Officers often relied on 'consent', in many cases securing it by bluff and/or the householders' ignorance (*ibid.*, paragraph 3.41; Lidstone 1984). A common police tactic has been to obtain 'consent' by threatening to obtain a search warrant if they are not allowed entry.[29] In New South Wales, consent searches are a matter of course, with warrants usually obtained if the subject is likely to refuse consent, and for defensive purposes. An officer explained:

Most of the time they just let you in. . . . The main reason you use a warrant is you don't get any allegations against you . . . I've used warrants where I didn't really need to, but it's better for court purposes . . . because all they do is throw up allegations that they haven't given you permission, whereas if you had a piece of paper saying you had the right to do it, it's a lot easier.

The Australian Law Reform Commission reported that 'in practice, very many of the searches of premises undertaken by police officers . . . are made, or are claimed to be made, at the "invitation", or at least with the consent, of the occupier in question' (ALRC 1975: paragraph 195). Courts typically overlook the unlikely nature of some claimed 'consents'.[30]

The original PACE Code B required a formalization of the granting of consent and its recording (in very much the way that the ALRC had recommended that Australian law should be changed: ALRC 1975: paragraph 205). Normally,

if it is proposed to search premises with the consent of a person entitled to grant entry to the premises the consent must . . . be given in writing. . . . Before seeking consent the officer in charge of the search shall state the purpose of the proposed search and inform the person concerned that he is not obliged to consent and that anything seized may be produced in evidence.[31]

Details of all searches had to be entered in a search register at a police station: in the case of consent searches, the record had either to

---

[29] For discussion of the legality of this in Canada, see *Meyers* (1987) 58 CR (3d) 176.

[30] See, e.g., *Filippetti* (1978) 13 A Crim. R 335.

[31] Code B (1995), ss. 4.1–2. Circumstances where it would be impractical to obtain written consent, e.g. for brief checks of a garden at night, are allowed as exceptions.

include the written consent or to specify where it was kept (normally, the officer's notebook). Like other recording requirements, this could benefit police by preventing subsequent disputes about the legality of their entry to property.[32] None the less, we found that many consent searches were not recorded (Bottomley *et al*. 1991: ch. 3).

The main reason for this was that the legal requirements could not easily be reconciled with standard practice in searching premises. Our observational research suggested that the process of obtaining consent from householders relies upon a potent combination of three factors—their ignorance of the law; their unquestioning belief in the power of the police; and their implied guilt if they refuse. A requirement for officers to tell a householder that they do not have the power to do what they want (and, more to the point, intend) to do is seen as being quite unrealistic. A serious loss of face would be threatened if a suspect decided not to consent to a search. An officer summed up the police perspective admirably: '[b]y asking someone for consent, you immediately infer that they have the right to say no. So, if they are happy in their ignorance . . ., I confess I would use that to my advantage.' One incident was observed in which consent was refused; however, its particular characteristics reinforce the general point. Two detectives wanted to search rooms in a hostel for electrical equipment which they had been informed was being kept there after a burglary. The warden refused to allow them to search: she was experienced and confident in dealing with the police and knew that they had no power to search. The more senior detective accepted her refusal. However, the junior tried, unsuccessfully, to slip away from the warden while she was talking to the senior officer. The junior was angry at the loss of face suffered when the warden insisted that he did not attempt to enter and search rooms. He told me that he would have searched irrespective of the warden's consent if the senior officer (whom he thought too cautious) had not been there.

The substance of consent may be particularly questionable when it is obtained from suspects in custody. Lidstone and Bevan's study found that 32 per cent of recorded searches in two force areas were described as consensual. Most of these consents were 'obtained from a person in custody in circumstances which were suggestive of duress or in which the detainee was not made fully aware that he [*sic*] could

---

[32] See, e.g., the incident reported in *Police Review*, 5 May 1989, 924.

refuse' (nd: 47, cf. also *ibid.* 158). Such detainees' houses could usually have been searched under the power in PACE, section 18.[33] Like stop/searches, search of premises is resistant to legal regulation because of its processual, fluid nature. Consent and power are often not clearly distinct. Officers will typically attempt to get consent even when a power is available to them, e.g. they have obtained a warrant (cf. Ericson 1981a: 154) or have arrested a suspect. Indeed, 95 per cent of officers in our interview sample said that they would do this. Lidstone and Bevan found that consent was an administratively convenient alternative to section 18, relieving the investigating officers and the inspector who has to give section 18 authorization from the need to justify reasonable suspicion and consequently protecting them from any potential 'come-back' (nd: 44, 47–8). Their study was of recorded searches: consent plays an even greater part in those which are not recorded, and these illustrate other benefits of relying on consent. Officers in our research force often preferred to search 'by consent' because it makes dealing with householders easier. This is illustrated by one detective's comments:

The thing is, particularly in the CID, we tend to deal with the same people all the time, and if you knock on somebody's door and say—'Under section so-and-so of the Police Act we're coming to search, like it or not', you antagonize them, and if you are back there a few weeks later, you are going to pay for that. That is why I, and most CID lads [*sic*], try and do it with an air of consent and try and do it friendly. You still get your search done but it's much easier if everybody gets on isn't it?

This reference to an 'air of consent' suggests that what is at issue here is civility rather than consent: '[s]uch interactions may . . . be sociable exchanges, but they are never equal exchanges' (Collison 1995: 64). As in the case of stop/search, an officer's 'request' for consent is not really a question, but rather an easing tactic, a way of handling the situation in a non-conflictual manner. Getting consent has other advantages. At the simplest level, working with consent is 'simply a less bothersome procedure'. But, Ericson continues, it also has

tactical and legal advantages. . . . If a suspect consented to a search, it gave the enterprise a character of voluntariness. . . . The detectives had a psychological edge because suspects were then obeying on the basis of the detectives' pervasive authority as police officers rather than on the displaced

[33] It authorizes search of the premises of a person arrested for an arrestable offence, subject (with exceptions in s. 18(5)) to the authorization of an inspector.

authority of another legal agent. Moreover, the voluntariness component could be employed in arguing at the court stage that any evidence seized was provided with the apparently uncoerced co-operation of the suspect (1981a: 154).

Decisions and requests to search are often not distinct incidents to which legal regulation can more appropriately be applied. Officers are often in premises for various reasons (such as dealing with noise complaints, or talking to or taking statements from parents, suspects, or witnesses) before the issue of search arises. They may then ask for a 'look around' before they go. As a NSW officer commented, 'you've got to . . . have a bit of wit about you. . . . You don't say "Let us come in, I'm looking for this". Sort of bluff them a little bit. Just say "Look, I'm here for another matter" and they say "Oh come in". And as soon as you're in, have a look around.' Informal searches can also be carried out by, for example, coming in the front door, and then asking to leave by the back door, and having a look around on the way through the house. Just as they differentiate types of stop/search, so officers typically distinguish between 'a quick look around' from a full house search. The former would usually not be recorded: only the latter is considered to need either formal consent or legal author- ity. The result was that consent searches amounted to only 15 per cent[34] of those recorded: our observations and interviews made clear that this was a substantial under-representation (see Bottomley *et al.* 1991: ch. 3).

When they felt that recording was necessary, many officers in our research force had developed a simple method of coping with the requirement that consents should be obtained in writing. Entry would be gained in the traditional way, beginning with a 'request' such as '[w]e'll just have a quick look around, OK?' The consent would only be put in writing at the end of the search. Typically, this involved officers asking householders to 'sign for the search' in the officer's notebook immediately before they left the premises. The householder usually had little appreciation of what he or she was signing. Legal requirements were fulfilled, but in a way which effectively emptied them of usefulness.

The 1991 revisions of Code B attempted to counter these tactics by

[34] This is less than half the percentage found by Lidstone and Bevan: our research force did not use formal consent as an alternative to s. 18 to the same extent, record- ing substantially more searches as carried out under ss. 18 and 32: see Bottomley *et al.* 1991: 54; Lidstone and Bevan nd: 7–8.

clearly requiring that written consent must be obtained 'before the search takes place'.[35] This must be on a standard Notice of Powers and Rights (introduced as a result of problems illustrated by *R. v. Badham*[36]) which officers must provide to occupiers of premises (normally before the search begins). It must state, *inter alia*, whether the search is by consent or under a power, and it summarizes powers of search and occupiers' rights.[37] This requirement was said (in an earlier draft of the 1991 revisions) to be 'designed to smooth relations between the police and those whose property is to be searched'. Welcome as this provision is, it seems unlikely that police officers will stand waiting at the front door while the householder reads the notice provided.[38] If the consent is obtained from a suspect in custody, its substance seems particularly doubtful.

iv. Consenting to Arrest, Detention, and Questioning

(a) *Detention and Voluntary Attendance*

Issues of consent have attracted considerable attention in the area of pre-charge detention and questioning in both Britain and Australia. Before the Criminal Justice (Scotland) Act 1980 and PACE, it was very common for British suspects to attend police stations 'to help police with their enquiries' and, subsequently, to make 'voluntary' confessions. As the next chapter will show in detail, consent was a necessary part of policing practice because of the doubtful legality of pre-charge detention for questioning until *Holgate-Mohammed* v. *Duke*[39] and because voluntariness was the common law's principal test for the admissibility of confessional evidence.

Similarly, in Australia, officers often relied (and in several states which have not provided statutory powers to detain for questioning continue to rely) on voluntary attendance (ALRC 1975: paragraphs 64–71; Coldrey 1986: paragraph 2.8). The Australian Law Reform Commission found that 'voluntary co-operation' (which was 'the normal vehicle of police investigation') 'would appear to be very much stretched in Australian police practice' (1975: paragraphs 9,

---

[35] S. 4.1.   [36] [1987] Crim. LR 202.   [37] S. 5(7).

[38] No significant research has been carried out on search of premises since our (Bottomley *et al.* 1991: ch. 3) and Lidstone and Bevan's (nd) ESRC studies of policing under the original Code B.

[39] [1984] 1 All ER 1054: see Ch. 4 below.

65). 'Voluntary attendance' became a particularly useful device following the High Court's refusal (in *Williams* v. *R.*) to follow the English judiciary in 'developing' the common law in order to allow extensive pre-charge custodial interrogation.[40] A NSW officer commented, 'there's some constables I work with, I've never heard them say the words, "You're under arrest". I've never heard them say the word arrest. They always invite them back to the station, "You're going to have to come back to the station" '. In the United States, increased reliance on consent was perceived as an early effect of American courts' development of exclusionary evidential rules (LaFave 1965: 351). In Japan, securing voluntary attendance is common practice in police investigations (Miyazawa 1992: ch. 6).

The reality of voluntary attendance at stations was made clear by the ALRC:

> The fact that no shoulders may have been touched, or incantations mouthed, does not mean for a minute that a very large number of people indeed who were in the past 'voluntarily co-operating with police' or engaged in 'assisting police with their inquiries' were just as surely arrested as if they had been bound in chains (1975: paragraph 71).

However, Australian state courts have not been prepared to be so realistic in the handful of reported cases in which defendants have challenged the admissibility of alleged confessions on the ground that they were made during unlawful detention rather than, as police claimed, during voluntary attendance at stations (Aronson and Hunter 1995: 220–7). For example, in *O'Donoghue*, the New South Wales Court of Criminal Appeal insisted that a suspect's belief that he or she was under arrest must be 'conveyed by anything said or done by the police officer' and not merely be 'a product of his own mind'.[41] This neat individualistic dichotomy left no room for a decisive cultural factor which the Court itself mentioned—'the common belief or assumption that a mere request from a police officer constitutes a command or an order to be obeyed'. So, in the Court's view, O'Donoghue was not arrested, even though the police (on the investigating officer's own account) told him 'I would like you to come with us to the King's Cross Police Station where I can interview you about this'. O'Donoghue's accurate, culturally-formed view that the only choice left to him was whether or not he would be wearing

---

[40] (1986) 66 ALR 385. See Ch. 5 below for details.
[41] (1988) 24 A Crim. R 397, at 402.

handcuffs on the way to the station was legally irrelevant.[42] He was cautioned and would have been arrested formally if he had refused to co-operate. When asked why he went with the police, O'Donoghue told the court that he 'felt that he did not have much option really, because there was an officer on either side of him at the time when he was asked to go'.[43] It would be naïve to suggest that police are unaware of such suspects' perception, whatever they say to them. A NSW officer commented: '[s]ee, a lot of people, if the police say "Come back down to the station", they don't know. They're not going to say "No", like they can refuse. They're not under arrest, so they don't have to come. But they all come.'

While, according to the NSW Court of Criminal Appeal in *O'Donoghue*, there is 'no duty on the police officer who wishes to avoid an arrest to disabuse a suspect of any error about his or her status', some South Australian decisions suggest that there is a duty to tell the suspect that he or she is not under arrest if a reasonable person would have understood that he or she had to go with the police.[44] If this is not done, 'the apparent invitation or request may constitute an apprehension'. However, the legalistic limits of this must be noted: a suspect may still be treated as consenting 'even though the police officer would have made an arrest if suspect had not complied and even though the suspect believed that that would be the result of non-compliance'.[45] As the case of *S and J* demonstrates, suspects may feel that they have no option even though police satisfy the court that the lack of arrest was communicated.[46] The cultural contexts of 'consent' are especially important when, as in *S and J*, the subjects of police attention were young Aboriginal people. A police statement that they were not under arrest meant little given the history of relations between police and Aboriginal people and the officers' conduct towards them in 'separating, searching, watching, guarding and driving here and there in different cars'. The 'inference that they were free to not comply with requests, indeed were free to go, was not only improbable but highly improbable in the circumstances'.[47] Meanwhile, in Tasmania, the Court of Appeal invented a legal form of 'non-arrest detention' to provide for cases in which a

---

[42] *Ibid.*   [43] *Ibid.* 400.   [44] *Laws of Australia* v.11.1, division 5, p. 20.
[45] King CJ in *Conley* (1982) 20 SASR 226, at 239–40; see also *Harris* (1995) 64 SASR 85.
[46] (1983) 32 SASR 174. Cf. *Trotter, Sutherland and Jordan* (1992) 60 A Crim. R 1.
[47] White J dissenting in *S and J*, n. 46 above, at 189.

volunteer is in *de facto* custody.[48] This was an unconvincing attempt to avoid the law's characteristic dichotomy. More importantly, suspects' experiences of being taken to stations often do not correspond to a neat legal division: some do not appreciate that they have actually been arrested, while others feel a compulsion to accompany officers irrespective of anything the latter do or say (CJC 1994: 678–80; 1996). As Chapter 5 will argue in more detail, 'consent' has been an important route by which Australian police forces have by-passed their lack of power to detain for questioning. The state trial and appeal courts have prioritized crime control in their unwillingness to be realistic about 'voluntary attendance'. Such decisions (in addition to, as in Britain, the potential for evasion of statutory restrictions on custodial interrogation) demonstrate the need for legal regulation of the volunteer's status.

In two Australian jurisdictions—Victoria and the Commonwealth—an attempt has been made to discourage police from using voluntary attendance to evade restrictions on detention before charge. A wide statutory definition of 'persons in custody' is adopted which is intended to include the volunteer as well as arrested suspects. Similarly, the NSW Law Reform Commission recommended that a person should be treated as being in custody if he or she has been arrested or is 'in a police station, police vehicle or police establishment in the company of a police officer, or is otherwise under police control, and is—(i) being questioned; or (ii) to be questioned; or (iii) otherwise being investigated—to determine his or her involvement (if any) in the commission of an offence' (1990: 59). The Commission's intention was made plain: ' "consent" to police detention for the purposes of investigation, and the "voluntariness" of that detention . . . will no longer be the principal determining factor on the question of the lawfulness of the detention. . . . [A]ll persons in the custody of the police must be dealt with according to the same regime' (1990: 59; see also *ibid.* 66–9 and the Queensland Criminal Justice Commission's recommendations: CJC 1994: 701–3). Problems caused by a lack of provision for volunteers continue in the jurisdictions which have not legislated in response to *Williams* (notably, New South Wales, Queensland, and Western Australia) and in those whose legislation does not face the issue (the Northern Territory,

---

[48] *Sammak* (1994) 18 Crim. LJ 167; cf. Henning 1994; Aronson and Hunter 1995: 220–7. Contrast the New Zealand Court of Appeal's decision in *Goodwin* [1992] CRNZ 1, discussed in J. November 1993.

Tasmania, and South Australia). These are illustrated by a South Australian case, *Leecroft*,[49] in which volunteers were held not to be eligible for rights to counsel during interrogation which had been provided for apprehended suspects.

This Australian concern to provide a legal regime for 'voluntary attendance' was to some extent informed by experiences in Britain, where the success of legal provisions in regulating 'voluntary attendance' has been mixed. The Criminal Justice (Scotland) Act 1980 preceded PACE in permitting pre-charge detention for questioning (for up to six hours). A Scottish Office study of its effects on policing found that many officers were continuing to rely on voluntary attendance rather than using statutory powers of detention. One third (and, in one area, over half) of suspects attending at stations were volunteers in 1981–4 (Curran and Carnie 1986). This experience encouraged fears that the PACE provisions for and controls on detention for questioning before charge might be evaded in the same way.[50]

There are significant contrasts between the experiences in Scotland and in England and Wales. First, the period for pre-charge questioning is potentially much longer south of the border, so there is less incentive to use voluntary attendance. Secondly, there were differences in the way in which the new provisions were discussed and communicated to the police. In Scotland, the new detention procedure was presented in Parliament 'not as a straight replacement of the old system but rather as a supplement to it. Guidance to the police from the Lord Advocate reinforced the view that voluntary attendance remained a possibility and Chief Constables, in their Standing Orders, reiterated the point' (Curran and Carnie 1986: xi). By contrast, PACE introduced a new, virtually all-encompassing procedure for detention and questioning. Custody officers normally (see the next but one paragraph below) expect officers to present suspects to them under arrest so that their detention and questioning can be accounted for in custody records.

Thirdly, recognizing that the PACE regime could be avoided if the practice of 'helping with enquiries' continued, some provision was made for the 'volunteer' who is at a police station (or elsewhere) 'for the purpose of assisting with an investigation'. The volunteer 'shall

[49] (1987) 46 SASR 250.
[50] e.g. Baldwin and Kinsey 1986. For similar concern in Australia, see ALRC 1975: para. 65.

be entitled to leave at will unless he is placed under arrest [and] shall be informed at once that he is under arrest if a decision is taken by a constable to prevent him from leaving at will'.[51] Bland as this seems, its inclusion in the statute (rather than the Code or other subordinate rules) is of considerable symbolic importance. Code C echoes this and also provides that a volunteer who is arrested in the police station must be 'brought before the custody officer, who is responsible for ensuring that he is notified of his rights in the same way as detained persons'. If a volunteer is cautioned, but not arrested, he or she must be told of the right to obtain free legal advice. Until caution, the volunteer has a right to legal advice if requested, but there is no duty on the police to inform him/her of it otherwise.[52] Following the implementation of the 1991 Code, our research force provided a leaflet advising volunteers who were not under arrest of their right to free legal advice.

It is not possible to provide statistics on the use of voluntary attendance by our research force: a recording form was provided, but was not completed consistently and did not show whether a volunteer was a suspect, witness, or other, or whether he or she was subsequently arrested and charged. However, our observations suggested that voluntary attendance was relatively little used, and attempts to evade the PACE system thereby could provoke a custody officer's displeasure. Discussions with officers from other forces and a survey by McKenzie *et al.* (1990) suggest that this is fairly typical. There is at least one significant exception: in three divisions of one force, almost a third of suspects dealt with in stations were volunteers.[53] This informal procedure is claimed to be in the interests of many suspects because they can be processed (and bailed or otherwise released) more quickly than if the PACE procedures of documentation and offering of rights had to be completed (*ibid.*). However, the propriety of treating as volunteers people who, for example, have originally been arrested by private security officers in shops is very doubtful.

Some investigations may be very difficult to deal with inside PACE time constraints, leading officers to resort to 'voluntary attendance':

---

[51] PACE, s. 29.   [52] 1991 and 1995 Codes, ss. 3.15–16.

[53] This is the only research report of systematic use of voluntary attendance. This does not, of course, mean that it does not happen elsewhere. But without more evidence of this, Sanders and Young are not justified in taking Curran and Carnie's Scottish study to back a claim that 'when the police wish to process suspects as "voluntary attenders", it appears that s. 29 has little inhibitory effect' (1994a: 117).

examples usually cited are large-scale fraud inquiries and some child abuse cases (McKenzie *et al.* 1990: 27). Rather than relying on fictions of voluntariness, procedures should be formulated which provide for such circumstances. There may be occasions when it is appropriate for someone to be questioned as a volunteer at a police station about his or her involvement in an offence: if so, legislation should require officers to explain their legal rights to potential volunteers and obtain written acknowledgement that this has been done (ALRC 1975: paragraph 66). However, 'voluntariness' is usually as inappropriate in the context of attendance at police stations as it is in that of confessions (see subsection (c) below). It should be clearly established that the expected normality is questioning under arrest, with full protection of suspects' rights. The opportunity to deal with concerns such as these passed by the Royal Commission on Criminal Justice, whose Report failed even to acknowledge the practice of 'voluntary attendance'.

(b) *Take-up of Rights*

As noted above, PACE provides a number of rights for suspects in police custody. The suspect who does not take up an offer of such a right will be regarded as having consented to detention and questioning without its protection. Here, attention will focus on the most important of these rights—access to legal advice.

In the later 1980s, researchers found that a quarter of suspects were requesting legal advice. However, there were considerable variations between stations, and some requests were not met, for a variety of reasons (Brown 1989; Dixon *et al.* 1990a; Sanders *et al.* 1989). Revisions to Code C in 1991 and increasing popular knowledge of the right increased the rate of requests. Brown *et al.* (1992) reported a request rate of almost one third in 1991, while Phillips and Brown found that, by early 1994, this had increased to 38 per cent (1997; Brown 1997: ch. 6). On the basis of these findings, it can be claimed that at least three-fifths of suspects 'consent' to being detained before charge without the benefit of legal advice. This is not just a semantic point: '[a]sking people what they want when they cannot be expected to know what is best for them is analogous to the problem of asking people to consent to search or detention' (Sanders and Young 1994b: 146). Officers justify practices in detention and questioning by pointing out that legal advice is available to those who want it. It provides a useful example of the inappropriateness of treating such 'consent' as the product of a rational, autonomous decision. For a number of cultural, social, and psychological reasons (Dixon *et al.* 1990a; Sanders *et al.* 1989; Sanders and Young 1994b: 146), most people do not respond in this way when the custody officer asks if they want legal advice. Intimidated by the situation, distrusting or unused to dealing with lawyers, assuming that legal services are costly (despite any formal reassurance that in-station advice is free), fearing that asking for legal advice implies guilt, and in some cases being discouraged by the way in which the offer is made, most suspects feel that the appropriate response in the situation is to decline. Revisions of Code C in 1991 and 1995 improved matters by requiring custody officers to inform suspects that initial legal advice in custody is free[54] and to point out to a detainee who declines such advice that the right to it 'includes the right to speak to a solicitor on the telephone and [to] ask him if he wishes to do so'. If the detainee continues to decline, the officer must ask him or her 'the reasons for doing so, and any reasons shall be recorded'.[55] However, many of the factors which lead suspects to decline legal advice are not susceptible to change of this kind. This is an area where adequate information should be available for the suspect; but the reality of their situation in the police station is such that many lack the power to use it. The Royal Commission on Criminal Justice made several recommendations on recording waivers of legal advice (1993: 35–6; for a critique, see Sanders and Young 1994a: 137).

If suspects will not ask for legal advisers to be brought to the station, it can be argued that legal advisers should be based at stations. The Royal Commission saw 'little prospect of introducing such a scheme in the foreseeable future' and, characteristically, looked for improvement in the present system by 'training, education, supervision and monitoring' by the legal profession (1993: 37, 38; for a critique, see Sanders and Young 1994a: 137). Perhaps underlying the Commission's conservatism was an appreciation that a scheme of permanent legal advisers would require a fundamental change in the structure and priorities of the solicitors' profession (McConville *et al.* 1994: 292–8) and a substantial improvement in the quality of service currently provided by some legal advisers in stations (Dixon *et al.*

---

[54] S. 3.1 (see also s. 6.1 in the 1995 Code). A note (3E) to this effect in the original Code was routinely overlooked in our research force area.
[55] Code C (1995), s. 6.5. This offer of telephone advice must be made whenever access to legal advice is declined, e.g. at the resumption of an interview.

1990a; McConville and Hodgson 1993; McConville *et al.* 1994). The fate of a proposal to shift a decision about legal advice out of the suspect's responsibility is illustrative of resistance to substantial change in this area. When suspects request legal advice, they are often subjected, during the period before the legal adviser reaches the station, to some pressure from officers to change their minds and to agree to being questioned immediately. In our interview study of solicitors and clerks who regularly provide legal advice at stations (Dixon 1991a; see Ch. 6, below), a regular complaint encountered was that the adviser would arrive at the station, only to be informed that the prospective client had changed his or her mind, the interrogation had already taken place, and a confession had been made. In an attempt to deal with this, draft Home Office revisions of the original Code C would have allowed interrogation to commence before the arrival of a requested lawyer only in exceptional circumstances: a 'change of mind' by the suspect would no longer by itself be enough. It was considered that this was the only way to deal with the potential pressure on suspects. By the time a new Code was issued in 1991, this had been watered down: investigating officers have now merely to record the suspect's agreement to being interviewed without receiving legal advice and to secure the approval of an inspector.[56]

(c) *Consent to Providing Evidence*

A significant appearance in PACE of a requirement for formal consent comes in the provisions for taking 'intimate samples' (such as bodily tissue or fluid). Taking these requires, among other things, the suspect's written consent. In addition to the general pressures to cooperate which detention puts on a suspect, PACE originally included a very potent, specific incentive: a court might 'draw such inferences . . . as appear proper' from a refusal of consent 'without good cause'. Such a refusal can corroborate other evidence against the accused.[57] The substance of 'consent' in these circumstances is very dubious. In 1994, the reference to corroboration was removed, in line with the

---

[56] S. 6.6(d). The Royal Commission on Criminal Justice's Report led to inclusion of relatively minor changes in the 1995 Code: the authorizing officer must inquire 'into the suspect's reasons for his change of mind', and the officer's name and any reason given 'shall be recorded in the taped or written interview record at the beginning or re-commencement of interview'. Such authorization may be given over the telephone (n. 6I).

[57] S. 62.

general abolition of corroboration requirements.[58] However, evidence of a refusal will continue to be admissible and refusal could still be corroborative in a general sense.

The taking of intimate samples is at present rare, although likely to become much more common with the use of DNA testing.[59] However, the issue of consent raised thereby is directly comparable[60] to the currently much more important questions of consent to interrogation and confession, or, in other words, the issue of the right of silence. This is discussed in some detail in Chapter 6. Here, it is appropriate to draw attention to just one issue. Critics of the right of silence often claim that allowing inferences to be drawn from silence would not affect the suspect's ability to remain silent if he or she chose to do so: 'it is not suggested that anyone should be obliged to speak under questioning' (Gibbs 1987: 50; contrast ALRC 1975: paragraph 146). Such assertions ignore the pressures on a suspect to speak if not doing so is likely to be counted as detrimental evidence.

In the common law, consent has notionally played a central role in judicial consideration of the admissibility of confessions, for which the traditional test was 'voluntariness'.[61] The product was unsatisfactory case law and practice. The Royal Commission on Criminal Procedure accepted the argument in Irving's research study of interrogations (Irving 1980) that 'voluntariness' was an inappropriate criterion in the context of police interrogation because of the psychological pressures to speak and to confess. Consequently, PACE abandoned the test of voluntariness, and instead provides for the admissibility of confessions to be decided on criteria of lack of oppression, reliability, and fairness.[62] While some judges may in practice refer to pre-PACE cases (e.g. assessing fairness as indicated by 'voluntariness'), the statutory change is significant. In largely similar fashion, the Australian Law Reform Commission criticized and recommended replacement of the 'voluntariness' test (ALRC 1987:

---

[58] Criminal Justice and Public Order Act 1994, sched. 11.

[59] The Royal Commission on Criminal Justice recommended several extensions of the power to 'require or request' samples (1993: 14–16). In order to facilitate DNA testing, the Criminal Justice and Public Order Act 1994, s. 58, changed the definition of 'intimate sample' so that, in particular, samples from the mouth are no longer included (Zander 1995: 149–51).

[60] The Royal Commission on Criminal Justice (1993: 14) did not agree. See also *Smith* (R.W.) [1985] Cr. App. R 286. Contrast Easton 1991.

[61] Contrast the US Supreme Court's decision in *Miranda* (384 US 436 (1966)) which is founded on the appreciation that custodial interrogation is inherently coercive.

[62] Ss. 76 and 78.

paragraph 156–9) and this was implemented in the major reform of evidence law in New South Wales and the Commonwealth in 1995.[63] Terminology such as 'voluntary confession' and 'consensual interrogation' (Review Committee 1989: paragraph 3.6) should surely now to be regarded as just more of the euphemisms which conjure up a comfortably misleading image of policing practice (along with talking about 'interviews' rather than questioning or interrogation; 'baton rounds' rather than plastic bullets; and 'the custody suite' rather than the charge room and cells).

v. Consent to Policing and Policing by Consent

This Chapter has attempted to illustrate some problems which 'consent' produces for a strategy of legal regulation of policing. As a matter of policy, is it preferable to replace consent with legal regulation? Of course, the question puts the issues too simply. It depends, first, whether a category of genuine 'consents' can be identified and distinguished in practice. Lidstone and Bevan suggest that consent should be used as an adjunct to, rather than as a substitute for, police powers, and that 'it must be based on a free choice with full knowledge of the circumstances and in the absence of any feeling of constraint' (nd:160). This appeal to a legalistic concept of full consent sidesteps the problem that the messy reality of interaction between police and suspects resists the law's neat dichotomies. Secondly, it depends how effective the legal regulation will be. Baldwin criticized PACE on the ground that it provided wide discretionary powers and restrictions which could be circumvented by relying on 'consent'. He preferred the pre-PACE situation in which police had to obtain (however illusory) 'consent', to use bluff and deception, and to rely on courts to endorse their actions: the 'advantages of these methods are that they are primarily consensual and, where they are not, involve police officers in "looking over their shoulders" ' (Baldwin 1985: 19). Baldwin's prediction that PACE would be ineffective as a control on policing has proved to be somewhat overstated. However, his pessimism was justified at the time by the experience of the Criminal Justice (Scotland) Act 1980 (Baldwin 1989: 162; Baldwin and Kinsey 1980). The significance of specific contexts is emphasized by Australian debate about regulating custodial investigation. A strong

[63] Evidence Act (NSW) 1995; Evidence Act (Commonwealth) 1995, parts 3.4 and 3.11.

body of opinion in New South Wales and Queensland has argued that statutory powers to detain for questioning should not be introduced. Experience in Victoria suggests that limiting such detention by a 'reasonable time' provision gives *carte blanche* to the police. Such critics prefer to retain the common law prohibition on detention for questioning (see Ch. 5). Knowing well that police do detain suspects by relying on 'consent' and other legal 'gimmickry' (NSW LRC 190: 15; for details see Ch. 5, below), they acknowledge the hypocrisy of this. However, they consider that police practice is more effectively regulated by the common law than it would be by statute. Policy choices have to take account of such local determinants.

More fundamentally, the issue's complexity stems from the desirability of (in a general sense) consensual policing, which may often (specifically) entail operating with consent rather than invoking legal powers. It is clear that operational police officers are expected to obtain consent whenever possible. The Royal Commission on Criminal Procedure stated, in introducing its discussion of the powers which police officers needed to carry out their duties, that in 'many cases they should and will achieve their objectives with the consent (which should be free and genuine) of the person concerned' (1981: paragraph 3.2). Similarly, in commenting on a police officer's use of legal power to enter and search premises, Lord Donaldson insisted that: the 'first hurdle which he will have to overcome in justifying force will be by providing an answer to the question: "Why did you not ask to be allowed in?" ' (quoted, Pike 1985: 114). Such sentiments are echoed by police officers who justify the use of consent (Lidstone and Bevan nd: 159). Policing requires some level of public consent. Criminal investigation largely depends on the flow of information to the police from the public (as victims, witnesses, and informants). More specifically, the exercise of police powers itself requires an environment of consent: this has been shown to be particularly so in the case of stop and search powers (Willis 1983: 23).

It is necessary to see the issues in a broader historical perspective. Consent to policing is, of course, not just a series of individual instances, but an ideological practice which has been constructed and reconstructed since the mid-nineteenth century. The history of policing in Britain has largely been about the negotiation and maintenance of relations between the police and the working class which, for short, is usually referred to as 'policing by consent' (Brogden 1982; Cohen 1979; Ignatieff 1979). The irony is that the police institution largely legitimated itself by claiming subordination to (a formalistic interpretation of) the rule of law, while everyday street policing was legitimated by the use of discretion (Dixon 1991c: ch. 7). An important part of 'policing by consent' was (and is) not automatically invoking legal powers and inflexibly insisting on one's legal authority, but instead seeking co-operation and developing personal authority. This finds new resonance in contemporary developments in policing, and particularly police training. An image strongly promoted here is that of the police officer as a new 'professional' who uses discretion (in both senses) and interactive skills to achieve his or her objectives. Inflexible resort to a comprehensive rulebook is regarded as an undesirable feature of 'pre-professional' policing (see Ch. 1, above). A move towards 'consensual' policing may be linked to general trends in the nature and uses of power. For example, Leo argues that the replacement of coercion by persuasion and deception in US interrogations is a feature of 'a broad cultural shift from harder to softer processes of control' (1992: 36) and 'a profound shift in the technologies of modern police power' (1994: 95). However, such developments are complex: while police violence in the interrogation room may have declined, elsewhere (notably in public-order policing) the capacity for coercion has greatly increased. The precise, directed, and controlled beating of Rodney King (Skolnick and Fyfe 1993) is an exemplar of a new form of police violence which co-exists with shifts towards consensual policing.

It is also necessary to see 'policing by law' in historical context. The 'common sense' in which policing is about law enforcement and is essentially legal work has been undermined by research showing that most patrol work is concerned with public-order and service duties (see Ch. 2, above). As Chapter 1 suggested, law is an emergent quality in the processing of cases. As Manning observed a 'preliminary definition of policing must be . . . analytically separated from the law. . . . [T]he legalistic basis of police authority must be seen as evolving in Anglo-American societies as not an essential part of policing, and as something that is only occasionally related to the police function. . . . It has been a recent development that has seen the police as an appendage of the law' (1977: 39–40). As suggested in Chapter 2, the 'new police' of the early/mid-nineteenth century in England and Wales were legitimated in part by stressing their role as a preventive force and as a supplement to 'traditional' policing by citizens (Manning 1977: 40). While law enforcement subsequently was promoted as the *raison d'être* of policing, a broader conception of the role continued to inform policing practice. Against this background, it is possible to see 'policing by consent' as the residue of older conceptions of policing. 'Policing by law' is an essentially modernist conception. While in no way diverting attention from its conscious use to evade legal regulation (which has been discussed above), this may provide some explanation for the recurrence and persistence of 'policing by consent' in a variety of national contexts.

However, there is a more fundamental way in which the identification of policing as legal work can be challenged. The resurgence of private policing has made researchers appreciate that policing is not just a state function and that the state's attempt to monopolize it was a historically discrete phenomenon (Johnston 1992; Bayley and Shearing 1996). In general, private policing does not have available to it the specific legal powers held by state police. This does not necessarily mean that it is disadvantaged: for example, private security officers 'enjoy a *routine* access to the property which they are paid to protect that is formally denied to the public police' (South 1989: 94–5, original emphasis). In a period characterized by the spread of 'mass private property' (Shearing and Stenning 1982: 20) the significance of this must not be underestimated. The authority of private police derives from consent which is provide by or implied from legal relations established in civil law:

The sources of their most significant powers . . . are to be found in such areas of law as the law of property (governing, for instance, the rights of property owners to control access to, and conduct on, their property), employment and labour-relations law (defining the rights of management to control activities in the work place and the conduct of workers), and the law of contract (whereby submission to various security procedures can be made a condition of access to various facilities and services). The powers which private security personnel derive from these sources . . . may be described as quasi-legal powers, in the sense that they are exercised in relation to persons who, through the use of various legal fictions, are often deemed in law to have 'consented' to their exercise (Shearing and Stenning 1982: 21–2; see also Sarre 1994; South 1989: 95).

The neat allocation of private powers to private police and public powers to public police is not the whole story. Public police, too, may use private powers. For example, it may not be clear what kind of power is in use when an officer allocated to a sports ground on a 'user pays' arrangement searches an individual within the ground.

More significantly, in Chicago, Housing Department and city police may carry out sweep searches for weapons in public housing project apartments on the authority of consent provisions in housing leases. If signing such a lease is in practice a precondition of access to public housing, then the implications for police powers are considerable.[64] A common concern about developments in private security is that it will leave the public police with responsibility for policing only parts of society: it would be ironic if, in this mass public property, private law were used to by-pass the restrictions on public police powers.

It is important to stress how the balance between 'policing by law' and 'policing by consent' varies across national (and regional and local) contexts. Soon after beginning research in New South Wales, I became aware that my preconceptions were inappropriate: I was looking for legal regulation in a system dominated by informality. Policing in NSW is, in contrast to that observed in England, a variety in which the constraints of criminal procedure play a relatively insignificant role (see Ch. 5, below). This was exemplified by the heavy dependence on 'consent' to searches and 'voluntary attendance' at stations. It may be objected that use of such procedures is a reaction to inadequate legal powers. While this may be a 'common sense' conclusion, it is inaccurate: in this context, 'consent' is simply the usual way of operating. Officers need concern themselves with legal powers only when dealing with people who may cause problems for them by complaining ('challengers': see Reiner 1992a: 119–20). Others who try to stand on their rights may be less successful.

For example, decisions to apply for a search warrant are often influenced more by the likely reaction of the occupant of the premises than anything else: an NSW officer explained that '[y]ou only really need a search warrant if you know they're arseholes and you know you're not going to get in.' Treatment of suspects who do not have the means to complain about police activity was illustrated in an incident which I observed. Some juveniles suspected of an attempted burglary were located at an apartment. Officers entered and took a number of them back to the station for questioning. They were not arrested; but the 'request' to accompany the officers was put in the form: '[w]e'll go back to the station and sort this out.' When the

[64] See Press Briefing by Secretary of Housing and Urban Development Henry Cisneros and Acting Associate Attorney General Bill Bryson, White House, 16 Apr. 1994 and the *People's Tribune* (Chicago), v. 21 (18), 2 May 1994.

officers' authority to enter the premises was questioned by the girl-friend of one suspect, she was sharply rebuked and told '[y]ou said we could come in. We are investigating a crime.' Officers' subsequent comments made clear that they were simply not accustomed to being challenged by such people in operating by 'consent'. While this method of working may be altered by legal change (e.g. the intro-duction of powers to detain for questioning), it would be a mistake to suggest that a process of evolution is at work, that 'policing by consent' is a predecessor of 'policing by law' which will inevitably replace it. Rather, the two are continuing modes of policing which can co-exist. Their co-existence is an example of legal pluralism: '[n]ot the legal pluralism of traditional legal anthropology in which the different legal orders are conceived as separate entities coexisting in the same political space, but rather the conception of different legal spaces superimposed, interpenetrated and mixed' (Santos 1987: 297).

In future debates, the mutual implications of consent and legal regulation should be fully considered. Some practical suggestions are that proper provision should be made for consent in police proced-ures, so that officers would be obliged to record consents and to pro-vide suspects with information about rights and powers, and legislation should provide procedural rights for those consenting (e.g. real access for volunteers to legal advice). Also, while some scepti-cism about rights in the context of street policing was noted above, there is value in attempts to educate people about the law. Provision has also to be made for giving such rights practical substance—so that, for example, legal advice in police stations is not only available, but is delivered effectively and competently.

However, the problems cannot be dealt with simply as issues of appropriate legal regulation. As suggested in the introduction, a fea-ture of the current strategy is its articulation with what are, at best, corporatist versions of community consultation and with the weak-ening of political accountability. Such developments are, of course, not distinct from other broader shifts in state composition and regu-lation. In addition, discussion of changes in policing must, as argued above, acknowledge that many practices are not contingent, but are products of police culture and of the policing mandate. Nevertheless, that does not make them unchangeable and permanent. They are not constituted independently from legal rules: such rules form part of the environment in which they develop. Fundamental change in policing would have to be a product of democratization of police accountability. By this is meant not simply the increase (or restoration) of the powers of local authorities in their present form in England and Wales,[65] but a more general democratization of state and communal practices and institutions. The product of that kind of process might be policing in which consent could have its full meanings.

[65] Meanwhile, the excesses of the NSW parliament and the inadequacies of NSW local government provide little room for enthusiasm about directive control of police by democratic institutions in their current form.

4
Detention for Questioning in England and Wales

to appreciate the dynamic is to be able to recognize the opportunity to affect it (Rothman 1980: 11).

A central argument of this book is that legal regulation and policing practices are inextricably entwined: their relationship is interactive, one cannot be understood without the other. This theme will be explored in this and the following chapter through examining in some detail the relationship between a key policing practice—detention for questioning—and its legal regulation in two jurisdictions, England and Wales and New South Wales.[1] In each case, historical analysis will be followed by consideration of research into current policing practices. This comparison focuses on how two jurisdictions which began from the same legal basis (the common law's insistence that an arrested person should be taken without delay before a magistrate, thereby effectively proscribing custodial interrogation before charge) developed differently in providing legal powers to the police. The analyses begin with discussion of crucial cases in which the legality of detention for questioning was considered.

i. Judicial Approval of Custodial Interrogation

In England and Wales, the courts constructed a power to detain for questioning out of 'common sense', gaps and inferences in the law, perceived policy requirements, and historical misinterpretation. The crucial decisions were *Dallison* v. *Caffery*[2] and *Holgate-Mohammed*

---

[1] In contrast, the length of pre-charge detention has not been a significant legal issue in the US despite *Mallory* v. *US* 354 US 449 (1957); cf. Barrett 1962. Attention has concentrated on *Miranda* warnings (Bradley 1993: 102–3).

[2] [1964] 2 All ER 610.

v. *Duke*.[3] In the former, Dallison was arrested in April 1959 after being identified from a group of photographs shown to the witness of a theft. He was charged nine hours later at a station thirty-four miles away. During the intervening period, investigating officers travelled to collect Dallison from the arresting officers and then took him (in order to test an alibi) to a place where he claimed to have been working at the time of the offence, and then to his house, which was searched. When the officers and their prisoner eventually arrived at the police station, an identification parade was held. Although it seems that the point was not raised, he could theoretically have been taken before magistrates immediately: he had been arrested at court after being found guilty of an unrelated offence. Subsequently, Dallison's alibi was confirmed, and the prosecution was abandoned. He took action for false imprisonment and malicious prosecution. The case reached the Court of Appeal in 1964. In *Holgate-Mohammed* v. *Duke*, some jewellery was stolen in 1979 from a house in which Holgate-Mohammed was a lodger. A jeweller who subsequently bought it described the vendor as resembling Holgate-Mohammed. In April 1980, she was arrested and detained for some six hours at a police station: she was questioned but not charged. She sued for false imprisonment. The case was considered by the Court of Appeal in 1983 and by the House of Lords in 1984.

In *Dallison* v. *Caffery*, Lord Denning concluded that when 'a constable has taken into custody a person reasonably suspected of felony, he can do what is reasonable to investigate the matter, and to see whether the suspicions are supported or not by further evidence'.[4] He gave examples of searching premises, testing alibis, and holding identification parades, as had occurred in the case under consideration. Questioning is not mentioned only, it would seem, because no evidence was given of Dallison having been interrogated.[5] In *Holgate-Mohammed* v. *Duke*, one further step was taken. *Dallison* v. *Caffery* had confirmed that police could detain an arrested person before charge while investigations were carried out. However, it was not clear whether such investigations had to be intended merely to confirm, or whether they had to be expected to add substantially to, existing police suspicion. In other words, was there a distinction between the level of suspicion required for an arrest and for a charge, and, if so, was it legitimate to arrest a person in order to obtain

---

[3] [1983] 3 All ER 526 (CA); [1984] 1 All ER 1054 (HL).
[4] N. 2 above, 617.   [5] For a thorough critique, see Teh 1973: 32–5.

evidence which would justify a charge? The court answered both questions affirmatively. The fact that the suspect was more likely to confess if questioned at a police station rather than at her home was regarded as a factor which the police could properly take into account in deciding to arrest.

For how long could such detention last? The only relevant legislative provisions were those dealing with bail in the Magistrates' Court Act 1952, section 38,[6] which required that an arrested person should be 'brought before a magistrates' court as soon as practicable'. If the offence was not a serious one, this should be within twenty-four hours: otherwise, the suspect had to be bailed. Neither 'practicability' nor 'seriousness' was defined. Legitimate reasons for delaying release, bail, or a court appearance were not specified. There was no statutory maximum for 'serious cases'. In 1981 in the Queen's Bench Division case of *Holmes*, Donaldson LJ suggested that 'about 48 hours' was an appropriate maximum period of detention in 'serious cases'.[7] Forty-eight hours was thought appropriate by analogy to the Prevention of Terrorism (Temporary Provisions) Act 1976. Ironically, while effectively making law by approving the forty-eight-hour limit, Donaldson LJ argued that changes in law (e.g. to allow police to delay charges) 'must be achieved in a constitutional manner and not by a process of modification in practice' and that 'both we and the police have to live not only with but by the law as it is'.[8]

ii. The Judicial Background and the Judges' Rules

These decisions provide useful examples of some techniques of judicial creativity. In *Holgate-Mohammed* v. *Duke*, it was suggested that the issue was 'surprisingly and indeed perhaps significantly bare of direct authority'.[9] This apparent lack of a history of dispute allowed the courts to suggest that detention for questioning had always been accepted in modern policing. According to this account, since the nineteenth-century reorganization of policing, arrested people had been taken to police stations for investigation and questioning (rather than directly to a magistrate) and could be bailed from there by the police: the 'practice of interrogating persons under arrest for the pur-

---

[6] Subsequently the Magistrates Court Act 1980, s. 43(4).
[7] [1981] 2 All ER 612, 616; cf. *Hudson* (1981) 72 Cr. App. R 163; and *Mackintosh* (1983) 76 Cr. App. R 177.
[8] Donaldson in *Holmes*, n. 7 above, 615, 616.   [9] Latey J. at 533 (CA).

pose of obtaining a statement while they are in custody is of course wholly familiar . . . and there is no doubt that it is perfectly common practice' which was 'long-established and widespread'.[10]

Lord Diplock emphasized this history, claiming that detention for questioning had been implicitly recognized and approved in the first Judges' Rules, issued in 1912, and that the practice was also acknowledged in the bail provisions of the Magistrates' Court Act 1952.[11] Although he did not make the point explicitly, this implied a much longer history, for the 1952 legislation re-enacted a section from the Summary Jurisdiction Act 1879. Lord Diplock was familiar with detention for questioning from the 1950s, when he had had experience of trying criminal cases. Both Diplock and Sir John Arnold[12] quoted the *Report of the Royal Commission on Criminal Procedure* as authority for the legitimacy of detention for questioning (RCCP 1981b: paragraphs 3.65–6). Cases which had been cited by Dallison's counsel suggesting that suspects could not be detained before being taken to a magistrate were dismissed as being relevant only to arrests by private citizens: police officers had greater powers which, it was said, included detention for the purposes of investigation. This was treated as being self-evident and too familiar to require authority. Indeed, familiarity bred caution: Latey J argued that

where the power . . . has for a long period been so exercised without apparently any question or challenge . . ., I do not myself think that it would be right for the courts, at any rate below the level of the House of Lords, to say that it has been wrongly exercised and by inference has always been wrongly exercised.[13]

The power was accepted by the courts as established by practice and legitimated by necessity.

iii. An Alternative History

This mode of assertion allowed the courts in these crucial cases to ignore more than a century of controversy about the issues involved. While a detailed history cannot be provided here, it is worth sketching some outlines of an alternative account. At the heart of the matter is the relationship between magistrates and police. In a

---

[10] N. 3 above, *per* Sir John Arnold at 531, Latey J at 533 (CA).
[11] N. 3 above, 1059 (HL).   [12] N. 3 above, 532 (CA).
[13] *Ibid.* 534.

lengthy process beginning in the fourteenth century, justices of the peace established dominance over criminal investigation, directing inquiries, and questioning suspects. Constables played an inferior role: their duty was to bring arrested suspects before a magistrate as soon as practicable (see Ch. 2, above). This common law principle was confirmed in *Wright* v. *Court* in 1825.[14] But a fundamental reorganization of criminal justice soon followed, in which the roles of both police and magistrates were transformed. As criminal procedure developed, magistrates withdrew from the investigation of crime into a narrower judicial role: the institution of magistrate was transformed from 'public prosecutor' to one of 'preliminary judge' (Stephens 1883: 221; Wolchover and Heaton-Armstrong 1996: 110–11). Legal rights of defendants (to cross-examine and call witnesses, to remain silent, to have legal representation, to see depositions against them) began to develop, and magistrates were responsible for upholding them (Stephens 1883: 220–1, 228–9; Skyrme 1991: ch. 5). In a separate but parallel development, police forces were reorganized, supplanting both magistrates and private prosecutors in the investigation of crime (Hay and Snyder 1989). Practices evolved of police taking arrested suspects to stations for questioning and charging before their presentation to magistrates. However, no provision was made in the law for this enormously significant change in practice (except in regard to police bail) and, as will be shown below, key concepts such as arrest and charge became ambiguous. As the police monopolized crime investigation and promoted it as their fundamental task (Manning 1977; RCP 1962: paragraph 82), this omission became of great significance. The law continued to assume that police had no role in criminal investigation after arrest: the 'principle from which the courts at least started' was not that detention for purposes of investigation was legitimate, but rather that an arrested person was to be taken before a justice without delay (Leigh 1985: 34; see also *id.* 1975: ch. 8). This attitude was consistent with judicial distrust of police power, with the lack of legal distinction between evidential requirements for arrest and for charge, and with a concern that to allow suspects to be questioned while in custody would be to undermine their right against self-incrimination.

The courts had to decide how to deal with confessions given by suspects in police custody. In the later nineteenth century, judicial

---

[14] (1825) 4 B & C 596. See NSW LRC (1990: 1–3) for a discussion of the context of this case.

practice became increasingly inconsistent (Berger 1990: 10–11; J. Hunter 1994: 14; Wolchover and Heaton-Armstrong 1996: 111–12). Some judges excluded all statements made by prisoners: as courts no longer questioned prisoners, they 'were loathe to accept that what was a low status body should have greater powers of interrogations than judicial officers' (Lidstone and Early 1982: 496). However, others 'less tender to the prisoner or more mindful of the balance of decided authority, would admit such statements, nor would the Court of Criminal Appeal quash the conviction thereafter obtained, if no substantial miscarriage of justice had occurred'.[15] One clear and influential attempt to resolve the problem was provided in 1882 by Lord Brampton's preface to *Vincent's Police Code*, one of the principal legal guides used by police: '[w]hen . . . a constable . . . is about to arrest a person . . . or has a person in custody for a crime, it is wrong to question such a person touching the crime of which he is accused.' The constable's duty 'is simply to arrest and detain him in safe custody. . . . For a constable to press any accused person to say anything with reference to the crime of which he is accused is very wrong' (quoted, RCCP 1981a: 162). Brampton's approach was affirmed in *Gavin*, in which the court stated clearly that when 'a person is in custody, the police have no right to ask him questions'.[16] This statement was the forerunner of the Judges' Rules.[17]

The Judges' Rules originated in advice provided in 1906 by the Lord Chief Justice, who was replying to the Chief Constable of Birmingham's request for guidance after further inconsistent judicial rulings on the propriety of police practices, notably cautioning (RCCP 1981a: 163). The abiding problem was that the judges were primarily interested in and able to speak authoritatively upon the admissibility of evidence, but not on the regulation of police investigative practices. The rules were formalized and extended in 1912 and 1918, but the result was unclear, self-contradictory, and incomplete. A lack of conceptual clarity in distinguishing between arrest and charge allowed the implication that questioning of suspects in custody was permissible after caution, although apparently the intention had been to permit 'questioning in custody only to clear up

---

[15] Lord Sumner, in *Ibrahim* [1914] AC 599.
[16] (1882–6) 5 Cox CC 656. Similarly, a legal guide for the Metropolitan Police insisted that 'constables have no right to ask questions of prisoners or cross-examine them as to statements that they may voluntarily make' (Archibald *et al.* 1901: 473)
[17] RCCP 1981a: 163. For their history, see Abrahams 1964; Gooderson 1970.

ambiguities in statements made prior to charge and custody' (Lidstone and Early 1982: 502. See below on the confusion of arrest and charge). However, cautions were treated as part of the charging process, and after charge any questioning was usually forbidden. This apparent contradiction, combined with the effects of the First World War on the self-confidence of the police who enjoyed unprecedented authority under the Defence of the Realm Acts (RCPPP 1929: paragraph 267), encouraged some officers to extend their powers: 'some Chief Constables, relying on the Rules, allowed questioning of prisoners after caution. Others adhered to the stricter view, found in many judicial dicta, to the effect that the police have no right to question a person in custody, and permitted no questioning whatever after the constable decided to arrest' (Smith: 1959: 447).

This uncertainty contributed to the considerable controversies about policing in the 1920s, especially involving the CID, which led to the Royal Commission on Police Powers and Procedure of 1928–9 (Dixon 1991c: 242–8). It reported that detention for questioning was a 'practice followed not infrequently in the Metropolitan Police' and occasionally in a few large provincial towns during investigations of serious crimes, particularly murder (RCPPP 1929: paragraph 151). However, other forces 'emphatically repudiate "detention" which they regard as an illegal practice' (RCPPP 1929: paragraph 152). 'Of the 49 witnesses examined orally by the Commission, only one chief constable claimed such a right to question, while eight chief constables, and other police and magisterial witnesses did not consider that any such right existed' (Gooderson 1970: 272). As regards questioning, there was a variety of practices:

The great majority of Police forces . . . follow Lord Brampton's advice, at least as the fundamental principle governing their action. Some will admit no questioning of prisoners on any matter connected with a criminal offence. Others limit the application of the principle to the charge for which the prisoner is in custody, and approve the questioning of prisoners regarding any other offence. Some few, on the other hand, have claimed . . . a right to question prisoners on the charge for which they are in custody, although even these are agreed that it should be done very sparingly (RCPPP 1929: paragraph 162).

Lord Brampton's advice against questioning was taken as reflecting existing 'best practice' (RCPPP 1929: paragraph 137).[18]

---

[18] My reliance on the Commission's obviously inadequate data about practices reflects the dearth of research on these crucial aspects of 20th-century police history: see Dixon 1991c: ch. 7.

The Commission felt unable to give a clear statement of what the law on detention and questioning was. However, it had no doubts about what it should be. Its Report recommended 'a rigid instruction to the Police that no questioning of a person in custody, about any crime or offence with which he is or may be charged, should be permitted' (RCPPP 1929: paragraph 169). This instruction appeared in the form of a Home Office circular issued with the approval of the judges in 1930. It explained that the Judges' Rules were

> never intended to encourage or authorize the questioning or cross-examination of a person in custody after he has been cautioned, on the subject of the crime for which he is in custody, and long before this rule was formulated, and since, it has been the practice for the Judge not to allow any answer to a question so improperly put to be given in evidence.[19]

The circular did, however, go on to provide (unsatisfactory) examples of exceptional circumstances in which post-caution questioning was permissible.

These were the administrative rules approved by the judges and the Home Office which were supposed to guide police practices between 1930 and 1964 (when they were revised: see the next paragraph below). Far from the legality of custodial questioning being universally accepted in the 1950s, a leading criminal lawyer could confidently assert in 1959 that questioning of suspects about an offence for which they had been arrested was impermissible, a view confirmed by two serving police officers.[20] Devlin's contemporary study of the criminal process stated: '[t]he police have no power to detain anyone unless they charge him [sic] with a specified crime and arrest him accordingly. . . . The police have no power whatever to detain anyone on suspicion or for the purpose of questioning him' (Devlin 1960: 68). In this account, arrest and charge were regarded as being legally identical. The police role was simply to deliver the arrested person to the magistrate: it was impossible even for a suspect to be 'de-arrested' if suspicion was dispelled. Devlin stated that a suspect 'cannot be arrested without being charged'[21] and thought that

---

[19] Circ. 536053/23 of 24 June 1930, quoted Brownlie 1960: 299.
[20] See J. C. Smith's comment on *Powell-Mantle* and letters from G. C. Payne and I. V. Packman in [1959] Crim. LR 445–8, 673–9. See also Brownlie 1960: 298–324; Leigh 1975; Gooderson 1970: 272–3; Williams 1962: 42, 185–8; and the comment on *Sargant* in [1963] Crim. LR 848 at 849.
[21] 1960: 29; see also Sanders and Young 1994b: 136; Smith 1964: 180, and, for a more recent example of the same argument, CJC 1993: 611. Contrast *Wiltshire* v. *Barrett* [1966] 1 QB 312. In the late 1980s, 'no further action' was taken against a quarter of arrested suspects (McConville *et al.* 1991a: 102–5; Sanders 1994: 795).

suspects were charged immediately on their arrival in custody at a police station (1960: 67). This effectively excluded custodial interrogation, as questioning after charge was impermissible. It appears that such accounts disguised a substantial discrepancy between theory and practice, and a change in the use of arrest (Sanders and Young 1994b: 136). Police detained and questioned suspects as a matter of course. They were able to do so because the courts had 'given up enforcing their own rules' in the 1950s and confessions were 'almost uniformly' admitted as evidence, wherever they had been obtained.[22] Bevan and Lidstone concluded bluntly that the Judges' Rules 'had by 1960 ceased to exist as a legal constraint on custodial questioning' (1991: 216).

These problems could have been investigated by the Royal Commission on the Police which was appointed in 1960. The Commission was asked by Justice and other witnesses to examine the Judges' Rules and police questioning[23] (or, in the preferred terminology, 'the methods employed by the police in obtaining statements from suspected persons', RCP 1962: 2). Contemporary concern about police investigative practices was illustrated by Colin MacInnes's typically vivid (and optimistic) comment:

it looks as if the hallowed myth that English coppers never use violence, perjury, framing of suspects . . . is at last being shattered. . . . Now, what has been foolish about this legend is not that coppers *do* do these things . . . but that national vanity led many to suppose that our coppers were far nicer men than any others.[24]

However, an important opportunity for thorough review was lost. It was agreed by the Home Secretary, the Lord Chief Justice, and the Commission's chairman that the Judges' Rules should instead be referred to the judges for consideration (RCP 1962: 3). Justice had argued that, as one of the Commission's terms of reference was to consider police–public relations and complaints, police questioning could not be excluded. The Commission conceded that there was 'a

---

[22] Williams 1960: 331–2; cf. Baldwin 1985: 27; Gooderson 1970: 274–81; Zuckerman 1991: 500. Subsequently there were occasional exclusions e.g. in *McGregor* [1975] Crim. LR 514, when unlawful detention was accompanied by a failure to repeat the caution, and *Hudson*, n. 7 above, when detention for 5 days was accompanied by other breaches of the Judges' Rules.

[23] For details of cases in 1959 involving mistreatment of detained suspects, see Williams 1960: 343–4.

[24] Quoted Skolnick 1975: 69.

body of evidence, too substantial to disregard, which in effect accused the police of stooping to the use of undesirable means of obtaining statements and of occasionally giving perjured evidence in court'. Such evidence came not just from Justice and the National Council for Civil Liberties, but crucially also from the Law Society which 'suggested that the police sometimes use guile, and offer inducements, in order to obtain confessions . . . and that occasionally police officers colour, exaggerate, or even fabricate the evidence against an accused person' (RCP 1962: 110). However, the Commission turned its back on the issue. Its discussion, buried in the soggy depths of the Report's chapter on police–public relations,[25] considered it purely as a matter of isolated individual deviance (focusing on the punishment of officers guilty of misconduct: 1962: 110–12). The Commission was primarily concerned with police accountability in terms of structural arrangements between local and central government, and did not want to be distracted.[26] But, more importantly, the Commission's deliberations were permeated by an ideological view of the police which its report would do much to entrench. Serious analysis of investigative practice could find no place in the celebration of an institution. Their concern was the protection of the police's reputation 'in an age when certain elements of society are not as amenable to discipline as in the past'.[27]

By referring the Judges' Rules to the judges for consideration, the issue of controlling police questioning was removed from public debate. This was fortunate for the police, as more serious incidents of police misconduct in police interrogation were very soon to emerge (notably the Challenor and Sheffield 'rhino whip' affairs: Bottoms and Stevenson 1992: 26–7). What mattered was not what the police did, but what the judges thought. By 1964, when the new Rules emerged, Lord Denning's views in *Dallison* v. *Caffery* were representative of his colleagues'. The first of the 1964 rules gave explicit approval to the questioning of arrested suspects before charge. In retrospect, this was an extraordinary use of administrative rule-making power. Notwithstanding the limited legal significance of the Judges'

[25] On the controversy over the Commission's use of its survey data on police–public relations, see Brogden 1982: ch. 9; Reiner 1992a: 59.

[26] On the role of the Commission's secretary, T. A. Critchley, in this, see Bottoms and Stevenson 1992: 26. Critchley, who had great influence on the Commission, was to go on to write the key Whig history of the police: see Critchley 1978.

[27] Quoted with approval from evidence by the Justices' Clerks' Society (RCP 1962: 112).

Rules, this amounted to the announcement of a major change in criminal procedure which was made 'quietly and unobtrusively without any express discussion or justification of the new policy or even an indication that a new policy had evolved' (Gooderson 1970: 270). In the 1980s, there was considerable criticism that PACE legalized police malpractice: in fact, the 1964 Judges' Rules were a better example of doing so. There is a nice irony that, while English judges were compliantly approving custodial interrogation, the US Supreme Court was deciding *Miranda* v. *Arizona*.[28]

iv. Police Practices in Detention for Questioning 1964–86

The uncertainty surrounding detention for questioning in the first half of the century had encouraged the police in many areas to develop practices which allowed them to question suspects. These continued after 1964, because 'not all police officers are aware of the extent of their powers and old habits die hard'. In addition, they were a means of questioning in custody suspects against whom there was not sufficient evidence to justify arrest (Lidstone 1978: 340). There were three principal methods.

The first of these was to avoid the restraints on post-arrest questioning by not formally arresting, but by informally detaining people 'to help with enquiries'. This invention of a stage between freedom and arrest was legitimated by invoking the suspect's supposed 'consent' (Lidstone 1978: 340; Lidstone and Early 1982: 502). As Chapter 3 argued above, this largely fictional concept has been a crucial and under-scrutinized mode of police work. It would be wrong to suggest that there was a clear distinction in everyday policing between arrest and the treatment of a suspect 'helping with enquiries'. Many suspects were simply detained according to a customary process in which the legal formalities of arrest rarely figured. Such details would become relevant only in the unlikely event of a complaint or legal action. Indeed, consent should be understood as being intimately linked to the breadth and obscurity of law which officers were (and in some respects still are) able to use to their benefit in dealings with potential and actual suspects. In commenting on matters such as arrest and search of premises, Grimshaw and Jefferson refer to

[28] 384 US 436 (1966).

the blurring of exactly which powers and duties the police have. . . . Since the police do not communicate about their powers and purposes, members of the public can regard what they do only in terms of an arbitrary power which it is safer to assume is legal than not. . . . What appears as informality on the police's part also contains a mystificatory element which multiplies the potential power of the police (1987: 96)

A second method of detaining suspects was to use holding charges: suspects were arrested and charged with one offence, and questioned about others.[29] This evaded the restriction on questioning suspects about the offence for which they were arrested. Despite the manifest dangers for suspects of this approach, courts did little to restrain the use of holding charges. Indeed, it had some high official approval: the Director of Public Prosecutions told the 1928–9 Royal Commission that he considered that 'from the point of view of the public it is a first rate procedure' (quoted, RCPPP 1929: paragraph 159). The Commission disagreed and strongly criticized the use of holding charges: but this opinion was translated into neither legislation nor administrative directions. The practice continued to be 'approved by many forces' and was 'always . . . regarded as correct by the courts' (Abrahams 1964: 35, 44).

In some areas, police developed the practice of taking suspects to magistrates to be remanded in custody for up to three days *before* being charged. While this was not done in London (and was regarded as being unlawful: Zander 1977), the procedure was 'increasingly used in the provinces' in the 1970s.[30] The main importance of this practice is to show how unsatisfactory was the state of the law, when it was not even clear whether or not suspects had to be charged before or at a court appearance, and courts would return uncharged prisoners to the police for questioning.

The volunteer, the prisoner on holding charge, and the remanded suspect would, typically according to police evidence, provide a 'voluntary statement'. This was preferable to a record of interview, in that it helped to avoid complaints about police questioning and satisfied the fundamental requirement that a prisoner's evidence should be voluntarily provided. Indeed, while warning against interrogation, Lord Brampton had approved this practice:

[29] For a useful review of law and practice, see Gooderson 1970: 276–81.

[30] Lidstone 1981: 468; see also Wolchover and Heaton-Armstrong 1996: 116–17; cf. current provisions for the 'three day lie-down' in the Magistrates Courts Act 1980, s. 128(7) and PACE, s. 48, which allow detention for questioning after charge about other offences.

There is . . . no objection to a constable listening to any mere voluntary statement which a prisoner desires to make and repeating such statement in evidence. . . . Perhaps the best maxim for a constable to bear in mind . . . is
'Keep your eyes and your ears open, and your mouth shut'. By silent watch-
fulness you will hear all you ought to hear (quoted, Abrahams 1964: 14).

Advice such as this, woefully ignorant of police practice and the pressures on arrested suspects, encouraged police to act deceitfully, constructing 'statements' out of answers to questions and presenting
them to court as if they had been volunteered by the suspect
(Abrahams 1964: 29. For good examples, see Kee 1986: 29, 60).

While these devices provided an important reservoir of police
power, the 1964 Rules allowed detention for questioning to become
an overt and standard police practice (Lidstone 1978: 342; 1981: 463).
It was encouraged by the extension of power to arrest on reasonable
suspicion effected by the Criminal Law Act 1967 (Lidstone and Early
1982: 503) and subsequent court rulings on the (minimal) requirements of such suspicion.[31] According to Bevan and Lidstone, these
changes 'led to arrest on reasonable suspicion becoming the rule
rather than the exception, and to arrest for questioning becoming
accepted practice' (1991: 217).

As noted in section i above, the courts in the early 1980s established a forty-eight hour limit for detention. However, the significance of this should be qualified in several respects. First, such a limit
was generous. Data on the use of PACE detention powers are illustrative: for example, in 1995, only 156 suspects in England and Wales
were detained for longer than forty-eight hours (Home Office 1995:
table 3). While authorization from magistrates is required for such
lengthy detention (see sect. vi, below), the relevant point is that there
appears to be no great demand for detention beyond forty-eight
hours. Before PACE, most police objectives could be met within
forty-eight hours. Secondly, the point at which the detention period
started could be confused (e.g. by the 'voluntary attender' who was
subsequently arrested) and there was no regulation of detention
length within that period. Thirdly (as noted above at p. 137),
uncharged subjects in some areas were remanded by magistrates back
to police custody. Fourthly, the courts were inconsistent and decisions approving detention for a considerably longer period could be
found (Wolchover and Heaton-Armstrong 1996: 115–16). Fifthly,

---

[31] *Hussein v. Chong Fook Kam* [1970] AC 942.

even if detention was found to be excessive, this did not necessarily lead either to exclusion of evidence or to a successful appeal.[32]

Officers with pre-PACE policing experience in our research in a northern police force area spoke fondly of 'the old days' when, one explained, 'it was "We will see you in 5 or 6 hours" . . . People were locked up on a night, and it was "We will see you at 9 o'clock in the morning" '. A retired police officer[33] talked about how

the job got done [when] you had a bit more leeway and you weren't hauled over the coals for the way you interrogated a prisoner. . . . He'd probably have been sitting in a cell overnight. . . . You'd arrest someone and then talk to them for a couple of hours or so and get nothing from him, so you'd go away. . . . A night in the cells has a very sobering effect on certain people. That was the psychological side of the job in those days. It was a very psychological job then.

Another made a similar point: 'I remember arresting people, putting them in the cells and then going off for tea. You'd just leave them in the cells to soften up. The police have got to have some tactics or they would never convict anybody.' As these quotations suggest, the threat of judicial or magisterial criticism was rarely a serious one. Officers did not need to expect that a court would scrutinize their activities, so long as they stayed within bounds of reasonableness which were largely culturally rather than legally prescribed. In this context, *Holmes* is interesting for the reaction of the investigating officer to being brought to court to answer an application for habeas corpus after detaining suspects without charge for two days. When the unrepentant officer eventually appeared in court, he explained that the suspects could have been charged on the morning of their arrest, but charges had been delayed while other offences were investigated. At the hearing, Lord Donaldson concluded that such delay displayed 'a complete disregard of [a] fundamental principle of the common law' that suspects should be charged as soon as sufficient evidence was available. He went on to comment that, far from being contrite, the officer made clear his 'surprise at our anxiety' and 'quite genuinely could not understand what the fuss was all about and that he was a good police officer doing his duty as he saw it'. This disregard and ignorance of what the judges considered the law to be led

---

[32] See *Mackintosh*, n. 7 above.
[33] Now a solicitor's clerk, who was interviewed in research on relations between police and defence lawyers: see Ch. 6, below.

Lord Donaldson to comment critically on 'those in command of the Metropolitan Police whose systems and standing orders had allowed such a situation to develop'.[34] Similarly, the judicial inquiry into the investigation of Maxwell Confait's death (which had led to the wrongful conviction of three young people) found that many police and lawyers were unaware of important provisions in the Judges' Rules. It was reported curtly that the requirement to inform suspects of their right to legal advice 'was unknown to counsel and to senior officers who gave evidence. . . . In the Metropolitan Police District it is not observed' (Fisher 1977: 13).

These examples illustrate the marginality of law to policing practices in this period. It is sometimes assumed that cases like *Holmes* limited policing practice (Ewing and Gearty 1990: 29–30; Leng 1995: 209), but there appears to be little evidence to establish this interpretation which legalistically overstates the effect of judicial decisions on policing practices. By contrast, Clayton and Tomlinson suggest that, in practice, *Holmes* 'was often ignored' (1992: 4). In laying the ground for their account of the descent into Thatcherite repression, Ewing and Gearty provide a quaint picture of a pre-PACE 'benign vagueness in the law. . . . [P]olice practice drifted benevolently in the uncertainty' (1990: 29). A harsher, but more accurate, judgement would be that the courts generally turned a blind eye to police malpractice, accepting that the ends justified the means (Rose 1996: ch. 1).

Relying on Home Office evidence which was rather less frank than the officers quoted above, but which confirmed the prevalence of custodial interrogation, the Royal Commission on Criminal Procedure reported in 1981 that detention for questioning to dispel or confirm suspicion 'has not always been the law or practice but now seems to be well-established as one of the primary purposes of detention upon arrest' (RCCP 1981b: paragraph 3.66). This drew on a misleading account of the issue's history: the accompanying *Law and Procedure* volume, based on Home Office evidence, ignored the history of controversy which has been sketched above and, like the judges in *Dallison* v. *Caffery* and *Holgate-Mohammed* v. *Duke*, presented a history of convenient consensus. Lord Brampton's contribution to *Vincent's Police Code* was misrepresented, while the Report of the Royal Commission on Police Powers and Procedure and the 1930 cir-

[34] N. 7 above, 614; cf. *Houghton and Franciosy* (1978) 68 Cr. App. R 197.

cular were ignored (RCCP 1981a: paragraphs 68–9). The significance of this is that it fitted with the Commission's general strategy, which was to assess what powers the police needed and then to place safeguards on the exercise of such powers (Brittan 1983: 390). This 'balancing' exercise could have been done another way: the Commission could have assessed what were essential rights, and then provided police with powers which fitted with those rights (McBarnet 1981b: 448; Ashworth 1994). In context, such an approach was unpalatable. The historical account was, therefore, presented in a way which fitted the priorities of the day. The Commission's report of practice was taken by courts as a statement of law.[35] In this way, informal practice came to give authority for judicial extensions of the law.

These legal developments have to be considered in the context of concurrent developments in policing organization and practices. The need to appreciate the interaction and possible contradiction between developments in law and in policing is emphasized by the US experience: while the Warren Court was active in extending due process protections, serious policing problems continued and indeed intensified (Dawson 1982: 348). Meanwhile, in the 1960s and 1970s in Britain,

a new emphasis was placed upon reactive and pre-emptive policing . . . as systematic intelligence collection was introduced and increasing weight was placed upon evidence gained by police questioning suspects in preference to methods premised upon active cooperation and supply of information from the public (Kinsey and Baldwin 1982: 304; cf. Reiner 1992a: 73–104).

The effect on patrol strategies and police–public contact of this shift towards reactive policing is well documented. Less often appreciated is its impact on investigative techniques. There was an 'increasing tendency to arrest first and ask questions afterwards' (Lidstone 1981: 464). Arrest and questioning before charge increasingly became the routine method of handling cases.[36]

[35] See e.g. Lord Diplock in *Holgate-Mohammed* v. *Duke*, n. 3 above, 532.
[36] In 1978, 24% of persons who appeared in court for indictable offences had been summonsed. Practice was notoriously inconsistent, with 4 forces (including the Metropolitan Police) summonsing 1% or fewer, while 8 summonsed 40% or more (RCCP 1981b: 42). By 1993, the overall percentage for indictable offences had fallen to 10% (Zander 1995: 82; note that, throughout, many of these will have been arrested at some point: McConville *et al.* 1991a: 38; Brown *et al.* 1992: 108). However, the use of summonses for non-motoring non-indictable offences increased from 55% in 1978 to 76% in 1993. Suspects who are arrested but not proceeded against are not included in these figures (Brown 1997: ch. 4). In McConville *et al.*'s research areas, 98.2% of adults in their sample were arrested (1991a: 39).

v. Policing and Criminal Procedure

In retrospect, the developments outlined in section iv constituted a highly unsatisfactory way to develop law and policy in an area of great importance. They contributed to the malpractice in police investigations which occurred regularly through this period. This section examines some contributory aspects of judicial, legal, and political attitudes and activities.

Judicial attitudes to the police were inconsistent. Interpretations of the requirement that confessions should be made voluntarily on occasions produced decisions on inducements to confess which exasperated police. This approach declined in the 1970s and early 1980s.[37] As challenges to police evidence became more common, judges lost enthusiasm for civil libertarian gestures. In general, judges in postwar England and Wales became increasingly accommodating to police demands for additional powers: they retreated from control of police, while senior American (in the 1960s) and Australian (in the 1980s) judges attempted to advance (Abrahams 1964: 25–6; Dawson 1982: 547). Leigh dignifies the main vehicle of this by calling it the 'ancillary powers doctrine', which meant that the police were allowed to expand their powers 'where to do so seemed necessary in the investigation of crime' (1985: 36; cf. Ch. 2, above). A good example was Lord Denning's reasoning in *Dallison* v. *Caffery*: the police have a power to arrest; to do their job properly they must be able to detain those arrested for investigation; so they have the power to do so.

Similarly, the courts chose legal analytical tools which allowed the police wide discretionary powers. For example, judges insisted that police powers of arrest without warrant[38] and of subsequent detention for questioning were subject to the requirement that they be exercised reasonably. The limitation set by this 'rule of reasonableness'[39] was largely rhetorical: 'reasonableness' was assessed according to the notoriously permissive standard applicable to executive officers in administrative law (the 'Wednesbury' rules: see Ryan and Williams 1986). In *Dallison* v. *Caffery*, Lord Diplock insisted that reasonableness had to be judged on contemporary rather than on historical standards, so giving the courts interpretive room to legitimate developments in police practice which had no statutory basis.[40]

---

[37] See cases cited by Russell 1990: 4–5 and e.g. *Rennie* [1982] 1 All ER 385.
[38] Criminal Law Act 1967, s. 2(4).
[39] Lord Diplock in *Dallison* v. *Caffery* , n. 2 above, 619.   [40] *Ibid.*

Reasonableness was employed in a syllogistic argument. Police had a statutory power of arrest. It was accepted that detention for questioning was necessary and legitimate. So, to arrest for the purpose of detention and questioning must itself be a reasonable use of the power. Finally, courts were very reluctant to exercise the discretion to exclude evidence (other than confessions) which had been improperly obtained, a reluctance formalized by the House of Lords in *Sang*.[41] It was argued that it was not the court's role to discipline the police, and that courts should be limited to the matter before them and be prepared to deal with any good evidence presented.

In these circumstances, it was hardly surprising that the Judges' Rules did not have much impact on policing: the judges had issued them as guidance on what had to be done to ensure that evidence was judicially acceptable, but then failed to sanction breaches. The courts became less rigorous in their requirement for the admissibility of confessions. The results could be seen in a case such as *Houghton and Franciosy*. Despite criticizing police for a 'flagrant disregard' of the Judges' Rules in detaining a suspect for five days incommunicado, the Court of Appeal agreed with the trial judge that the resulting confession should be admissible.[42] These examples of judicial interpretation were just part of wider processes which included the expansion of state power, the decline of civil liberties, the subservience of the judiciary in post-war decades to executive priorities, changes in policing, and concerns about the ability of the system to deal with perceived threats to law and order. Often judges employed a familiar account of criminal justice: police powers were made acceptable by being 'balanced' with restrictions on the power to arrest and limitations on permissible detention (contrast Ashworth 1994). Thus, the community's interest in security was balanced against the individual suspect's interest in liberty. In some judges' view, these 'balances' unfairly favoured the suspect as against the police (and, increasingly in modern law and order discourse, the victim).

From time to time Parliament and the courts have deprived the police, no doubt rightly, of weapons which might otherwise be in their armoury, but this is surely a time when further deprivation should only be made for cogent reasons, if, that is to say the interest of the law-abiding citizen (the victim or the potential victim) is to be given at least as much consideration as the liberty of the reasonably suspected person.[43]

[41] [1979] 2 All ER 1222.   [42] N. 34 above, 205 (Lawton LJ).
[43] Latey J, n. 3 above, 534 (CA).

Similarly, Lord Denning insisted that detention powers were 'an important adjunct to the administration of justice', which should mean 'justice not only to the man himself [*sic*] but also to the community at large'.[44] While it may be inevitable that judges develop a world weariness about defence pleas, there was a deeper antagonism towards defendants which, for example, expressed itself in the long debate about the right of silence (see Ch. 6, below and references in Dixon 1991b: 29), and, indeed, appears to continue: according to a member of the Court of Appeal, there 'will always be the unscrupulous policeman. I believe him to be a comparatively rare phenomenon. There will always be the unscrupulous suspect. I do not believe that he is such a rare phenomenon' (Russell 1990: 18).

A striking aspect was the courts' and many legal commentators' ignorance (real in many cases, apparently feigned in others) of the realities of policing practice. There was a simplistic and misleading conflation of what the law required and the police did: for example, Devlin claimed that 'in practice it is nearly always possible to bring the accused before a magistrate within a day. . . . So it is safe to say that as a general rule the police do not hold a man for more than a day without judicial sanction' (1960: 71). In one voice, judges said that law should be extended to legitimate necessary policing practices: in another, they said that policing practices were determined by the law. The confinement of criminal justice issues within a narrowly doctrinal and court-focused approach to criminal law (Dixon 1997) bears much responsibility for these inadequacies. There was little evident understanding of the transfer of investigative duties from magistrates to police in the mid-nineteenth century, or of the subsequent production of crime investigation as the priority and reserve of police (see sect. iii above). Yet both these developments were crucial to any understanding of the phenomena with which the courts were expected to deal.

From the mid-nineteenth century through to PACE, a major problem was the failure or inability to make fundamental conceptual distinctions between arrest, caution, and charge. It is apparent that the separate stages were not properly understood in many cases and debates, or indeed even by the various authors of the Judges' Rules. A series of interconnected but separate issues were run together and confused: evidential requirements for legal arrest; arrest procedure;

---

[44] In *Dallison* v. *Caffery*, n. 2 above, 617.

when (and what kind of) cautions should be given; the length of time
for which suspects could be detained between arrest and court
appearance; evidential requirements for charge; what could be done
during this time; and the admissibility of confessions.

Such difficulties were exacerbated by insisting on artificial concepts
of voluntariness and consent, and using the awkward terminology of
judicial and executive functions. Much of this was due to a simple
lack of familiarity or contact with the routine of everyday policing.
This, in turn, was a product of lawyers' traditional attitudes to criminal law, particularly the everyday administration of ordinary cases,
as low-status, intellectually unchallenging work (McBarnet 1983:
143–53). According to Blom-Cooper and Drewry, 'criminal law has
long been . . . the jurisprudential Cinderella of the English legal system; although the part it plays within the system has not been so
much despised as disdainfully ignored' (1972: 276). Yet they echo
familiar prejudices: 'the criminal law is a branch which the first-class
intellect can quickly grasp; it is by and large free from technicalities
requiring any great measure of expertise' (1972: 275–6). If lawyers
had been sufficiently interested (and remunerated), criminal law and
procedure would have provided ample material for theorizing and
conceptualizing, in 'minor' public order cases as much as in murder
cases (Brown *et al.* 1996; Dixon 1997).

The development of the law also depended significantly on the
expertise and interest of lawyers and their willingness to argue crucial points. In neither *Dallison* v. *Caffery* nor *Holgate-Mohammed* v.
Duke did defence counsel argue squarely that detention for questioning between arrest and charge was unlawful. Dallison's counsel
had suggested, not that he should have been taken immediately
before magistrates, but that he should have been taken directly to the
investigating officers' station.[45] It had been argued for Holgate-
Mohammed that custodial interrogation was permissible, but was not
in itself a legitimate cause of arrest unless it was necessary to prevent,
for example, the destruction of other evidence or because there were
no other investigative methods available to the police.[46] Similarly,
despite 'the breaches committed in the Confait case, no defending
counsel invited the Judge in his discretion to exclude any of the confessions on the ground of such breaches' (Fisher 1977: 17). This

---

[45] N. 2 above, 621.   [46] N. 3 above, 531 (CA).

clearly illustrated how a suspect's interests may be harmed by inadequate legal representation.[47]

The problem was also one of procedure and the organization of criminal justice. In a system built around the guilty plea and the avoidance of contested cases (Sanders 1994a: 805–7), remedial tactics such as challenging the admissibility of evidence are marginalized. Police were encouraged to interrogate for confessions, knowing that the likely result was a guilty plea: how a confession was obtained would rarely be scrutinized, so there was little incentive to stick to the rules (Williams 1960: 328). Other methods of raising such issues in court were (and are) equally limited. Detention for questioning could be challenged by an application for habeas corpus; but the result would usually be an adjournment during which the suspect would be released or, more likely, charged.[48] Civil actions were possible, although unlikely to be taken if the suspect was acquitted and particularly unlikely to succeed if he or she was convicted. In the 1950s and 1960s, courts were unsympathetic to civil actions against police, the policy being not to discourage police from attempting to do their duty: however, this tendency appears to have diminished in recent years, as civil actions have increased (Clayton and Tomlinson 1992). Problems of cost, legal access (by prisoners), and cultural attitudes towards the use of law also limited the practical availability of remedies. In addition, important issues could often be raised only indirectly, e.g. the legality of an arrest might be an issue in a case about an assault on police.[49] This inevitably affected judicial or magisterial treatment of the matter.

An important additional factor was parliamentary and governmental neglect. There was no comprehensive legislation on detention or questioning. On the contrary, the legislation which the courts were asked to interpret was poorly drafted and only obliquely relevant to the issue, being primarily concerned with arrest and bail. This contributed to the tendency of courts to concentrate on issues which were really of secondary relevance, such as the requirements of a proper arrest. As was commented in an Australian context, it is 'highly unlikely that an area of law which dealt with the ownership of property would have been allowed to remain in this state without urgent legislative attention' (NSW LRC 1990: paragraph 1.62).

---

[47] See generally Baxter and Koffman 1983; McConville et al. 1994: 3–5; Ch. 6, below.
[48] See, e.g., *Holmes*, n. 7 above.   [49] e.g. *Kenlin* v. *Gardner* [1967] 2 QB 510.

Similarly, Lord Devlin (referring to arrest, search, and detention laws) complained that it 'is quite extraordinary that these should be so obscure and ill-defined. It is useless to complain of police overstepping the mark if it takes a day's research to find out where the mark is' (1967: 12). Devlin assumed that a 'mark' was there to be found, that the law was potentially certain: the account above would suggest that this owes more to rhetoric than to reality. Similarly, elsewhere, Devlin attempted to account for the law's uncertainty within what is almost a caricature of Whig history, in which there is

a constant drift, always in the same direction from unfettered administrative action to regulated judicial proceeding. . . . If it is asked whether the police can do such-and-such a thing with impunity, the answer may be, 'Possibly, but in practice they do not do it.' That means either that a practice is maturing or that a fully grown practice is not yet ripe enough to be termed a rule of law. (1960: 10).

From more critical perspectives, such uncertainty may be seen as neither temporary nor contingent, but rather as structural (Grimshaw and Jefferson: 1987; McBarnet 1983; Ch. 1, above).

vi. Statutory Detention for Questioning

In 1986, the Judges' Rules and much common law were replaced by the Police and Criminal Evidence Act 1984, which provides explicit powers to detain suspects for questioning and other investigation between arrest and charge. Such detention may be for up to twenty-four hours in most cases or four days in the case of 'serious arrestable offences'.[50] This maximum can be reached only after a series of reviews by progressively more senior authorities: an inspector must authorize continued detention after no more than six hours, and again after no more than fifteen hours; a superintendent after no more than twenty-four hours; and a magistrates' court after no more than thirty-six and again after no more than seventy-two hours. A suspect must be charged as soon as there is sufficient evidence for a successful prosecution and he or she 'has said all that he wishes to say' about the offence or offences for which he or she was detained.[51] After being charged, he or she must be taken to court 'as soon as is

---

[50] PACE, ss. 41–44. In addition, the Prevention of Terrorism Act allows detention for up to 7 days.

[51] Code C, 1995, s. 16.1.

practicable and in any event not later than the first sitting after he is charged with the offence'.[52]

During pre-charge detention, suspects have various rights to which PACE provisions give some substance. Most importantly, suspects must be informed of a right to free legal advice, including the attendance of a legal adviser during interrogation. The keystone of the PACE system is the custody officer, who has statutory responsibility for the suspect's detention. In this way, the duties of detaining suspects and investigating offences are supposed to be kept quite separate, with the custody officer controlling and supervising the access of investigating officers to the suspect. Custody officers have a crucial role in making the legislation work by controlling practices such as the use of holding charges. PACE, section 37(2), makes clear that a suspect can be detained before charge only for questioning and investigation of the 'offence for which he is under arrest'. This does not prevent suspects being questioned about other offences after having been charged. In one case in our research study, two suspects were charged with what was openly termed a holding charge and were subsequently questioned at length[53] about related large-scale theft and drug offences. They were unlikely to complain, because their co-operation was to earn them better treatment and reduced charges. As custody officers control access to such suspects, it is for them to decide whether what is done is acceptable and reasonable. The utility of holding charges is limited to some extent by the rule that access to legal advice cannot be delayed once a suspect has been charged with any offence.[54] They have been made less necessary (in police terms) by PACE's provision of lengthy, legal pre-charge detention for questioning. PACE's provisions dealing with another evasive tactic—the use of 'voluntary attendance'—are discussed in Chapter 3, above.

How has PACE affected the practice of detention for questioning? There is space here for only a brief summary of the extensive research on PACE's effects on this and related matters.[55] In providing arrest

[52] PACE, s. 46(2).

[53] Before and after being remanded for a 'three-day lie down': see n. 29, above. Such practices have been inadequately studied in PACE research to date (cf. Bottomley *et al.* 1991: 95–6).

[54] PACE Code C, Annex B.

[55] See Brown 1997 for summaries, interpretation, and extensive references to the PACE literature. References will frequently be made below to this as a conduit to other studies.

powers, PACE provided a compromise: when a less serious ('non-arrestable') offence is suspected, an arrest can be made only if one of a number of arrest conditions is satisfied. In practice, officers regard this as a substantial extension of power: they can be more confident about the legality of arrest without the detailed consideration of inconsistent arrest powers which was notionally needed in pre-PACE days. We found little evidence of officers devoting much consideration to whether or not arrest conditions had been satisfied. As in the case of stop and search, legal regulation of street policing is of limited effect (Bottomley *et al.* 1991: chs. 2 and 4; Brown 1997: chs. 2 and 4; Dixon *et al.* 1989).

This makes even more important the major check which is supposed to be provided by the custody officer's scrutiny before a suspect is admitted to detention at a police station. While they provide differing explanations (see sect. vii below), researchers have agreed that this scrutiny is minimal. Reception into police custody has become an essentially routinized process, with custody officers failing to inquire in any detail into the circumstances of arrest or the need for detention (Brown 1997: ch. 4).

As regards the time for which suspects are detained, our research confirmed other findings that PACE has had a dual effect: crudely, suspects in more serious cases are detained for shorter periods, while those in less serious cases are now detained for longer periods than before 1986 (Brown 1997: ch. 4).[56] A significant factor in this increase was time consumed by requests for legal advice. Such advice may be free, but its cost is additional time spent in custody, which some suspects will always be unwilling to pay.

Like the authorization of initial detention, many reviews of continuing pre-charge custody lack substance, and compliance with PACE requirements is largely presentational. The right of suspects and their legal advisers to make representations to review officers often amounts merely to an inspector asking the suspect 'All right, mate?' through the hatch in the cell door. Solicitors comment that their representations rarely influence inspectors, who treat early extensions of detention as routine. However, as the period of detention nears twenty-four hours and reviews require the approval of a superintendent, investigating officers no longer can assume that their applications will be granted.

---

[56] It is important here to note the problems of such comparisons: data on pre-PACE practice are often unavailable or unreliable.

In our research sample, almost three-quarters of suspects were charged or released within six hours. A further fifth were dealt with before the second review is required at no more than fifteen hours. Most of the rest were charged or released before the twenty-four-hour review, with less than 1 per cent detained for longer without charge (Bottomley *et al.* 1991: ch. 6). These findings are broadly replicated by other research (Brown 1997). This may suggest that detention powers can be effectively limited by the involvement in review decisions of officials who (unlike shift inspectors) are further removed from the investigation of the offence, and that earlier involvement of more senior officers (e.g. at fifteen-hour reviews) would be desirable. In 1995 in England and Wales, 220 applications to magistrates were made to detain suspects without charge for more than thirty-six hours: eleven were refused. (Home Office 1996: table 3). This could be interpreted as suggesting either that magisterial supervision is superficial, or that managerial controls mean that cases are scrutinized closely before applications are made, or simply that police find no great need for very lengthy pre-charge detention. Fears that four-day detentions would be routine have been allayed, while predictions that, once granted, powers would be increasingly pushed to their limits are belied by a substantial decrease in detentions beyond thirty-six hours since 1986.[57] A cause for concern here, as elsewhere, is regional variation in the legislation's application. Of the 310 applications in 1993, no fewer than forty-one were in South Wales, while a further twenty-six were in Lancashire. Thirty-three of the forty-three forces applied for ten or fewer warrants; six of these made no applications at all.[58]

Among the suspects' rights which PACE provides or strengthens, access to legal advice is most important. Substance is provided by public funding and the organization of duty-solicitor schemes (Cape 1993). While it is not possible to provide precise numbers of requests before 1986, there is no doubt that they were substantially increased by PACE, and that rates continued to increase at least to early 1994, when the most recent research was carried out (Phillips and Brown 1997). This steady rise was due to broadening public knowledge about the right and revisions of Code C in attempts to ensure that

[57] In 1986, there were 684; there has been a steady, if not linear, decline to 209 in 1995 (Home Office 1996: 7).

[58] Home Office 1993: table 3. In 1995, 37 forces made fewer than 10 applications, with 12 making none (Home Office 1996: table 3).

information about it was properly communicated to suspects. In a study of the processing of over 4,000 prisoners at ten police stations in 1993–4, Phillips and Brown (1997) report that 38 per cent requested legal advice. Again, it is important to note the wide regional variations: request rates at thirty-two stations in 1987 ranged from 14 to 41 per cent (Brown 1989: 21), while at ten stations in 1993–4 the variation was from 22 to 50 per cent (Phillips and Brown 1997). Researchers have emphasized the need to look beyond request rates to rates of actual provision which can be substantially lower (Brown 1996: ch. 6; Sanders *et al.* 1989; Sanders and Young 1994a: 124–46) and, even more importantly, to the quality (or lack thereof) of advice provided. Substantial deficiencies in legal advice provided to suspects have been reported and are discussed in Chapter 6, below.

Apart from legal advice, a major safeguard is the requirement that 'vulnerable suspects' including juveniles, the mentally ill and the intellectually disabled should be attended by an appropriate adult, other than in exceptional circumstances (Brown 1997: chs. 9 and 10). There are two major problems here. The first is the identification by custody officers of suspects who are intellectually handicapped or mentally ill: it seems undeniable that more training is required here. Secondly, there is the ability of those who act as appropriate adults for juveniles to perform the role envisaged in the Code of Practice. Experience would suggest that many parents and social workers do not do so effectively and that trained social work teams which are available at all hours are required. An appropriate adult who is passive may serve principally to preserve the integrity of evidence obtained, while one who actively assists investigating officers may do more harm than good to a suspect's interests (Dixon 1990).

PACE controls interrogations by having custody officers limit the access of investigating officers to suspects and by requiring recording, originally in contemporaneous notes, now overwhelmingly on audiotapes. Enthusiasm for videotaping was dampened by the Royal Commission on Criminal Justice's lukewarm assessment (1993: 26, 39–41; Brown 1997: ch. 7; but contrast Pollard 1996: 155) in marked contrast to developments in Australia (Dixon and Travis 1997). Practices vary amongst custody officers. More generally, there was some relaxation after initial strictness on PACE's implementation. In our PACE study, one commented that custody officers 'have realized that they are still police officers. . . . When we first started, we tried to stick to that "independent" thing. . . . As long as you stick to the rules, if there is evidence to get, then get it.' This quotation also provides a good example of a more general realization that PACE benefited rather than obstructed police work in significant respects. This emerged most clearly in attitudes to tape-recording: 91 per cent of interviewed officers reported favourable or very favourable attitudes towards it because of its expected effects in producing unchallengeable evidence and reducing accusations of malpractice (as well as providing an escape from contemporaneous note-taking). Preparing audio-taped material for use in court can be problematic: researchers have found significant deficiencies in the records of taped interviews which officers create (Brown 1997: ch. 7).

These methods of control are inevitably limited. There is always an incentive to interrogate while a house is being searched following arrest or in the car on the way to the station (Brown 1997: ch. 7). Limits on admissibility of evidence are avoided if the suspect is persuaded to repeat admissions during a formal interview. Similarly, officers routinely prepare suspects before recorded interviewing: in our study, 71 per cent of officers reported that they sometimes, often, or always did this. Such practices are probably impossible to eradicate, not least because it is suspects who are sometimes unwilling to have what they say recorded. However, appropriate measures would be to strengthen the custody officer's position and to increase the deterrent against malpractice by amending section 78 to provide a presumption that evidence collected in breach of the Codes of Practice should not be admissible.[59]

vii. Professionalism or Pessimism?

The summary in section vi represents a critical, but guardedly positive, assessment of PACE. There are, however, two other (markedly different) views. The first presents PACE as a 'sea-change' in policing: it argues that PACE fundamentally changed criminal investigation, shifting towards a supposedly American model of due process (McKenzie 1990; McKenzie and Gallagher 1989: 11, 136–7). Much of the research upon which such claims are based has been produced by police officers. It must be considered in the political context of police reactions to PACE, which included arguments for increased resources to accommodate the extra work, resistance to the controls on police

---

[59] For a detailed statement of such a provision, see NSW LRC 1990: 145–54.

practices, arguments that PACE had rendered redundant the 'right to silence', and even a claim from a prominent commentator that PACE was 'the true reason' for 'the crisis in policing and for the public's loss of confidence in the police' (McKenzie, 1990b). Methodological problems evident in much of this research cannot be divorced from this political context.

According to Tom Williamson, a key figure in police responses to PACE,

There has been a sea change in the way that police officers question suspects. . . . The Police and Criminal Evidence Act 1984 . . . and the Codes of Practice regulating police questioning, the tape recording of interviews and police organisational policies aimed at promoting ethical values represent the most important developments in the questioning of suspects since the formation of the police over 150 years ago. A new climate has been created in which there is strict adherence to the new rules. . . . The new legislation is succeeding in its intention of making the questioning of suspects less coercive and more a process of enquiry rather than purely one of persuasion to confess (1990b: 1, 6).

The evidence for these claims comes from a questionnaire administered to eighty detectives. Williamson acknowledges the inevitable objection that 'there could well be a gap between what they say and what they do'. Given that Code C (at the time of the research) clearly stated that the 'purpose of any interview is to obtain from the person concerned his explanation of the facts, and not necessarily to obtain an admission',[60] it is hardly surprising that detectives responding to a senior officer's survey should have replied appropriately: when 'asked to rank order truth, evidence and confession, 72 put truth first, 27 put evidence first and only 5 put confession first' (Williamson 1990: 2, *sic*). The perception of PACE which the police tried to establish as common sense was captured well by another police researcher: 'PACE and the Code of Practice are being religiously followed' (Mackay 1990: 63).

Some academic backing for police assessments of PACE was provided by Irving and McKenzie's study of detention and questioning (1989; see also McKenzie 1990a). A particularly significant feature of this research is that it was a partial replication of Irving's study of interrogation (1980) for the Royal Commission on Criminal Procedure and, as such, can claim to be the only 'before and after'

---

[60] N. 12A.

observational study. In addition, Irving's earlier work had demonstrated the vulnerability of suspects during custodial interrogation and the use by police of manipulative interviewing tactics. His exposure of the myth that confessions secured during custodial interrogation can ever properly be considered 'voluntary' considerably influenced the debate about rules of evidential admissibility from which sections 76 and 78 emerged (see sect. viii, below).

Irving and McKenzie's initial report (1989: part 1) suggested that PACE had very substantially affected detention and questioning: in 'all cases observed prisoners were informed of their rights exactly as stipulated in the code of practice and . . . the procedures laid down to safeguard these rights were also closely adhered to' (1989: 42). As the PACE strategy required, custody officers 'had taken a firm grip on the management of the cell block and CID officers had submitted to the new formalities about access to prisoners and the other regulations governing interrogations' (1989: 117). Custody officers 'were not prepared to allow any contact between suspect and investigating officer, save in the formal interrogation situation' (1989: 102). There were 'dramatic and unexpected' changes in interrogation practices (1989: 103). Contemporaneous notes were taken in full and had 'more or less eliminated the use of persuasive interrogation tactics' (1989: 118). More evidence was collected before arrest than had been the case before, and interrogation was concerned more with confirming such evidence than with obtaining a confession as primary evidence (1989: 98, 194). In the second year of their study, Irving and McKenzie found the initial effects of PACE were waning; notably, there was a resurgence of 'tactical interviewing' as officers became familiar with the legislation. None the less, the overall conclusion from Irving and McKenzie's study was that PACE had changed the interrogation process in the direction which the legislators had intended.

These findings were met with some surprise by other researchers. Sanders *et al.* commented tersely: '[e]ither Irving and McKenzie were badly misled or the police station in which their research was done was unusual' (1989: 142). While they were aware of the danger of being misled (1989: 28–9), some of their comments on the issue were somewhat naïve. For example, it was suggested that McKenzie's 'previous experience as a police officer made it unlikely that he would cause behaviour to be edited' (1989: 29; see also McKenzie 1990a: 185–9). This gives insufficient weight to police resistance to oversight by others (including senior serving as well as retired officers) as well as to the antagonism of many towards social science research (Young 1991: 20–1). Irving and McKenzie claim that sometimes custody officers did not know who the researchers were, and assumed that they were detectives (1989: 42). This underestimates the spread of knowledge about the presence of outsiders within a station, and particularly in a charge room. Their practice of collecting copies of the contemporaneous notes made by interrogating officers (1989: 32) must surely have affected the way in which such notes were compiled.

The database of the research was small—sixty-eight cases were observed in detail in each year, with supplementary studies including analysis of custody records. The research was all conducted in Brighton police station. Irving and McKenzie do not deal adequately with the problem of studying only one station, simply asserting that their before and after study is all—and therefore the best—that we have (1989: 30). It is hard to believe that the return to a station of a researcher (strongly backed by senior officers) whose earlier study had been critical and politically significant would not radically have affected the way in which the station operated, particularly when some of the officers studied in the earlier project still worked there. In brief, Irving and McKenzie discuss the likelihood of individual editing of behaviour: they do not deal with organizational editing of behaviour. What they report may be an accurate picture of practices in Brighton (although there is room for considerable doubt about this). It seems doubtful that the findings are generalizable.

In very considerable contrast, the second view to be considered suggests that PACE has been 'easily absorbed by the police' (McConville *et al.* 1991a: 189). The Warwick School has presented influential and highly critical assessments of PACE which have to be set in the context of their theoretical analyses of relations between law and policing which were discussed in Chapter 1. From this perspective, the dominance of police priorities, culture, and crime-control commitments has been little affected. 'Apart from changes to bureaucratic recording practices . . . the basic message from our research is of the *non-impact* of PACE on police practices' (McConville *et al.* 1991a: 189, original emphasis). Rather than regulating policing, PACE has served to facilitate and legitimate powers and practices adopted by the police in their culturally-driven commitment to crime control. According to this account, there is a fundamental similarity between policing on the street and in the station;

PACE has changed procedures, but not substance; police dominate the process by which cases are constructed and processed; police resist and evade attempts to control their activities; supervisory and managerial controls are largely ineffective, particularly in an adversary system; provisions which notionally protect suspects' rights (such as legal advice and electronic recording of questioning) tend to degenerate into contributions to crime control; and criminal justice is operationally biased against the socially and economically marginal.[61] The implications for law in policing are made clear: '[t]he assumption underlying the reforms of the 1980s is that police and prosecutors are susceptible to control by law and administrative guidelines, and that the practices of these agencies may be changed by tightening the law. . . . Our major finding is that these assumptions are wrong.' (Leng *et al.* 1992: 134–5).

This account, and particularly its presentation in the major work *The Case for the Prosecution* (McConville *et al.* 1991a) has been both influential and controversial. The debate around it provides an exception to Rock's assessment that British criminology 'has entered a newly quiescent phase: it is less strident, less acrimonious [and] less argumentative' (1994: xxii). The debate is fully rehearsed elsewhere (Dixon 1992; Noaks *et al.* (eds.) 1994: chs. 9–13), and it is appropriate here to comment on only some of the more prominent issues. Some critics misunderstood or failed to engage with the theoretical project underlying the empirical findings: the results varied from naïve empiricism to claims that the Warwick School constructed its case in a similar manner to the police (McConville and Sanders 1995: 194). Such criticisms were easily dealt with by reference to McConville *et al.*'s clear statement of constructionist methodology (1991a: 13; see Ch. 1, above). In many respects, the Warwick School's empirical findings are similar to those of our research. However, some significant differences in interpretation have emerged which overlie some theoretical differences, and it is on some of these, rather than the areas of agreement, that it is most worth focusing.[62]

First, we differ in our beliefs about how institutions change and can be changed. Central to the Warwick School's assessments is scepticism about the dependence of PACE on supervisory and manager-

---

[61] This is an attempt to summarize the main features of often complex, sometimes ambivalent, arguments which appear in slightly different form in various publications.

[62] Some more detailed differences are discussed in Dixon 1992; Noaks *et al.* (eds.) 1995: chs. 9–13.

ial control within police organizations. 'PACE's controls on the police are largely controls exercised by the police. There are . . . more laws for the police to conform to (which is why the police find PACE irksome) but they comprise, at best, due process ornaments on a crime control edifice' (Sanders and Young 1994b: 130). It is argued that custody officers are 'no safeguard for suspects' and, as an institution, 'do more harm than good' (Sanders 1991: 11–12; contrast Dixon 1992: 532–4). Miscarriages of justice, such as the Irish cases, 'not merely remain possible. . . . They would actually be more likely to happen now than before' (Sanders 1992: 26). Sanders accepts that police will remain committed to 'crime control' and argues that, rather than trying to inculcate due-process values (which assumes they can be 'successfully schizophrenic'), it is better that the criminal justice 'system as a whole should embody both goals but establish different agencies pursuing different goals. . . . The challenge would be to establish truly powerful defence agencies . . . which would engage . . . on equal terms' with police, prosecution, and prisons (1994b: 675–6; cf. 1994a).[63]

The accumulated research certainly illustrates the limited effectiveness of PACE's control mechanisms, including the routinization of supervisory controls (Dixon *et al.* 1990a) and the under-use of disciplinary sanctions (Clayton and Tomlinson 1992: 432; RCCJ 1993: 48). However, this must not be overstated: Maguire and Norris's research illustrates well its possibilities and limits (1992; 1994). As will be argued in more detail in Chapter 7, external controls and accountability mechanisms (desirable as they are) cannot be expected to be effective unless police organizations are themselves involved in the process of control: this is the clear lesson to be learnt from studies of regulation in other areas. Criminologists should hardly be surprised by evidence that punitive sanctions and deterrence tend to be ineffective. Change in institutions is a complex phenomenon: people may change their behaviour without being culturally or ideologically committed to such change, but values and beliefs may then shift too. At the same time, attempting to change by using highly prescriptive and punitive rules may well provoke cultural resistance rather than change. Compliance has to be sought by a blend of negotiation and imposition (cf. Goldsmith 1991; Ch. 7, below).

[63] Cf. Smith's critique (1995 and Ch. 1, above) of this crime control/due process dichotomy.

Secondly, I find difficulty in the way they attribute motive and intention: it oversimplifies complex and sometimes inscrutable processes.[64] An example is McConville *et al.*'s discussion of record-making requirements. They claim that '[e]very feature of policing which enters the official domain is grounded in and based upon a paper reality created to authenticate and legitimate the police version of events, and to insulate police action from critical review' (1991a: 98). In such attributions of motive, the use of the passive sidesteps the thorny issue of agency: whose designs and intentions are so deliberate and effective? In another context, individual responsibility is made clear: suspects are deterred from requesting legal advice by 'ploys' used by custody officers (1991a: 47–54; see also Sanders *et al.* 1989). In our observations of custody officers at work,[65] we encountered most of the activities which are categorized in this way. However, it seems to be misleading to call all of them ploys. Deliberate discouragement of requests is only one among several factors, including routine performance of familiar tasks without appreciating the suspect's dilemma, and well-meaning but inappropriate assessment that requesting legal advice would not be in a suspect's best interest. To acknowledge this, but to insist that custody officers 'are able and willing to be obstructive whenever investigating officers wish them and/or need them to be' (McConville and Sanders 1995: 199) is a circular argument which other researchers' observations of custody officers do not support (Brown 1997: ch. 10).

Perhaps the best example concerns the way in which custody officers accept suspects for pre-charge detention. It is frequently observed that custody officers do not examine the need for detention (as PACE requires), but instead ritually authorize the detention of almost everyone brought to stations under arrest (Dixon *et al.* 1990a: 129–30; Morgan *et al.* 1990: 17–20). McConville *et al.* explain this by arguing that 'custody officers, with some exceptions, readily go along with the wishes of the case officers because they are emotionally committed to believing their version of events, and because they share the instrumental goals of case clearance which underpins all policework.

---

[64] See Dixon 1992: 523–6. As Leng points out (1995: 206–7), our research report (Bottomley *et al.* 1991) was also guilty of this.

[65] Dixon *et al.* 1990a; Bottomley *et al.* 1991. This is the 'empirical grounding' which McConville and Sanders complain that my criticisms lack. If, as they say (1995: 202), their interpretation is based not on attribution of motive but on 'what custody officers told us in interview', then our data are inconsistent.

. . . [G]roup solidarity, police culture and professional friendships dictate mutual reinforcement of authority' (1991a: 42, 44).

However, initial detention decisions can be seen from a less one-dimensional perspective. As Morgan *et al.* point out, another factor is the bureaucratic reality in which it is easier and safer to accept a suspect into custody than to refuse (1990: 18–19). Procedures are designed for accepting suspects, not for turning them away. Once a custody officer begins to write a custody record (by asking the suspect's name, even though the item 'reasons for arrest' precedes this on custody records), the bureaucratic expectation is that it will be completed. In addition to cultural and bureaucratic factors, there are legal pressures to accept suspects. PACE has standardized custodial interrogation: it is expected that most suspects will be 'interviewed'; it is regarded as desirable that this should take place at a police station; and the pressure of custodial interrogation can be properly considered by officers in deciding to detain for questioning.[66] Consequently, officers can legitimately claim that the conditions of section 37 (which allows detention for questioning if this is necessary to obtain evidence by questioning) will almost always be met (Sanders and Young 1994b: 139). The importance of this example is that it is not simply countering a structural with a bureaucratic account.[67] Rather, it suggests that their structuralism tends to over-simplify complex processes which have several determinants. Elsewhere, Sanders points correctly to another example of the law's role: different criteria govern arrest and detention for questioning, so that 'arrests can lawfully be made in circumstances where custody officers should decline detention and negate the arrest'. Not surprisingly, custody officers resolve the dilemma by authorizing detention (1994a: 784).

Thirdly, they over-generalize about policing practice (Dixon 1992: 526–9). By contrast, I would suggest the need to appreciate differences which are: functional (notably the need to distinguish between the potential[68] for regulation of policing on the street and in the station); geographical (the significant variation in PACE practices both

[66] See PACE, s. 30(1); Code C (1995), s. 11.1; *Holgate-Mohammed* v. *Duke*, n. 3 above.

[67] Cf. Sanders' contrast between explanations in terms of 'bureaucratic pressures or societal structures' (1994a: 811).

[68] While the Warwick School usually stresses the unity of policing practice in the station and on the street (Dixon 1992: 526; Leng 1995: 211–12; Sanders 1994a: 793), Sanders (1993) accepts that regulation should focus on the station.

locally and regionally); and cultural (police culture is not immutable, and is characterized as much by division and sanction as it is by more familiar characteristics such as cynicism and suspicion). While it is certainly true that sociological explanation must look for patterns and generalities, it must also take account of discontinuities and inconsistencies. It may be that they are the pattern: that 'is not throwing up one's hands and saying "anything can happen in history", but, rather, finding the "reasons" of social unreason' (Thompson 1995: 303). To take one example from those discussed in more detail elsewhere (Dixon 1992), a notable feature of PACE has been its uneven usage across the country: for instance, very long pre-charge detention, investigative methods, and rates of requests for legal advice[69] all vary substantially (see sect. vi, above). This invites caution about suggestions that there has been a unitary, culture-based response to PACE and, possibly, that policing cannot be changed by legal reform. Identifying the factors which produce such variations will be an important task for future research.

There is also a tendency (linked to the pessimism to be discussed later in this section below) to take what may be 'worst cases' as representative. For example, Sanders and Young claim that '[m]any' officers evade the PACE restrictions on detention length by continuing to exploit the fiction of 'voluntary attendance', thereby 'driving a coach and horses through the attempt by PACE to regulate police–suspect encounters' (1994b: 142). They cite McKenzie et al.'s finding that volunteers constituted a third of suspects in three stations in one of the three forces which they studied (1990). Yet none of the (numerous) other studies of PACE (including The Case for the Prosecution) reported voluntary attendance to be common.[70] It may be (despite the considerable accumulation, PACE research has inevitably been geographically limited), but the available evidence does not suggest this.[71] Indeed, it might be regarded as surprising if this were to be the case: given the claimed amenability of PACE to police desires, there would seem little need for them to evade its provisions (Sanders and Young 1994a: 117).

---

[69] McConville and Sanders do not comment on these matters when brushing aside evidence of variations as sociologically insignificant 'minutiae' (1995: 197).

[70] Cf. Sanders and Young 1994b: 143: it is implied that 'volunteers' were common in one of their research areas, but no details are given.

[71] Sanders and Young (1994a: 117) look to Scotland for evidence of extensive use of volunteers, but fail to take account of the very different and specific conditions which produced this: see Curran and Carnie 1986 and Ch. 3, above.

In part, my unease with the Warwick School's portrayal of police stems from what is apparently a different experience of observing of operational officers.[72] Their attribution to police officers of commitment to crime control overstates, in my experience, the commitment of many to anything, and to understate the extent to which policing is a job, in which other more profane concerns (having a good time, getting to the end of the day/night without trouble, etc.) are as important.[73] There seems little room for the 'incompetence, shiftlessness, and boredom' which other observers have found characteristic (Smith 1995: 14). Just as Dennis Wrong wrote of the 'over-socialized conception of man in modern sociology' (Wrong 1961), here we have an 'over-socialized' conception of police officers.

Fourthly, their implicit history of criminal justice locates PACE as a part of a more general, relentless drift towards law and order in which law was 'increasingly brought into line with police practice, legitimating . . . dubious or illegal behaviour. . . . [L]aw reform has largely been a matter of empowering the police in relation to the suspect' (1991a: 200). This linear account understates the breadth of police powers before PACE, partly by overstating the real impact of judicial decisions such as *Holmes* (see 128 above). When PACE specified the length and conditions of pre-charge detention, this was experienced by many officers as a limitation of what had previously been a matter of their discretion (cf. Wolchover and Heaton-Armstrong 1996: 114–17).

To treat PACE as an unproblematic extension of police powers undervalues the pressures for reform in the interests of organizational (by which I mean structural, not just bureaucratic) efficiency (notably, a reduction in disputes about police evidence) which preceded it. One product of the largely unregulated conditions of pre-PACE detention and questioning of suspects was inefficiency in criminal justice (as defined by its managers) as police activities were increasingly challenged in court. At times, alleged confessions were contested so regularly that the utility of confessional evidence could

---

[72] Contrary to Leng's suggestion (1995: 208), my assessment is based not just on interview data, but also on extensive observation (for details, see Bottomley *et al.* 1991: ch. 1).

[73] NSW police have provided some notable illustrations: the Wood Royal Commission (see Ch. 5) has found that officers on surveillance duties in even very serious, high profile cases (such as the murder of a MP) have spent much of their 'working' day on the golf course and in other recreation.

be doubted and court delays were seen as a real problem.[74] Codification and clarification of both police powers and suspects' rights could be seen as being in the system's interest. This instrumental concern combined with 'liberal bureaucratic' (Bottoms and McClean 1976) opinion in sections of the Home Office.

Part of the problem here appears to be the continuing influence of oppositional politics understandably provoked by the excesses of Thatcherism which, in its application to the analysis of policing, too often resulted in slogans and inaccuracy (Dixon 1992: 529–31) and theoretical and political pessimism (Brogden 1992). According to Scraton, PACE was part of a legislative package which 'consolidated and embodied the Thatcherite programme within the law' (1987: viii). In a notable feat of hyperbole, Ewing and Gearty describe the PACE detention regime as 'a bureaucracy of incarceration beyond the dreams of the bleakest writer' (1990: 31; cf. Bridges and Bunyan 1983; Christian 1983; De Gama 1988). Such descriptions illustrate the common degeneration of analyses of Thatcherism into empty rhetoric and exaggeration. (Indeed, this degenerative, provocative effect was one of Thatcherism's more notable and regrettable achievements.)

Showing significant links to this approach, Sanders and Young present a functionalist account: the 'social and political discontent created within disadvantaged sections of the working class, and the homelessness and disorder thus generated, required the continued development of the "Strong State" of which PACE was part' (1994b: 129). The political implications of this are unclear: Sanders and Young discuss various means of bringing policing within the rule of law, but conclude by equivocally noting that 'we are not necessarily advocating rigorous due process laws aimed at controlling the police' (1994b: 156 note 118) because they recognize the conjunctural inevitability of 'relatively effective but repressive policing' (1994b: 156; cf. Smith 1995). They do not, course, accept it, regarding it as a 'fundamental undermining of the rule of law. . . . The task for those who believe in the rule of law must be to consider afresh the kind of society within which such a notion could be made meaningful for all' (1994b: 156). In the meantime, watch 'for a century or two before you cut your hedges down' (Thompson 1977: 266).

---

[74] See, e.g., the evidence given to the Royal Commission on Criminal Procedure by Mervyn Griffith-Jones and by the Senate of the Inns of Court and the Bar. However, Vennard's study (1984) suggests that this may be overstated.

Their analysis of police culture also raises difficulties of historical perspective.[75] No adequate history is available, but policing has changed considerably in recent decades, and police culture has changed with it. When officers speak of a new 'professionalism' in police work, their terminology may be questionable,[76] but they do refer to a perceptible shift. This must not be overstated: I do not (as has been suggested) argue that 'PACE has ushered in a new era of police professionalism' or new professionalism is 'sweeping though the ranks' (Leng 1995: 206, 208). It is altogether a more modest claim, one which accords with Maguire and Norris's perceptive discussion of detective work (1992).

They found that some detectives maintain 'the "traditional detective culture" of secretiveness, individualism and beliefs in the "Ways and Means Act" ' (1992: 41). This is not a homogeneous group: as well as the 'TJF dinosaurs',[77] it includes some more influential officers.[78] A larger group (a majority of Maguire and Norris's interviewees) displayed the effects of PACE as what the PSI called 'inhibitory' rules (Smith 1986): they 'followed the rules because they had to, rather than because they believed in them' (Maguire and Norris 1992: 42; cf. White's 'rule-appliers' 1972: 74–5). There has been no mass conversion to due process: as Matza comments wryly, '[p]olice professionalism includes many things, but rarely an unbounded faith in the preeminence of legality' (1969: 191). Indeed, it can be argued that such a change would be impossible (Smith 1995). However, alongside the grumbling acquiescence, there have been some attitudinal and behavioural shifts (Rose 1996: 216–17). As time passes, PACE becomes normality, rather than an imposition, particularly for younger officers (Maguire and Norris 1994: 82). This process of normalization has been noted in studies of the long-term effects of procedural reform in the United States:

virtually all of today's police interrogators have known no law other than *Miranda*. The discourse of *Miranda* has . . . by now suffused police consciousness so much that it has become second nature to them. . . . *Miranda*

---

[75] It is also subject to the theoretical criticisms noted in Ch. 1, sect. ii, above.

[76] For searching critiques of the concept of police professionalism, see Cain 1972; Manning 1977: 127–31; White 1972.

[77] TJF (The Job's Fucked) is a standard police colloquialism used by (and as an adjectival description of) cynical officers.

[78] One of the latter was a Detective Sergeant who realized that I had seen him leaving a cell after a 'welfare' visit to a suspect. His lengthy inquiry into 'what my brief was' provided a good insight into this group.

has helped generate a professional ethic of physical restraint in policing that has changed the social organization and moral ordering of detective work (Leo 1994: 114; cf. Skolnick 1994: 279).

For a time at least, constitutional requirements were 'normalized': while officers grumble about restraints upon them, 'underneath the veneer of "prime time" cop talk, one discovers that police at all levels demonstrate a routine awareness of procedural tasks that have become as much part of the job as using the radio or completing paper work' (Skolnick 1993: 196; cf. Orfield 1987; Walker 1993; Wasby 1976: 218; Ch. 7, below).

Maguire and Norris found that officers spend less time drinking, a change which only someone ignorant of police culture would underestimate (1992: 43). There are 'signs of genuine commitment among junior officers, in principle at least, to the new styles of working, centred around the concept of "crime management" ' (Maguire and Norris 1992: 42). Crucially, there has been a shift in evaluations of investigative methods: the tradition of arresting on hunches, interrogating, and giving weak cases 'a run' has been challenged by according status to officers who investigate and collect evidence more carefully before arrest, rely less on interrogation, find ways of working within the rules, and produce convictions which cannot be successfully challenged on appeal (Dixon et al. 1990a; Maguire and Norris 1992: 42). One has by no means replaced the other; but there is a significant tension which indicates shifts and variations within police cultures. It is such tensions within a changing institution which are among the most sociologically significant themes in this area. Obviously, this is not a declaration of a simple faith in 'progress'. It is not necessary to say that things have changed for the better to accept that there has been change: change requires recognition (not necessarily applause), so that analysis can address the new situation. The 'new professional' is not necessarily a 'nice cop' (contrast Williamson 1990b). He or she may be one who resents the restrictions of PACE (Maguire and Norris 1992: 42) and who ruthlessly exploits the resources which it provides, in very much the way that McConville et al. describe.

A similar account of American policing is provided in Richard Leo's work: he charts a shift in interrogation practice from coercion to 'manipulation, deception and persuasion' (1996a: 284; cf. 1992; 1994; 1996a; 1996b; 1996c). Simple moral judgements are unhelpful: while 'contemporary interrogation tactics are undeniably more

humane and civilized than the coercive practices they have replaced'
(Leo 1994: 117), they are ethically questionable, notably in their
reliance upon deception.[79] These tactics legitimate the use of interrogation and represent more effective modes of police power (Leo 1994:
115; 1996a: 285). Yet they also provide the possibility of their further
transformation by being opened to the influence of 'legal institutions,
professional standards and social norms' (Leo 1994: 117).

Again, developments are rarely linear: such change as there has
been can be reversed or undermined. The detrimental effect which
the 'war on drugs' has had on the 'legal professionalism' of US police
provides sad evidence of this (Skolnick 1993: 205; cf. id. 197–205;
1994; Allen 1996: 31–2, 36–47). Maguire correctly stresses that the
toe-hold of reforms in English policing is not firm: they are 'by no
means so well established, nor is the commitment to them by the
police service so secure, that one can be confident that the momen-
tum will be maintained. Priorities in the police service change
quickly, and are strongly influenced by the political "mood" ' (1994:
47). In 1993, the focus and priorities of the Royal Commission on
Criminal Justice's Report and the appointment of Michael Howard
as Home Secretary[80] ended a period during which the police had been
on the back foot from public and judicial criticism resulting from the
miscarriage of justice cases (Reiner and Leigh 1994: 100; Rose 1996).
In the mid-1990s, the message from government was approval of a
simple-minded 'toughness' on crime: '[i]f such messages were accompanied by firm statements of commitment to fair and open investigations and the protection of suspects' rights, there would be less reason
to fear backtracking by the police from commitment to investigative
reform. However, not only are statements of this kind virtually
absent, but specific proposals appear to send out quite opposite messages' (1994: 48; see also Maguire and Norris 1994; Rose 1996).
Among these, the restriction of the right to silence in 1994 (see Ch.
6, below) is emblematic. Maguire warned that it 'could have the
effect of encouraging a reversal of the move away from reliance upon

---

[79] See Skolnick and Leo 1992. Courts in England and Australia have disapproved
some deceptive tactics: see *Hawkins* (1994) 124 ALR 366; *Mason* (1988) 86 Cr. App.
R 349.

[80] He 'rapidly came to the conclusion that the balance in our criminal justice system had tilted too far in favour of the criminal and away from the rights of law abiding citizens' who were outraged and threatened by organized criminals, drug dealers,
and 'professional burglars who use the motorway system rather as the Vikings used
rivers to pillage and spread misery' (Howard 1995).

confessions as the central plank of investigative strategy. . . . [i]t returns the focus to the interview room, with all the attendant dangers of oppressive questioning, false confessions, and so on' (1994: 48; see Ch. 6, below). Encouraged by success in the long campaign against the right to silence, senior police officers in the mid-1990s launched renewed and increasingly sophisticated campaigns against the 'imbalance' of the criminal justice process (e.g. Pollard 1996).

Fifthly, the Warwick School's distinction between reform and more fundamental change is essentialist and leads to unnecessarily pessimistic political conclusions. In *The Case for the Prosecution*, McConville *et al.* explicitly distance themselves from reformism:

When we began our research we anticipated as one tangible product a set of reform proposals. . . . We do not, however, intend to pursue this kind of analysis because we think it counter-productive. . . . [R]eformist strategies embody . . . the false promises of liberal legalism. . . . Attention should be focused away from extending ineffective 'protections' to a captive and largely unchanging suspect population, and towards altering the composition of this suspect group, by removing the bias of state legality against the weak and powerless. Within the legal system a start in this can be made by overturning police culture, by redefining the policing mandate and by instituting new forms of accountability (1991a: 191, 205–6).

The hopelessness of this programme is soon acknowledged:

[i]t is, of course, hardly necessary to emphasise that there is no real possibility of major changes to police culture or forms of police accountability. Law reform does not have a dynamic separate from and independent of state interest. . . . [T]here is no constituency of any note for reform which involves real protections for vulnerable citizens or substantive changes to existing modes of policing. For the state, existing modes of law enforcement work (1991a: 208).

For those who might be surprised to learn that the scandals and embarrassments of the early 1990s constitute success, there is a neat functionalist answer: existing modes work 'even when they sometimes fail or encounter resistance: indeed, occasional failure and the possibility of resistance is a *requirement* for an effective *legal* system' (McConville *et al.* 1991a: 208, original emphasis).

This is not mere scepticism (contra Boyle 1993: 577): I find it impossible to interpret these statements as anything other than political pessimism which, if taken seriously, would entail either political abstention or engagement with elements of the social structure which are less rigidly determined. In fact, active involvement in reform activities by members of the Warwick School belies this position. Elsewhere, their concern has been to identify potential for progressive change (e.g. Sanders 1993; 1994a) and to engage in 'reform' by, for example, preparing research papers for the Royal Commission on Criminal Justice (Leng 1993; McConville 1992). To respond by claiming that they are proposing structural rather than presentational reforms (McConville and Sanders 1995) simply leads back to a problematic dichotomy which in turn is unhelpful in understanding and contributing to processes of change (Brown 1987: 263; Dixon 1992: 535–6), and which provides no criteria for distinguishing their reform proposals from those which leave 'the underlying structure of society (race, class, economic inequality, police culture, etc.) untouched' (McConville and Sanders 1995: 199). Despite their evident impatience with critics, their attitude to reform is ambiguous.

More specifically, their attitude to legal reform is particularly problematic. Sanders and Young's ambivalence (1994b) about the rule of law has been noted 162 above (see also Ch. 7, below). Elsewhere, McConville and Sanders insist that the issue is not whether rules work, but rather which rules will work (1995: 195). It is accepted that 'changes in legal rules have had some effect on the behaviour of state officials and that further rule revisions and fine tuning might have a wider impact . . . and that legality . . . may place limits on the extent of illegal behaviour by the police', but the distinction of this from 'meaningful legal regulation' is left unclear (Leng 1995: 211, 214). If this turns on the issue of whether the control is external rather than internal to the police organization (Sanders and Young 1994b: 130), first, objections to this view have been suggested above, and secondly, the special potency of some external (legalistic) reforms which they suggest such as a corroboration rule (McConville 1992) remains obscure, while others (such as making provision of legal advice automatic 'unless it is positively refused by the suspect', making improperly obtained evidence inadmissible, and a 'genuinely independent' complaints body: Sanders 1993: 105–7) develop, rather than diverge radically from, a broader reform movement.

In turn, such proposals sit uneasily with a deeper pessimism about law, in suggestions that using law as a tool of change is particularly prone to producing superficial and counter-productive results (McConville and Sanders 1995). Is this limited to 'liberal legalism'

(McConville *et al.* 1991a: 191) in which case their critique adds little to earlier work on the limits of law and legal-bureaucratic approaches (cf. Scheingold 1974; Ch. 1, sect. i, above) or is there an even deeper problem in the form of law? This case can be made (as feminist writers, notably Carol Smart (1989), have done) but it has to *be* made, explicated, and justified.

A better approach[81] to reform would be one which uses law pragmatically and tactically (e.g. Scheingold 1974: 5–9, 203–5) and is aware of the dangers of deflection, co-optation, and legitimization, but in which specific successes or failures are not considered in isolation: '[t]he point is that such developments have a multitude of effects. . . . And further that these effects are not fixed once and for all but are the subject of continuing struggles which seek to overturn, subvert or bypass a particular balance of forces . . . which in turn generate fresh struggles' (Brown 1987: 260). This is an argument for 'a conception of reform as partial, limited, continual struggle' (Brown 1987: 267) which must be pursued with a clear appreciation of the structuring forces which provide its context. Success in using law to change policing will depend, *inter alia*, upon the clear expression of desired standards, effective training, favourable political circumstances, the backing of effective sanctions for non-compliance, public knowledge of rights and police powers, and a skilful, adaptive use of legal techniques designed to maximize compliance.[82]

As McConville and Sanders suggest, it is at the theoretical and political level that, ultimately, differing interpretations of PACE must be considered (1995: 195–6). It was suggested in Chapter 1 above that the Warwick School's work was flawed by theoretical inconsistency in the use of the due process/crime control dichotomy.[83] There is a similar inconsistency in their attitude to reform activity.[84] Whereas in the first case the problem was a failure to apply their own theoretical insights in their analysis of data, here the problem appears to be an unwillingness to abandon a political position which, *inter alia*, their own subsequent writings show to be untenable. These problems are

[81] One which their own reform activities adopt.

[82] Dixon *et al.* 1989: 43; see Ch. 7, below. Contrary to McConville and Sanders (1995: 200), this is neither 'a plea for a new society' (welcome as that might be) nor 'a rejection of reform through law'.

[83] McConville and Sanders suggest that, in this respect, I unfairly quote conclusions and summaries which 'inevitably sound like overgeneralizations' (1995: 204).

[84] McConville and Sanders suggest that their critics are 'seriously confused' on this issue (1995: 199). If so, perhaps, the fault is not all the critics'.

not resolved by dismissing their critics *en masse* as completely wrong,[85] theoretically obtuse, conservative, and (worst of all) 'administrative' criminologists (McConville and Sanders 1995).

viii. PACE and the Judges

How have the courts responded to the new regime for detention and questioning introduced in 1986? Under PACE, confessions must be excluded from evidence if they are obtained by oppression or in circumstances rendering them unreliable. If challenged, the prosecution must prove beyond reasonable doubt that they were not so obtained (section 76). This replaces the specious 'voluntariness' test: a 'court will now look not so much at the state of mind of the suspect . . . but rather whether, in all the circumstances, the confession can safely be relied upon' (Russell 1990: 6). In addition, there is a discretionary power to exclude a confession (and other evidence) if its admission 'would have such an adverse effect on the fairness of the proceedings that the court ought not to admit it' (section 78(1)). While this discretion is wide, it must be related to the fairness of proceedings: it was not intended by the Government to be an exclusionary discretion inviting judges to consider public policy (Leigh 1986; Sieghart 1985). Also, a demonstration of unfairness and potentially adverse effect is not enough: the quoted subsection allows for degrees of unfairness and adverse effects which the court must assess. Common law powers to exclude are also preserved by section 82(3).

Given the courts' previous record, it was not surprising that, in predicting judicial use of these sections, most commentators were sceptical. Section 78 was said to be 'couched in language of the greatest opacity . . . almost a caricature' (Leigh 1985: 421). Baldwin was confident that those 'who demand evidence for use in court can be assured that breaches of the code (of practice) will not interfere with conviction' (Baldwin 1989: 164; see also Dixon *et al.* 1989: 201; Lustgarten 1986: 131). This was an expression of a broader concern that the regulatory strategy of PACE represented 'a wholesale retreat of the law' (Kinsey and Baldwin 1985: 96), the 'deregulation' of policing (Baldwin 1989: 161); 'a shift from policing under the law towards self-regulated policing' (Baldwin 1989: 164; see also Grimshaw and Jefferson 1987: 289; Baldwin 1985: 22). It was argued that PACE put

---

[85] McConville and Sanders acknowledge their work has 'significant shortcomings', but apparently these are not those discussed by their critics.

'all faith . . . in managerial control and internal disciplinary and supervisory systems' (Kinsey and Baldwin 1985: 96), leaving the police 'to get on with the job in the shadow of discipline rather than in the spotlight of the law' (Baldwin 1989: 162). As regards the contribution of the judiciary, the 'position . . . is bleak. Instead of acting as a check on executive action, judges . . . are likely to operate as agents of legitimation for policing by unbridled discretion' (Baldwin 1985: 27). These claims that something was being lost sat uneasily with Baldwin's own recognition that the courts had 'long abdicated from disciplining the police in the collection of evidence' (Baldwin 1985: 27).

Scepticism about the courts' likely application of PACE has proved to be overstated, and there has been considerable judicial activity in interpreting sections 76 and 78, as well as other sections of the Act and the Codes.[86] According to Feldman, the 'measured but active use which the English courts have made of sections 76 and 78 . . . has shown a surprising but welcome commitment to the idea of using evidential rules to protect rights' (1993: 246–7). Some reasons for this may be suggested. The context of judicial laxity towards police misconduct and willingness to extend the law was the lack of legislative attention to what were regarded as legitimate police needs. Once PACE provided an adequate framework for crime investigation, judges were more disposed to enforce rules of procedure. An example of this is the important case of *Samuel*[87] in which the Court of Appeal narrowly interpreted the power to delay a suspect's access to legal advice. This showed a willingness to recognize that the right to legal advice would be undermined if police were able to broaden the grounds for delay. Superintendents in our research area took note of this decision, recognizing that, in future, they would have to be chary in approving delays (Bottomley *et al.* 1991). Operational officers soon learnt the lesson, although for them the significant influence was not

[86] For surveys of the case law, see Berger 1990; Birch 1989; Feldman 1990; May 1990: ch. 9; Sanders and Young 1994a: 416–27; Wolchover and Heaton-Armstrong 1996: ch. 4; Zander 1995: ch. 8.

[87] [1988] 2 WLR 920. As Dennis points out (1993: 310), it may not be coincidental that Hodgson J, who gave the CA's judgment, had been the judge in the Broadwater Farm murder trial: he was very critical of the treatment of some suspects in that case. For details, see Rose 1992. In addition, Sanders and Young point out that, in *Samuel*, 'the solicitor concerned had recently been appointed a Crown Court Recorder and imputations of dishonesty or incompetence would have been extremely hard to substantiate' (1994a: 127).

Samuel, but its application in *Guest*, an unreported case in which a confession to the murder of a police officer was excluded, leading to the defendant's acquittal.[88] *Samuel* was reflected in the 1991 PACE Code of Practice C Annex B which specified the conditions under which access to legal advice can be delayed. Brown *et al.* found that the 'difficulty of satisfying these conditions is manifested in the almost total non-use of the delaying power' (1992: 9).

This tendency was encouraged by the wider political atmosphere during this period in which police investigations (including many conducted before PACE) came under severe criticism (Rose 1996: 8). The judicial and political rearguard action against acknowledging the wrongful convictions of the Guildford Four and Birmingham Six was finally abandoned. As evidence of police malpractice continued to emerge, it became unrealistic to claim that the problems were all in the past, that the 'Irish cases' were irrelevant products of the unreformed system. As well as examples of specific miscarriages of justice, there was evidence of systemic abuse in some areas (Kaye 1991). In this context, the courts could hardly let pass cases in which there was evidence of deliberate disregard of the Code such as *Canale*.[89] Among a series of breaches of PACE and Code C by Metropolitan Police Flying Squad officers (including a failure to carry out at least five post-charge detention reviews), that regarded as most serious concerned requirements for the recording of interrogations. The officers did not make a contemporaneous note or record the reason for not so doing in their pocket books. They gave as justification just two letters, 'BW', which they later explained stood for 'Best way'. This was provided on an Incident Report Form rather than in their pocket books, which were said to have been left at home or not issued, an explanation which the Court of Appeal clearly disbelieved. The Lord Chief Justice made his distaste clear:

In the officers' view the reason for failing to record the interview contemporaneously was that the best way was not to record the interview contemporaneously, which of course is no reason at all. [It] demonstrates a lamentable attitude towards the Police and Criminal Evidence Act and the rules made thereunder. . . . [The] rules were flagrantly breached.

The officers displayed a 'cynical disregard of the rules': these were 'flagrant . . . deliberate and cynical breaches'. He also took the

---

[88] This a significant example of how case law may be communicated to operational officers. For details of *Guest*, see M. Hunter 1994: 563–4.

[89] (1990) 91 Cr. App. R 1.

opportunity to comment on the incidence of other such cases: '[i]f, which we find it hard to believe, police officers still do not appreciate the importance of [PACE] and the accompanying Code, then it is time they did.'[90] Systemic problems exemplified by the numerous instances of cases involving the West Midlands Serious Crimes Squad led the courts to accept that the reliability of officers' evidence of admissions could be challenged by evidence of their previous malpractice.[91]

More significantly for present purposes, there have been cases in which officers thought that they were working within PACE, but the courts have disagreed, resulting in much-publicized acquittals. A crucial case was *Paris, Abdullahi, and Miller*, the 'Cardiff Three'.[92] In ruling that Stephen Miller's 'confession' should have been excluded from evidence as having been obtained by oppression in a 'travesty of an interview', the Court of Appeal stated that they were 'horrified' by the interrogation: '[s]hort of physical violence, it is hard to conceive of a more hostile and intimidating approach by officers to a suspect'.[93] Yet the investigating officers presumably thought their tactics were unexceptionable, in that the interviews were recorded on audiotape; Miller's solicitor sat passively through the objectionable interrogations; and, at trial, Miller's counsel did not have the judge listen to the crucial sections of the tapes. This was merely business as usual, the way that the criminal justice system was accustomed to dealing with this kind of defendant (three black men from Cardiff's 'notorious' Butetown).

The *Paris* decision achieved real impact on many police officers through its application in another murder case, *Heron*.[94] (This was perhaps not unrelated to the fact that, while the victim in the former was a drug-using prostitute, that in the latter was a 7-year-old girl). In *Heron*, the trial judge excluded the defendant's 'confessions' as

---

[90] Lane LCJ in *Canale*, n. 88 above, 4, 5, 6.

[91] *Edwards (John)* [1991] Crim. LR 372. Note, however, Pattenden's criticism (1992) of the narrowness of this decision.

[92] (1993) 97 Cr. App. R 99; see also Williams 1993.

[93] Taylor LCJ, at 103, 104.

[94] Unreported, Leeds Crown Court, 1 Nov. 1993. The decision in *Paris* came between George Heron's interrogation and his trial. Discussion of this case below also draws on George Heron's interview records, the report of an inquiry into the case (Northumbria Police 1994) and interviews with the principal investigating officer, Detective Superintendent John Renwick, and Heron's counsel, Mr Roger Thorn QC and Mr Robin Patton. I am grateful to them for their assistance, but the interpretation is mine.

oppressive because the investigating officers misrepresented the strength of the evidence against Heron, repeatedly asserted his guilt, asked offensive questions about his sex life, and suggested that it was in his own interest to confess. Heron had been questioned for a total of almost eight hours in five interviews over three days, during which he denied the murder some 120 times. As the Northumbria Police's report on the case commented drily, the decision 'undoubtedly came as a surprise to many of those involved in the case' (1994: 25). Here, the principal interviewers were a Detective Chief Inspector and a Detective Inspector (rather than the detective constables in the Cardiff Three case); again, a legal advisor[95] had been present during audio-taped interviews and made no complaint; and the tapes were 'vetted' by the CPS and a psychologist acting as an 'independent assessor'. Subsequently, the investigating officers' superior insisted that '[t]hese interviews were conducted properly by police in accordance with the Police and Criminal Evidence Act and much of the lines and styles used in the questioning of the suspect have been used over a number of years'.[96]

Decisions such as these add weight to Feldman's assessment that there is:

a shift away from the traditional notion that it is not the judiciary's job to discipline[97] the police. . . . This seems to reflect a growing disillusionment with police pretensions to professionalism and self-regulatory capacity, a determination to make a go of the balance struck by PACE, a renewed judicial commitment to rule of law principles and the ideal of legal accountability for the exercise of public powers, and the failure of other forms of legal control over the police (1990: 468).

There is a degree of wishful thinking in this assessment, but it is an important balance to the scepticism of the early commentators. Limited research has been done, and that depends largely on reported cases (Zander 1995: ch. 8). One study of a Crown Court suggested that trial judges were frequently excluding evidence under section 78,

[95] However, the judge strongly criticized the fact that this was not a qualified solicitor.

[96] Detective Superintendent Barry Stewart, head of Northumbria CID, quoted in *The Times*, 2 Nov. 1993, 3. See reports and letters in *The Times* on 23 and 24 Nov. 1993.

[97] Despite regular disavowal of such intent (e.g. *Oliphant* [1992] Crim. LR 40), 'there is, inescapably, a whiff of a disciplinary principle in the air . . . and this is not surprising in the light of some of the scandalous conduct which has come before the Court of Appeal' (Birch 1990: 330; cf. M. Hunter 1994: 563).

but noted the importance of specific local factors and suggested that, as so often in criminal justice, practice elsewhere is probably inconsistent (M. Hunter 1994).

There are several problems with judicial responses to PACE. First, access to the Court of Appeal continues to be difficult (Malleson 1993; RCCJ 1993: ch. 10; Sanders and Young 1994a: 433–45). Secondly, the concept of oppression under section 76 is unclear, while the courts' discretion under section 78 is broad: the requirement of breaches which are 'significant and substantial' leaves very considerable room to move.[98] Even if breaches pass this standard, they may not lead to the quashing of a conviction if the Court of Appeal considers no miscarriage of justice resulted.[99] The situation would be worsened by implementation of the recommendation by the Royal Commission on Criminal Justice that 'the Court of Appeal should not quash convictions on the grounds of pre-trial malpractice unless the court thinks that the conviction is or may be unsafe'.[100] 'Unworthy' defendants fare badly in the courts. The effects of *Samuel* have been reduced by a series of decisions in which it has been held that experienced criminals were not disadvantaged by the improper refusal of access to legal advice. Lane LCJ used one of these, *Alladice*,[101] as a platform for his opposition to the right of silence. Such decisions exemplify 'a proclivity towards announcing a healthy principle while, at the same time, proceeding to disregard it under a camouflage of legal niceties' (Zuckerman 1991: 499; cf. Sanders and Young 1994a: 461 and the discussion of McBarnet in Ch. 1, above).

Of most concern is the failure of the courts to develop clearly either principles or detailed guidance to the police about what is expected of them. Traditional judicial techniques sometimes can lead judges not to look beyond the instant case, or to provide otherwise narrow rulings. Taylor LCJ's criticism of police in the *Heron* case (English 1993) was hardly justified following his failure in *Paris*[102] to

---

[98] e.g. *Walsh* [1989] Crim. LR 822; *Matthews* [1990] Crim. LR 90.

[99] Criminal Appeal Act 1968, s. 2(1). Some 10% of unsuccessful appeals are dismissed under the 'proviso' (Malleson 1993: 11). See, e.g., *Cox* [1993] Crim. LR 382.

[100] RCCJ 1993: 172; see the withering critique in Michael Zander's dissent (RCCJ 1993: 233–5) and Sanders and Young (1994a: 426).

[101] (1988) 87 Cr. App. R 380; see also *Dunn* [1990] Crim. LR 572; *Dunford* [1991] Crim. LR 370; *Oliphant* [1992] Crim. LR 40. The irony of assertions that it was abuse of the right to legal advice by professional criminals which made abolition of the right to silence necessary should not be lost: see Ch. 6, below.

[102] N. 92 above, 103.

go beyond quoting a dictionary in defining 'oppression'.[103] Investigating officers were (as the officer who carried out the subsequent inquiry into *Heron* commented) left in 'a sea of uncertainty'.[104] This lack of judicial guidance encourages police cynicism about the justice process.[105] The courts must recognize that at the heart of the issue is a fundamental difference between what has traditionally been accepted as appropriate interaction between investigating officer and suspect in the interview room and that between prosecutor and defendant in the court room. Electronic recording means that interrogations are available for the court to hear (and perhaps see). Procedure in the police station and at the subsequent trial can no longer be distinct (Feldman 1990: 470–1). Restrictions on cross-examination by prosecutors have little value if the court is presented with an audiovisual record of cross-examination and vigorous interrogation by police officers. The seemingly inevitable outcome is the dominance of curial standards.[106]

The implications of this have to be faced squarely. As regards trial judges, the result may be to deepen the gap between the rhetoric of legality and the practical administration of law. As for police, uncertainty in what they should do is unhealthy for crime investigations. It may be helpful to take a specific example. How, for example, *should* the officers who 'interviewed' George Heron have proceeded? His apparently untrue statements (about his knowledge of the dead girl and his movements on the night of the murder) to officers carrying out house-to-house enquiries provided good grounds to treat him as a suspect, even though these would later appear to be probably innocent products of George Heron's personality and his cultural wariness of police.[107] Those suspicions had to be discounted, or

---

[102] Similar difficulties have been encountered in cases involving undercover police operations: the condemnation of deceptive conduct and the extension of PACE to cover 'interviews' between police officers and suspects in this situation requires fundamental re-examination of undercover tactics: cf the unsuccessful prosecutions of Keith Hall and Colin Stagg, reported in *The Times*, 15 Sept. 1994.

[104] Northumbria Police 1994: 9. The phrase is John Baldwin's: see Baldwin 1992c: 13; cf. Zuckerman 1991: 500.

[105] See comments by Birch on *Kingsley Brown* [1989] Crim. LR 500 at 502 and Zuckerman 1991: 498–9.

[106] For a discussion by the Victorian Court of Criminal Appeal of cross-examination and audio-visual evidence, see *Pritchard* (1990) 49 A Crim. R 67.

[107] Heron lived in Wearside's Hendon, 'an area which suffers from chronic social and economic deprivation' (Northumbria Police 1994: 13). For the best account of relations between police and people in these post-industrial 'domestic disaster areas', see Campbell 1993: xii and *passim*.

resolved at a level which a court would accept as proof of guilt beyond reasonable doubt. While other kinds of evidence had to be investigated,[108] Heron had to be questioned. Again because of personal and cultural factors, he was difficult to interview. In context, academic cynicism about an officer's argument that it is 'rather difficult to establish the truth by pussyfooting about' is unhelpful.[109] While the investigating officers may be criticized for 'a poorly conducted interview',[110] it is easier to point to faults than it is to say what should have been done. (The need to shift attention to what constitutes good policing will be revisited in Ch. 7, below). For all the commitment to 'investigative' and 'ethical' rather than 'persuasive' interviewing,[111] officers faced with similar investigative duties will face a dilemma of where 'the line is to be drawn between proper and robust persistence and oppressive interrogation'.[112] The case may suggest a fundamental problem in using confessional evidence: the point at which interrogation could become effective in difficult cases is also the point at which its results become potentially unreliable.[113] If interrogation were to be severely restricted or abandoned, the implications for change in substantive criminal law[114] and in the development of other (possibly more reliable but much more intrusive) investigative methods need to be squarely faced.

[108] The notable lack of such evidence in this case provides ammunition for those who favour a corroboration rule (cf. McConville 1992).

[109] Detective Superintendent Stewart, quoted Sanders and Young 1994b: 151.

[110] Tom Williamson's report on the questioning of George Heron in Northumbria Police 1994, app. L, 56.

[111] See Home Office circs. 22/1992, 'Principles of investigative interviewing' and 7/1993, 'Investigative interviewing: national training package'; Central Planning and Training Unit, 'A guide to interviewing'; Gudjonsson 1992; Memon et al. 1995; Shepherd (ed.) 1993; Williamson 1993.

[112] Mitchell J's ruling on voir dire in Heron, n. 94 above. Cf. Baldwin 1992c; 1993b.

[113] As suggested in interview about Heron by Roger Thorn QC; cf. Sanders and Young 1994b: 153. However, please note Baldwin's scepticism regarding the value of vigorous, 'persuasive' interrogation (1992c: 8–9; 1993a), about which police officers have often deluded themselves. As Baldwin also makes clear, 'difficult', resistant suspects are a minority.

[114] See Sanders (1993) on the consequences which tight restriction of interrogation might have for substantive criminal law (e.g. requirements of mens rea) and evidence (the balance and standard of proof) which might encourage the least desirable characteristics of contemporary 'technocratic' justice (Dixon 1997). It is surprising to see Sanders arguing that '[c]onsideration should be given to putting the onus in relation to intent on the defendant'. To suggest that this 'would change the emphasis from the police trying to construct their case . . . to the suspect constructing theirs, returning some control to suspects' (1993: 106) seems rather sanguine.

Characteristically, the Royal Commission on Criminal Justice did not deal with the implications of a shift to curial standards for investigative practice. Rather than attempting to define the limits of proper police questioning,[115] it limited itself to recommending the inculcation of interviewing skills by way of training,[116] repeating the reference to a dictionary definition of oppression, and expressing satisfaction with 'the way in which section 78 has worked in practice' (RCCJ 1993: 58). The Commission did not bother to explain how it was working; nor, apparently, was it even aware of the contradiction between this and its recommendation on limiting appeals against convictions involving pre-trial malpractice (Sanders and Young 1994a: 426–7). Despite the evident problems for police, legal advisers, and suspects in knowing what is and is not acceptable in police questioning, the Commission's report 'makes no real contribution to resolving these difficulties' (Baldwin 1993b: 1195).

[115] As, e.g., the Law Society's evidence suggested it should do. Michael Zander has defended the Commission's approach, arguing that the line between acceptable questioning and oppression can be drawn only retrospectively by the courts, and that reliance must be placed on effective training (Clarke 1993).

[116] 1993: 13. As Maguire and Norris (1994: 81) point out, training is an ineffective stategy if the policing organization remains otherwise unchanged.

5

The Legal (Non)Regulation of Custodial Interrogation in New South Wales

> You're not meant to detain anyone for questioning, but it always happens. It's the best way to do it: get them back on your turf.[1]

> I . . . reject the findings of the High Court of Australia.[2]

This Chapter deals with the ways in which New South Wales police have conducted criminal investigation without legislative authority to detain suspects between arrest and charge. Research for it began as a study, by observation and interviews, of policing in NSW. However, the principal focus is not on the police: the need soon became clear to locate policing in the legal environment provided by the courts and the legislature. As will be seen, New South Wales provides a strong case for McBarnet's argument that attention should be shifted from those who administer the law to those who make it (1976: 199; see Ch. 1, above).

New South Wales provides a useful comparison to England and Wales. Building on a shared legal foundation (see Ch. 2, above), the jurisdictions have developed distinctively. There are notable contrasts in the roles of the senior judiciaries and of government. In Australia, criminal law and procedure are primarily matters for the states and territories, although there is a body of federal law dealing with offences (notably, illegal drug importation) relating to matters within the Commonwealth's responsibilities. Federal law is increasingly significant as a model for reform and codification in the states and

---

[1] A NSW police officer in an interview.
[2] From an internal memorandum supplied by Detective Sergeant Liversidge to Internal Affairs investigation of conduct criticized by the High Court in *Foster* (1993) 113 ALR 1, quoted NSW Ombudsman 1996: iv.

territories. A notable example is the Commonwealth's regime for investigative detention.[3]

i. Detention and Questioning of Suspects in Australia

In Chapter 4, the English judges' development of the common law in order to allow police to detain and question suspects was discussed. Such judicial activism was, eventually, resisted in Australia: a clear distinction between the approaches of the senior English and Australian judges was emphasized in *Williams*, a Tasmanian case which went on appeal to the High Court.[4]

It is important to set this case in the context of debate in Australia about police 'verbals' (the fabrication of confessional evidence) which has been more frank, widespread, and public than in Britain. This is not to suggest that police verballing has not been an issue in Britain.[5] However, there was generally an official refusal to admit to the existence of a serious problem. For example, the Royal Commission on Criminal Procedure expressed the issue as being the inaccurate recording of confessions, rather than their fabrication (McConville and Baldwin 1982: 296). Concern about the *Confait* case (which sparked the Commission's establishment: see Baxter and Koffman 1982) centred on the under-protection of vulnerable suspects, rather than the source of the incriminating material in their false confessions. In the parliamentary debates on the PACE Bills, much more attention was paid to search powers (particularly those which might affect powerful élites such as doctors and lawyers) than to interrogation. In the early 1990s, publicity given to miscarriages of justice in the Guildford Four and the Tottenham Three cases and to the activities of the West Midlands Serious Crimes Squad focused attention on verballing (Kaye 1991; Rose 1992). However, the official response

---

[3] See Crimes (Investigation of Commonwealth Offences) Amendment Act 1991. This was the product of the Review of Commonwealth Criminal Law Committee (Gibbs 1989) and, more distantly, the Australian Law Reform Commission's report on Criminal Investigation (ALRC 1975). The latter's grasp of principles and understanding of practices makes it an impressive document.

[4] (1986) 66 ALR 385.

[5] Indeed, the General Council of the Bar commented in 1973 on 'the current prevalent mischief of the invention of false oral admissions' (quoted, McConville and Baldwin 1982: 296).

has been to claim that verballing is a problem of the past which has been solved by PACE and tape-recording.[6]

By contrast, in Australia, concern about verballing has a considerable history (Finnane 1994: 84–92), including public campaigns, gaol 'strikes', and other political activity (Zdenkowski and Brown 1982: 337–51; Anderson 1992). The term 'verbal' is common currency in popular discourse. According to Roger Rogerson, sometime star of the NSW Police and now disgraced, 'verbals are part of police culture. Police would think you're weak if you didn't do it.' Like 'loading-up' suspects, 'it was all done in the interests of . . . truth, justice and . . . keeping things on an even keel, and keeping the crims under control' (quoted, Anderson 1992: 43). In Australia, the emphasis has been so much on verballing that the question of the accuracy of confessions which undoubtedly were made has been neglected. More generally, confessions have dominated debate to the exclusion of other issues and problems in investigative activity, for example in identification and search and seizure (Bradley 1989: 202). Verballing has been publicly acknowledged in a series of official reports[7] which influenced judicial perceptions and policy at the highest level. In the High Court, Deane J stated: 'In the context of modern inquiries and experience, . . . it would be to fly in the face of reality to deny that there is, throughout this country, a real and substantial risk of fabrication of police evidence of the making by an accused of oral admissions in the course of interrogation while held in police custody'.[8] Legislatures were slow to respond: the reform of criminal investigation was described by Kirby J as 'a graveyard of reports' (1979: 628). It is in this context that, in a number of cases, the High Court explicitly tried to deal with the problems of verbals by tightening requirements for the admissibility of confessional evidence (Aronson and Hunter 1995: 212–14; ch. 11; Brown *et al.* 1996: 197–234; J. Hunter 1994). While the specific issue in *Williams* was the legality of pre-charge detention, Williams' lawyer insisted that the case 'has always been about "verbals" . . . it arose because of the need to seek . . . legal solutions to the factual difficulties and injustices caused by alleged police verbals' and the need 'to limit the opportunities during

---

[6] As suggested in Ch. 4, 'confessions' made away from interview rooms continue to cause problems (Moston and Stephenson 1993a; Leng 1994a).

[7] e.g., Fitzgerald 1989: 206–7; Beach 1976: 83–7; Lucas 1977 14–15.

[8] *Carr* (1981) 81 ALR 236, at 251.

which disputed confessional evidence could come into existence'
(Kable 1989: 17, 25, 27).

The origin of the case was Williams' arrest following three burglaries in May 1984 in Tasmania. He was arrested at 6am and taken
to a local police station. Detectives were called in, and they took him
back to their 'headstation', where they interrogated him between
1.10pm and 8.30pm about the offences for which he was arrested and
about numerous other thefts and burglaries. He was taken to court
the next day at 10am. Echoing the common law, Tasmanian legislation required police to take arrested people to a magistrate 'as soon
as is practicable' and 'without delay'. At his trial, Williams pleaded
guilty to the three burglaries for which he had been arrested.
Confessional evidence relating to the other charges was excluded as
having been obtained during unlawful detention.

The case eventually reached the High Court. By a majority of four
to one, it was decided that Australia should not follow the developments in English common law associated with *Dallison* v. *Caffery*
and *Holgate-Mohammed* v. *Duke*[9]. The case provides an important
example of the High Court's liberalism (expressed here, ironically, as
legal conservatism), its willingness to break with English precedent,
and its impatience with the failure of Australian legislatures to
address crucial issues. Mason and Brennan JJ reviewed the English
case law unfavourably, making oblique criticism of the English judiciary's attitudes towards civil liberties and the extension of police
power.[10] They preferred to affirm a line of Australian authority (consistent with nineteenth-century English common law) which made
clear that the common law provided no power to detain for questioning and that the desire to question arrested suspects did not justify delay in bringing them before a justice.[11] It was made clear that
the purpose of arrest was to bring the suspect into the judicial system. This was to be done without delay, so any time spent in custody before a court appearance should be minimal.[12] There was no
power to arrest for questioning and, consequently, there was no
power to detain in custody for questioning.[13] The duty of the police

[9] [1964] 2 All ER 610; [1984] 1 All ER 1054; see Ch. 4, above.
[10] N. 4 above, at 398–400.
[11] Mason and Brennan ibid 396–8. On the definition of a 'justice' for this purpose,
see *Zorad* (1990) 19 NSWLR 91; Crimes Act 1900 (NSW), s. 352.
[12] Wilson and Dawson JJ, n. 4 above, at 405.
[13] Mason and Brennan JJ, ibid, at 397.

was simply what the law required: to bring an arrested person before a magistrate without delay. The justification for this approach was made clear. The limitation of a fundamental right of personal liberty needed clear authority which was available neither in case law nor in statute. If the law was to be changed, this was the legislature's job: 'it is not for the courts to erode the common law's protection of personal liberty in order to enhance the armoury of law enforcement . . . the right to personal liberty is not what is left over after the police investigation is finished'.[14] It was the legislature's responsibility both as a matter of constitutional principle and because it 'is able—as the courts are not—to prescribe some safeguards which might ameliorate the risk of unconscionable pressure being applied to persons under interrogation'.[15] These safeguards could include 'precise limits' on detention length.[16]

Mason and Brennan JJ recognized the problems which their interpretation of the law created for the police: the 'jealousy with which the common law protects the personal liberty of the subject does nothing to assist the police in the investigation of criminal offences'. None the less, there was no great judicial enthusiasm for legislation: they thought that officers could do their job within the existing law which was 'by no means incompatible with efficient investigation'. As the law stood, the police required as much evidence to arrest suspects as they did to charge them, so custodial interrogation was unnecessary.[17] Wilson and Dawson JJ were wary about the possible direction of reform:

legislative change should take place against the background of the common law as it has been understood in this country, which has consistently viewed detention for the purpose of investigation as an unwarranted encroachment upon the liberty of the person. The experience of the common law . . . should be borne steadily in mind if and when the changing needs of society appear to require statutory adaptation of the existing rules.[18]

In form, *Williams* was a conservative decision, simply restating 'principles of long standing' in the common law. However, 'it brought

---

[14] Mason and Brennan ibid, 398, 400.   [15] Ibid. 398.
[16] Wilson and Dawson JJ, *ibid*. 410.
[17] *Ibid*. 398, 400–1. The need to respond to this reassertion of the common law's traditional evidentiary requirement for arrest has been consistently ignored in subsequent debates and legislative changes which have simply assumed that arrest can be made on the lower level of suspicion approved in *Hussein* v. *Chong Fook Kam* [1970] AC 942.
[18] N. 4 above, at 410.

home that those principles had, for all practical purposes, been forgotten. For years, police had been interviewing suspects in detention which was in fact unlawful' (Hidden 1993: 38).

A minority judgment by Gibbs CJ took a very different approach, effectively arguing that Australia should follow the guidepost set by *Dallison* v. *Caffery* which he approved as stating the common law position.[19] While agreeing with his colleagues that arrest and detention merely for questioning were unlawful, Gibbs argued that the police could investigate and interrogate suspects who had been arrested properly on reasonable suspicion before taking them to court. He would have allowed the police considerable discretion in the length of such detention: the determination of what was 'reasonably practicable in a particular case is a question of fact',[20] and various considerations such as time, place, and conditions of arrest, and the availability of justices, transport, and escorting police were relevant. Also, the police could (indeed, should) take 'time to make such inquiries as are reasonably necessary either to confirm or dispel the suspicion upon which the arrest was based', including questioning, searching premises, testing alibis, and conducting identification parades. In his view, police could detain suspects for a period which 'is reasonably necessary to make inquiries to enable charges to be laid, to prepare the necessary papers and to bring the arrested person before the justice'.[21] Given judicial unwillingness to interfere with executive determinations of reasonableness in such matters (Ryan and Williams 1986), this would be to provide the police with considerable freedom of action.

Despite the Chief Justice's dissent, the majority's judgments left little room for doubt that detaining a suspect between arrest and charge for investigative purposes was unlawful. However, the court was less successful in clearly spelling out either what the police could lawfully do in pre-trial criminal procedure or what the consequences of unlawfulness should be. The following sections deal with these problems in turn.

ii. Authorization and Police Practices

A key difficulty was the partial nature of the law's regulation of police practices in this area: 'the Australian common law cases do not

[19] *Ibid.* 389.   [20] *Ibid.* 388.   [21] *Ibid.* 389.

prohibit questioning or investigation of the arrested person by the police. Rather, they prohibit delaying the processing . . . of the accused person . . . for these purposes' (NSW LRC 1990: 12). They dealt with delay, when the real issue was the use to which delay was put. In *Williams*, the High Court conceded that the police could properly investigate (including interrogation of suspects) in the period following arrest, so long as the court appearance was not thereby delayed: '[w]here no delay is involved, there can, of course be no objection to the occasion of the arrest and subsequent detention being used for the purpose of further investigation of the offence in question or, for that matter, any other offences'.[22]

This approach was consistent with the authorities; but the judges failed to comment on the artificiality of this distinction between (acceptable) interrogation which did not delay a court appearance and (unacceptable) detention for questioning. The problem had been illustrated well by Cox J when *Williams* was considered by the Tasmanian Court of Criminal Appeal:

The test seems to be whether or not the arrest or detention is used solely or primarily for the purposes of furthering police inquiries. If on the other hand those inquiries occur not by virtue thereof but concurrently with a detention of which the prime purpose is the bringing of an alleged offender before the court to be dealt with according to law for the crime for which he was arrested, the detention remains lawful. Even if the making of such inquiries has the effect of delaying his presentation to the court it does not automatically follow that his detention will then become unlawful.[23]

Apparently, according to this account, two processes can be concurrent, but one can last longer than the other. In the High Court, Gibbs CJ tried to distinguish between a detention for the purpose of bringing a suspect before a magistrate (which incidentally included questioning) and a detention 'solely for the purpose of questioning'. He commented that the 'line may be a fine one, as it often is when a discretion has to be exercised in sensitive matters'.[24] The problem is not that the line drawn is 'fine', but that it is drawn on a fictional subject—a quite unrealistic account of the process in which police construct cases.

---

[22] Wilson and Dawson JJ, *ibid.* 405, affirming *Bales* v. *Parmeter* (1935) 35 SR(NSW) 182. The High Court muddied the water somewhat in *Michaels* by suggesting that a suspect could be detained for questioning so long as there was 'no undue delay' [1995] ALJR 686, at 688.

[23] Quoted, Mason and Brennan JJ, n. 4 above, at 394.   [24] *Ibid.* 390.

These judicial formulations suggested an artificial distinction between crime investigation and the preparation of papers for court, as if different officers would carry out each task, so that the former could be regulated by the time consumed by the latter. It also showed a failure to understand the central role of questioning in modern criminal procedure. Questioning is a distinct (and not merely secondary) part of the process. Its principal function is to raise the reasonable suspicion on which a suspect is arrested to the level of a *prima facie* case required for a charge. There is no recognition[25] that police practice has produced a distinction between reasonable suspicion and a *prima facie* case. Such factors must be set in a broader context of judicial attitudes to criminal procedure. As in England and Wales, a striking aspect of many Australian cases is the judges' limited understanding of policing practices or of the nature of custodial interrogation.[26]

In particular, there is inadequate discussion in the cases of in-station charging and police bail. Some judges fail to appreciate the significance of the fact that, as a result of shifts in the allocation of functions between courts and police in the mid-nineteenth century (see Ch. 4, above), the significant point of charge is not at the court, but in the police station. Charges are laid and bail determinations are made by police officers. The duty to bring arrested suspects to court is effectively (and legally) made redundant if they are charged at and bailed from the station. While bail has been regulated by statute, in-station charging developed informally in Australia (as in England). Despite its great importance (not least as the point at which the Judges' Rules and NSW Commissioner's Instruction 37.14 require that questioning of the suspect must normally cease), judges usually ignore it. For example, only Mason and Brennan JJ even mentioned that Williams was charged on the evening of his detention.[27] Gibbs CJ[28] seems to confuse the procedures for charging with those for adoption of an interview record by a suspect (by answering questions from a senior officer about the way in which it was made). The role of in-station charging was not investigated or explained.[29]

[25] Contrast *Holgate-Mohammed* v. *Duke*, n. 9 above.
[26] The High Court judgments of Deane J provided a notable exception: see e.g. n. 8 above.
[27] N. 4 above, at 392.   [28] *Ibid*. 387–8.
[29] The issue was considered in *Burns* (unreported 256/1987, 19 Aug. 1988), when the NSW Court of Criminal Appeal made clear that the duty to bring an arrested person before a Justice was not satisfied by the actions of an officer at a police station

Similarly, there is no acknowledgment in the cases of the significant role played by interrogation in both discovering and clearing up offences other than those for which the suspect was arrested (Ericson 1981a: 156–7; McConville and Baldwin 1981: ch. 8). This takes two forms. First is the use of holding charges: an example is *Kushkarian*,[30] in which a suspect was arrested for possession of a firearm, then detained for twelve hours while police investigated an armed robbery. As Aronson and Hunter comment, such holding charges allow 'the police to flaunt the spirit of the law (that is no arrest until a reasonable suspicion has been established and no arrest for questioning) whilst keeping within the strict letter of the law' (1995: 226–7; cf. CJC 1994: 667; Teh 1973: 23–9). The NSW Court of Criminal Appeal's failure to comment adversely gave implicit encouragement to the practice.

The other involves secondary investigation of other offences. The courts' ignorance in this instance may be more understandable: there have been no Australian studies such as those in the United Kingdom, notably by Bottomley and Coleman (1981), who reported that one-quarter of detected crimes were cleared up by being 'taken into consideration'. For some offences, the proportions were high: 39 per cent of burglaries and 58 per cent of frauds and forgeries. More than half of offences taken into consideration were unknown to the police until admitted by suspects under interrogation (Bottomley and Coleman 1981: 99; see also Brown 1991: ch. 6; Steer 1980: 69, 75). It could be said that factors such as this are irrelevant to judicial reasoning; and, in formal terms, they are. In other terms, they are significant, in showing many judges' lack of real understanding of the processes on which they were adjudicating.

Such ignorance seems to be genuine, however unfortunate. Elsewhere it was apparently feigned, in a familiar judicial deceit. A good example is a trial judge's 'improbable description of a police interrogation room resembling rush hour at central station' (Brown *et al.* 1996: 196) in comments to a jury discrediting a defendant's claims of mistreatment:

The accused has firmly told you he was taken in handcuffs to the police station and there handcuffed to a chair. . . . Suppose they did that. . . . How would it look if the Police Minister made a call and saw the accused sitting

who, in form, takes a quasi-judicial role in making a bail determination. See also *Zorad*, n. 11 above; Crimes Act 1900 (NSW), s. 352.

30 (1984) 16 A Crim. R 416; cf. *Heiss* (1992) 111 FLR 362.

there handcuffed? Suppose the Superintendent had called? Suppose an undoubtedly honest police officer had walked in? Suppose a member of the public had walked in . . . suppose a newspaper or television reporter had walked in? What then, if the police had left a man handcuffed like that?[31]

Similarly, judicial hostility to cross-examination of police officers about verballing has been notorious. Misrepresenting both reality and the burden of proof, some judges 'used to tell the jury that their task was to decide which side was telling the truth, and that they would have to ask why police officers with unblemished records would jeopardise their careers to secure the conviction of this one accused' (Aronson and Hunter 1995: 347; cf. Freeman 1988: 104).

There is comparable disingenuity in judicial comments on the purposes of custodial interrogation. Suspects may well be surprised to learn that detention for questioning is for their benefit, providing them with an 'opportunity to dispel' police suspicion 'before being taken before a Justice'.[32] In McKinney and Judge, the NSW Court of Criminal Appeal accepted uncritically the evidence of police witnesses that they thought it 'proper and permissible, as a matter of fairness, to give the accused an opportunity, if he wished, to answer the relevant allegations before the formal step of being charged and placed before a Justice was taken'.[33] In turn, this reflected a Commissioner's Instruction which states that, in deciding whether or not to charge, 'it may only be fair to question the arrested person . . . to confirm or dispel the suspicion on which the arrest was based'.[34] The reality, in which police questioning is used to confirm suspicions, harden case theories, and construct cases (McConville et al. 1991a), does not intrude into such accounts. Until McKinney and Judge and Foster,[35] Australian judges generally failed even to acknowledge the significant role which is played by unlawful detention in a system constructed around interrogation and guilty

---

[31] Quoted by Brennan J in Duke (1989) 63 ALJR 139, at 142. Suspects frequently claim that they were drug-affected or handcuffed during interrogation. For another example, see Zorad, n. 11 above, at 94. On the potential unreliability of confessions made by heroin-affected suspects, see Murakami et al. 1996.

[32] Wood J in McKinney and Judge (No 2), 60335/92 and 60342/92, unreported, 6 Sept. 1993, NSW Court of Criminal Appeal, 37.

[33] Ibid. 32.

[34] #1.10 (since 1995, #37.14). A long, inglorious history of claims that custodial interrogation is 'really in the suspect's interest' could be written. See, e.g., Holmes [1981] 2 All ER 612, at 613; I. D. Packman, letter to Criminal Law Review, 1959, 675; Holdane-Mohammed v. Duke [1983] 3 All ER 526, at 534.

[35] See Judge and McKinney (No 1) (1990) 49 A Crim. R 7 and Foster, n. 2 above.

pleas.[36] While these cases marked a significant shift in the High Court's approach, state judges at trial and appeal level continued to take a narrow view structured by crime control commitment.

As suggested in Chapter 3, courts have often turned a blind eye to detention masquerading as voluntary attendance (Odgers 1990: 225; see also Aronson and Hunter 1995: 220–6). Even in cases where compulsion was made evident, some resultant rulings seem to have a weak grasp on reality For example in *Van der Meer*, a majority of the High Court found that suspects were not in custody despite having been at a police station for most of a day, during which they attempted to exercise their right to silence, were subjected to persistent interrogation, had some clothing removed for forensic examination and testing, were put on an identity parade, and were confronted with the victims of the alleged crime.[37] The court's teleological view was that there was no detention because the suspects had 'consented' to assist the police with their inquiries and, according to the police, were free to leave prior to the point when they were formally arrested.[38] The majority agreed with the trial judge's determination that reasonable suspicion did not arise until inquiries were well under way. In so doing, they arguably exaggerated the level of suspicion required for arrest[39] and ignored the possibility that the detention followed an unlawful 'constructive' arrest. As will be shown below, such decisions encourage police to evade legal controls by disguising arrests as voluntary attendances.

iii. Consequences of Unlawful Police Investigative Activity

A crucial weakness of the majority's judgments in *Williams* was their failure to make clear what the consequences of unlawful detention

---

[36] A rare exception was Murphy J, who argued that there were 'very powerful social considerations in deterring police from unlawfully imprisoning persons' and that confessional evidence so produced should generally be excluded: *Cleland* (1982) 151 CLR 1, at 16–17. See also Deane J in *Cleland*, at 26.

[37] (1988) 35 A Crim. R 232; Wilson, Dawson, and Toohey JJ at 249. These events are described by Deane J (at 260–1), who criticized the investigation in very strong terms.

[38] Similarly, see *Boucher* (unreported 11/A59/1993, 28 July 1993) in which the Supreme Court of Tasmania approved the fiction that a suspect in a rape case would not have been prevented from leaving a police station where he was being questioned as a 'volunteer' if he had chosen to do so.

[39] *Hussein* v. *Chong Fook Lam*, n. 17 above.

should be, so leaving their rhetoric about unlawful detention lacking teeth.[40] Typically, Mason and Brennan JJ approved Deane J's statement in *Cleland* that 'the restraints which the law imposes on police powers of arrest and detention [should] be scrupulously observed', but did so as a general exhortation rather than as guidance to trial judges on how deal with the matter in practice.[41]

Establishing that detention was unlawful is only one step in challenging the admissibility of a subsequent confession. The court must then be persuaded to use its powers to exclude evidence. Until 1995, this could be on grounds of involuntariness, unfairness, or public policy.[42] Although illegality was doctrinally distinct from involuntariness, the defence might attempt to convince the court that a confession obtained during unlawful detention was involuntary.[43] If this was done, the confession must be excluded. If not, the judge has discretion to exclude on grounds of fairness or public policy. In 1995, Commonwealth and NSW law was reformed in almost identical Evidence Acts, products of the move towards a codified national law of evidence. The voluntariness rule is replaced by mandatory exclusion for 'violent, oppressive, inhuman or degrading conduct' or threats.[44] Secondly, a confession must be excluded 'unless it is unlikely that anything said or done by the interrogator adversely affected the truth' (Aronson and Hunter 1995: 345). The unfairness and public-policy discretions are given statutory form.[45] Significant as the Evidence Acts are, it seems inevitable that concepts and understandings developed under the common law will continue to be highly influential.

In the traditional formulation which has a long history in the common law,[46] voluntariness entails 'the exercise of [a suspect's] free choice to speak or remain silent'.[47] Brennan J insisted that '[p]roperly understood, the requirement of voluntariness gives extensive

[40] See Vincent J in *Narula* (1986) 22 A Crim. R 409, at 412; Freckelton 1987.
[41] N. 4 above, at 395, quoting *Cleland*, n. 36 above, at 26.
[42] These are merely some bare bones of a complex body of evidence law: see Aronson and Hunter 1995: ch. 11; J. Hunter 1994.
[43] Formally, the burden of proof lies on the prosecution. In Australia, this is only the civil test of probability, not, as in England, beyond reasonable doubt. In both countries, a significant burden in practice falls on the defence.
[44] s.84. This draws on PACE, s. 76, and international human rights provisions (Aronson and Hunter 1995: 345).
[45] Ss. 90 and 138.   [46] *Ibrahim* [1914] AC 599.
[47] Mason CJ in *Van der Meer*, n. 37 above, at 238.

protection to a person from whom a confession is sought'.[48] Indeed, if one took at face value rulings that a confession is involuntary if it is the product of sustained pressure,[49] the results of many interrogations would be excluded. Custodial interrogation itself might be impermissible: 'the whole point of interrogation is to persuade someone to tell the police things which, usually, he does not wish to tell them. "Manipulative tactics" are . . . required of the police if interrogation is to be allowed at all' (Sanders 1987a: 210). The central weakness of 'voluntariness' is that it was a test which was developed in the context of public confessions to magistrates, not those in 'the closed environment of police custody' (J. Hunter 1994: 17). However, only very rare judges followed the logic of this, questioning the voluntariness of any confession obtained while the suspect was in detention, 'lawful or otherwise'.[50] Instead, 'voluntariness' degenerated into narrow and often artificial concern with the effects of threats and inducements (J. Hunter 1994). Despite arguments for its potential recuperation,[51] the reality is that the criterion of 'voluntariness' is as inappropriate in the context of police interrogation as it is in the context of detention (ALRC 1987: 87–8; Ch. 3, above). In practice, voluntariness has been a limited, artificial, and psychologically discredited test. One benefit of video-recording is that it has made some judges see for themselves how suspects who 'volunteer' confessions are actually treated in interrogations. An early example was *Pritchard*, in which the Victorian Court of Criminal Appeal expressed distaste for some fairly standard techniques, such as the interrogating officer's 'undisguised ridicule and derision' of the suspect.[52] None the less and symptomatically, the conviction was not disturbed.

Judges have discretion to exclude evidence of a 'voluntary' confession if 'it would be unfair to the accused to admit the evidence because of unreliability arising from the means by which, or the circumstances in which, it was procured'.[53] It might well be expected that unlawful detention would be sufficient to establish unfairness,

---

[48] In *Duke*, n. 31 above, at 141.

[49] One of the conditions cited by Dixon CJ in the leading Australian statement of principle, *McDermott* (1948) 76 CLR 501, at 511.

[50] Murphy J in *Cleland*, n. 36 above, at 15.

[51] In *Foster*, n. 2 above, McHugh J attempted to rehabilitate voluntariness, shifting attention away from the investigating officer's actions to more subjective issues of the likely effects of, e.g., threats on specific suspects (cf. J. Hunter 1994).

[52] (1990) 49 A Crim. R 67, at 77.

[53] Dawson J in *Cleland*, n. 36 above, at 36. See now Evidence Act 1995, s. 90.

but this view has been taken only in minority judgments by the more critical, such as Deane's forceful statement in *Duke*.[54] For reasons discussed below, the important case of *Foster*[55] does not provide an exception. In practice, 'the courts have been very conservative in exercising the discretion'.[56]

In *Foster*, the majority of the High Court began what may be the development of a significant fairness discretion.[57] Deane J's increasing influence was shown by the majority's acceptance of the argument which he had made in *Duke*.[58] Unlawful detention, particularly if combined with unrecorded interrogations and denial of access to rights such as legal advice, should make judges consider excluding evidence on grounds of unfairness. Unfortunately, *Foster* is marred by familiar weaknesses of case law as a vehicle for reform which are discussed below. The opportunity for a clear, comprehensive statement about the relationship between voluntariness and the exclusionary discretions was missed. Despite the unprecedented attention which has been paid to police interrogation by the High Court in recent years, 'this has certainly not produced any great clarification of the law. Issues remain unresolved, doctrines imprecise, new uncertainties introduced' (Odgers 1990: 220).

Australian courts developed a further discretion to exclude illegally obtained evidence, including confessions, on grounds of 'public policy'.[59] This is important in allowing explicit consideration of factors other than those relating to the individual suspect or defendant. Perhaps not surprisingly, the courts have been very cautious in using this discretion: from the beginning, it was made clear that it would be 'most exceptional' to exclude on public-interest grounds a voluntary confession which it would be fair to use against the defendant.[60]

---

[54] N. 31 above, at 144; see also Odgers 1990: 232–3.   [55] N. 2 above.

[56] Odgers 1990: 229. For examples of the many cases in NSW and other states in which unlawful detention did not lead to the exclusion of evidence obtained therein, see *Narula*, n. 40 above; *Foster* (unreported, NSW Court of Criminal Appeal, 60614/1990, 19 Aug. 1991); *Salihos* (1987) 27 A Crim. R 319; *Mansted* (unreported, NSW Court of Criminal Appeal, 60253/1989, 20 Oct. 1989); *Ainsworth* (1991) 57 A Crim. R 174; *Hawkins* (unreported NSW Court of Criminal Appeal, 92/1992, 17 Dec. 1992).

[57] N. 2 above.   [58] N. 31 above.

[59] *Bunning* v. *Cross* (1978) 141 CLR 54; *Cleland*, n. 36 above. Please note the High Court's vigorous interpretation in *Ridgway* (1995) 129 ALR 41 in which a 'controlled importation' of heroin was castigated as 'grave and calculated police criminality'. See now Evidence Act 1995, s. 138. Contrast English common law in *Sang* [1980] AC 402.

[60] Gibbs CJ and Wilson J in *Cleland*, n. 36 above, at 9. Note, however, the minority opinions that confessions obtained during unlawful detention should normally be excluded: Deane J at 27, Murphy J at 16.

While *Foster*[61] is more positive, the reluctance of trial judges to exercise the exclusionary discretions (and of state appeal courts to interfere therewith) is likely to continue to be a significant problem (J. Hunter 1994: 19–20).

iv. Unlawful Detention and (Non)Exclusion

The law of evidence provides judges with an apparently powerful set of devices for scrutinizing the confessions presented to them and, by implication, influencing the conduct of police investigations. The reality is that powers to exclude are rarely used: this section discusses some of the reasons for this and some of the methods of avoiding the exclusion of confessions obtained during unlawful custody.[62]

Trial judges who misunderstand the approved relationship between law's rhetoric and its practice have been corrected by their superiors. For example, trial judges in Victoria who followed the approach of Murphy and Deane JJ by excluding confessions obtained during unlawful detention[63] were brought into line by the Full Court of Victoria's sharp disapproval after police protests.[64] When *Williams* reached the High Court, Wilson and Dawson JJ[65] criticized trial judges in some earlier (unspecified but presumably the Victoria) cases who had exercised the public-policy discretion for having 'perhaps a somewhat expansive view of the effect' of *Bunning* v. *Cross* and *Cleland*. The clearest direction to trial judges was given by Gibbs CJ, who reaffirmed his view in *Cleland* that the public-policy discretion would appropriately be used only in 'a most exceptional case'.[66] He criticized the trial judge in *Williams*, who, in excluding the confessions on grounds of public policy as well as of fairness, had been 'significantly influenced' by Deane J's opinion in *Cleland* (Kable 1989: 27). The result was to leave the High Court majority's criticism of the English judicial approval of custodial interrogation looking somewhat hypocritical. The Australian judges condemned the practice of unlawful detention without providing inferior courts with directions on how to deal with it. In these circumstances, it is hardly

---

[61] N. 2 above; see also Deane J in *Pollard* (1992) 67 ALJR 193, at 208.

[62] This sect. tends not to respect the doctrinal distinction noted above between mandatory and discretionary exclusion: in practice, decisions on voluntariness or under the Evidence Act 1995, s. 84, are every bit as discretionary as the others.

[63] For references, see Bradley 1989: 199, n. 97.

[64] *DPP's Reference No 1 of 1985* [1984] VR 727; Willis and Sallman 1985: 219.

[65] N. 4 above, at 409.   [66] *Ibid.* 390.

surprising that unlawful detention rarely leads to the exclusion of confessions.

Few trial judges need to be persuaded not to exclude evidence, despite the fact that the public-policy discretion's main purpose is to prevent police illegality being encouraged or approved by judicial acceptance of illegally obtained evidence.[67] Ideologically, the issue is 'the threat which calculated disregard of the law by those empowered to enforce it represents to the legal structure of our society and the integrity of the administration of criminal justice'. It is argued that, in some circumstances, the courts must exclude illegally obtained evidence:

In part, this is necessary to prevent statements of judicial disapproval appearing hollow and insincere in a context where curial advantage is seen to be obtained from the unlawful conduct. In part it is necessary to ensure that the courts are not themselves demeaned by the uncontrolled use of the fruits of illegality in the judicial process.[68]

However, most judges give preference to more profane policies. During its investigation of criminal procedure, the NSW Law Reform Commission

received many submissions from members of the judiciary which emphasized that there is a compelling community interest in ensuring that accused persons who are factually guilty are found guilty by a court. Thus, there is a real reticence about excluding probative evidence at trial in order to 'punish' the police for some wrongdoing (NSW LRC 1990: 17).

Such sentiments were strongly held by judges who felt that the law on custodial interrogation (as stated in *Williams*) was contrary to established, unproblematic practice[69] and that the anomaly would, sooner or later, be rectified by providing police with statutory power to detain for questioning. In the meantime, 'guilty' suspects should not profit from the combination of the High Court's liberalism and the state government's procrastination.[70] If, as a result, judicial

---

[67] *Cleland*, n. 36 above, Gibbs CJ at 7, Deane J at 20.

[68] Deane J, in *Pollard*, n. 61 above, at 207. The significant influence of American judicial reasoning is evident here.

[69] See, e.g. comments in *Curry and Curry* (NSW CCA, unreported, 15 Feb. 1991).

[70] Cf. *Walsh* NSW Court of Criminal Appeal 60257/89 (unreported, 18 Oct. 1990), in which Samuels JA (after criticizing police for 'irrelevant and tedious' arguments about the law making their job impossible) considered that 18 hours 'was capable of amounting to an unreasonable delay', but saw no reason to exercise the fairness discretion, and did not consider public policy.

rhetoric sounded 'hollow and insincere' and the courts were 'demeaned', *tant pis*.

These policy considerations surface only rarely in judgments. They do so when judges weigh the seriousness of the defendant's alleged offence against the unlawful detention: the 'more serious the crime committed, the greater is the public interest in securing a conviction, and the more likely that a court's discretion will be exercised against excluding the evidence unlawfully obtained'.[71] From a trial judge's viewpoint, this is, no doubt, mere common sense. From the viewpoint of an officer investigating a serious offence, it is an invitation to justify means by ends. From the viewpoint of a person suspected of a serious crime, judicial protection shrivels when it is most needed.

The broader context is that of judicial politics. At the level of the High Court, there is increasing attention to the implications of commitments to protect human rights and a willingness to acknowledge and attempt to counter police malpractice. Lower in the judicial hierarchy, the picture is often very different. Zdenkowski and Brown argue that 'a key factor' in the longevity of police verbals 'in the face of official law reform commission condemnation and increasing exposure . . . is the support given by appellate courts, and the NSW Court of Criminal Appeal in particular, which sustains the practice by accepting such evidence' (1982: 345; cf. Finnane 1994: 89). They quote Street CJ's withering response[72] to an argument that uncorroborated, unsigned records of interview should not be admitted into evidence:

I find this submission unpalatable and wholly unacceptable. It denigrates, absolutely unjustly and unjustifiably, the police force of this state. This community can count itself fortunate to be served by a body of men and women who comprise a police force of which it can be justly proud and of which we are indeed proud. In the face of difficult odds and often, alas, badgered by ill-informed and unfounded criticism, our police have a fine record of achievement in preserving for the citizens of this state the civilities that are necessary for life in a law abiding community. To suggest the evidence of all police officers is inherently suspect to such an extent to require corroboration is, in my view, offensive and wholly without justification (quoted, Zdenkowski and Brown 1982: 345).

---

[71] *Ainsworth*, n. 56 above, at 187: note the assumptions that a crime had been committed and that the defendant was responsible, which are, of course, exactly the issues which the trial is meant to determine. See also *Hawkins*, n. 56 above.

[72] In *Burke* NSW Court of Criminal Appeal (unreported, 30 Nov. 1978).

In a case soon afterwards, the Chief Justice complained about defence challenges to the admissibility of evidence which wasted the court's time in 'tedious and pointless fishing expeditions'.[73] Hindsight challenges this view: the investigating officers in the case were Roger Rogerson and his well-known colleagues in the Armed Hold-Up Squad. Such attitudes to evidence of malpractice (and public knowledge thereof) in state courts make quite clear the commitments and priorities of many judges at this level.[74] Such scepticism about defendants' complaints was widespread in the criminal process: a Crown Prosecutor opined complacently that 'at seasons, to allege beatings, threats and concoction [of confessions] is so much the vogue that a genuine complaint may fail to win due regard. . . . The underworld may be ever keen to shake confidence in police evidence; but there can be too much smoke for any natural fire' (Kidston 1960: 369–70). In fact, defendants often do not challenge police evidence for fear that doing so would be 'balanced' by admitting evidence of their previous convictions. Ironically, when defendants and appellants are emboldened by public controversy about police practices associated for example with Royal Commissions, they are dismissed as voguish expediency.[75]

In practice, police in states like New South Wales which did not provide statutory detention powers were able, despite *Williams*, to carry on unlawfully holding suspects for questioning in the knowledge that courts would rarely penalize them.[76] (In any event, most suspects plead guilty without contesting police evidence.) This might seem an ideal situation for the regular application of the exclusionary discretions, but this has not happened.[77] Even when confessions are excluded, it may be done without suggesting any criticism of the police or their masters. For example, in a case in the NSW District

---

[73] *Lattouf and Carr* NSW Court of Criminal Appeal 287/1978 (unreported, 13 Mar. 1980).

[74] There are, of course, exceptions. Compare, for example, Kirby J's dissenting judgment commenting on police verbals with the views of the majority in *Savvas* (1991) 55 A Crim. R 241, at 269. Symptomatically, Kirby has since left the NSW Court of Appeal for the High Court.

[75] e.g. from that on the *Studley-Ruxton* case in 1954–5 (Kidston 1960; Finnane 1994: 168–9) to the Royal Commission into the NSW Police Service in the mid-1990s.

[76] Queensland and Western Australia share NSW's lack of post-arrest detention legislation. A variety of schemes has been adopted in the other jurisdictions: for details, see Aronson and Hunter 1995: 227–34; CJC 1994, app. 10.

[77] See cases cited in n. 56, above. Courts may take a stricter attitude when the suspect is a juvenile, e.g. *McKellar v. Smith* [1982] 2 NSWLR 950.

Court in 1996, the judge felt 'bound to apply the law as it has been authoritatively enunciated' by the High Court, but said that he approached the task of excluding 'with no enthusiasm' and 'no little reluctance' even though the officers had not merely acted unlawfully, but had done so under the instructions of the Crime Commission.[78] There has been a longstanding consensus between judges and police (and most lawyers) that, so long as they behaved 'reasonably', police could detain and question suspects before charge. In his dissenting judgment in *Williams*, Gibbs CJ was providing a clear expression of that consensus.[79] In New South Wales, 'regularly, records of interview conducted some hours after arrest were received into evidence, without question as to the lawfulness of the detention of the accused at the time of the interview'.[80]

The origins of this approach require more detailed examination than is possible here, but they can be traced at least to the 1930s, when Jordan CJ was noting critically that in NSW 'the same strictness has not been observed with respect to the interrogation by a police officer of persons who have been arrested . . . as now obtains in England'.[81] By 1947, 'much prominence' was being given to questions of police powers to detain and question, and Jordan's concern had grown: it appeared that the common law was

being disregarded, and that arrested persons are being taken, not to a magistrate to be charged, but to a police station, where they are questioned by the police, sometimes for many hours, in the hope of extracting from them something that can be used in evidence against them. . . . Indeed, there seems to be a growing impression in police circles that so long as a constable, after making an arrest, gives the usual caution, there are no limits to the extent to which he may go, short of violence, threats, promises, or lies, in endeavouring to extract admissions from his prisoner. If these methods are tolerated,

[78] The judge commented: '[i]n ten years, I don't think I have *ever* excluded a record of interview': NSW District Court, unreported, 27 Feb. 1996 (case #27, Dixon and Travis 1997). After arrest, the defendant had been taken to his flat for two hours (in clear breach of Commissioner's Instructions 2.07 and 37.06), where he was questioned, before being taken (following Crime Commission guidelines, but contrary to the Crimes Act 1900, s. 352, and Commissioner's Instructions 2.07) to the Commission for electronically recorded questioning. See 209–10 below for discussion of the Crime Commission's role.

[79] N. 4 above. See Lee AJ, quoted by Wood J in *McKinney and Judge* (No 2), n. 32 above, at 31; see also *Henning* NSW Court of Criminal Appeal 406/1988 (unreported, 11 May 1990), at 60.

[80] Wood J in *McKinney and Judge* (No 2), n. 32 above, at 36.

[81] *Bales* v. *Parmeter*, n. 22 above, at 189. His contrast with English practice was overstated: see Ch. 4, above.

it is a short step to the moral, if not physical, tactics of the Gestapo and the Ogpu.[82]

Jordan CJ would have excluded a confession obtained from the defendant during unlawful detention. However, his was a minority judgment: the majority were concerned less with traditional common law than with fears about crime which are now familiar. The law had to be adapted because it

> has been recognised that in modern conditions when . . . many dangerous criminals are wont to conceal their activities with great subtlety, . . . it is necessary in the interests of the public that the guile of these directing minds should be combated, so long as the Judge is equipped with the power of controlling the exuberance of over-zealous or unscrupulous police officers, of which fortunately there are not many.[83]

As long as suspects were cautioned and treated fairly, their voluntary confessions made during custodial interrogation could be given in evidence against them.[84] Soon afterwards, the solicitor who instructed the prosecution in *McDermott* can be found informing a police audience that the decision (usually cited for its foundational definition of voluntariness) should remove doubts about their power to question detained suspects before taking them to magistrates (Cleland 1949). As Finnane suggests, 'the decision was relayed by a court official in ways which mandated a police freedom to interrogate in custody' (1994: 90). By 1989, the Chief Justice could say, without apparent awareness of self-contradiction: '[a] person who has been arrested must be taken before a magistrate without delay. The arrested person may be questioned and then charged.'[85] By then, this approach had become so institutionalized that an authoritative study of the developing case law in New South Wales could conclude that 'the discretion to exclude unlawfully obtained confessions seems to have become a dead letter' (Odgers 1990: 227; cf. Bradley 1990).

---

[82] *Jeffries* (1947) 47 SR(NSW) 284 at 288–9. See also Mann CJ's comments on the 'growing evil' of custodial interrogation, quoted *The Argus Law Reports*, 22 Dec. 1936, 519; cf. Finnane 1994: 86.

[83] Davidson J at 302; see also Street at 313 on the interests of the community in crime investigations not being 'unduly hampered'. The 'dangerous criminal' in the case was a 69-year-old man who had been gaoled for 7 years for offences of consensual homosexual intercourse with an 18-year-old. As Jordan CJ remarked, even the police officers' own account of the interrogation 'makes ugly reading' (*ibid*. 294). For more recent concerns about dangerous criminals, see Twining 1973 and Ch. 6, below.

[84] Jeffries, n. 82 above; Street CJ, at 309–14.

[85] Gleeson CJ in *Hull* (1989) 16 NSWLR 385, at 390.

When trial judges refuse to exclude evidence and when appeal judges decline to disturb such refusals, various devices are available. It may be argued that it is impossible to distinguish the effect of a disputed confession from that of other undisputed evidence, such as that of witnesses. In such circumstances, appeal courts will be reluctant to overturn a jury's decision.[86] Secondly, it may be argued that exclusion is unnecessary because the defendant was not disadvantaged by any illegality.[87] The dangers of such an approach are illustrated by *Percerep*, in which the Victoria Court of Criminal Appeal suggested that failure to provide a suspect with his statutory right of access to legal advice could be treated as insignificant because he 'showed an acute awareness of his right to refuse to answer questions, a fact which might be thought to raise the question of whether . . . even had he been given a proper opportunity to communicate with a solicitor, it is likely that he would have been in any different position'.[88]

In cases following *Williams*, the NSW Court of Criminal Appeal used traditional techniques of legal reasoning (notably the law–fact distinction) in order to avoid interfering with trial judges' rulings. Similarly, appeal judges insisted on their limited capacity to overturn discretionary judicial decisions. A good example of these processes is *Kyriakou*. Here, the court refused to interfere with the trial judge's finding of fact that a confession was made voluntarily, even though the defendant claimed that he had been assaulted, had suffered heroin withdrawal, and had been promised heroin. He had certainly been in custody for several hours before being charged. The breadth of the discretion reserved by the law–fact distinction is illustrated by the statement that, while it would not interfere with findings of fact, it would intervene 'in order to prevent injustice' if 'there is no evidence to support a finding, or if a trial judge has applied wrong principles, or if the evidence is all one way'.[89] In this case, the trial judge (and, by its lack of criticism, the Court of Criminal Appeal) treated the legality or illegality of the detention as being almost irrelevant

---

[86] See Russell 1990: 2 and e.g. the Chamberlains' case: Brown *et al*. 1996: 296–307; Young 1989.

[87] See e.g. *Henning*, n. 79 above, at 60.

[88] (1993) 65 A Crim. R 419, at 431. The decision is very similar to the much-criticized decision of the English Court of Appeal in *Alladice* (1988) 87 Cr. App. R 380 and its progeny: see Ch. 6, below. See also *Bishop* NSW Supreme Court (unreported, 8 Sept. 1994).

[89] (1987) 29 A Crim. R 50, at 57 (Yeldham J); see also Loveday J in *Foster*, n. 56 above, 7; and Brennan J in *Duke*, n. 31 above, at 142.

(Odgers 1990: 228). The supposedly authoritative and crucial decision in *Williams* was simply brushed aside by judges who evidently preferred the minority view of Gibbs CJ to that of the majority. Despite what was virtually a challenge to its authority, 'the High Court refused special leave to appeal' (Odgers 1990: 228).

Trial and state appeal court judges usually choose one of two methods of dealing with arguments that unlawful detention should lead to evidentiary exclusion: either they refuse to find involuntariness or to exercise the exclusionary discretions, or they simply refuse to treat pre-charge detention as illegal.[90] An example of the latter is *Mansted*,[91] in which a suspect was arrested at 7.30am, interrogated until 11am, and taken to court at 1pm. While the prosecutor conceded that 'technically' the detention was unlawful, the trial judge (even after considering *Williams*) concluded that it was lawful. This result can be achieved either by doing no more than asserting the detention's legality[92] or by minimizing the illegality. For example, in *Zorad*, the NSW Court of Criminal Appeal rejected a complaint of unlawful detention, treating as relevant only the period before interrogation commenced (a delay 'of little over an hour' which 'could hardly be regarded as serious') and ignoring the subsequent three hours and fifty minutes between the beginning of questioning and the time of in-station charge.[93] Similarly, in *Henning*, the suspect was arrested at 2.00pm (after being at the station 'voluntarily' for two and a half hours), interrogated between 4.32pm and 7.42pm, charged at 11pm and taken to court at 10am next morning. The court suggested that only the period between the arrest and beginning of questioning was relevant to the question of illegality.[94]

In exercising the exclusionary discretions, judges have frequently treated the police officers' motivation and knowledge of the law as being crucial. For example, in *McKinney and Judge*,[95] three suspects were detained without charge for lengthy periods. Under interrogation by different officers, each 'confessed' to having fired the single shot which seriously injured a man during an attempted robbery. They claimed that the confessions were fabricated. One was acquitted after showing that he had scratched on the interrogation

---

[90] Good examples of reaching the same destination by different routes are the respective decisions of Samuels J and Gleeson CJ in *Walsh*, n. 70 above.

[91] N. 56 above; see also *Ainsworth*, n. 56 above.

[92] e.g. Gleeson CJ in *Walsh*, n. 70 above.

[93] N. 11 above, at 99.

[94] N. 79 above, at 60.

[95] N. 32 above.

room table a statement that he was innocent and was not answering questions.[96] Here, the Court of Criminal Appeal refused to overturn the trial judge's decision not to exclude McKinney's and Judge's unlawfully obtained 'confessions'. A claim was accepted that the police did not realize that their actions were unlawful: they held a genuine but mistaken belief that detention for questioning was lawful. This somewhat unusual insistence on the relevance of subjective attitudes to legal obligations posed problems for defence counsel, who had to try to elicit from the officers a clear statement of what they considered the law to be. Given that a central problem in such officers' attitudes to the law is their failure to regard it as a significant factor in decision-making, it is hardly surprising that the results were inconclusive. This provided room for the court to decide that, being neither deliberate nor reckless, the officers' breach of the law should not affect the admissibility of evidence.[97]

Given the guidance provided by courts (see sect. ii above) and by Commissioner's Instructions (see sect. vi below), officers' uncertainty about the law might be understandable. However, a further step was taken in *Curry*, which suggests that breach of the law must be not just conscious and deliberate, but also 'defiant' before it will have legal consequences. Here, the officer who detained a suspect for twelve hours was aware that he had no legal power to do so, but 'truly believed it was a proper exercise of his duty to investigate the facts fully . . . before charging the accused' and was not acting 'deliberately in defiance of the law'.[98] The way in which Victoria, Tasmania, and the Northern Territory responded legislatively to *Williams* by permitting detention between arrest and charge for a 'reasonable time' means that such arguments will continue to be made. The lack of clarity of the Northern Territory's statutory power led the Supreme Court in *Heiss*[99] to refuse to exclude evidence of an

---

[96] This acquittal was somewhat shadowed by a subsequent judicial comment that to suggest the confessions were fabricated was 'Gilbertian': see Lee J, quoted with approval by Wood J in *McKinney and Judge (No 2)*, n. 32 above, at 26. Note also how evidentiary rules operated against the defendants: 'the jury was not entitled to have had regard to the interview of Judge when considering the case against McKinney and vice versa', *ibid*. 16; cf. J. Hunter 1994: 117.

[97] See also *Salihos*, n. 56 above, at 332; *Narula*, n. 40 above, at 415.

[98] N. 69 above. Cf. the US Supreme Court's unfortunate development of a 'good faith' exception to the exclusionary rule in *US* v. *Leon* 468 US 897 (1984) and *Massachusetts* v. *Sheppard* 468 US 981 (1984).

[99] (1991) 101 FLR 433; see also the Court of Criminal Appeal's decision in *Heiss*, n. 30 above.

unlawfully detained suspect's confession which was made to officers who were acting in good faith. Similar responses are invited by the jurisdictions (the Commonwealth and South Australia) which provide power to detain for a specific period discounting 'time-outs', the calculation of which is sure to become a matter of dispute.

v. The High Court and the Future of Judicial Supervision of Custodial Interrogation

McKinney and Judge appealed successfully to the High Court. But they did so not on the ground of the unlawfulness of the detention: this and the lower courts' effective dismissal of *Williams* were all but ignored. Instead, the High Court developed another tool against unreliable confessions by requiring a warning to be given whenever confessions are not electronically recorded or otherwise corroborated.[100] Despite the controversy which this decision provoked, the court was dealing with an issue which has in practice been (or soon will be) resolved by the introduction of electronic recording of interrogations in most jurisdictions, and the statutory inadmissibility of most non-recorded confessions (Dixon 1991d; Dixon and Travis 1997).

Unlawful arrest and detention were again discussed by the High Court in *Foster*. Here, an Aboriginal suspect was arrested (at around 12.30pm on Friday) by being ordered to '[g]et into the back of the police truck', taken to a police station, and questioned about a fire at a school. The basis for the arrest was a statement by one of his alleged companions which 'impliedly included him among persons whom it alleged to have been involved . . . by referring to a "Steven" as being a participant in a preliminary conversation'.[101] In less than two hours, Stephen Foster had (according to the police) shifted from emphatic denial of involvement in the fire, signed a confessional statement, and been charged. He was held in custody over the weekend and first appeared before a magistrate on Monday. The New South Wales Court of Criminal Appeal dealt briefly with Foster's appeal against conviction, using several of the techniques discussed above. It was argued, *inter alia*, that: any police mistake or malpractice did not affect the making of Foster's confession; the finding that

---

[100] For criticism of this conflation of confirmation (of a confession being made) and corroboration (of its content), see Dixon 1991d.

[101] N. 2 above, Mason CJ *et al.*, at 1, 2.

the confession was voluntary was 'peculiarly a matter for the trial judge. . . . This Court is not a fact finding tribunal and it is not for this court to consider whether it would have found differently on the same facts'; the discretion to exclude voluntarily made confessions should only be used 'in exceptional circumstances'; and there was no significant delay in taking Foster before a Justice.[102] The decision exemplified the Court of Criminal Appeal's narrow approach and its unwillingness to supervise trial judges actively.

The case was approached very differently by the High Court. The tone of the majority's judgment deserves comment. It begins significantly by referring to the appellant as 'Mr Stephen Foster'. He was mistreated by the police in a way which was 'deliberate and reckless'. The judges refer, not to police 'interviews', but to 'interrogation'. They speak, not as if they are considering procedural technicalities in the treatment of a criminal, but rather in terms of the 'appellant's rights', specifically, 'the right to personal liberty under the law . . . "the most elementary and important of common law rights" '.[103] The discussion of applying the public policy discretion made clear that unlawfulness of the police officers' actions was no mere technicality: 'it could scarcely be thought that unlawful arrest and detention in custody by police for the sole purpose of interrogation does not, in this country, constitute "exceptional circumstances" '.[104]

The majority's judgment strongly reiterated *Williams*, condemning the arrest, the detention, and the questioning. Police could arrest suspects only to take them to a magistrate to be charged. Consequently, they had to have sufficient grounds to charge before an arrest could be made. Foster's arrest was unlawful—indeed, there was not even enough in the unspecific reference to 'Steven' to amount to reasonable suspicion. The post-arrest detention was necessarily unlawful because the arrest was unlawful, and also because there was no power to detain for questioning even after a lawful arrest. As in *McKinney and Judge*, the arresting police had justified their action by claiming that they 'believed that it was lawful to arrest a person solely for questioning'. The argument which the NSW Court of

---

[102] N. 56 above, at 7–8 (Loveday J). The reasoning on the final point was particularly unconvincing: it was said that there was no evidence of the availability of a Justice between Foster's arrival at the station and his 'confession', and delay thereafter was irrelevant.

[103] N. 2 above, Mason CJ *et al.*, at 8, quoting Fullagar J from *Trobridge* v. *Hardy* [1955] CLR 147.

[104] *Ibid.* 5.

Criminal Appeal had accepted in *McKinney and Judge* was dismissed almost contemptuously by the High Court: officers, according to their Commissioner's Instructions, had 'a basic obligation . . . to be and remain "fully acquainted" with the limitations upon police powers of arrest. . . . In the context of the clear law and of the content of the "Police Instructions" . . . that explanation is simply unavailing by way of excuse'.[105] The questioning was carried out by officers whose attitude was that Foster would remain in custody for as long as they liked. The arresting officer had agreed with defence counsel that, having made up his mind that the suspect was guilty, he set out to break Foster down to a point where he would tell him 'something that [the officer] believed'.[106] In these circumstances, there had to be a 'real question' about the voluntariness of Foster's alleged confession:

Inevitably, the subjection of a person to involuntary and persistent interrogation by the police while he or she is unlawfully detained in police custody gives rise to a situation in which there are likely to be grounds for concern about whether any confessional statement has been voluntarily made since the unlawful detention in custody is likely to carry with it an implicit threat of continued unlawful detention unless and until the questions of interviewing police are answered to their satisfaction.[107]

Although McHugh J was alone in formally setting aside the finding of voluntariness, the majority concluded that Foster's 'confession' should probably have been excluded as involuntary; certainly fairness required its exclusion, as did public policy. State trial and appeal court judges are clearly expected to exclude evidence collected by the kind of arrest, detention, and questioning experienced by Foster.[108]

Optimistic expectations may be tempered by noting some limitations of the decision. It was, in the majority's view, an extreme case, in which 'the police infringement of [Foster's] rights . . . was both serious and reckless' and their actions displayed 'deliberate or reckless disregard of the law'.[109] It was the combination of unlawful arrest, unlawful detention, and the absence of any possibility of independent confirmation of the accused's allegations about mistreatment and the fabrication of Foster's 'confession' which made the

---

[105] *Ibid.* 8–9.   [106] *Ibid.* 10.   [107] *Ibid.* 10–11.

[108] The decision came too late to benefit Stephen Foster directly: by the time it was reached, he had already served his full term of imprisonment (NSW Ombudman 1996: ii).

[109] *Ibid.* 8, quoting *Bunning* v. *Cross*, n. 59 above.

police actions so reprehensible. It is not made clear what, in the future, the outcome should be if only one of these factors, unlawful detention, is present.[110] If police can point to evidence justifying arrest and videotape the interrogation, courts may continue refusing to exclude evidence obtained during unlawful detention. This is particularly so because the High Court repeated the artificial *Williams* formulation, in which questioning is permissible so long as it does not delay presenting the suspect to a court.

These limitations were manifested by the first occasion on which the NSW Court of Criminal Appeal had to consider *Foster*. Ironically, this was McKinney and Judge's appeal against their conviction at the retrial ordered by the High Court in their successful appeal. There was no dispute that McKinney and Judge had been illegally detained, but it was thought not to be an appropriate case for the exclusionary discretions to be applied. There was no challenge to the legality of the arrest, the unlawfulness of the detention was said not to be not deliberate, the suspects had none of Foster's characteristics which made him especially vulnerable, they were not treated unfairly, and 'the crimes charged were particularly heinous'. Treating a suspect who is charged with serious offences and has experience of the criminal justice system as requiring less legal protection than others is justified as a judicial balancing of social interests.[111] Alternatively, it might be seen as a denial of judicial protection to suspects who need it at least as much as others, but who are seen as undeserving. It is a familiar expression of the disjuncture between legal rhetoric and legal substance (McBarnet 1983). In sum, it was felt, *Foster* 'was a decision on its own facts, which were very much more powerful than the present case'.[112] It is likely that this will be a common refrain from trial and state appellate judges.

This process by which trial and appeal courts and police accommodate High Court pronouncements on suspects' rights is examined further in the following sections, which consider reactions to *Williams* in New South Wales. In *Foster*, McHugh J 'doubted that public policy would require the exclusion of the statements in this case even if the police officers were guilty of the conduct alleged against them.' However, '[a] different result might ensue if the ille-

---

[110] Cf. *Bishop*, n. 88 above.
[111] *McKinney and Judge (No 2)*, n. 32 above, at 21, 23, 33, 27, 36 (Wood J). For comparative examples, see n. 87 above.
[112] *McKinney and Judge (No 2)*, n. 32 above, 27 (Wood J).

gality or impropriety was part of a systematic course of conduct knowingly done in breach of the law or the public interest, particularly if it was carried out with the approval of high ranking police officers. But that is not this case'.[113] As will be shown below, this *was* the situation in New South Wales.

vi. The Police Response to *Williams* in New South Wales

'Police, naturally enough, have little time or inclination to read the decisions of superior courts concerning the limits of their powers. Even if they did read such judgments, it is doubtful if they would fully comprehend their significance without "sustained expert guidance" ' (Kirby 1979: 631, quoting Burger). Kirby J went on to comment that, for example, reliance on an exclusionary rule 'assumes greater attention to judicial pronouncements than may exist in police practice' (1979: 644). The reception by police of a judicial decision depends, not surprisingly, on its origin, content, and context, and the interaction between these variables. So, for example, decisions of superior courts may attract publicity and attention; but equally, they may be unknown to operational officers if they are not communicated or may be ignored when custom and practice are strong in a particular procedure.[114] By contrast, the lower courts with which operational officers have more regular contact can set informal precedents, when, for example, it is known that a particular judge or magistrate has a strong view about particular evidential requirements or legal arguments (LaFave 1965: 429). As suggested in Chapter 4, cases with local or emotional connections may make more impact than cases which lawyers and law reporters notice. Judgments are communicated down to operational officers through various legal, prosecuting, and training departments, via instructions, circulars, updating bulletins, directions from supervisors, advice from colleagues, and rumour. The result is often rather like the apocryphal whispered message which changes in the telling.[115]

The reaction of the New South Wales police to *Williams* developed as its potential impact on practice became clear and it became a cause

---

[113] N. 2 above, at 25.

[114] Apparently, the investigating officers in *Foster* were not even aware that the case had gone to the High Court until they saw a newspaper report.

[115] See Ch. 7 below for fuller discussion of the communication of law to police.

for concern amongst officers. This led the Attorney General to ask the Law Reform Commission to focus an inquiry which was under way into criminal procedure on a review of 'the whole question of the rights and powers of police following arrest' (NSW LRC 1990: viii). The immediate product was a Discussion Paper which proposed that police should be given power to detain between arrest and charge for an initial period of no more than four hours, extendable by a court for such time as the court considered reasonable (NSW LRC 1987: 103–10). The NSW Police Commissioner's response began by ignoring the reasonable time extension and treating the four-hour period as if it was the maximum proposed: this was castigated as 'an unjustified and unwarranted hindrance to effective law enforcement' (NSW Police 1988a: 60). It was argued that 'detention for the purposes of investigation should be for a "reasonable time" unfettered by the imposition of time limits, or legalistic technicalities designed for the unwarranted advantage of the individual offender [sic] at the expense of the community' (NSW Police 1988a: 57). It should be for the police, not the courts, to define 'reasonableness'. The possible extension of detention was then considered (apparently as an after-thought) as if it was a quite separate matter and criticized by raising potential procedural and practical problems (1988a: 67–9). The context was a wholesale critique of the Commission's proposals, expressed in traditional police terms, counterposing the rights of the community and of the 'offender'.

Similarly unfavourable responses to *Williams* emerged from the legal and training sections of the police. The *Digest* of cases prepared by the Police Prosecuting Branch[116] reported the decision correctly, noting that 'the law in England and New South Wales on arrest is now quite different'. In an apparent attempt to deal with the court's lack of comment on in-station charging, the *Digest* suggested that if 'no justice is available . . . the person should be taken before an authorized officer for a bail determination, after charging, without delay'. However, rather than advising on how the substance of the judgment should be complied with, the *Digest* indicated how its effects could be mitigated: it was pointed out that 'Williams' case is only applicable where the suspect has been arrested', so voluntary attendance was not affected. In addition, it was explained that confessions or admissions obtained in breach of the ruling were not nec-

---

[116] ii, issue 26 (Dec. 1986), 453–5.

essarily inadmissible. Comments from Gibbs CJ were quoted, indicating that voluntary confessions, however obtained, would be excluded only in 'a most exceptional case'. A contemporary note in the *Education Officer's Digest*[117] summarized the case, explaining it as being consistent with earlier High Court decisions. It was noted that this was in contrast to the approach taken by the NSW Supreme Court, which tended to follow *Dallison* v. *Caffery* when considering exclusionary discretions regarding detention for investigative purposes.

Meanwhile, a memorandum on the case was sent to detectives which stated the decision and went on to comment: '[f]rom a practical point of view, there is nothing to stop you from questioning the offender after the arrest, taking admissions, Record of Interview, statement, etc., but having regard to the decision, BE PREPARED TO LOSE THE BRIEF'. The negative, critical tone in which the decision was made known was exemplified by training materials for a crime investigation course. In commenting on *Williams*, these cited the Gundy case as 'an example of how a court can interpret police activity'. This apparently bland reference was, in fact, highly charged. It was to a case in which the courts had decided that a person could be regarded as being in police custody when, although he had not been formally arrested, his house had been surrounded and entered by armed police officers.[118] The importance of this decision is that it granted jurisdiction to the Royal Commission into Aboriginal Deaths in Custody to investigate the killing by police of David Gundy. The Commission's eventual Report was highly critical of the police, and was a considerable embarrassment for the NSW Police Service (see Wootten 1991 and sect. viii below).

A change to police instructions in order to deal with *Williams* was precipitated by a case in which confessional evidence against a defendant was excluded on grounds of unlawful detention. There was said to have been a delay of six days between his arrest and his court appearance. (He also complained that police delayed him access to medical attention for a bullet in his knee for six hours.) The problem became public when a civil action for unlawful imprisonment against the investigating officers began. The response was a protest by drug squad officers who refused to make arrests for fear of being sued. The

---

[117] ii, issue 27, 1 Dec. 1986.   [118] *Eatts* v. *Dawson* (1990) 93 ALR 497.

Police Association called for legislation to provide a power of pre-charge detention.[119]

In response, the Police Commissioner issued a circular, 'Instructions to police as to the effect of Williams case on police investigations of criminal offences',[120] which provided guidance on the decision's implications. The Commissioner's Instruction then in force stated: '[w]hilst in custody, and before being charged, a person may, after the usual caution, be questioned as to any offence in respect of which he/she has been arrested or may be charged.'[121] Like instructions issued to Victoria Police (Willis and Sallman 1985: 216), this reflected official police approval of Dallison v. Caffery. The Commissioner's circular replaced it and, with minor amendments, was re-issued as a new Commissioner's Instruction in July 1989.[122] This was said to have been approved by the Attorney General: it is therefore surprising to find that it was based on the minority judgment of Gibbs CJ in Williams, rather than the decision of the majority.[123] Police were informed that 'they do not have any general power to detain a citizen merely for the purpose of questioning. . . . An arrested person must be brought before a Justice without unreasonable delay.' While this is accurate, the Instruction goes on to relate 'reasonableness' not to the availability of a magistrate, but to the requirements of police investigation. Questioning and other inquiries could properly be used 'for the making of a decision to prefer a charge or not' and to 'anticipate defences which may be raised . . . and to obtain evidence which may negate them'. The Instruction goes on to list fourteen factors by which questioning (presumably meaning delay in presenting the suspect before a magistrate) 'may . . . be occasioned'. These include the time and place of the arrest, the making of a statement by the suspect, interviews with co-offenders, vic-

[119] See 'Police may get tougher arrest powers after week of protest', *The Australian*, 9 May 1988; 'Anger at Govt plan for police', *Sydney Morning Herald*, 9 May 1988; 'Man sues three officers for unlawful detention', *Sydney Morning Herald*, 10 May 1988; 'New guidelines on powers of arrest', *Sydney Morning Herald*, 7 June 1988.

[120] 88/98, 15 June 1988.   [121] #31.10.   [122] Now #37.14.

[123] In other jurisdictions which have not legislated in response to *Williams*, similar methods have been adopted to allow the decision's effect to be sidestepped or ignored. For example, in the foremost commentary on criminal law in Queensland, the s. dealing with the duty to take arrested suspects before a justice (s. 552 of the Criminal Code) gives as authority *Dallison v. Caffery*. *Williams* is mentioned merely in passing (Carter 1992: 7388). For a similar approach in New Zealand, see *Alexander* [1989] 3 NZLR 395. This decision, with considerable disingenuity, suggested that those dissatisfied by a court not excluding evidence could find remedies in tort or police disciplinary action.

tims, and witnesses, preparation for conducting interviews with the suspect, provision of legal advice to officers on what charges would be appropriate, waiting for the attendance of experienced or specially skilled investigators, interpreters, lawyers, or appropriate adults, or conducting medical or other examinations, 'the necessity to convey the arrested person to some location for the purpose of obtaining evidence relevant to the suspected offence', identification parades, searching, fingerprinting, and photographing. The High Court might be surprised to see how openly the NSW Government's law officers and the police were willing to express their preference for the minority view of Gibbs CJ and the English Court of Appeal's decision in *Dallison* v. *Caffery*.

The circular reminded officers of the Crown's vicarious liability 'for police acting in accordance with the directions of the Commissioner of Police'. The Commissioner added that he would 'accept responsibility for the actions of police, performing their duties in good faith and in accordance with the Statement of Values'. In effect, police officers were given an authoritative direction to ignore or evade the High Court's decision in *Williams*. This approach was backed by further executive and judicial support. When it was pointed out that the 1989 Instruction was contrary to *Williams*, a draft was prepared which reflected the decision accurately. However, the government's law officers delayed giving their (informal but necessary) approval, while the government apparently waited for an opportunity to provide police with a statutory power to detain for questioning (see sect. ix).

Finally, another example of official encouragement to ignore *Williams* can be found in guidelines given to police officers carrying out investigations for the NSW Crime Commission, an independent statutory authority established to tackle illegal drug trafficking and other organized crime. Officers were directed to bring suspects to the Commission's premises (rather than to the nearest police station or a court) where questioning could be electronically recorded. There are no charging facilities at the Crime Commission, so a suspect would have to be taken subsequently to a police station.

It is appreciated the decision in William's [*sic*] case exists . . . but it should be appreciated that the NSW Court of Criminal Appeal has recently pointed out to trial judges that that decision does not demand rejection of evidence. I take the view that rejection is unlikely to occur when police working with this Commission are endeavouring to produce an untaintable record of interview in the interests of justice and fairness.[124]

These guidelines were in the name of the Commission's chairman, formerly a prominent judge. Once again, the message which police officers received from their superiors was very different from that sent by the High Court.

vii. The Survival of Detention for Questioning since *Williams*

The law provided several methods by which the police could avoid the effects of *Williams*. First, as noted above, the courts have routinely not excluded unlawfully obtained evidence. As it was unlikely that doing so would have legal repercussions, police could simply ignore the High Court's version of the law: one officer told me, '[y]ou're not meant to detain anyone for questioning, but it always happens. It's the best way to do it: get them back on your turf.' By comparison to processes under PACE, such detentions were remarkably informal: officers could bring suspects into stations without having even to inform supervisors: this duty arose only when questioning had been completed and suspects were to be charged.[125]

While police could often rely on the law being toothless, more creative and safer alternatives soon became available. The New South Wales Court of Criminal Appeal approved a practice which evaded *Williams*. In *Burns*,[126] a suspect was arrested at 6.15pm. Interrogation began sometime after midnight, and an admission was made at 3.45am. He was taken to a magistrate later that morning. When the legality of the detention was challenged in an appeal against conviction, the court found that magistrates were not available in the evening or overnight, so the detention was not unlawful. A very narrow approach was taken. The issue was simply the practical availability of a magistrate: none was available, so there was no failure of duty by the police. An obvious conclusion might have been that, if the law was to be effective, there was a need for round-the-clock services: but no comment of this kind was made (NSW LRC 1990: 14). A different approach was suggested in *Attorney General* v.

---

[124] B. R. Thorley, Crime Commission memorandum, 'Video Interview Facility', 4 July 1990.

[125] See criticisms of these arrangements in NSW Ombudsman 1996: v–xi.

[126] N. 29 above. The decision was followed in *Zorad*, n. 11 above.

Dean, in which the Court of Appeal stated that it was 'highly desirable' that arrangements should be made for suspects to be taken before a justice during weekends and after hours.[127] Some provision was made following these obiter dicta in a contempt case, although these were not sufficiently widespread to prevent officers continuing to cite *Burns* as authority for detaining suspects.

Burns exposed the inadequacies of the majority's judgments in *Williams*: as noted above, they had made no comment about what the police could or should do if no magistrate was available, circumstances which were obviously likely to occur. The result was that 'at least as seen through the eyes of the NSW Court of Criminal Appeal, "the jealous protection of personal liberty accorded by the common law of Australia" is limited to non-holiday weekdays between 10.00am and 4.00pm, when the local court is sitting' (NSW LRC 1990: 14, quoting Mason and Brennan JJ in *Williams*). Police were thereby encouraged to delay arrests of suspects whom they wished to question at length. One detective's answer when asked what effect *Williams* had had was: '[a] little, but not much. People tend to ignore it. A lot of people, especially in the squads, have a tendency to lock people up at night time. . . . That gives you an outer, you can get around it. You've got no magistrate to put him in front of at night.' The law had been reduced to doggerel: '[a]rrest on the night and you'll be all right.' This resort to 'gimmickry' (NSW LRC 1990: 15) was reinforced by advice from legal officials. In the *Blackburn* case,[128] the investigating officers planned to make an arrest at 6.00am, but were advised by public prosecutors to delay until 4.00pm 'so as to avoid difficulties arising from R v Williams' (Lee 1990: 360, see also *id*. 219). The effect of *Burns* is to confirm that the high principles of *Williams* are rendered largely rhetorical by legal interpretation and by the practical arrangements of criminal procedure: it provides an excellent example of McBarnet's argument about the relationship between law and its rhetoric (1979; 1983; see Ch. 1, above). An officer explained to me: '*Williams* says, no, you can't arrest anybody for questioning and gathering evidence, and the other precedent [*Burns*] says you can. Just proves the law's flexibility.' Such perceptions must affect broader police attitudes towards law and legal procedures.

---

[127] (1990) 20 NSWLR 650, at 653; cf. Aronson and Hunter 1995: 231.

[128] In which a senior police officer was accused of a series of rapes: see Lee 1990 and below, sect. viii.

Arrests are also delayed in another way. In training materials for a crime investigation course, officers are advised: '[i]n order to comply with the *Williams* decision, an arrest should only be made when sufficient evidence becomes available. Often this occurs during an interview when the suspect admits the offence.'[129] What begins apparently as simply a statement of the requirements of a lawful arrest is something different: officers are encouraged to get suspects to the station as 'volunteers' and to arrest them formally only when a charge is about to be laid.[130] An officer whom I interviewed explained that, because of *Williams*, 'you have to use it that way. You can always ask them if they want to come down and if they do, you don't place them under arrest until you're sure you are going to charge them.' Another gave an example:

You might grab them with reasonable cause or suspicion or whatever, but they're not actually under arrest, if you know what I mean. They are brought back here [to the station] to clear it all up. . . . You might go to a scene and he's there, he's got a knife in his hand and witnesses saying, 'That's him'. That's enough for me to arrest him. You might go to a scene and he hasn't got a knife. There's no witnesses saying anything, but the victim says, 'Yeah, that's him.' I suppose you've got enough to arrest him there and then, but you prefer to say 'Would you come back to [the station] where we can clear this up?' And most of the time they will. If they want to kick up a barney, you just arrest them anyway.

Delayed arrests of this kind restore, in form, the congruence of arrest and charge which the common law used to require (see Ch. 4, above), but only at the cost of police having to maintain the fiction that people brought to stations in order to 'help with inquiries' are not suspects under arrest.

Finally, some officers were encouraged by the decision to interview suspects before bringing them to a station, in the mistaken belief that this was a way of avoiding the requirement to take an arrested suspect to a magistrate without delay.[131] While the dangers of this practice for the suspect are obvious enough, there are disadvantages for

---

[129] Unit 3.26: *Investigation Practice and Procedure*, para. 7.3.

[130] This practice means that the recording of arrest times does not provide a reliable basis for assessing detention periods, in the way that was attempted in a survey reported in NSW Police 1988a: 58. On voluntary attendance, see Ch. 3, above.

[131] This may well be a foretaste of how officers will respond to a statutory scheme of custodial interrogation in the unlikely event that it includes features regarded as undesirable, such as access to legal advice. On British experiences of similar practices, see Curran and Carnie 1986; Moston and Stephenson 1993a; Leng 1994a.

police also, particularly the difficulties of getting advice from more experienced or detective officers. As one experienced officer suggested, junior officers 'attending crime scenes and speaking to suspects must have a maturity and an investigative knowledge well beyond their years'.

Among the officers whom I interviewed and observed, knowledge about *Williams* varied. While one supervisory officer did not recognize the name of the case, others frequently raised it during discussions with me. Not surprisingly as a result of the nature of their work, detectives knew more about it than general duties officers. In turn, it is likely that officers in squads dealing with more serious offences and potentially longer investigations would have most knowledge. The most common view expressed by officers at patrol level[132] was that they were allowed a reasonable time for investigation and interrogation between arrest and charge. While this is contrary to *Williams*, it is effectively what their Commissioner's Instructions tell them (see sect. vi above) and also can be regarded as an accurate perception of the effective limits on their authority. Those who had come across *Burns* would have seen the court also stressing that the common law duty to bring a suspect to a magistrate was 'tinged . . . with an element of reasonableness'.[133] Again, the High Court might be surprised by an officer's comment: '*Williams*' case . . . at first caused a furore, but I don't think it's as hard as it's really made out. I think "reasonable time" is fine'. Another's response to an inquiry about investigative detention was blunt: '[y]ou can interview them as long as you want.'

The working definition of reasonableness is constructed by reference to what 'common sense' regards as 'unreasonable'. Here, inaccurate beliefs about the facts of *Williams* played an important part. Several officers thought that Williams had been detained for several days without charge: one said that it 'was almost like South Africa where a bloke was incarcerated for a long time and then questioned'. In fact, the illegal detention was (according to the varying interpretations in the High Court) between eight and twenty hours. By exaggerating the facts of *Williams*, officers were able to dissociate their own practices from the case. When I suggested to one officer: '[i]n practical terms, people are detained for questioning, aren't they?,' his response was:

---

[132] Roughly equivalent to an English sub-division.   [133] N. 29 above.

Oh yeah, shit yeah. They always are. But with the *Williams* case, . . . everyone got all excited about it, but it didn't really mean anything. . . . [I]t was a stuff up because no reasonable copper would have done it anyway . . . just questioning him for 24 or 48 hours or whatever it was, which is absolutely ridiculous.

The second major component of the working definition of reasonableness is an assessment of whether supervisory officers, particularly the Patrol Commander, will 'back up' an officer. It was expected that, as long as 'common sense' was used and he or she 'didn't do anything stupid', this would be the case. This overlapped with a willingness to take a chance in the interests of securing evidence: as a senior supervisory officer explained, 'if I want to keep someone for two days I will, and it will be for the courts to deal with subsequently'. The unlikelihood of either such behaviour being sanctioned or a defendant pleading not guilty made it a risk worth taking (NSW LRC 1990: 15). As noted above, this approach was supported by the Commissioner's commitment to back officers who acted 'in good faith and in accordance with the Statement of Values'.

Police misinterpreted *Williams* in another respect. It was widely believed that the decision made a significant distinction between offences for which suspects were arrested and others about which police might want to question them: while a reasonable period was allowed for the former, this was not possible for the latter. This had been the approach taken by the trial judge,[134] but the High Court had rejected it. In its view, suspects could be interviewed about any matter, so long as this did not delay taking them before a magistrate.[135] This was consistent with the High Court's artificial distinction between investigation and preparing papers for court. Perhaps it is wrong to describe these police readings of *Williams* as misinterpretations. While not reflecting the High Court's view, they did reflect practical limits on police activity.

viii. Law in NSW Policing

Symbolized by its titular transition from Force to Service, NSW Police underwent substantial reform between 1984 and 1991 under the direction of a Commissioner, John Avery, of some international

---

[134] N. 4 above, at 387 (Gibbs CJ).
[135] *Ibid.* 390; see also Wilson and Dawson JJ at 405.

repute (G. Jackson 1991; NSW Police 1988b; Sparrow *et al.* 1990: 72–7). There were organizational changes and anti-corruption drives, notably the disbandment of the centralized detective agency, the CIB, and the introduction of linked policies of community policing and regionalization with devolution of responsibility to patrol commanders. Cultural change was also attempted by means including new training and promotion systems (Chan 1997).

None the less, the everyday practice of crime investigation appears to have survived these changes relatively unscathed. Ironically, the reform movement provides some spurious justification for resistance to legal regulation: it promotes a model of 'professional policing' which devalues rules (see e.g. G. Jackson 1991; NSW Police 1988b: 5–6, 26; Sparrow *et al.* 1990; see Ch. 1, above). The place of law in NSW policing practice was illustrated by four notable embarrassments experienced in the early 1990s.

In the report of the Royal Commission into Aboriginal Deaths in Custody into the shooting of David Gundy during a search for another person who had killed a police officer, there is scathing criticism of police attitudes towards legal requirements. Senior detectives and Special Weapons and Operations Section officers treated 'the law and its processes disdainfully' (Wootten 1991: 2). Search warrants were obtained by 'the making of patently untrue statements' in an attempt to get a 'general warrant' (Wootten 1991: 3, 53). Even if the warrants had been obtained properly, the house in which Gundy was shot was entered unlawfully, before the time specified in the warrant: this was one of several ways in which officers 'demonstrated their lack of respect for the law. . . . One detects an assumption that the law will look after police acting to catch a serious criminal, and inconvenient legal rules can safely be ignored. . . . Police felt entitled to make their own law. . . . [I]n the whole operation, the extent of their legal powers does not seem to have been considered' (Wootten 1991: 4, 17, 18, 130–1). Such attitudes and practices were subsequently supported and defended by senior officers (Wootten 1991: 17–18). This was not a case where the police could legitimately feel constrained by the law: '[t]heir problem was not that the law gave them insufficient powers—their problem was that they had insufficient information about Porter's whereabouts to justify action and were not prepared to wait for further information' (Wootten 1991: 92). The Aboriginality of the subjects of police attention was significant: how the abuse of police powers exacerbated bad relations between police and Aboriginal people was further demonstrated by the mass raid on the Aboriginal area of Redfern in 1990 (Cunneen 1990).

A second major contemporary inquiry was the Royal Commission on the *Blackburn* case. Its Report (Lee 1990) shows that the investigation of Blackburn's suspected involvement in two series of sexual assaults was almost a caricature of police operating on a 'case theory' (McConville 1989). This led to 'the falsification and distortion of virtually all the evidence brought against him and complete suppression of the evidence pointing to his innocence' (Lee 1990: 473). One officer's hunch that Blackburn resembled descriptions of the assailant turned into an investigation in which basic procedures of recording were ignored in a way which was thought to be 'rife throughout the Force' (Lee 1990: 408). Authorization for a listening device was obtained improperly (Lee 1990: 224–31). Search powers were abused (Lee 1990: 232–90). Evidence which did not fit the case theory was suppressed (Lee 1990: 312). Blackburn was unlawfully arrested (Lee 1990: ch. 19), and the arrest was arranged in order to avoid restrictions on detention for questioning. Tony Lauer (Commissioner 1991–6, then 'the head of the "Professional Responsibility Section of the Police Department", of all things') lauded 'the achievements of the Task Force involved in [Blackburn's] arrest merely for questioning' and said that 'it is probable that [he] would be charged following the questioning'.[136] As in the Gundy case, a person quite unconnected with the suspected crimes was also unlawfully detained for questioning (Lee 1990: 313; Wootten 1990: 124).

Charges against Blackburn were dropped only when the investigating officer was seriously injured in a road accident following celebration of the arrest. The flimsiness of the case was discovered and exposed by his replacement, 'who found the evidence in support of the prosecution to be in a state of disarray' (Lee 1990: 24). This officer then had to suffer accusations that he had 'gutted the brief' in a corrupt attempt to embarrass the force leadership. The Royal Commission found not only a serious lack of professionalism by the investigating officers, but that 'the police officers of all ranks involved in the investigation into Mr Blackburn's guilt [*sic*], from the

---

[136] *Blackburn v. The State of NSW* NSW Supreme Court, 13944/1990 (unreported, 31 Jan. 1991), Hunt J, at 24.

Commissioner down, failed lamentably to exercise the supervision which their rank demanded of them'.[137]

Thirdly, there is the charging, conviction, and ultimate acquittal of Timothy Anderson on three counts of murder arising from the 'Hilton bombing' in 1978.[138] The most charitable explanation of this episode is that, once again, the authorities convinced themselves of a suspect's guilt, and pursued a conviction relentlessly (see Carrington *et al.* (eds.) 1991). The result was the construction of a case by the provision of information from police to witnesses, which was then re-presented as their evidence. As the defence demonstrated its flaws, the prosecution's case was reconstructed during the trial. The case is a complex one, with many facets which will not be considered here, where there is space to deal just with three points.

Anderson was arrested (according to the Crown) on the highly unreliable (and subsequently discredited) evidence of a man described by the Court as 'a notorious prisoner'.[139] The senior investigator (then one of the state's most renowned detectives) explained that 'he was working on this principle: "One old detective used to say, 'When you haven't got much, pull them in. The brief will only get better.' This was certainly true in our case." '[140] This was a remarkably honest admission about how powers supposedly dependent on reasonable suspicion are used.

Prosecution counsel apparently became equally committed to the case theory and manipulated evidence in a way which earned the disapproval of the Court of Criminal Appeal. This illustrates again that it is wrong to focus just on the police: their attitudes towards prosecutions and the law can be shared and shaped by others, including their senior officers, officials in other parts of the criminal justice process, and the media. As Hogg argues, there has been an 'entrenched legal, political and popular indulgence of police illegality in NSW, if it is undertaken in what are seen to be the interests of effective law enforcement' (1991b: 253). The Court of Criminal Appeal quoted, with apparent approval, defence counsel's comment

---

[137] Lee 1990: 19; see also 472. For a summary of the 'faults and misconduct' of police in the case, see Lee 1990: 311–15.

[138] *Anderson* (1991) 53 A Crim. R. 421. A bomb exploded, killing two people, outside a hotel at which Commonwealth heads of government were meeting.

[139] *Ibid.* 424. On the use of prison informants, and their development as an alternative to confessions (genuine or otherwise) during police questioning, see Brown and Duffy 1991.

[140] A. Tees, quoted, *Sydney Morning Herald*, 26 Oct. 1990.

that 'from time to time it was necessary to make a positive effort to remind oneself that this had been a criminal prosecution in which the Crown carried the onus of proof beyond reasonable doubt. . . . [O]n occasion, it was easy to get the impression that the relevant search was for some hypothesis consistent with guilt'.[141] Anderson's conviction was quashed, with the court refusing to order a retrial on the ground that the prosecution should not be given 'a further opportunity to patch up its case. . . . It has already made one attempt too many to do that'.[142] Such prejudice had also been a notable feature of media reporting of the trial (Carrington *et al.* (eds.) 1991). Few lessons had been learnt from the Chamberlain case (Brown *et al.* 1996: 296–307; Young 1989).

Although Anderson's appeal succeeded, a notable feature was the narrowness of the Court of Criminal Appeal's vision. While (contrary to many expectations) the judges quashed Anderson's conviction, their analysis of the police role in the affair was deficient. On two occasions, it is noted that the evidence of the main prosecution witness 'appeared to have been modified, under pressure of police interviews, to make his story accord with other evidence upon which the prosecution intended to rely'.[143] However, there was no sustained discussion of how the case was constructed and how other evidence which the court took at face value may well have been the product of witnesses being provided with information by the police. As in the Blackburn case, there appears to have been a serious deficiency in the supervision of what was a very controversial and publicized arrest and investigation.[144]

Finally, the police response to the High Court's criticism of officers' 'serious and reckless' misconduct in *Foster* deserves comment. A report by the NSW Ombudsman[145] found that of one of the senior investigating officers attitude was far from contrite: in a memorandum to Internal Affairs investigators, he wrote 'I . . . reject the findings of the High Court of Australia . . . and deplore the findings without being given the courtesy of addressing the Court as to the reasons of [*sic*] my actions' (quoted, NSW Ombudsman 1996: iv). As the Assistant Ombudsman concluded, the officer's comments demon-

---

[141] *Anderson*, n. 138 above, at 426.   [142] *Ibid.* 453.   [143] *Ibid.* 446.

[144] Anderson had already spent 7 years in gaol for another offence before being released when the charges were shown to have been the product of fabrication by a police informant: see Carrington *et al.* (eds.) 1991; Anderson 1992.

[145] Which was presented as 'only one example' of many cases revealing problems in arrest and detention practices (NSW Ombudsman 1996: i).

strated 'both his arrogance and ignorance of the law' (*ibid.* 16). Less dramatic, but as indicative of police attitudes to law, were institutional responses. Officers responsible for investigating the matter following the decision recommended that no action should be taken; the senior officers in the case were promoted; the Ombudsman had to tolerate long delays in obtaining material; and changes to Commissioner's Instructions regarding treatment of suspects were inadequate and insubstantial (Ombudsman 1996). The High Court's caustic criticism was met with a combination of inertia, defensiveness, and resentment that anyone should feel qualified to tell them how to police.[146]

Despite the problems identified in the reports noted above, the New South Wales Police Service presented a complacent face in the early 1990s and enjoyed some international recognition (Sparrow *et al.* 1990: 72–7). An application for an Australian Quality Award (itself some indication of self-confidence) reported on a ten-year programme of developing 'professional, accountable, responsible and innovative police officers' (NSW Police 1994: 3). The Police Service sought to 'perform as a "good corporate citizen" ', providing 'leadership in the community' and considered itself to be 'at the fore-front of implementing Community-based policing world-wide and so are trail blazing' (*ibid.* 5, 7). When, in May 1994, an independent MP convinced Parliament that a Royal Commission into allegations of corruption was necessary,[147] this was opposed by the government[148] and dismissed by the Police Service as unnecessary: according to Police Commissioner Lauer, 'in today's Police Service, institutionalised corruption does not exist'.[149] The Royal Commission's investigation found otherwise: from its inquiry (which is still under way at the time of writing) has emerged a picture of venality which has extended throughout certain squads, across whole areas, and reached

---

[146] Disciplinary charges were subsequently brought against two officers.

[147] Parliamentary Assembly, 11 May 1994, 2286–97 (J. Hatton).

[148] The Minister for Police described the motion as 'an attack on the very institutions of our State that have achieved direct results in cleaning up the Police Service . . . which . . . may ultimately jeopardise the future of policing in New South Wales', n. 147 above, 2308 (T. Griffiths). The Deputy Premier said that instead of 'launching this unwarranted attack on the New South Wales Police Service' John Hatton 'should be acclaiming the service as one of the finest in the world. He should be thankful for the law and order it provides to him and to the community': n. 147 above, 2316 (I. Armstrong).

[149] In evidence to the Royal Commission, quoted *Sydney Morning Herald* , 22 Oct. 1996.

very senior officers. More banal, but as significant, has been evidence of bureaucratic inefficiency and a gulf between managerial claims and policing practice. Illustrative examples include a surveillance squad which, even when investigating the highly-publicized murder of a local politician, routinely played rather than worked; a senior officer who provided a commendatory reference for a colleague who had been dismissed in disgrace; fabrication of injury compensation claims; and theft of drugs and money from suspects and property from crime scenes. The disrepute into which the police fell was illustrated by a conservative journalist's comment: '[t]he worst thing that could happen to any crime victim in Sydney's outer west was to call police. Dial the Home Guard, dial an ambulance, dial the fire brigade or dial a pizza. But do not dial the police. They were a bigger menace than the criminals' (Chesterton 1996). As for 'law in policing', the Royal Commission found evidence of mistreatment of suspects, unlawful searches and interrogations, planting of evidence, fabrications of confessions, and institutionalized perjury (Brown *et al.* 1996: 209). An Interim Report concluded that 'a serious state of corruption exists' and that 'management, both at senior command and supervisory levels, has failed the Police Service' (Wood 1996a: 2, 3). There was significant evidence of ' "process" corruption, in which police powers are abused, evidence is fabricated or tampered with, or confessions are obtained by improper means in order to procure the conviction of persons suspected of criminal or anti-social conduct, and others' (*ibid.* 33). Such corruption was 'routine' in some stations: 'the "police verbal" and "loading" of accused' had 'become an art form within certain sections of the NSW Police Service' (*ibid.* 39, 40). There was 'a widely held perception that the NSW Police Service is . . . a law unto itself' (*ibid.* 116).

The Commission had to trace the link between investigative practices and corruption. If officers justify acting unlawfully by pointing to the inadequacy of their powers and by insisting that the end justifies the means, then process corruption is born. While this does not suggest the opening of some inevitable slippery slope into other forms of corruption, the significance of a general atmosphere or culture in which deviance is encouraged and tolerated must not be under-estimated: such corruption is 'often the first step in the destruction of the values of junior, able and enthusiastic police' (Wood 1996a: 46). As the Australian Law Reform Commission had commented two decades before, '[h]ypocrisy does breed cynicism. The tension between law and reality in present police practice is nowhere more apparent than in the area of custodial investigation' (1975: 3). The variety of instances discussed above suggests that criminal investigation and policing generally in New South Wales are at a stage where law is often regarded as a flexible resource and is sometimes ignored, but is rarely taken as a constitutive and directive part of professional policing. Policing in New South Wales is deeply ambivalent: some elements of the Police Service are as good as it may be realistic to hope, while others could come from a bad nightmare. In the continuing process of reform, legal regulation must play an important part, both instrumentally in providing an effective legal framework, and ideologically, in shifting police cultures towards better understanding of the appropriate relationship between police and citizens in a democratic society. A major problem in policing and criminal justice more generally is a failure by many practitioners to appreciate the political significance of their powers and responsibilities. For a state official to detain a citizen without charge for investigative purposes is a major incursion into a liberty which is a constitutive part of liberal democracy. This does not make it unacceptable: it simply requires that such powers be clearly defined and be no more extensive than necessary.

ix. Legislating Powers to Detain for Questioning

In 1990, the NSW Law Reform Commission completed the inquiry which it had begun in 1987 (see sect. vi, above) into post-arrest detention. Founded on a good understanding of history and principle, it provided a scathing critique of contemporary law and practice and (drawing from PACE and the Bill soon to be enacted by the Commonwealth[150]) recommended that police should be empowered to detain for investigative purposes suspects who were to be provided with substantial protective rights.[151] The Commission found it 'remarkable that an area of law of such fundamental importance to personal liberty has been left in a state which is so informal, so uncertain and inconsistent for so long' (1990: 18). However, opposition from the Police Service to the proposals for time-limited detention

---

[150] See n. 3 above.
[151] On the general acceptance of the need for custodial interrogation, see also Gibbs 1989: 30; New Zealand Law Commission 1992: 149; RCCP 1981a: 18–19.

and legal advice for suspects saw the report swiftly on its way to the well-stocked 'graveyard' (Kirby 1979: 628).

This reaction must be set in the context of a strong antipathy felt by Australian police forces towards externally imposed reform of criminal procedure.[152] As Willis and Sallman commented in Victoria, it 'almost seems as if . . . the police have come to treat police powers questions as industrial relations issues to be negotiated . . . on a semi-private basis with government'.[153] Another, related, context is the highly politicized nature of 'law and order' in the state. This has often obstructed rational and constructive debate about change in policing by discouraging the major political parties from going beyond simple-minded commitments to toughness on law and order.[154]

These problems were demonstrated in the Police Commissioner's response to the Law Reform Commission's earlier Discussion Paper (NSW LRC 1987). As noted above, implicit in this was a distinction between the community and the criminals, and a belief that the police can mobilize the former against the latter. Throughout, uncharged suspects are described as 'offenders'. The comment on a proposal for a reverse onus exclusionary rule was symptomatic: 'changes in corporate culture with concurrent promotion of ethical behaviour and integrity, together with a ruthless excising of those who fail to conform with such standards, has more to offer the citizens of NSW than

---

[152] Another example is the history of public-order offences in New South Wales. In the late 1970s and early 1980s, police campaigned publicly against legislation which delimited their powers in this area, and eventually secured further legislative change. The powers which the police had were never less than wide-ranging and adequate: their objection was largely a political and symbolic one (Egger and Findlay 1988; see Ch. 2, above).

[153] 1985: 228. The analogy is appropriate, given the prominent and powerful role played by police associations in Australia (Finnane 1994: 44–51). See, e.g., the Police Federation President's threat of a police strike against the reforms of criminal investigation proposed by the Australian Law Reform Commission: *Reform* (1982), 63; cf. ALRC 1975. At the time of writing, NSW officers are 'working to rule' in protest against proposed changes in dismissal procedures. In the context of evidence collected by the Royal Commission into the NSW Police Service (Wood 1996a) concerning police practices, the suggestion that police should work to rule has attracted some predictably cynical responses.

[154] The NSW Labor Party's hand-me-down promise in 1994–5 to be 'tough on crime and tough on the causes of crime', attacks on criminologists who questioned claims that Sydney was suffering a crime-wave, and labelling of young people wearing baseball caps back-to-front as gang members are examples: see *Sydney Morning Herald*, 13 July 1994. Commitments to reform policing in the wake of the Wood Royal Commission are combined with proposals in a Street Safety Bill [*sic*] to give police power to 'move on' groups of 3 or more people.

the blind application of an arbitrary and unthinking exclusionary rule' (NSW Police 1988a: 4). One of the authors of the response commented that '[m]any of the proposals border on turning police investigative procedures into a legalistic game fraught with technicalities, with offenders being constantly presented with the opportunity to rely on procedural rules to escape conviction' (Drew 1989: 59). Similarly, this officer responded to the Law Reform Commission's Report by claiming that time-limited detention had been tried and had failed elsewhere, that giving substance to suspects' rights was unacceptable because it would obstruct police inquiries, and that some lawyers would 'deliberately seek to frustrate police from conducting an investigation' if the right to a lawyer was given legal substance.[155]

Eight years after *Williams* and three years after the Law Reform Commission reported on the matter, a Crimes (Detention after Arrest) Amendment Bill was finally published in 1993. The government rejected the schemes of legally regulated detention length introduced for investigations of Commonwealth offences and proposed for New South Wales by the NSW Law Reform Commission. Rather than providing specified maximum periods of detention, the Bill allowed police to detain suspects for a 'reasonable period', as the Police Service had demanded. The Attorney General claimed the experience of other states in justification for rejecting fixed time detention: '[t]hat model was first trialled [*sic*] in Victoria. Victoria rejected it and changed the law as it was unworkable. All the other States have rejected the concept as unworkable.'[156] This argument was specious. As the Law Reform Commission had explained, the Coldrey Committee found the Victorian scheme to be working successfully, but 'surprisingly recommended its abandonment on the basis that it had "the potential to cause problems in the future" ' (NSW LRC 1990: paragraph 4.18). Such problems as there had been were due to a strange provision which required a suspect to consent to an extended period of detention and to suspects' use of their right to silence: the former could have been remedied by legislative amendment, while the latter had nothing directly to do with the detention regime. It would seem that the rejection of fixed time periods in Victoria was due more to the political influence of the Victorian

---

[155] Quoted Beun-Chown 1991; see also NSW Police Press release, 10 Sept. 1991.
[156] *Sydney Morning Herald*, 28 Aug. 1993. Cf. NSW Hansard (LC), 21 Apr. 1994, 1584.

Police than to its inherent weakness. In other jurisdictions, fixed times have been used successfully. The Law Reform Commission reported that South Australia's police were satisfied with that state's fixed-time provision (1990: paragraph 4.17; McEniery 1995). The Commonwealth's legislation provides a fixed-time model very similar to that recommended by the NSW Law Reform Commission, and no evidence of problems in its operation has been made public.[157] As Chapter 4 suggests, the fixed-time system in England and Wales has been more successful than sceptics expected.

Far from the 'reasonable time' model being preferable, experience elsewhere illustrates its deficiencies. In *Heiss*, the Northern Territory Supreme Court strongly criticized the lack of guidance to police in that jurisdiction's reasonable-time provision, rejected suggestions that the courts should clarify reasonableness, and suggested that this was properly a legislative function.[158] In the NSW Bill, 'reasonable time' for detention was to be determined by the investigating officer, with no requirement for involvement of supervisory officers. The real issue was not that a fixed-time regime could work, but that the police objected to the constraints that they expected it to put upon them. The government's priority was acknowledged: it was not the unlawful detention of suspects, but 'the uncertainty now faced by police at operational level as to the extent of their powers [which] clearly required a response from the Government'.[159] In addition, the Bill did not deal with the problem of 'volunteers', despite the Law Reform Commission's clear exposition of the need to do so (NSW LRC 1990: paragraphs 3.27–37).

Control of detention practices was to be provided by guidelines and by 'judicial supervision'. Given the record of NSW courts, there were few grounds for expecting the latter to be effective.[160] There was no suggestion that real substance would be given to suspects' rights, for example by providing a right to free legal advice during custody backed by a duty-solicitor scheme and rules requiring police

---

[157] Despite pressure from the Federal Police for a 'reasonable time provision', an official review favoured continuing the fixed time regime (Attorney General's Department 1995: 18).

[158] N. 30 above, at 455, 457–9 (Nader J).

[159] Attorney General's Press release, 7 Aug. 1993.

[160] It must be acknowledged that the English judiciary's performance did not meet similar gloomy predictions made before PACE: see Ch. 4. The difference, however, is that PACE has specific provisions for judges to employ, and the political context made it more likely that they would employed.

to enable suspects to contact it (NSW LRC 1990: paragraphs 5.20–36). Police were not to be able to refuse access to legal advice (in contrast to access to family and others, which could be refused in specified circumstances), but lawyers were to be given only two hours to get to a station before the obligation to delay questioning or other investigation expired. This would encourage officers arresting suspects thought likely to be able to employ a lawyer to do so at inconvenient times. It is ironic that, while a principal argument against fixed detention lengths was that they would be impractical in rural areas, a short period was considered adequate for the arrival of legal advice. While the Bill borrowed some of PACE's terminology, referring to custody officers and custody records, it left elaboration of arrangements to police management and subordinate legislation. Special groups were dealt with only in permissive sections on interpreters and by providing that a suspect's age and physical, mental, and intellectual conditions should be taken into account in determining a 'reasonable' detention length. Notably, no reference was made to Aboriginality. The duty to inform suspects of their rights rested with 'the police officer concerned', presumably the investigating officer.

The proposed legislation could properly be described as offering the legal non-regulation of detention for questioning: the law was to be used merely to authorize and legitimate what police do, leading to 'the worst of all worlds . . . a benighted department exercising the maximum discretion under invisible standards' (McGowan 1972: 676).[161] In the event, the Bill lapsed with a change of government in 1995. At the time of writing, another Bill is before Parliament.[162] In introducing it, Andrew Tink MP (a member of the opposition) claimed that his Private Member's Bill would implement the Law Reform Commission's proposals: however, he overlooked the first recommendation, which was that powers of investigative detention were acceptable only as part of an integrated package which included

[161] The Director of the Attorney General's Department stated that the Bill 'does not authorise police to do anything that they cannot lawfully now do': letter to J. McCrudden (South Coast Aboriginal Legal Service), 16 June 1994. It is questionable whether such provisions would satisfy the International Covenant on Civil and Political Rights which, while not precluding investigative detention between arrest and charge, does require that such detention should be brief and police powers should be clearly specified (cf. New Zealand Law Commission 1992: 143–5).

[162] Crimes Amendment (Police Detention Powers after Arrest) Bill 1996, introduced by Andrew Tink MP to the Legislative Assembly, 17 Oct. 1996.

suspects' rights which were 'meaningful, realisable, and enforceable' (NSW LRC 1990: 53). While the argument against 'reasonable time' has prevailed, the suspects' rights and safeguards which are provided have no substance in procedure, regulation, or resource provision. In particular, a right to legal advice is not complemented by anything to make this more substantial or effective. It was made clear that the priority was to satisfy demands from the Police Service for clear powers: substantial reform of criminal procedure was not on the political agenda. Similar proposals are apparently made in a Bill drafted by the Attorney-General's Department. Although not yet publicly available, it has received the imprimatur of the Royal Commission into the NSW Police Service (Wood 1996b: 17–18). Its priorities are suggested by the Royal Commission's note that the Bill was prepared 'following extensive consultation with the Police Association' (Wood 1996b: 17). Given the Royal Commission's support and the apparent political consensus, legislation providing significant powers but insubstantial suspects' rights is likely to be enacted.

The fate of the Law Reform Commission's report illustrates the character of criminal justice politics in New South Wales. Debates are dominated by hackneyed juxtapositions of suspects' rights and police powers. Politicians, judges, and police struggle with the idea that suspects should have rights which need to be given substance. Their primary concern is the demands and desires of crime control. This narrow view was expressed by the then Chair of the Police Board's comment on calls for legislative reform: 'I confess that I sometimes wonder if it matters very much. With the present powers, our police manage to keep the criminal courts quite busy and the prisons full' (G. Jackson 1991: 15). Such corrosive cynicism has blighted criminal justice in New South Wales. There is some civil libertarian opposition, but this tends to be legalistically obsessed with 'the grand rhetoric of the common law' (NSW LRC 1990: 14) and with 'rights' which are of little practical relevance in the criminal process. This connects with a conservative preference for 'the way we've been doing it right through',[163] which is a product either of complacency or of fear that any change is likely to be for the worse. More per-

---

[163] A phrase symptomatically used by a senior Queensland law officer resisting proposals for reform which were eventually brought forward in CJC 1994. In depressingly familiar fashion, the Queensland Government rejected the CJC's central recommendations after a notably obtuse and ill-informed commentary by a parliamentary committee (Parliamentary Criminal Justice Committee 1995) and attempted to introduce a 'reasonable time' regime for detention. As in NSW, a state election intervened.

ceptive critiques come from the margins of political debate, notably from groups representing those who have experienced criminal (in)justice.[164] But, of course, their influence is limited. In a manner still surprising to someone brought up on a diet of the English House of Lords and Court of Appeal's conservatism, the High Court provides the only powerful, significant opposition. It is, inevitably, limited by the legal tools available to it (Dixon 1991d; cf. Bradley 1993: 4).

Criminal justice is increasingly and crudely politicized: in the mid-1990s, politicians' wilful misrepresentation of the crime problem and manipulation of the fear of crime exemplified a cynicism which must be related to the deep cultural ambivalence about crime, law, and authority in Australia which is discussed further in Chapter 7, below. In the context of this Chapter, the central issue is the way in which police practices of detaining and questioning suspects at or beyond the margins of the law must be addressed not merely as the products of 'police culture', but as the expression of legal and political cultures and structures. Police have been able, indeed have been encouraged, to detain suspects unlawfully or by means of legal trickery and loopholes, because legislators neglected the issue, judges routinely allowed unlawfully obtained evidence to be used in their courts, prosecutors advised police to exploit legal shortcomings, and defence lawyers routinely advised their clients to plead guilty.

---

[164] Cf. Anderson 1992; Prisoners Action Group (PAG) 1989; and *Framed*, the quarterly magazine of Justice Action.

6

Silent Suspects and Police Questions

the so-called right of silence . . . is contrary to common sense. It runs counter to our realisation of how we ourselves would behave if we were faced with a criminal charge (Williams 1987: 1107).

the very habit and faculty that makes apprehensible to us what is known and expected dulls our sensitivity to other forms, even the most obvious. We must rub our eyes and look again, clear our minds of what we are looking for to see what is there (Malouf 1993: 130).

The Criminal Justice and Public Order Act 1994, section 34,[1] permits courts and juries in England and Wales to 'draw such inferences . . . as appear proper' from a suspect's failure to mention to a police officer investigating an offence a fact relied upon in his or her defence. In other words, it severely restricts the right to silence during police questioning. The caution is transformed from warning to threat,[2] and its implications go beyond the specific legal provisions on which it is based. With some significant judicial support, senior police officers had campaigned for such a change in the rules of evidence for almost thirty years.[3] One Metropolitan Police Commissioner claimed that

[1] Hereafter, 'the 1994 Act'.

[2] 'You do not have to say anything. But it may harm your defence if you do not mention when questioned something which you later rely on in court. Anything you do say may be given in evidence': (Code C (1995), s. 10.4). The Criminal Justice and Public Order Act, ss. 36 and 37 similarly allow inferences to be drawn from (inter alia) failures to account for possession of an object or a substance, or for marks on clothing, or to account for being in a particular place. Silence at trial is similarly dealt with in s. 35. My focus here is restricted to pre-trial silence. For commentary, see Wasik and Taylor 1995: ch. 3; Zander 1995: 303–23.

[3] Dixon 1991b. See Lord Lane's address to the 1987 Bar conference and his subsequent comments in Alladice (1988) 87 Cr. App. R. 380, at 385; Imbert 1988; Lawton 1987; 'The Police and Criminal Evidence Act: review of operations: summary of

'abolition of the right of silence would be the most important single step legislators could take to control and reduce crime'.[4]

Examining the 'right to silence debate' in a somewhat sceptical light, this Chapter looks first at how empirical evidence was used (and abused) in the production of the 1994 Act. Secondly, it comments on the role of legal advisers whose increasing presence at police stations following PACE, it was claimed, had increased reliance on the right to silence and made its restriction imperative. Finally, the Chapter suggests some reasons why silent suspects have attracted such attention and why the 'debate' has been so unsatisfactory. Understanding of the relationship between law and policing in this area has been limited by an insistent 'common sense' which misrepresents the practices and perceptions of police officers, defence lawyers, and suspects.

i. Evidence, Research, and Policy Formulation

(a) Silence before PACE

Critics of the right to silence had to face the difficulty that the image which they invoked (of professional criminals escaping conviction in increasing numbers by using the right to silence) found little support in the research literature. The main response was to ignore inconvenient evidence, providing a depressing example of official debate and decision-making.

A number of pre-PACE studies agreed that very few suspects exercised their right of silence.[5] Research for the Royal Commission on Criminal Procedure found that doing so was rare: 4 per cent of Softley's sample (1980) refused to answer any questions of substance, while 8 per cent refused to answer some. These findings facilitated the Commission's recommendation that the right should be maintained. Similarly, an analysis of cases heard by Worcester Crown Court in 1978 showed that 4.3 per cent of suspects had exercised the right of silence: equal proportions of these had no previous convictions and had served prison sentences, suggesting that silence was not a particular characteristic of the more experienced suspect (Mitchell

responses', Home Office memorandum, 1 Sept. 1987, POL/87 2/24/26; and *Report of Her Majesty's Chief Inspector of Constabulary for the Year 1987*, HC 521 1988.

[4] Peter Imbert, quoted Pickover and Greaves 1989: 2239; cf. Mark 1977: 39, 72.

[5] These studies used varied sampling strategies and took identification of uses of the right to silence as unproblematic (Brown 1996: ch. 8).

1983: 600). Zander's study of Old Bailey cases reported a 4 per cent silence rate. Silence was not an effective bar to conviction: only a quarter of silent suspects were acquitted (1979: 211–12). McConville and Baldwin found no statement recorded in the committal papers of 3.8 per cent and 6.5 per cent of defendants in Birmingham and London respectively. Their analysis also showed that many of these 'silent' suspects pleaded guilty; that 'ambush' defences were rarely responsible for acquittals; and that 'those defendants viewed by the police as professionals . . . confessed at about the same rate as others' (1981: 112; cf. *ibid.* 117–25). In the course of their lengthy observations of the Metropolitan Police, the Policy Studies Institute's researchers 'never saw anyone remain silent under questioning' (Smith and Gray 1985: 472). Walkley studied sixty interviews: 'only one person was observed who made a determined effort to say nothing . . . but this ploy quickly crumbled in the face of a proficient police interviewer' (1987: 100). The Home Office field trials of tape-recording interrogations were carried out in 1984–5, when several forces were anticipating PACE in their procedures: no evidence was obtained from 3 per cent of questioned suspects (Willis *et al.* 1988: 34).

(b) The Effects of PACE

Claims that PACE completely changed the situation were belied by early academic studies of its impact. Research for the Lord Chancellor's Department found only 2.4 per cent of suspects exercising their right of silence. Access to legal advice did not, contrary to police claims, dramatically increase this. Suspects were rarely advised to remain silent. 7.3 per cent of those whose legal advisers attended their interrogations did so (Sanders *et al.* 1989: 135–6). In interviews conducted in our study of a Northern police force, a large majority (78 per cent) of the operational officers said that PACE had not affected suspects' exercise of the right of silence (Bottomley *et al.* 1991: 152).

Irving's research on interrogation was unique in being able to compare findings from research carried out before and after the legislation's implementation.[6] In 1979, only one of sixty suspects under interrogation 'refused to answer any of the questions put to him and four refused to answer questions relating to the crime' (1980: 149). In

---

[6] Albeit in only one, rather untypical, police station: see comments in Ch. 4, above.

1986–7, total silence was still extremely rare. Suspects refused to answer all questions of substance in up to 5 per cent of cases, and refused to answer some questions in up to 11 per cent of cases (Irving and McKenzie 1988: 97–8). Irving and McKenzie suggested that a fall in admissions in serious cases (which was used as ammunition against the right of silence) was due not to silence resulting from legal advice, but to the 'reduced availability of persuasive interrogation tactics and coercive custody conditions in cases where pre-interrogation evidence is not in itself overwhelming'. As officers learnt to work with PACE and to exploit its possibilities and grey areas, such tactics began to re-emerge (1989a: 171–2). A careful and detailed survey of the literature found (with appropriate Home Office caution) 'no evidence that the rate of silence has risen since the introduction of PACE' (Brown 1994: 74).[7]

The results of these independent academic studies would seem to suggest few grounds for the authorities' concern about either the right to silence or the effects of PACE. However, this would be to overlook the political and symbolic dimensions of these issues. The move against the right of silence was legitimated by internal police research. Much was made of a 'limited survey' by the Metropolitan Police which found the silence rate to be 20 per cent of suspects questioned about serious offences in 1987 (Police Review 1988). It was with some relief that the critics of the 'right to silence' found further apparent support for their case in research carried out by Tom Williamson, a Metropolitan Police officer.[8] An imprimatur was given to Williamson's work when it was relied upon by a Home Office Working Group, which was asked to report on how the 'right of silence' should be restricted. (The Home Secretary's commitment to the need for change had already been made public, and the Group was not asked to consider this fundamental issue of principle.) No other relevant research was considered,[9] except a complementary survey by West Yorkshire police (Williamson 1990b: 306–35). Here, at last, the case against the right of silence found some more favourable statistics. 12 per cent of London suspects and 5.1 per cent of West

---

[7] Brown's subsequent research suggests that the silence rate has increased: see n. 15, below. However, the quoted comment reflects the state of knowledge at the time of the 1994 Act.

[8] Whose research later appeared as a Ph.D. thesis: see Williamson 1990b.

[9] Reference was made to Brown's survey (1989), but only in regard to the recorded take-up of legal advice.

Yorkshire suspects failed to answer any questions at all or any questions relevant to the offence.[10] Legal representation increased these figures to 27.2 per cent and 10 per cent respectively.[11] (It is important to note that only 21 per cent and 31 per cent respectively of these suspects were legally represented: the silent, legally represented suspect was a small sub-category.) There was no strong relationship between silence and either offence seriousness or previous convictions. Silence was more commonly followed by charge in London than in West Yorkshire: suspects who failed to answer any questions at all were charged at rates of 56.4 per cent and 37.1 per cent, while, for those who failed to answer any questions relevant to the offence, the rates were 53.2 per cent and 27.6 per cent respectively (Home Office 1989; Williamson 1990b: 287–337). These findings were enough to legitimate the Working Group's *raison d'être*. Research had shown that something had to be done about the 'right to silence': it was assumed that, at some undefined point, usage of the right to silence became a problem requiring rectification. This conclusion dominated discussion of the issue for some time.

Unfortunately for those who seized upon it so readily, Williamson's research proved to be as unreliable as those who were initially surprised by his findings suspected. Writing with academic colleagues, he has subsequently acknowledged that his methodology was flawed: the questionnaires were badly designed and 'may have led to confusion and an over-estimation of the use of silence' (Moston *et al.* 1993: 40). They began by informing respondents that:

The Home Secretary and the Commissioner of the Metropolitan Police, among others, have recently expressed concern regarding the exercise of the right of silence. . . . There is little evidence of the full extent to which and in what circumstances the right is exercised. It is hoped that research will provide this evidence (Williamson, 1990b: 401).

This statement was hardly likely to ensure the validity of the research findings (cf. Brown 1994: 65). In addition, the survey counted inter-

---

[10] Home Office 1989: 61–2. Statistics were also collected of failures to answer some questions relevant to the offence: their limited relevance is noted at 262 below. Their main function appears to be to provide some politically useful, inflated percentages: e.g. '42.6 per cent of all interviewees who were legally represented exercised their right to silence in one form or another' (*ibid.* 61).

[11] It is not clear whether this means that legal advice was requested or actually received, or whether it was provided by telephone or in person. On the significance of these distinctions, see Sanders *et al.* 1989.

rogations, rather than suspects: 'if a fairly reticent suspect was interviewed five times, each time withholding some element of a story,
then this would have been recorded as five instances of silence'
(Moston et al. 1993: 40). Again, the result was to overcount 'silence'.

In a more rigorous, subsequent project, Williamson and his academic colleagues reported a 'silence rate' of 16 per cent in interrogations by detectives (Moston et al. 1993). They defined use of the 'right
to silence' very broadly, as encompassing 'any refusal to answer a
question', including evasion. Many instances which they classified as
uses of the 'right to silence' might not have been regarded as such by
a trial court, and defendants would not have received the right's limited protection.[12] Further, the relative seriousness of the cases (i.e.
those involving detectives) in their sample must be taken into
account. In the light of these factors, it is not surprising to find that
they concluded that PACE had not significantly increased use of the
'right to silence'. This important research also shows that 'silence'
does not reduce the rate at which suspects are charged or convicted:
if anything, silent suspects are more rather than less likely to be
charged (Moston et al. 1992a; 1993).

(c) The Restriction of the Right to Silence

Immediate implementation of the Working Group's recommendations was made impossible by the belated acknowledgement of a
series of miscarriages of justice. The right to silence was among the
issues specifically referred for consideration to the Royal Commission
on Criminal Justice in 1991. The Runciman Commission, like its predecessor, solicited a series of research studies. These provided further
evidence that attacks on the right to silence were misconceived. A
study of Crown Court cases found that 11 to 13 per cent of defendants had been silent in relation to all questions and that a further 9
to 17 per cent had been 'significantly' silent in relation to some questions (Zander and Henderson 1993: 3). Leng reported that 4.5 per
cent of suspects used the right to silence (1993: 17.) In McConville
and Hodgson's study of suspects who received legal advice, 2.5 per
cent answered no questions, while 27.4 per cent answered selectively
(1993: 176). However, these studies did not simply produce more statistics for the numbers game into which the debate was degenerating.

[12] Evasive or incomplete answers can found adverse inferences under the 1994 Act.
Problems in defining and identifying use of the right to silence are considered below:
see also Brown 1996; Leng 1993.

Much more importantly, Leng and, particularly, McConville and Hodgson provided the first analyses which did not assume an exercise of the right to silence to be a clearly defined, common-sense category. Some implications of their careful attempts to specify the right to silence will be considered in section iii below.

Leng's research made clear that the impact of the right to silence on case outcome had been misunderstood and exaggerated by its critics:

the right to silence is rarely exercised and . . . about half of those who exercise it are convicted. For cases which fail, there is little evidence to suggest that the prospects for conviction would be enhanced by inducing the suspect to speak or by treating his silence as evidence against him (1993: 79).

The 'ambush' defence was found to be largely mythical. Abolition of the right to silence 'would have a limited effect in enhancing the prospects of convicting guilty offenders in only a very small proportion of cases' (Leng 1993: 80). The Runciman Commission concluded that such an effect would not justify 'the risk that the extra pressure on suspects to talk in the police station and the adverse inferences invited if they do not may result in more convictions of the innocent'. They were particularly concerned about the implications for vulnerable suspects (1993: 54, cf. 54–5).

This was not what the Government wanted to hear. Engaged in a 'law and order' campaign to rescue plummeting electoral popularity and seeking to improve relations with the police (which were much strained by proposals for change in pay, conditions, and institutional arrangements), the Home Secretary found the right to silence a convenient target at the 1993 Conservative Party conference. Michael Howard's populism would be hard to caricature:

As I talk to people up and down the country, there is one part of our law in particular that makes their blood boil. . . . It's the so-called right to silence. . . . [It] is ruthlessly exploited by terrorists. What fools they must think we are. It's time to call a halt to this charade. The so-called right to silence will be abolished (quoted Zander 1994: 145).

In a decision which seemed to confirm the Government's disdain for Royal Commissions, the recommendations of Philips and Runciman were set aside and restriction of the right to silence was included in the Criminal Justice and Public Order Bill. Zander argued that this decision, by simply preferring personal and political opinion to the informed advice of the Commission on a topic which was specifically included in the terms of reference, 'verges on the unconstitutional'. It was 'a debasement of the process of public decision-making' (1994: 145,146).

As before, the police conveniently produced evidence apparently lending weight to the abolitionist cause[13] by countering the Runciman Commission's research which was 'not . . . accepted as representative by the police service'.[14] A survey carried out for the Association of Chief Police Officers (ACPO 1993) found that 10 per cent of suspects refused to answer all questions, while 12 per cent refused to answer some.[15] The right was more likely to be exercised in more serious cases and by experienced and professional criminals, and by those who receive legal advice. A familiar case was made: '[i]t is often argued that the "Right of Silence" is a protection for the weak and inexperienced. The reality is that it is a protection for hardened criminals. . . . [It] has a profound impact on the criminal justice system, and is used to the advantage of practised criminals in the course of their "professional" business' (Phillips 1993). The problem in assessing such findings is that they are all that was presented, even to a Home Office review of research (Brown 1997). In contrast to McConville and Hodgson's and Leng's careful discussions of the difficulties in researching silence, ACPO simply presented a set of figures, as if they spoke for themselves.[16] But because they said what was politically convenient, they could be adopted by the government, while the Royal Commission's research and conclusions could be pushed to the back of the shelf. The Bill duly became law. Naïve as it may be to be surprised by this episode, I still find it a profoundly disappointing example of how government uses research and makes policy and law.

[13] As Michael Zander points out (1994: 146, n. 7), this research was produced after the Home Secretary's announcement at the 1993 conference.

[14] Letter, J. D. Phillips, Chief Constable of Kent, to Michael Howard, Home Secretary, 10 Nov. 1993; see also Phillips 1993.

[15] Some support for these figures came in subsequent Home Office research on 2,000 cases from 10 police stations which found 10% of suspects refusing to answer all and 13% refusing some questions (Phillips and Brown 1997). Relying upon police officers to record and return information, this research has problems of reliability which are noted by Brown (1997: ch. 8). None the less, he appears to be justified in suggesting that silence has increased since the early post-PACE studies as suspects have become more aware of their rights (ibid.).

[16] See also the critique by Leng 1994: 25–8.

ii. Legal Advisers and the Right to Silence

As noted above, an important part of the argument against the right to silence was the claim that suspects in custody who were allowed access to legal advice would almost inevitably be advised not to answer police questions. Indeed, this became part of the 'common sense' which so distorted the debate (Dixon 1991a). This section challenges this 'common sense' by examining the activities of legal advisers at police stations and their effect on suspects' responses to police questions.[17] First, contrary to what 'common sense' tells us, advice to remain silent is not given as a matter of course when legal advisers attend police stations. Secondly, when such advice is given, any consequential silence may be a temporary, negotiating or sanctioning tactic rather than an entrenched position. Thirdly, silence may not be the result of legal advice.

(a) Police–Legal Adviser Relations

The provision of legal advice at police stations has to be understood in the context of continuing, long-term relations between legal advisers and the police. In the area which we studied, regular contact between groups of legal advisers[18] and investigating officers means that social bonds and co-operative expectations are perhaps stronger than elsewhere. None the less, our experience is broadly similar in this respect to that of other researchers (Sanders *et al.* 1989; Irving and McKenzie 1989b; McConville *et al.* 1994; McConville and Hodgson 1993).

Even within this relatively small group of legal advisers, there are significant differences (as indeed there are amongst the police officers with whom they deal). Some are committed to criminal work: some regard it as the poor relation of more prestigious assignments, such as commercial work (McConville *et al.* 1994: 24). Some expressed

[17] This section draws on my research with Bottomley and Coleman and on a related project, 'Solicitors, Suspects, Runners, Police', which I carried out with research assistance from David Wall. This project involved lengthy semi-structured interviews with 35 legal advisers who regularly provide services in the stations studied in the PACE project. Otherwise unidentified quotations below are from these interviews. The findings of these are compared to other research, notably by Sanders *et al.* (1989) and McConville *et al.* (1994).

[18] This term is used to indicate that advisers are often not solicitors, but their clerks, representatives, or 'runners': see Dixon *et al.* 1990a; McConville *et al.* 1994; Sanders *et al.* 1989: ch. 5.

strong civil libertarian views: some spoke in crime control terms of which any chief constable would be proud.[19] There are also important contrasts between the working practices and experiences of legal advisers according to distinctions such as city–small town, male–female, black–white, and between those acting as duty solicitors and those personally requested by the arrested person (Sanders *et al.* 1989: 20–3).

Moreover, police categorize legal advisers: police culture traditionally distinguishes 'good' and 'bad' legal advisers. Officers frequently talk as if all legal advisers are 'bad' (i.e. they take an adversary role and assert their clients' rights), overlooking not only the mass of generally co-operative 'good' solicitors, but also the minority who 'give advice which their clients cannot reasonably follow . . . or accept the police version of events and advise suspects to confess when the suspect could well have a plausible explanation or alternative to offer' (Sanders *et al.* 1989: 132; cf. McConville *et al.* 1994: chs. 3–5). However, officers make more complex distinctions when referring to specific people, rather than to advisers as an abstract group. As one solicitor commented, 'some legal advisers are respected, some are considered bobbies' men, some are considered just alright and doing a job'. Others are disliked because they are thought to be dishonest, corrupt, or simply pompous. Some 'good' solicitors earn little respect for their co-operativeness, while even some 'bad' solicitors can be liked because of their personalities, if not the advice which they give their clients.

A simple but vital point to make is that criminal justice has to be seen as work, for legal advisers and police alike. This has several aspects: it means that police–legal adviser dealings have to be understood as social and as economic relations, and that such relations have specific histories. In the first place, criminal justice is subject to the same limitations of commitment and pressures for maintenance of social relations as most other work: developing a reasonably comfortable, unstressful relationship with officers may be, at the level of everday social interaction, as important as the legal adviser's formal duties. So, for example, many legal advisers deal with the pressures of working in police stations by developing a 'working relationship'

---

[19] One told us: 'I'll tell you about PACE, without any doubt the most retrograde step of legislation from moribund politicians who have never set foot on the street in the dark. . . . It's a total impossibility to implement the provisions of the Act even if you understand them.'

with officers. One explained: 'I tend to breeze in and out and have a laugh . . . and say "Oh bloody hell, what's he in here for?" and have a bit of a chuckle. That's just to oil the wheels, and it is a social thing.' Entering police territory (Cape 1993: 1; Holdaway 1983) makes some adaptation necessary. However, many legal advisers lack the self-confidence and status of the solicitor quoted above. McConville *et al.* present a starker picture, in which legal advisers' relationship with police allocates them a subservient and marginalised role (1994: chs. 3–5).

The 'fact that . . . police stations are not just legal institutions but the daily work-places' of officers and advisers contributes 'to the development of stereotypes, networks of shared understandings, alliances of alleged adversaries, techniques for routinising the work of policing or processing cases' (McBarnet 1983: 4). These ordinary social relations are important: such 'continuing organizational and informal relations, . . . in their intricacy and depth, range far beyond any priorities or claims a particular defendant may have' (Blumberg 1967: 31). Advising a suspect not to answer questions threatens these significant relations, inviting hostility and non-co-operation from police (McConville and Hodgson 1993: 89, 170; Baldwin 1992a: 45).

These working relations between police and legal advisers are not just social: fundamentally, they are economic relations, with significant historical roots. Before the implementation of PACE in 1986, police directed work to certain solicitors by recommending them to suspects. Contact would usually be made after charge and bail, but on some occasions legal advisers would be called to see a client at the station. Perhaps inevitably, work tended to be directed towards solicitors who had reputations for 'going in and getting coughs for the police'. This also provided an incentive for solicitors to employ ex-police officers as representatives or 'runners': they could use their contacts with people still in the job to get work (cf. McConville and Hodgson 1993: 28; McConville *et al.* 1994: 30–2). PACE formalized the process of providing access to legal advice, and thereby 'improved relations between the police and solicitors. Everyone knows where they stand; they've got a well defined set of rules to work within'. However, pre-PACE practice inevitably has a continuing influence on police–legal adviser relations. While the potential for impropriety is reduced, there is continuing need for collaboration in order to 'make the system work'.

From the police perspective, a suspect's request for legal advice means more work for charge-room staff. It also entails a sometimes frustrating delay in the investigation (although this may be useful if time spent in the station puts pressure on the suspect to confess). It is helpful if the suspect requests a legal adviser who will attend promptly and who 'knows the ropes'. While officers 'have preferences because some people give the police a hard time and others just sit back', the priority is getting on with the case. The division of responsibility made by PACE between charge-room staff and investigating officers is significant here: guidance on legal advice is more likely to be given by the former, whose direct interest is in having the suspect processed, rather than in securing a confession (Bottomley *et al.* 1991: ch. 5; Dixon *et al.* 1990a).[20]

From the legal adviser's perspective, co-operation with police is important as a means of meeting the demands of criminal legal aid practice. For the city firms (or units within firms) specializing in such work, a high turnover of clients is indispensable. For general practice firms (particularly those operating in small-town and rural areas), legal advice to suspects at police stations has to be accommodated with other work. In all cases, station work must be provided economically and is subordinated to court work. McConville and his colleagues provide compelling accounts of structural, cultural, and economic factors affecting the solicitors' profession and producing criminal defence arrangements in which the client is an economic unit to be processed according to the prosecution's case with minimal commitment or intervention by the legal adviser. The main purpose of attending police stations is not to defend a suspect's rights, but rather 'to acquire or retain clients' (McConville and Hodgson 1993: 20). Their picture is of 'a criminal defence practice seemingly concerned with the efficient management and processing of its clients through the "machinery of justice" than with the delivery of justice itself' (McConville *et al.* 1994: 295, ch. 11).

Sanders *et al.* found that 'many 24–hour duty solicitors are not prepared to substantially disrupt their practices and lives to meet the needs of suspects at police stations, particularly to have a legal advisor present for police interrogations' (1989: 190). These joint interests of police and legal advisers produce mutually convenient

---

[20] Until the practice was disapproved in the 1991 revisions to Code C, custody officers relied on legal advisers to act as appropriate adults when parents and social workers were unavailable (Dixon 1990: 107).

arrangements (which will be of increasing importance as criticism of the quality of legal advice leads to action restricting the use of unqualified and junior staff in a solicitor's place: see Bridges and Hodgson 1995; Cape 1993). Although officers are 'nowadays . . . very, very careful' about recommending particular solicitors, it can be done, for example by providing the suspect with the list of lawyers who do criminal work and saying: '[r]un your hand down it and stop when I say so, because he will come out'.[21] Police may short-cut the system by suggesting to a suspect that he or she should see a legal adviser who is already in the station dealing with another client. Similarly, some legal advisers try to pick up work in stations: when informal arrangements with police allow and accusations of touting can be avoided, they check the custody records and even the cells to see 'who else is in and what is going on, to see if there is any . . . more work available'. Another mutually beneficial arrangement involves charge-room staff allowing a firm, when a named solicitor is not immediately available, to arrange a time for attending the station or to offer an alternative (typically, a clerk). This is better for both sides than following the rules to the letter by asking the suspect to nominate another solicitor or offering the duty solicitor scheme or the list of lawyers.

Similarly, demands for legal advice can be filtered by charge-room staff. When PACE was first implemented, legal advisers found themselves being called to stations at all hours of the night to see people whose cases were so simple that detailed advice was considered unnecessary, or who were too drunk to understand it. Subsequently, custody officers usually got such suspects to 'agree' that contact should be delayed until the morning. More generally, the inconvenience (for police and legal advisers) of personal attendance can be avoided by officers encouraging suspects to speak on the telephone to the legal adviser. It may be argued that this is also convenient for the suspect, in that time in detention may well be reduced: however, the inadequacy of the telephone as a means of providing advice means that such 'convenience' may be costly.[22] Co-operation is also wide-

---

[21] Cf. Code C, n. 6B.

[22] See Sanders *et al.* 1989: ch. 6; Dixon *et al.* 1990a: 124; McConville *et al.* 1994: 81–3. Concern about reliance on telephone advice and its limitations led to amendments to the Legal Aid Board Duty Solicitor Arrangements which require a duty solicitor to speak to a suspect on the telephone (subject to a few exceptions) when they receive the initial call and also require attendance in certain circumstances. Advisers who are not duty solicitors are recommended by the Law Society to adopt a similar approach.

spread in arranging times at which suspects will be questioned: if legal advisers do not get the investigating officers to give (and stick to) a time for the interrogation, they may waste valuable time waiting at the police station. The benefit for police is that the investigation can be planned and expedited.[23]

In making such arrangements, the police are without doubt the more powerful party: it is legal advisers who would suffer most by their suspension. Inconvenient early-morning telephone calls and time spent in station waiting rooms remind them of their dependence on police co-operation. More seriously, police may discourage a suspect from requesting legal advice either by employing the 'ploys' identified by Sanders, such as suggesting that it is unnecessary in the circumstances or failing to inform suspects properly of their rights (Sanders *et al.* 1989: 56–64; Sanders and Bridges 1990: 500–1; contrast Dixon 1992: 524–5) or, more overtly, by denigrating the legal adviser requested by the suspect. One solicitor reported that there were 'instances when I have gone down to see a kid and he's said, "I asked for you" and they told him I was crap, "What the fuck do you want him for?" ' In these negotiations between police and legal advisers, the suspect's interests may not be well served. Another solicitor put it candidly: '[y]ou've got to do the best for your client, but you've still got to live with the system many years on. So . . . most solicitors do their best for their clients, but they also . . . won't generally upset the police'. Such contacts may involve accepting the police account of the alleged offence, even presuming the client's guilt rather than innocence (Ericson and Baranek 1982: 94; McConville *et al.* 1994).

(b) *Benefits to Police of Legal Advice to Suspects*

This equivocal, potentially contradictory, negotiated role played by legal advisers strongly influences both their activities in stations, and police attitudes towards them. 'Common sense' tells us that legal advisers obstruct police work by asserting rights and demanding due process: this is hard to reconcile with the fact that officers often perceive considerable advantages from a legal adviser's presence.

A legal adviser can effectively be used as a witness of an interrogation. His or her presence may make it difficult successfully to make

[23] As McConville and Hodgson point out, attributing increasing detention length to delays in legal advisers' attendance overlooks the effect of police deciding when it is appropriate for an adviser to attend the station (1993:39).

allegations of mistreatment,[24] although in some notorious cases, the legal adviser's passivity has been criticized and complaints of mistreatment upheld.[25] An adviser's presence is likely to enable a court to feel justified in drawing an inference from a suspect's silence.[26] Officers often see benefits from the legal advice which suspects receive. Apart from inducing earlier confessions (see immediately below), legal advisers can explain the situation to the suspect and improve communication with the police. One officer put it graphically: '[m]ost prisoners are brain dead and we get more sense out of them if they've got a solicitor'. 72 per cent of officers in our interview survey reported that a legal adviser's presence did not affect—at all or very much—the way they conducted interrogations (Bottomley *et al.* 1991: 119; cf. Sanders *et al.* 1989: 137, 149, 186). Research by Greater Manchester Police reported similar findings. When legal advisers did have an effect on interrogations, this was more likely to be beneficial than detrimental to police interests: 'the widespread assumption that PACE and the duty solicitor scheme load the dice against the police must be challenged' (1988: 18).

For police, a significant benefit of suspects receiving legal advice is that often they are advised to confess or are presented with a set of options of which confession is clearly the most attractive. At the very least, investigative time is saved thereby: officers do not have to do the job 'the hard way', i.e. collecting witness statements and forensic evidence (Sanders *et al.* 1989: 134). As in other settings, clients are discouraged from standing unnecessarily on their rights. In a criminal justice process whose 'single most important feature . . . is its fundamental dependence on the guilty plea' (McConville and Baldwin 1981: 7; cf. Sanders and Young 1994a: chs. 6 and 7), the best advice is often to make an early confession and to cooperate in other ways, such as implicating co-offenders, for which courts give credit in sentencing. Confession may be particularly important if silence might lead to a heavier charge: for example, confessing to possessing drugs in order to avoid accusations of supplying. Similarly, confession can minimize a client's involvement in an offence and distance him/her

---

[24] *Dunn* [1990] Crim. LR 572.

[25] e.g. *Paris, Abdullahi and Miller* (1993) 97 Cr. App. R 99.

[26] The Criminal Justice and Public Order Act 1994, s. 34, provides that, in order for an inference to be drawn, it must have been reasonable in the circumstances for the suspect to have mentioned the fact subsequently relied upon in evidence. The presence of a legal adviser might encourage a court to come to this conclusion, especially after *Murray* v. *UK* (1996) 22 EHRR 29.

from aspects of it (e.g. the use of firearms in a robbery). Co-
operation is also likely to be beneficial when decisions on matters
such as bail, other charges, and the presentation of the prosecution's
case are considered. The adviser's economic interests are as significant as the suspect's rights: a 'good client' is often one who accepts
advice and is 'content to be processed on a guilty plea' (McConville
et al. 1994: 34). Hodgson concludes that 'the empirical reality of custodial legal advice is that it does not occupy a central role in the
adversarial process, but has been redefined by solicitors in essentially
non-adversarial terms' (Hodgson 1992: 861).

Therefore, standard advice provided to suspects is: '[i]f you did it
and they can prove it, you may as well admit it because it will help
at sentence'.[27] Given that, in most cases, there is non-confession evidence available against the suspect (McConville and Baldwin 1981:
ch. 7; Moston *et al.* 1993), most suspects are likely to accept this legal
advice. Clients might well have been informed or reminded of their
right of silence: but this should be distinguished from the less common advice to exercise it (Sanders *et al.* 1989: 129). McConville *et al.*
note the frustration which some suspects feel in being presented
merely with options (to speak or be silent) rather than with advice
on which to adopt (1994: 112–13). Even if silence is advised privately,
this may well not be reinforced during interrogation. McConville *et
al.* rightly stress the significance of this in the light of the legal implications of 'partial silence' (1994: 103–7).

Common sense assumes that legal advice will lead to a reduction
in confessions, charges, and convictions. However, the detailed analysis by Sanders *et al.* found that this connection is weaker than is
usually thought and that a causal link is not clearly established.
Indeed, their conclusion is that 'there seems to be little consistent
relationship between advice, advisor, and outcome' (1989: 146; cf.
Moston *et al.* 1993; Leng 1993: chs. 3–4). It may be that such a connection would be clearer in more serious cases involving more experienced suspects (Irving and McKenzie 1989b: 239, but cf. Ericson and
Baranek 1982: 97). Even if research concluded that this was the case,
it is not necessarily a cause for concern. The system has to have a

---

[27] Ed Cape points out that 'there have been significant efforts to change this culture' and suggests that an adviser who 'displayed the kind of approach referred to
. . . would be unlikely to pass' the accreditation scheme introduced by the Law Society
and Legal Aid Board for clerks and (from 1997) trainee solicitors (personal communication, 5 Mar. 1996; cf. Cape 1993; Bridges and Hodgson 1995).

normal setting, a 'default mode', for the mass of everyday minor cases and inexperienced suspects. PACE does include some special provisions for more serious offences, urgent investigations, and vulnerable suspects. But most rules will be general, providing powers and safeguards in all cases. PACE was supposed to change a system which allowed abuse and, *inter alia*, produced false confessions. The point was put well by one solicitor:

it's had some bad effects in that too many people who know the ropes can get away with things. But the other side of the argument is that those who don't know the ropes are far better protected. . . . You can't treat an experienced defendant and an inexperienced defendant any differently.

Overall, he considered the effects of PACE to be beneficial.

While confession is often advisable, this is not always the case. Considerable criticism has been made of the quality of legal services to suspects in police stations (Baldwin 1992a; Sanders *et al.* 1989; McConville *et al.* 1994; McConville and Hodgson 1993). Relying on representatives (many of whom are ex-police officers) and advising by telephone rather than attending the station personally attracted the displeasure of the Royal Commission on Criminal Justice (1993: 37–8). Characteristically, remedial action was left largely to the Law Society and the Legal Aid Board (RCCJ 1993: 37–9; cf. Bridges and Hodgson 1995).

Some legal advisers whom we interviewed were sharply critical of the priorities and abilities of others operating in the area. Similarly, some suspects express dissatisfaction with their legal advisers' activity on their behalf. McConville *et al.* studied contact between advisers and suspects before, as well as during, interrogation: in 'over three-quarters of all cases, nothing was said about the rights of the client, or the meaning of those rights, and co-operation with the police was assumed or encouraged' (1994: 106). During interrogation, advisers are often passive and unsupportive. Our and others' experience of observing interrogations attended by legal advisers confirmed what Sanders *et al.* found: 'two thirds . . . simply observed and/or made notes' (1989: 137; cf. Baldwin 1992a; Dixon *et al.* 1990a: 120–5; McConville and Hodgson 1993; McConville *et al.* 1994). The effects of such passivity were demonstrated in the Cardiff Three and *Heron* cases.[28]

---

[28] *Paris*, n. 25 above, *Heron* Leeds Crown Court (unreported, 1 Nov. 1993) (see Ch. 4, above).

Sometimes legal advisers act positively against the client's wishes, as field notes from one observed interrogation suggest. A solicitor stated that his client was 'pleased to help the police with their inquiries. The suspect went to argue, but the solicitor shouted him down. . . . The solicitor gave the impression of being pro-police in helping his client to talk'. In the area in which our research was conducted, some advisers had reputations (some of which were a legacy of pre-1986 arrangements) both with police and their colleagues for being too ready to accept the police account of events and to encourage clients to confess (cf. Sanders *et al.* 1989: 131; McConville and Hodgson 1993: 78–80).

Similarly, police and solicitors were often sharply critical of the priorities and practices of the legal advice scheme. One solicitor described it as 'a big machine . . . to churn around a lot of people. . . . It's designed for the big firms to send their legmen out to give naff advice in the cells, so that the punter, when he comes up, goes to that firm.' An officer's view of legal advisers' activity in the station was equally cynical: '[a]ll they want to do is get them signed up for legal aid and then piss off.'[29] Such problems result from negotiated legal adviser–police relations, the priorities of legal professionals, and the economics of criminal law practice. However, the important point for present purposes is that, as argued above, confessing often will indeed be good advice.

An experienced solicitor provided a useful summary of the state of police–legal adviser relations:

there has to be rapport. If the police know the solicitor and trust the solicitor—not to do them any favours or not to be pro-police or lean towards their side of the facts, but to be an honest man [*sic*] who will play it properly and straight—they will cooperate. . . . Years and years ago, the ideal advocate was a great antagonist who would battle and fight,—'You're lying officer' etc. . . . That's gone now. There is a different style of advocacy, a bit more laid back. And therefore a different type of relationship.

Criticism of legal advisers' priorities and practices has led to pressure for them to become more assertive and to act more adversarially. Ironically, this increased police concerns and encouraged action against the right to silence in order to neutralize this perceived development.[30]

---

[29] See also Hodgson 1992: 861; McConville *et al.* 1994.
[30] I am grateful to Ed Cape for suggesting this point.

(c) *Advising Silence*

The function of legal advisers is not (contrary to many suggestions[31]) limited to advising on whether or not to confess. They

must seek to identify misleading statements and prevent questions which are unclear, ambiguous, amount to more than one question, or seek answers about assumed events that have not taken place. They must stop irrelevant issues being raised and undue repetition. They must prevent assertion, comment and the use of technical language or language beyond the understanding of a suspect. They must be on guard for imperfect statements of the law, questions based on false premise, inaccurate recollection of what has already been said, and the whole range of psychological tricks. . . . They have to be firm to comment on bullying, threats, inducements and insulting behaviour. They must identify 'vulnerable' people (Edwards 1993: 33).

Advisers can also make representations about continued detention, charges, bail, and complaints. Suspects can be helped to give their accounts coherently, informed about the law and about rights during custody, and protected from misconduct (Sanders *et al*. 1989: 4, 86; McConville *et al*. 1994: 102). They should be given practical advice on how to deal with the police. As one solicitor explained, 'you have to get clear to your client . . . that nothing with the police is informal' and that they must be careful in talking to detectives who may 'nip into the cell and have a quick word'. They 'should also be advised about the conduct of the interview . . ., how they should read everything three times before they sign it, even if they are fed up and tired'. So advice on silence never exhausted the legal adviser's responsibilities; but it was an important part of them until the 1994 Act (and how much difference the Act will make in practice remains to be seen).

When, before the 1994 Act, were suspects advised not to answer questions? Sanders *et al*. encountered 'only the occasional solicitor' who 'said that s/he advised silence in the majority of cases' (1989: 130). None of the legal advisers whom we or McConville and Hodgson (1993: 87) encountered advised silence as a matter of course. They told us that only the inexperienced would give such advice, which typically was thought to be 'as a blanket rule, wholly pointless'. Some reported that they never advised silence, either because it was thought to be unhelpful to the client or because of principled

---

[31] See, e.g., *Dunford* [1991] Crim. LR 270; *Alladice*, n. 3 above, at 385.

objections to the right of silence. Most suggested that silence would be advised in particular circumstances (cf. McConville *et al.* 1994: 104–8; McConville and Hodgson 1993: ch. 5).

Thus, suspects would often be advised to remain silent when initial contact was made by telephone and the legal adviser arranged to come to the station to advise the suspect before, and to attend, the interrogation. Here, silence was expected to be temporary, a protection for the suspect until proper advice could be given. Such advice was important, because officers frequently tried to get the suspect talking during the wait for the legal adviser's arrival.[32] This should be distinguished from advice to remain silent, which is not followed by attendance at the station, advice which is useless to most suspects (Sanders *et al.* 1989: 130, 132).

In other situations, silence might be advised as a temporary measure because of a particular client's characteristics. If the legal adviser felt that the client was being reticent with or lacked full confidence in him or her, silence might be advised until there had been more time for discussion and consideration. Similarly, silence might be advised if the client was thought to be unfit to answer questions because of the effects of drink or drugs or 'when the suspect is confused or highly emotional and is not really sure what he's being . . . accused of'. Several solicitors stressed that their clients were often 'genuinely frightened' in stations and were 'under great pressure, . . . totally confused . . . and emotional'. In such circumstances, it might be in the interests both of the suspect and the police (in obtaining reliable evidence) for questioning to be delayed.

A more general category of advice was the recommendation of silence as a tactic in negotiations with investigating officers. Here, as elsewhere, it is vital to see criminal justice as a fluid, negotiated process, rather than a static confrontation. A solicitor interviewed by Sanders *et al.* illustrated the point: '[m]y starting point isn't "Let's say nothing unless we absolutely have to". It's rather, "How can we use this interview constructively from our point of view?" ' (1989: 130). This is not to suggest equality of power or voluntary participation here: 'negotiation' is shorthand for a spectrum running though discussion, negotiation, manipulation, coercion, and bargaining.[33] There

---

[32] This partly accounted for the cancellation of 1 in 8 requests for legal advice (Sanders *et al.* 1989: 59, 62–3, 123). Revisions of the Code of Practice made weak attempts to regulate this practice: see Code C (1995), s. 6(6).

[33] Cf. Ch. 3, above.

may be sanctions (in treatment, charge and sentence) for non-co-operation. The suspect is often not involved in the negotiation: this is part of the way in which she or he becomes the subject of the criminal process, rather than an active participant in it (Ericson and Baranek 1982).

Investigating officers want their suspect to confess and to provide information about other offences and other suspects. The suspect wants to avoid being charged and, if this is impossible, to minimize the charges and subsequent penalty for him or herself, and usually to avoid the involvement of friends and family. The legal adviser wants to maintain relations with both client and police. The police have many resources which can be traded—decisions to charge, level of charge (is a broken window to be treated as malicious damage or as attempted burglary?), decisions on bail, implicit or explicit recommendations to the court (and so, effectively, on sentence), and treatment during custody (visits, quality of food, access to clean clothes). The suspect and, more importantly, the legal adviser have only one resource: information. Silence is a way of negotiating access to that information. Consequently, silence might be recommended on a variety of occasions as a tactic during the process of negotiation.

In order to discuss the allegations with the client properly, the legal adviser needs to be given information by the investigating officers about the nature of the available evidence, any admissions which have already been made, other associated suspects in custody, their attitude towards bail, and the level of charges contemplated. As a solicitor told Sanders *et al.*:

To tell a client to make no reply throughout an interview is too easy an option to take. You must find out as much information from the police as possible and then discuss with your client what he says happened. (1989: 130; cf. Irving and McKenzie 1989b: 160–1; RCCJ 1993: 36).

According to one legal adviser in our study, the mutual benefits of negotiated relations mean that

most officers will play straight with you if you play straight with them. They have no useful purpose served by keeping the solicitor in the dark because they know that if they have good strong useful evidence, the solicitor will in general advise their client to tell the truth. . . . Generally I find that the police will tell you what is what. They don't lie to you, but may not always tell you the whole truth. They know what they say will go back to my client and they have to hold something up their sleeve for questioning, and that's fair enough. I don't always tell them the whole truth either; I don't lie to them but I don't always tell them everything. I find that relationship works.

However, this again is the view of a self-confident, experienced solicitor: the activities and experiences of other legal advisers are different. In 45 per cent of McConville and Hodgson's cases, investigating officers were not asked for information (1993: 43). A principal reason was that many officers were not prepared to co-operate, preferring (however counter-productively) the power that information control gave them (McConville *et al.* 1994: 91, 105; McConville and Hodgson 1993: 90–3). A second is, once again, the inactivity of advisers: given that most do not even consult adequately with their clients (McConville *et al.* 1994: ch. 4), it is not surprising if significant attempts are not made to seek information from investigating officers.

If the officers are unco-operative, the legal adviser might respond in kind by recommending that the client should 'keep quiet for the time being. . . . They're not saying anything to me, so let's just listen to what they've got to say.' This approach might be particularly useful when complex offences were involved and the suspect was not in custody. In these circumstances, the legal adviser might formalize the negotiations, by arranging for the suspect to be questioned at the station or elsewhere, asking for a list of questions relating to 'some topics to be covered', and advising silence if the officers do not co-operate.

This was the other side of the legal adviser's willingness to encourage admissions:

I am quite happy, if the police are prepared to show me their evidence, to go into a cell and say to a lad, 'Look, how are you going to explain this? . . . You are going to be charged anyhow.' But the attitude of several police officers . . . is, . . . I'll say 'What have you got?' 'Oh, you'll find out during the interview.' So I will go to that kid beforehand and will say: 'Look, I haven't a clue what they have got. You might as well just keep your mouth shut'.

This result was seen by legal advisers, not as a desirable insistence on a client's rights, but as a product of a lack of police professionalism and investigative skills. These negotiations with investigating officers before questioning can be conducted only if there is some level of co-operation between the 'sides', even if this amounts simply to conceding that 'they've got a job to do'.

Silence may also be used in negotiating how much of an interview is recorded (manually or electronically). These records may give a misleading impression of what the suspect says (and not only in the more traditional form of 'verbals'). Far from being a complete account, the interview record is sometimes constructed in a process which involves the suspect. In some observed interrogations, it was suspects who insisted that answers to certain questions should not be recorded: they were prepared to talk to officers (giving an account of the alleged crime and, particularly, explaining the involvement of others), but only if no record was taken. When the formal record recommenced, the suspect replied '[n]o comment' to questions which had been answered, at least in part, earlier.

In the negotiated relationships between legal adviser, suspect, and police, silence could be used to sanction breaches of formal or informal rules and expectations. Thus if the legal adviser thought that the officers had so little evidence against a client that the legality of the arrest was doubtful, silence would be an appropriate response to questioning. A client who reported that officers tried to get him or her to talk while the legal adviser was not present (either before arrival at the station or between sessions of questioning) might be advised to remain silent until the relationship with officers was satisfactorily renegotiated. As noted above, refusal by officers to show at least part of their hand might be regarded as not playing the game, and countered by advising silence (e.g. Law Society 1988: 27). This was even more likely if officers tried to deceive the legal adviser, for instance by lying about what the suspect or witnesses had said or about the availability of evidence, for example, when it was clear that there has not been sufficient time for fingerprints to be collected and analysed.

During questioning, clients might be advised not to answer questions when officers 'throw something in' by asking about a serious offence which had not previously been mentioned and about which the legal adviser had not had an opportunity to speak to the client (cf. McConville and Hodgson 1993: 160). Advice to remain silent might be used to protect clients from repeated questioning about the same matter when an answer had already been given, or from 'hectoring, badgering, overbearing or over-insistent behaviour'.[34]

---

[34] Irving and McKenzie 1989b: 164. E.g. the defence solicitor in *Samuel* was reported as saying that 'it was not his policy always to advise a client not to answer questions put to him by the police. . . . [In] many cases, it was of advantage to someone in detention to answer proper questions put to him. However on this occasion,

(However, it must again be noted that some advisers do not intervene at all even when their clients are being treated in this way: e.g. Baldwin 1992a: 29–32; McConville and Hodgson 1993: 169.) Legal advisers argued that silence in these circumstances was the result of some officers' lack of professionalism: 'the police bring this upon themselves.'

Silence might also be advised when a client was not responsible for an offence which had been committed, but was connected with it in some way sufficient to justify the investigating officers' reasonable suspicion. 'Common sense' might suggest that the suspect in such circumstances should explain his or her involvement. But, once again, matters are not as simple: attempts to do so might carry real dangers for suspects (Ericson and Baranek 192: 51; McConville and Hodgson 1993: 93–5). Guilt and innocence often are not clearly distinguishable because of the subjective nature of constitutive criteria, such as intention and complicity. As Sanders *et al.* point out, 'the "truth" is not always objective or clear cut. It sometimes has to be worked out, constructed, rationalised, negotiated. Police interrogation is therefore not just a process of discovering the "truth", but is also a process of constructing it' (1989: 139). Once initial suspicion has been established, the working practice of many police investigators is to confirm that suspicion and prove the suspect's involvement, not to seek to establish the truth. In such circumstances, many suspects are unable to deal with questioning and literally talk themselves into trouble.

These examples suggest silence being recommended as part of a skilful strategy by a competent adviser. In contrast, there is the category of 'blanket' advice mentioned above—that given by inexperienced advisers, 'routinely advising the client to exercise silence as a safety-first measure in case they gave inappropriate legal advice' (McConville and Hodgson 1993: 32; see also *ibid.*: 95–7; McConville *et al.* 1994: 106). Such advice was often inappropriate, usually ineffective, and to be understood as a product of the structure and culture of criminal defence work.

Finally, there is the category of advice which is usually the only one considered in the right-of-silence debate. In some situations, legal advisers thought that silence was the best course of action for

knowing that his client had already been interviewed on four occasions and at each had strenuously denied complicity in the robbery and had already been charged with two serious offences, he would probably, after consultation, have advised his client, for the time being at any rate, to refuse to answer further questioning' ([1988] QB 615, at 629–30).

suspects who had committed an offence and against whom a prosecution would fail without evidence of a confession (cf. McConville and Hodgson 1993: 97–8). However, such cases were neither so common nor so straightforward as is usually suggested.

For one thing, the legal adviser would be aware of the potential .dangers of not answering questions (see subsect. (d) below) and so had to be confident that a prosecution was very unlikely without a confession. The adviser who has this confidence will presumably continue to advise silence, despite the Criminal Justice and Public Order Act 1994. Secondly, McConville and Baldwin (1981: ch. 7) demonstrated that confessions are a less significant component of cases than is usually assumed, and consequently that silence did not significantly 'obstruct justice'. It might be thought that this understates the significance of cases not taken to court because of a suspect's silence. Leng's research dispels this: he suggests that abolishing the right to silence would have potential relevance to only about 2 per cent of cases which do not proceed to trial (1994: ch. 3). On the other hand, it is now widely accepted that prosecutions based solely on confessional evidence are undesirable, and that police should develop other investigative techniques. PACE is at least partly responsible for a reported increase in the amount of evidence available against suspects brought into custody, resulting in a shift in the main purpose of many interrogations from obtaining a confession as main evidence to obtaining a confession as additional evidence (Irving and McKenzie 1989b: 145–50).[35] Two-thirds of the officers in our interview sample thought that arrests based on hunches were less common than before 1986 (Bottomley et al. 1991: 61). This trend was noted by a solicitor's clerk (or, as such advisers were usually known, a 'runner') who had had extensive experience as a senior operational police officer: he suggested that investigating officers

are doing their job better. They are getting evidence together and getting their act in order. . . . There is more evidence other than a confession. . . . [In] the old days, they used to just get the confession and that was it. . . . Now they do tend to have done their homework before they begin to interview. . . . If they lock somebody up now, it's generally on some hard evidence, as opposed to the old grass or the officer's suspicion.

It is true that confessions may be necessary to secure some convictions: child abuse and sexual offences are usually cited. This can

---

[35] The opposing view of McConville and colleagues is discussed in Ch. 4, above.

make for a strong emotional case against the right of silence (e.g. Williams 1987). However, no evidence has been produced about the rate at which suspects in such cases refuse to answer questions, or about the effect of such refusals on decisions to charge and convict. The suspect's silence was not included in a police officer's thorough discussion of problems in investigating sexual offences (Blair 1985). On the contrary, the problem is more likely to be the suspect's attempt to construct a defence (typically of consent) and the attitude of police and judges to victims of sexual assault. Such suspects hardly fit the image of the sophisticated, professional criminal whose abuse of the right of silence was the main subject of complaint. Furthermore, refusal to answer questions about sexual offences 'may not be due to the supposed advantages that might develop from exercising the right, but from more psychological reasons' (Moston *et al.* 1993: 40). Evidentiary protection of victims, judicial training, or improvements in police interviewing techniques could be more effective responses.

Finally, the restriction of the right to silence creates considerable difficulties for legal advisers in the context of their professional duties. If a client has committed an offence and refuses to confess, silence may be the only advice which can be given according to professional ethics: '[t]he only thing I can do is to advise them to tell the truth and if they're not going to tell the truth, then to keep their mouth shut'. If the latter option is hazardous (as may be the case following the 1994 Act), the legal adviser's role in encouraging responses to questions will, to some suspects, be indistinguishable from that of the investigating officers (Morton 1988). Alternatively, the legal adviser will have to tread the narrow line of encouraging the suspect, not to lie, but 'to find ways of answering questions without giving anything away' while not exposing him or her to inferences drawn when a defence is subsequently presented. If silence is still advised, legal advisers will have to ensure that an acceptable account of the reasons for so doing is recorded at the beginning of questioning (Cape 1993; Zander 1995: 315–16).

(d) *Advice Against Silence*

Against a background of legal advisers generally advising co-operation with investigating officers, we now consider specific factors which resulted in (relatively few) suspects[36] being advised not to

---

[36] 21.8% in McConville and Hodgson's sample (1993: 69).

answer questions. As suggested above, early confessions may benefit suspects, and silence may be traded away during negotiations with investigating officers. If a suspect has a viable defence or explanation or credibly denies involvement in an alleged offence, he or she would be advised to answer police questions (McConville and Hodgson 1993: 75–7). Also, some legal advisers believed that people arrested on reasonable suspicion should have to give an account of themselves. They felt little sympathy for their clients (McConville and Hodgson 1993: 79–80).

More importantly, such advice would not be easy for most suspects to follow. As several studies have shown, the psychological pressures of detention and questioning make a complete refusal to respond very difficult, particularly if interrogation is carried out by skilful, trained, or merely insistent investigators (McConville and Baldwin 1981:100–1; McConville *et al.* 1994: 108–11; Gudjonsson 1992). Suspects can be drawn into apparently innocuous conversation, not realizing that it forms part of the interrogation and not appreciating the legal dangers of selective silence (see 225 below). A solicitor explained:

However often you tell clients that they don't have to answer questions, they will nevertheless answer every question until they come to a question that incriminates them and then give no reply, thus negating the point of having the option to remain silent, because they are indicating in this way that they have done it.

Other suspects felt that remaining silent would be contrary to their immediate, and apparently paramount, interest of getting out of the police station (Sanders *et al.* 1989: 190), whatever the consequences: 'the client feels under pressure . . . most clients feel that they will only get out of the police cell if they make an admission'.

Questions may be pressed and suspects may be persuaded to speak: suspects are not protected in England and Wales from interrogation by stating that they refuse to answer.[37] Some police officers threaten to exclude solicitors who advise silence[38] and pressurize suspects who attempt to remain silent by asking questions about their refusal to answer questions (McKenzie and Irving 1988: 103; Mackenzie: 1990;

---

[37] See Code of Practice C (1995), n. 1B.
[38] The impropriety of this police practice was confirmed by Code C (1991), n. 6D, and this has survived the 1994 Act: see Code C (1994), n. 6D. None the less, such threats could still be effective against less experienced legal advisers.

McConville *et al.* 1994: 116–26; McConville and Hodgson 1993: ch. 8). In interrogations which we observed, officers asked questions such as: '[w]ould you say that your refusal to answer was an admission you were involved in burglary?' One officer reported that he would say to a silent suspect: 'I take it that by not answering any of my questions you can't give a reasonable answer for your actions . . . do you agree that a magistrate or judge would also form the opinion that your silence is tantamount to guilt?' (cf. McConville *et al.* 1994: 110–11). While the defence might object to the inclusion of such material in evidence, this would often be irrelevant: the questions would have had the desired effects of encouraging a confession and a guilty plea.

Even before the 1994 Act, suspects would have been misled if they believed that there was a straightforward right of silence and that their silence could not count against them in court. It provided an outstanding example of McBarnet's argument that the rhetoric of legality holds out certain rights, but that the reality of law and its practice do not include or protect these rights (see Ch. 1, above). Its value was limited by both the law of evidence and the realities of police, prosecutors', and courts' decision-making. Legally, a crucial issue was 'selective' silence: 'where a number of questions are answered, interspaced with others which the suspect refuses to answer, the whole dialogue is admissible in evidence . . . subject to the trial judge's discretion' (McConville and Hodgson 1993: 176). An adviser's presence could prejudice the suspect in this respect: see *ibid.*: 6). Officers could point this out to suspects (e.g. McConville and Hodgson 1993: 146). This accounted for legal advisers' insistence that clients answered 'all or nothing', as it did for police attempts to get suspects talking 'socially' about matters unconnected with the alleged offence.

Similarly, it is clear that a suspect's refusal to answer police questions might well practically affect the case outcome: it would increase police suspicion, might be commented upon openly or in coded fashion by the judge, and might influence decision-making by magistrates or jury (RCCP 1981: paragraphs 4.39 and 4.48; Zander 1988: 178). The *Crown Court Study* carried out for the Royal Commission on Criminal Justice (Zander and Henderson 1993) found that 'in the overwhelming majority of cases where the defendant had been silent in response to police questions the jury learnt of it' (Zander 1995: 304). Police officers routinely supported calls for removal of the right of silence. However, when asked to comment more specifically on its effects, many made clear that (so long as there was sufficient evidence to get a case into court) a suspect's silence was often helpful to the prosecution, certainly as much as a qualified or contestable confession. In addition, research which traced cases from interrogation through to court found that exercising the right of silence did not reduce a suspect's prospects of avoiding either prosecution or conviction (Moston *et al.* 1993).

(e) Silence Without Legal Advice

The Home Office Working Group on the right of silence assumed that there was a causal connection between legal advice and refusal to answer questions. However, the strength of this might be less than was thought (Brown 1996: ch. 8). It is misleading to assume that legal advice determines a suspect's response. McConville and Hodgson found that some 'may have very decided views about whether to answer police questions' (1993: 68). In 10.6 per cent of their cases, the suspect was silent despite legal advice, while 36.2 per cent chose silence unprompted (1993: 179). As noted above, there were many occasions when silence would not be advised and at least some silence was not attributable to legal advice.

In interrogations which we observed, two suspects who had not received legal advice refused to answer police questions, not for their own benefit, but in attempts to avoid implicating colleagues. When one discovered that his colleagues were also in custody, he confessed (cf. McConville and Hodgson 1993: 183; Baldwin 1992a: 37). It seems unlikely that restricting or even abolishing the right to silence will or could be relevant to such cases.

In other cases, the crucial factor was often the attitude of the suspect: suspects who considered their arrest to be illegitimate (McConville and Hodgson 1993: 100–2) or, more generally, those who were 'anti-police' would often refuse 'to give interviews',[39] or to co-operate in other ways, irrespective of the potential effect on charge and conviction decisions. One legal adviser suggested that the people who stayed silent were 'very anti-police, very anti-social in a general sense, and pretty bad bastards'. This overdramatized matters: in our experience, the anti-police suspect was likely to be, not a hardened,

---

[39] As a suspect, subverting the conventional euphemism, put it in McConville and Hodgson's study: 1993: 99.

sophisticated criminal, but a young male involved in persistent but fairly minor offences (cf. McConville and Hodgson 1993: 99–100). Such people are, from a police perspective, difficult and obstructive. In one interrogation, a young man accused of burglary said '[n]o reply' to a series of questions. After a while, the increasingly frustrated CID officer said:

Q: I take it that you won't answer any questions.
A: That's a bit of a daft question because I don't know what the next one is going to be.
Q: Very well, let me ask you a sensible question. Who were you with last night?
A: No reply.

The interrogation was then abandoned. Such behaviour from what are regarded as arrogant criminals is frustrating. However, a confession was not crucial in this case: the suspect had been witnessed breaking a shop window, had been arrested almost on the spot, and his clothes, which had been taken for analysis, were covered with glass fragments. The fact that he was already 'bang to rights' made his behaviour particularly annoying for the officer (cf. McKenzie and Irving 1988: 101). The detective was seeking his confession in order to avoid having to do the investigation 'the hard way'. Confessions and guilty pleas are the oil in the system: 'it is precisely because of the centrality of interrogation that the exercise of the right of silence' despite its rarity 'so often angers the police' (Sanders et al. 1989: 134).

If legal advisers have a role in cases involving such suspects (and others, such as those 'who think they have some sort of barrack room knowledge'), it is to explain the benefits of co-operation with the police and to discourage silence. However, such suspects often want a legal adviser at the station, not to offer advice, but 'to be there to ensure fair play and that nothing is recorded that isn't said'[40] and possibly to 'sus out what is going on' by talking to and negotiating with police. As Fenwick suggests, the 1994 Act is likely to emphasize this approach to work at stations more generally: the 'roles played by the adviser may become more exclusively those of referee and counsellor . . . to check on adherence to the PACE scheme . . . and to offer reassurance and support' (1995: 133).

According to interviewed police officers, PACE had relatively little effect on the behaviour of such suspects. Typical comments were:

---

[40] e.g. *Alladice*, n. 3 above, at 386.

'[t]he people who aren't going to speak to you wouldn't have spoken to you previously' and 'you always are going to get the obnoxious person who doesn't want to talk to you'. As noted above, three-quarters of these officers thought that, contrary to the prevailing wisdom, PACE had not increased refusals to answer questions. From this perspective, the significant element of PACE was not legal advice, but detention limits: suspects may be able to 'stonewall' more effectively if they know that it will be necessary to do so for a determinable period. In other words, it has given some substance to rights which were previously of largely rhetorical value. Equally, it seems unlikely that such suspects will be much affected by the Criminal Justice and Public Order Act 1994.

iii. Police Questions and Silent Suspects

It is ironic that, as the right to silence is severely restricted in England, Wales, and Northern Ireland, 'a principle of the common law which, on the face of it, is at odds with the inquisitorial traditions of much of continental Europe' should have been incorporated into European law (Dennis 1996: 371; see also Munday 1996). The European Court of Human Rights boldly interpreted the right to a fair trial as implying the privilege against self-incrimination in *Funke*[41] and *Saunders*.[42] However, this has been qualified by *Murray* v. *United Kingdom*.[43] While confirming that the right to remain silent and the privilege against self-incrimination were 'generally recognised international standards which lie at the heart of the notion of fair procedure'[44] in trials and deciding that a conviction could not properly be based solely or mainly upon a suspect's silence, the Court concluded that silence could be taken into account in appropriate circumstances in assessing the weight of other evidence. The acceptability of drawing inferences from silence depended upon the circumstances of a case and a trial court's interpretation of silence. A particularly significant aspect of the decision was the Court's insistence on the need for suspects to have legal advice when making a decision to (or not to) speak. So *Murray* again binds together the rights to silence and to legal advice. Its *direct*

---

[41]   (1993) 16 EHRR 297.
[42]   *Saunders* v. *UK* 19187/91, Report of the European Commission on Human Rights, 10 May 1994.
[43]   N. 26 above; see Wolchover and Heaton-Armstrong 1996: 679–84.
[44]   *Ibid.* 61.

implications are limited in England and Wales: access to legal advice may be delayed but not refused under PACE, and legally authorized delay has been rare since *Samuel*.[45] What, however, of the suspect who does not request legal advice or who is questioned before a legal adviser arrives? A *fortiori*, what of the suspect who refuses to answer or inadequately answers questions outside the police station? Inferences may be drawn from silence, although there is no right to (nor, usually, any practical availability of) legal advice. *Murray* seems to suggest that inferences should only be drawn from silence by a suspect who has received legal advice. If so, the implications for investigative practice should be considerable: officers may find that their interests are served by encouraging rather than discouraging legal advice at stations, especially if advisers continue to approach their duties in the ways noted above. Consequently, the decision also demonstrates the need for legal advisers who are active, capable, and committed to their clients' interests. While accurate prediction is hazardous, the 'only really safe wager is that, given the expansionist tendencies of the ECHR, the scope of the application of any right of silence is more likely to spread than to shrink' (Munday 1996: 384).

The implications of *Murray* for Australia also deserve comment. Pressures to follow the English example are growing[46] and opponents of the right to silence often uncritically refer to English debates, even though Australian suspects have no substantial rights to legal advice.[47] The High Court has, characteristically, been more concerned to defend the right than English counterparts.[48] The ECHR's development of the concept of the fair trial chimes with the High Court's vigorous insistence on its constitutional significance.[49] In both Australia and Europe, future discussion of the right to silence will have a significant constitutional context.[50]

---

[45] *Ibid.* None the less, informal means may be used to delay or obstruct access (Cape 1993: 39).

[46] e.g. Gibbs 1988; Odgers 1985; 'Judge urges removal of the right to silence', *The Age*, 29 Oct. 1994.

[47] i.e. there is no public funding for in-station legal advice or duty solicitor schemes: see Ch. 5.

[48] *Petty* (1991) 173 CLR 95. However, cf. the High Court's decision on silence at trial in *Weissenstiener* (1993) 178 CLR 217.

[49] *Dietrich* (1992) 109 ALR 385; Brown *et al.* 1996: 253–94. The right to silence has been consolidated by the Commonwealth and NSW Evidence Acts 1995, s. 89, which forbid unfavourable inferences being drawn from silence. See generally Aronson and Hunter 1995: 326–38.

[50] See Munday 1996. More generally on the potential influence of the ECHR, see Ashworth 1994 and Feldman 1993.

How will the restriction of the right to silence affect the interaction between police and suspects? As in Northern Ireland where the right to silence was similarly restricted in 1988, 'little thought seemed to be given to what the consequences . . . would be' (J. D. Jackson 1991: 413). It was simply assumed that the mythical, rational 'silent suspect'—the product of legal advice and professional criminal experience—would be dealt with. Reports from Northern Ireland suggest that things have hardly gone as planned, and conviction rates have not increased.[51] If, as has been argued above, the restriction of the right to silence was founded on an inaccurate conception of how criminal justice works, it is not surprising that the change did not have the expected effects.

In their enthusiasm for action against the right to silence, the police may have underestimated its implications for them, particularly the impetus which it may give to developments in interrogation practice. If, as Addison suggests, 'suspects can only reasonably be expected to mention facts about which they were actually questioned', then officers will have to plan questioning and 'ensure the points are put whether the suspect is answering or not. . . . [They] must be precise, clear and unambiguous in their questions' (1995: 21). Police interview techniques are all too often inefficient and ineffective (Baldwin 1993a).

Too often, questioning is rambling and vague, and officers can quickly get angry with suspects who are being unhelpful, sarcastic or simply say 'no comment' to everything. That has got to change . . . if officers make their disdain apparent, it may be difficult to hold any subsequent silences against the suspect. It would not be difficult for a defence lawyer to argue that a suspect who is disbelieved has a good reason to remain silent (Addison 1995: 21).

This beneficial effect of the 1994 Act may be counterbalanced by one less welcome. An important feature of PACE (as developed by the Codes of Practice) is controlling police interrogation by insisting that, if evidence of it is to be used, it should be conducted in a police station where recording and supervision are available. Requiring a suspect to give information to officers at or before arrest in order to avoid adverse inferences inevitably provides fertile ground for dis-

---

[51] See J. D. Jackson 1991; 1993. The suppression of a police officer's study of the right to silence in Northern Ireland because of its apparently inconvenient conclusions (Zander 1994: 144, n. 4) contrasts starkly with the publicity given to the English police research discussed at 235 above.

putes about what was (or was not) said.[52] Failure to consider such systemic effects of restricting the right to silence is characteristic of how debate on the issue proceeded.

What of the 'hardened' professional criminals whose 'abuse' of the right so infuriated its critics? Twining's ridicule is still apposite, as officers warn of 'new age' criminals 'exploiting the weaknesses of the judicial processes'.[53] Unfortunately, while criminals have become more sophisticated, 'progress, it seems, has not affected our police in comparable fashion'. Just as two decades ago, we are confronted with

The New Criminal Class Problem . . . Diagnosis: There is a new class (of unspecified size) of sophisticated criminals who abuse (with unspecified frequency) the safeguards designed to protect the (uncounted, countless?) weak, stupid, illiterate, spontaneous or slow-witted, accused. Prescription: remove safeguards for all accused (1973: 349).

Even setting aside doubts about this stereotype of the professional criminal,[54] it is unlikely that the 1994 Act will have the desired effect. As the Royal Commission on Criminal Justice suggested, '[t]he experienced professional criminals who wish to remain silent are likely to continue to do so and will justify their silence at trial by stating that their solicitors have advised them to say nothing at least until the allegations against them have been fully disclosed' (1993: 54). Focusing on professional criminals can inadvertently raise awkward issues. As Ashworth suggests, a claim about professional criminals' resistance to interrogation 'introduces conceptions of power into the debate. It implicitly recognises that the police have great power over suspects

---

[52] Hand-held recorders are unlikely to provide a satisfactory solution. It is notable that the Police Federation argued that inferences should be drawn from silence only in formal PACE interviews ('Judges force Howard into another justice Bill retreat', *The Times*, 12 Apr. 1994).

[53] David Phillips, Chief Constable of Kent, quoted *The Times*, 2 Dec. 1993.

[54] Some of the defendants whose use of the right to silence attracted judicial ire hardly fitted the image of the experienced professionals who allegedly abuse the right of silence. For example, in *Samuel*, a suspect was arrested after returning to and making a deposit at the Building Society which he had allegedly robbed. Photographs showing him 'kissing bundles of bank notes' were found in his house: *Samuel*, n. 34 above, at 618). Immediately after the robbery which he carried out, the defendant in *Alladice*, 'who was aged 18 and unemployed . . . spent almost £3000 on buying and insuring a BMW motor car and paying off debts'. As Lord Lane conceded, he 'could scarcely . . . be classed as a sophisticated criminal' (n. 3 above, at 382, 384). None the less, he used the case to fulminate against the right to silence. More generally, defining professionalism merely in terms of seriousness of offence and/or previous convictions is manifestly inadequate (cf. Brown 1997 ch. 8).

in most investigations, and that rights without the power to exercise them are a sham' (1996: 224).

What of other types of suspect? Account must be taken of the effect of the new caution on suspects who would not, even under the previous caution, have stayed silent. This may seem paradoxical, but it is crucial to appreciate that the change in the right to silence has important consequences for all suspects. While legal commentators rightly stress the specificity of the 1994 Act, to focus only on its effect upon 'ambush' defences is to fall victim to a legalistic, court-centred fallacy which overlooks the impact on the mass of other cases, most of which will be settled by guilty pleas. The old caution was a state-ment of warning (which is one reason why it was so often not given). The new caution is much more like a threat about the consequences of non-cooperation, thereby substantially increasing the power of an investigating officer over a suspect.[55]

As the discussion above suggested, there are various reasons why some suspects do not answer police questions. It is misleading to describe all these silences as exercises of a right: 'exercise' surely implies some consciousness by the actor. Some suspects who do not answer questions were not exercising a right: they were simply refus-ing to or were unable (for reasons of fear, vulnerability, etc.) to speak to police. This is not a semantic quibble: it speaks directly to the expected benefits of restricting the right to silence, for there was no consideration of how such suspects would react to the new caution. Further, it raises questions about the whole enterprise of counting exercises of the right to silence: researchers have quite misleadingly constructed a category and allocated disparate phenomena to it. Indeed, it could be argued that an exercise of the right to silence can only be identified retrospectively, i.e. when a court refused to allow inferences to be drawn from a defendant's silence (or police or pro-secutor abandoned a case in the expectation of such a refusal). What researchers study are, at best, attempts to exercise the right to silence, and these, as suggested above, can only be identified by subjective cri-teria.

To similar effect, McConville and Hodgson insist that the 'debate' has been misled by focusing on suspects' or (as they suggest is more appropriate: 1993: 198) detainees' responses, rather than on the ques-tions which they are asked. If these are illegitimate (by, for example,

[55] Shepherd *et al.* (1995) found that 80% of their sample 'saw the adverse inference as pressuring or threatening' (Munday 1996: 379; see also Wasik and Taylor 1995: 55).

seeking comment on matters beyond the suspect's knowledge), repetitious, irrelevant, improperly put (e.g. abusive or leading), there can be no obligation to reply, and no proper inference of guilt taken from silence. McConville and Hodgson conclude that when 'this more sophisticated analysis is made, at least one third of "silence" cases in conventional empirical terms do not in truth involve the assertion of a right to silence and ought not to be counted as such' (1993: 188–9). Leng's study admits a category of cases which opponents of the right to silence tended to ignore: instances when a suspect answers all questions, but 'fails to disclose a particular matter which he later raises or intends to raise in his defence'. (It is this failure, rather than silence, at which the 1994 Act's change is notionally directed.) However, if a charge does not follow or is dropped, this exercise of the right to silence is not amenable to empirical analysis (1993: 8). Different, but as great, problems would be involved in any attempt to measure exercise of the right to silence outside the interview room or, *a fortiori*, the police station. Even more problematic is the failure in the debate on the right to silence to define criteria by which use of the right to silence at a certain level is judged excessive. At some unspecified and unjustified point, silence is simply assumed to become problematic.

More generally, the deficiencies of the right-to-silence debate reflect features of criminal justice research which are products of theory (or lack of it), policy-orientation, and access arrangements. Taking an exercise of the right to silence as a common-sense category is characteristic of a research tradition which generally pays little detailed attention to suspects and defendants, and which rarely looks beyond its disciplinary boundaries. For example, there is a rich stream of anthropological literature which makes clear that 'silence, like any linguistic form, gains different meanings and has different material effects within specific institutional and cultural contexts' (Gal: 1991: 176; cf. Saville-Troike 1985). At the very least, the differential effects of race,[56] gender, age, intellectual ability,[57] and class on the uses and meanings of silence have to be acknowledged. Just as 'exercises of the right to silence' are not a unitary category, so it is necessary to specify and to distinguish suspects. More generally, it is important to acknowledge differential responses to criminal justice, for example

[56] See Eades (ed.) 1995.
[57] For some rare empirical work on how people with an intellectual disability understand the right to silence, see NSW LRC 1993.

gendered differences in responses to accusations (Worrall 1990: 74–5). Women in McConville and Hodgson's sample were much less likely than men to remain silent (1993: 177; cf. Ainsworth 1993). It is also important to note the significance of the characteristics of legal advisers: those who are women may be patronized or marginalized (e.g. McConville and Hodgson 1993: 152), while those who are black may suffer particular difficulties. Such observations, no doubt, will be dismissed by some as irrelevant to the practical world of policy-oriented research. Such a reaction would be short-sighted: formulating policy based on inaccurate stereotypes is more properly seen as unacceptable self-indulgence.

In conclusion, it is appropriate to comment on the wider context of the 'common sense' which distorts discussion of the right to silence. This common sense is typically constituted by court-focussed misconceptions of how the criminal process actually works, a translation of opinion into objective truth, and an inability to conceive that there are ways of experiencing the world other than one's own.[58] It assumes that a 'formal and hierarchical understanding of the criminal process . . . is reproduced in the minds, attitudes, motivations of defendants. It assumes that they experience the process—the procedures, safeguards, penalties—in the ways in which they are legally and conventionally prescribed' (Hogg 1991a: 10). As Hogg suggests, the suicides of so many Australian Aboriginal people during pre-trial detention for 'trivial offences carrying minor penalties' tragically make the point that the 'formal threats and safeguards prescribed by the legal process appear as nothing when compared to the apparent experience of the process by these prisoners in the context of the rest of their lives' (ibid.). More specifically, this common sense is a product of the dominant discourse of due process in criminal justice and 'the traditional legal conception of a criminal case as an adversary, combative proceeding, in which counsel for the defense assiduously musters all the admittedly limited resources at his [sic] command to defend the accused' (Blumberg 1967: 18). It is anachronistic that this discourse has retained so strong a hold in discussion of the right of silence. The concept of adversary justice corresponds to the prob-

---

[58] See, e.g., Cross, 'simply . . . giving tongue to the utterances of common sense', on how to deal with unjustified questioning by a police officer: 'slamming the door in his face' may be an option for a law professor, but it is not for those who usually encounter the police on their doorsteps (1970–1: 71, 72).

lematic metaphor of 'balance'[59] which provides the context for arguments that allowing suspects to have legal advice must entail restricting the right to silence.

The fundamental weakness of this approach is that it conceives of criminal justice essentially as a legal institution rather than as a social process, and does so in legalistic rather than sociological terms (Loader 1995; Walker 1996). A number of well-known studies of later stages in the criminal process showed the substantial gap between legal reality and the ideology of due process and adversary conflict (Baldwin and McConville 1977; Bottoms and McClean 1976; Carlen 1976; Ericson and Baranek 1982; McBarnet 1983; McConville and Baldwin 1981; McConville and Mirsky 1986–7). They showed that many cases are dealt with (not always in the suspect/defendant's best interests) by arrangement, compromise, and negotiation, in order to produce the guilty pleas around which the system is currently organized. Negotiated justice is neither deviance from the way in which the system is intended to work, nor is it simply produced by the imperatives of an overloaded bureaucracy. It is 'the system'. It is non-negotiated justice which is abnormal. (Recognition of this is a notable feature of the first significant general studies of criminal justice in England and Wales: Ashworth 1994; Sanders and Young 1994a.) These insights require a critical understanding of criminal justice, freed from the constraining and misleading dualities of crime control and due process.[60] As McBarnet argues, 'the pressures to plead guilty lie not just in negotiations, informal liaisons and bureaucratic interests, but also in the legal system itself' (1983: 78).

Advising a suspect in a police station is the beginning of this process. It should not be surprising to find that, here too, we often find negotiation rather than adversarial confrontation, and the arrangement of case disposition rather than an insistence on rights. The presence of the legal adviser in the station cell and the interview room may often be better understood, not as a disruptive introduction of due-process values, but as an earlier introduction of pressures for informal settlement (Bottoms and McClean 1976: 321). It is only when criminal justice is seen in this way that the right to silence, and the effect of legal advice upon its exercise, can be properly understood.

Debate about the right to silence has been populated by caricatures: the skilful, aggressive police interrogator; the committed,

---

[59] See critique in Ch. 7, below.   [60] See Chs. 1 and 7.

adversarial defence lawyer; and, of course, the manipulative silent suspect.[61] The unreality of these figures suggest that the debate has been about the right to silence only at a superficial level. On both sides,[62] it has been used as a touchstone by which broader commitments and opinions are tested. It is, of course, not unusual for legal debates to be conducted through myths and symbols.[63] However, the costs of distortion may be high. It may be that the Criminal Justice and Public Order Act, section 34, may, by providing a legislative conclusion to the long debate, open the way for more constructive, accurate, and principled discussion of legal regulation of, and policing practice in, the questioning of suspects.

[61] Cf. Baldwin's comments about the misconceptions, misunderstandings, and mythology about police questioning (1992c: 8). While providing a more realistic picture of suspects and legal advisers, Baldwin's work is particularly valuable in demonstrating the inefficiency and incompetence of many police interrogators (1992c; 1993a; see also Moston and Engelberg 1993).

[62] Of course, it has been more complicated than this dichotomy suggests: see Greer 1990.

[63] The controversy leading to the 1994 abolition of unsworn 'dock statements' in NSW had many of the characteristics of English debates about the right to silence: see Hunter and Cronin 1995: 264–5.

7
Legality, Regulation, and Policing

Even the least event had lines, all tangled, going back into the past, and beyond that into the *unknown* past, and other lines leading out, also tangled into the future. Every moment was dense with causes, possibilities, consequences (Malouf 1990: 296).

This final Chapter begins with discussion of how the practices and forms of law and policing intersect. The second section goes on to discuss the limits and possibilities of the legal regulation of policing.

i. Intersections of Law and Policing

This conclusion does not, as might be expected, set out to provide a new theory of law in policing. Such a theory is what seems to be expected when complaints are made about, for example, 'the mystery surrounding the rules/behaviour relationship' (Goldsmith 1990: 112; cf. Reiner 1992a: 212; Reiner and Leigh 1994: 79, 107). However, the research discussed above suggests that a general, formulaic theory of this kind is unlikely to be appropriate: relations between law and policing depend on the kind of policing, the kind of rules, and their socio-political contexts. While sociological explanation requires looking for patterns, it must allow for the possibility that discontinuities and inconsistencies are (or are at least part of) the pattern. This empirical pluralism may best be matched by theoretical pluralism. As Garland suggests in the field of penality, 'there is a real danger of singular—and hence reductionist—interpretations coming to dominate' (1990: 2). In understanding law in policing, various theoretical perspectives are of value, and the way forward is to draw on elements of various approaches without slipping into a naïve meccano model of theoretical formation.

Analysing the relationship between law and police practice requires a synthesis of the 'culturalist' and 'structuralist' positions. . . . The art of successfully regulating policing practice is dependent on understanding the complex relationship between formal rules and procedures, the sub-cultural rules of the police themselves, the structure of the police organization, and the practical exigencies of the tasks of policing (Reiner and Leigh 1994: 79; cf. Brown 1996: ch. 12; Walker 1993b: 47).

Significant variables are likely to include the ways in which rules are expressed and communicated, the immediate and long-term political contexts, the support for or opposition to change in police and other criminal justice agencies, the level of commitment to actively seeking compliance and the provision of effective sanctions for non-compliance, and the significance (or otherwise) accorded in popular culture and discourse to rights and the limits of police powers. In this section, some insights from the work surveyed in Chapter 1 will be expanded in the light of my research in England and Australia.

(a) *Making Cases*

First, building on the constructionist approach, the emergent quality of law in policing must be stressed. Police and lawyers work on the original material (hunch, suspect, physical evidence, witnesses), infusing it with law, translating it into legal categories, making a case. The work of detectives is, as Ericson's germinal account explains 'making crime' (1981b: cf. Miyazawa 1992). The point can be illustrated by examining how legality took material form when suspects were charged in one of the police stations which I observed in New South Wales. Such a procedure has conventionally come to be seen as a degradation ceremony (Garfinkel 1956). This stresses the negative; but it can also be seen as a constructive creation of legal matter. The suspect was placed in (and sometimes handcuffed to) the dock, a railed enclosure like that found in older courtrooms. The charge was read to the suspect and written into the charge book, using the stilted formalities of legal language.[1] The in-station charging process marks, both practically and symbolically, a new stage in the criminal process. An investigation produces incident report forms, crime reports, fact sheets, charge sheets, and a complete 'brief' for court: in this process, the matter becomes increasingly 'legalized'. As a matter takes on its legal appearance, it moves out of the control of investi-

---

[1] Convenient shortcuts were provided first by the provision of rubber stamps carrying details of some charges and, more recently, by computerized charging, in which the appropriate wording is available in an on-line system.

gating officers: they take on a new status, of witnesses who will appear in court to give evidence (in the rare cases not concluded by a guilty plea). As they lose contact with a matter, their knowledge about the system becomes more generalized and less experiential.[2] Their comments about criminal justice become increasingly abstract, and they tend to repeat familiar police complaints about the law's technicalities and chicaneries obstructing 'justice'.

As these observations suggest, bureaucratic processes play an important part in this, showing again how the legalistic and bureaucratic aspects of policing are entwined. An arrest becomes legal matter in tangible and recognizable, standard form, as a prosecution file is opened, information is entered and interpreted, previous files and documents (e.g relating to earlier inquiries or to search warrants) are included or cross-referenced, and revisions and additions are subsequently made (McConville *et al.* 1991a: 6–7). Chatterton has demonstrated the importance of 'paperwork' in policing: the time spent creating prosecution files 'produces the cases which enable the police organisation to interface with the courts and other organisations. Events, incidents and encounters are shaped, ordered and transformed through this paperwork into recognisable, typical cases' (1989: 110; see also Kemp *et al.* 1992: 99–108; Manning 1980: 220–4; Manning and Hawkins 1989: 151–2). Far from being residual or

marginal practices, mastery of paperwork and the ability to manipulate the 'paper reality' are core police skills. . . . The ability of the police to create a convincing paper record is a necessary part of successful case construction. Cases against individuals . . . are cases made out on paper, subject to assessment on paper and, for the most part, decided upon paper' (McConville *et al.* 1991a: 98, quoting Goffman).

Records are 'designed—implicitly or explicitly—to produce an effect in some kind of audience, which itself actively uses records to interpret events. . . . [They] serve as cognitive devices that order and frame, sort and name' (Van Maanen and Pentland 1994: 53, 81). 'Legalizing' a case involves the creation and transmission of 'paper',[3]

---

[2] For an extreme example of officers losing contact with 'their' case, see *Foster* ([1993] ALR 1) which is discussed at 279 below, and, in its legal context, in Ch. 5 above. See also Caplan 1974: 66.

[3] This is increasingly metaphorical with the introduction of other modes of storing and presenting data, notably video tape (Dixon and Travis 1997) and computer disk (see e.g. the discussion of information management in NSW Police 1995: issue paper 2).

not just to other parts of the formal criminal justice 'system', but also to other providers of security to whom police act as 'knowledge brokers, expert advisors and security managers' (Ericson 1994b: 153; cf. Ericson and Haggerty 1997).

When Bittner, Wilson, and others spoke of law as providing a resource for officers, they referred to the availability of legal categories in which to place social activity (see Ch. 1, above). Particularly in dealing with low-level disorder, police intervene to stop trouble, to regain control, to impose order, to harrass the marginal: only subsequently (if at all) is the law summoned to justify and classify the interventions.[4] But similar legal work goes on throughout the process, as an incident is transformed into a case. The individuals subject to police attention are also transformed, as they become first suspects, then prisoners, then defendants. Particularly valuable accounts of such processes of construction have been given by feminist writers' accounts of women in criminal justice (Smart 1995: ch. 11; Worrall 1990). Elements of the person's identity are identified and emphasized (and possibly supplemented by imputed characteristics of the person's group, race, or type) while others are omitted as irrelevant. These processes involve the construction of the person in a shape suitable for legal processing, a translation into an appropriate subject of legal discourse. This is not, as a simple labelling account might suggest, a linear process: some will drop out as they are bailed or cautioned, or as cases are designated as requiring no further action (NFA) or as charges are dropped (McConville et al. 1991a: 103–5).

In these processes, the legal nature of detectives' work has received much less attention than it deserves. Most detective work is not detection, but the transformation of an incident into a case and an individual into a defendant by the collection, categorization, and presentation of evidence (Bradley et al. 1986: 186–92; Burrows and Tarling 1982; Sanders 1977; Ericson 1981b). It provides a particular example of broader processes by which legal discourse provides and adapts categories (Burton and Carlen 1979). Interrogation is an especially important site for the 'legalization' of accounts, For example, McConville et al. point to the use of 'legal closure questions' whose apparent purpose is

---

[4] A critical perspective on police 'peace-keeping' is given by Kemp et al. (1992) who demonstrate how and why many incidents which could (and often should) be treated as crimes are ignored, downgraded, or 'decriminalized'.

to invite the suspect to provide information but in reality force information into a legally significant category in the hope that the suspect will 'adopt' it. This may involve introducing some matter not previously mentioned or it may reshape what has been said so that it now 'fits' into an appropriate legal category (1991a: 70).

Most importantly, suspects have to be led to speak an account of their actions which satisfies legal requirements of mens rea, so that, for example, reference is made to stealing, rather than simply to taking, or to acting recklessly, rather than accidentally (McConville *et al.* 1991a: 70–1). The legal (re)construction is of course not a neutral process: as the police and prosecution construct the case in their terms, so the suspect/defendant's version of reality is marginalized and she or he has to battle for a hearing within the formal dialogue. In fact, most do not do so: the process of marginalization alienates, all too often producing suspects and defendants who are mute and passive (Brogden and Brogden 1984: 42; McBarnet 1983: ch. 7; McConville *et al.* 1991a: 208). The experience in court of being treated as the subject of, rather than as a participant in, proceedings culminates in a process of being ordered and ignored. Physical treatment plays its part, as the suspect/defendant's body is appropriated by arrest, search, fingerprinting, and storing in cells.

Occasionally, accounts may be 'delegalized'. People attracting police attention may be steered away from criminal responsibility if, for example, they turn out to be police officers themselves. Some incidents are notoriously prone to delegalization: an obvious example is the traditional police response to domestic violence (Hanmer *et al.* (eds.) 1989; Kemp *et al.* 1992: ch. 6). Another example is provided by Ericson:

two detectives responded to a call dispatched to patrol officers regarding a 'break and entry in progress' at a school administration building. One of the detectives entered the building and emerged with a suspect who turned out to be an inarticulate mongoloid [*sic*] individual. . . . The detectives turned the culprit over to the patrol officers who had subsequently arrived, saying 'He's all yours.' (1982: 57).

As Ericson comments, this situation is the reverse of the usual in which detective officers take over patrol officers' cases, often much to the displeasure of the latter (1982: 56–7). The point is that a decision was made to treat the detective's 'culprit' as requiring not legal, crime-related work, but welfare, 'service' work: the characteristics of the suspect determined this result. In other situations, detectives may simply ignore occurrence reports submitted by patrol officers (Ericson 1981b: 8)

It has been argued above that law is an emergent feature of the police handling of 'a case'. What this 'legalization' means needs to be specified. As Ericson (1981b, 1994b) and Manning (1977, 1992; see also Manning and Hawkins 1989) suggest, the processing of a case is information and communication work. The rules of substantive and procedural law provide the language and framework of the accounts which must be given of police action. To Ericson, detectives are 'accountants' who 'explain, justify, and legitimate their actions with respect to what they think are the appropriate rules, and these rules are used in conjunction with their accounts to orient their actions' (1981b: 16–17; see also 1982: 13–14; 1994b; Manning 1977: 101, 141; Van Maanen and Pentland 1993). An important function of this accounting is to confirm the action's legitimacy and justification: law provides the pigeonholes into which the actions of suspect and police officer alike can be slotted (Bittner 1990: 194, 197, 246). For example, officers stop and search people for a variety of reasons, but only some of these are legally sufficient (Dixon *et al.* 1989). In completing a stop and search record (required under PACE), an officer in England and Wales may, like American counterparts, have to 'try later to figure out what the suspect did which might have justified the search' (Skolnick 1975: 220). 'Later' may mean on the street, where the form should be completed[5] or back in the station, where assistance may be available. Reinterpretation may be needed for arrests as well as for searches. As an English sergeant commented,

Often . . . the bobby out on the street . . . doesn't appreciate what the rules are until he's back in here. He's got to make an instant decision; sometimes the rules and regulations go by the board and he uses his common sense. Then he may find when he comes into the police station that he's done something he shouldn't have, or he's used a power that he didn't have. Then we have to sort of find a way round that—find him a power! (Dixon *et al.* 1989: 196–7).

More is involved here than mere legitimation: all describing and accounting for action involves active interpretive work. Incidents are

---

[5] Police skills should not be overestimated: our study of PACE stop and search forms found many entries which were legally inadequate: see Dixon *et al.* 1989; Bottomley *et al.* 1991: 40–2.

reconstructed as stories, in which legal definitions and requirements provide cues, plots, and character development (Manning 1992; cf. Bennett and Feldman 1981: 4–5; Shearing and Ericson 1991). To understand law in policing involves making a choice of viewpoint. In *Police Work*, Manning suggests a dichotomy: one can begin with the law and see how police work corresponds to or deviates from it; or one can begin with police work, and see how law is used. Manning criticizes Skolnick and Reiss for being too legalistic:

> That is, they see the legal template as a reality existing 'out there' somewhere from which police are obligated to draw authority, guidance, constraint, and justification. . . . [I]t is more useful to describe what the police do and how they rationalize it to themselves and others than to hold up a fictive comparative ideal such as 'the law' (1977: 204; see also Chatterton 1976: 114).

However, this distinction is too rigid: police activities and their rationalization cannot be understood apart from law. Even when (as the discussion in Chapter 3 of the relations between 'policing by law' and 'policing by consent' suggested) some police practices may be structured by extra-legal criteria, this is not to suggest that law does not affect what police do.

In subsequent research on legal decision-making, Manning has provided a fuller account by usefully adapting Goffman's concept of framing (1992; cf. Manning and Hawkins 1990; MacLachlan and Reid 1994: ch. 3). Policing activities are fitted into legal frames as cases are 'legalized'. Again, interrogation provides a good example: there is a significant (but, as yet, inadequately traced) link between the trend in areas of modern substantive criminal law towards requiring proof of subjective intention and police use of interrogation in order to obtain confessions (Sanders 1987; Fletcher 1976: 525–7; Tiffany *et al.* 1967: x). In addition to mens rea, officers know that they have other 'points to prove' (elements of actus reus) in relation to various offences (Calligan 1988). Such requirements affect the way officers work.

Lustgarten pointed out that frames may not be visible if, in culturalist fashion, the focus is tightly on 'the custom and practice of policework'. As he suggests, policing has 'evolved within contexts: it did not just "happen". One of these contexts is substantive law' (1986:180). Acknowledging the influence of McBarnet, he argued that, for example, police treatment of suspects 'is not simply the result of what the police think appropriate; it has flourished within a structure of rules and judicial attitudes that puts few restraints upon them' (1986: 180; cf. Remington 1967: ix). This echoes Grimshaw and Jefferson's suggestion (see Ch. 1, above) that the activities of resident beat officers was structured by law despite their apparent lack of legal work (1987: 179).

A problem with the 'framing' metaphor is that it can suggest the placing and presentation of given material within boundaries which provide definition without affecting substance. This limitation makes it more attractive to think in terms of law in policing as a discourse, allowing for a more active role for participants and for the interpretive shifts in constructing cases which have been suggested above. As Kemp *et al.* suggest in their analysis of police handling of disputes, officers 'translate complex situations in their unique and concrete specificity into . . . the structured vocabulary of organisational and legal discourse' (1992: 88). Law is activated in policing 'by the police officers who bring to bear on the incident their own interpretation of the relevant legal categories. . . . In the process of translation from one discourse to another (from commonsense to law) the "text" is filtered through the personal, occupational and organisational concerns of the patrol officer' (1992: 92; cf. Grimshaw and Jefferson 1987). This implies that what is required is study of the law 'in action'. This is not intended to revive the old distinction between law in the books and law in action, which really meant 'the police in action' (Kemp *et al.* 1992: 87). Rather, it suggests the need to study law as an active, constituting part of policing practice.

(b) *Distinctions*

The perspectives discussed in Chapter 1 indicate another sense in which 'law' must be disjointed. There is a clear need to appreciate that law can and does change, that it can take very different forms, and that this points to a need for specific historical, cultural, and legal analyses. Most obviously, there are distinctions between the procedural and the substantive. But there are also significant distinctions within these categories: for example, the differences between types of procedural rules have been noted in debates about regulation, including the strategy adopted in PACE (Baldwin and Houghton 1986). As has been noted above, some categories of substantive offences (e.g. disorderly conduct or offensive language) are infinitely flexible, while some include quite clear rules (e.g. a traffic speed limit). In the latter case, the significant discretion is not in interpretation of law, but in its application (and situational factors—time, place, type of car, perceived characteristics of occupants—will influence this discretion). Breaking the rule is the necessary (but not sufficient) reason for intervention, whereas in the former, police intervene to restore public order and police authority, with law as a classifying and disciplining resource.

A corollary is that law in policing varies greatly in terms of the possibilities of intervention: it is in this way that distinctions must be made between policing on the street and in the station. McConville *et al.* are ambivalent about this: while their general analysis treats street policing as the paradigm for police work in general (McConville *et al.* 1991a: 16–17), they also recognize that the 'degree of control enjoyed by the police over case production is not constant but varies according to a host of factors, including case seriousness, the nature of internal supervision, the structure of legal provisions and so on' (1991a: 37) and they go on to contrast the potential for regulation of policing in the street and the station. Leng claims that the distinction between supervision in and outside stations is invalidated by the cursory attention which in-station supervisors pay to stop/search records (1995: 212). This misses the point, which is to focus not on particular supervisory mechanisms, but on the nature and location of the activity supervised. While I do not (as he suggests) have a 'blind faith in the regulatory mechanism of PACE' (Leng 1995: 212), it would be merely dogmatic to equate a stop/search form with a custody record (Dixon *et al.* 1989, 1990a).

Generalizations must be also wary of national differences. For example, in New South Wales, there is not the contrast between activities outside and inside the station which was a notable feature of the policing observed in England (Dixon *et al.* 1990a; Bottomley *et al.* 1991). Largely because of the lack of legal regulation, there is not the same situational distinction which the transfer of responsibility from an arresting officer to a custody officer creates: people are brought to NSW stations and questioned or otherwise investigated while their status as 'volunteers' or arrested suspects is not clear (see Chapter 5, above). Unless they are charged, their presence in a station may never be recorded or even known to others than the investigating officers.

(c) *Legal Knowledge*

Various parts of the police organization have different contacts with and knowledges of the law. The most obvious contrast is between general duties and detective officers: as specialists in turning events into cases (see 270–1 above), detectives are usually more aware of legal categories. As such knowledge becomes more important, so it becomes more evident, among, for example, detectives in specialist fraud squads. Knowledge about law varies between police officers, not only because of functional specialization, but also as a result of individual differences in ability and interest.

At a more complex level, attitudes to law can vary significantly both among police officers and within an individual officer, depending on the level of abstraction or generality. The same officer can express 'an indomitable faith in "The Law" ' (Bittner 1990: 114) and, in the next breath, a familiar cynicism (Reiner 1992a: 113–14) about the legal system and lawyers. Yet these mid-level views, in turn, can be inconsistent with those expressed about specific laws and individual legal actors. This should not suggest a stable hierarchy: particular instances and experiences can provoke discordant views. This layering of apparently inconsistent beliefs can be found not only in police attitudes to law, but also, for example, in public attitudes to the police, politics, and law. A disjuncture between theoretical/ideological views, cultural 'common sense', and opinions based in personal or group experience is a characteristic product of tensions between dominant and subordinate ideologies (Brogden 1981; Mann 1970).

Not surprisingly, therefore, police views about law which are based on experiences rather than on broader belief systems tend to be very different. In my research in New South Wales, I encountered some criticisms of the criminal process, but when particular examples were requested or the discussion was about substantive areas, such criticism fragmented and became specific. For example, objection was taken to particular magistrates, while others were applauded. Following generalized complaints about legal restrictions on their activities, officers were asked if they had ever not done something (e.g. made an arrest or a search) because they lacked a legal power to do so. The great majority could not give any such instances.[6] Similarly, most officers perceived no need for significant changes in police powers to be made, with only a few asking for the clarification of detention for questioning. A representative response

---

[6] The only exceptions were those who were well-informed about *Williams* ([1986] ALR 385: see Ch. 5 above), whose answers may well have been affected by the notoriety which the case had attracted and by knowing of my interest in it.

came from a sergeant, whose answer was: '[n]ot really. What do we need? . . . We've got enough authority now. There's not much we can't do now.' Similarly in England, rhetorical complaints about the disabling effects of PACE were often followed by acknowledgment of its specific benefits to police (Dixon *et al.* 1990a; Bottomley *et al.* 1991.)

The PACE research also provided further examples of the complex nature of police attitudes towards law. One section in our questionnaire asked officers to respond to four statements which were designed to encapsulate distinct approaches to the law–police relationship. Responses were, on first analysis, senseless: for example, some officers rejected (or agreed strongly with) all four. In general, they gave inconveniently incompatible answers. In part, this result may just reflect the limitations of formal interviewing: but we had put hours of work into constructing this section, following all the rules of questionnaire design. It became clear that more was involved than faulty questionnaire construction when we heard the same kind of self-contradictory, incompatible comments while talking to officers during observation. These apparent contradictions and inconsistencies emerge as important data in themselves illustrating the complexity of attitudes to law.

Looking at how police learn about law suggests the need for further research on ways of legal (and non-legal) thinking about law.

Few police know much law, and seem to develop 'recipe knowledge' derived from tutelage by other constables, oral traditions within various subdivisions, and study for promotional boards. For the primary world of the street, information about the law is gained from other PCs, sergeants and inspectors, especially the charge sergeant when an arrest is made (Manning and Hawkins 1989: 152).

In recruit training, few police forces have paid sufficient attention to the difficult task of teaching law in a way which both transmits the necessary factual knowledge and prepares the recruit for practical application of law. Too often, the complexities of doing so are apparently not appreciated (Wasby 1976).

In police training sessions which I observed during the PACE research, two ways of thinking were identified. On one hand, probationary constables knew the law 'parrot fashion'—they could reel off a list of arrestable offences, for example. However, when considering hypothetical cases, they did not analyse the facts in the way that, for example, a law student would be expected to do (and, more importantly, legislators assume officers do). Rather than considering what the law was and then applying it to the facts, trainees made generalized normative statements: you can do this, she cannot do that. Decisions, for example, to arrest were a product of a mixture of legal knowledge, 'common sense', and general behavioural norms. While this is perhaps not surprising, the problematic aspect is the apparent lack of appreciation that these different types of norms were in play.

As Bittner observed cynically,

I am not aware of any descriptions of police work on the streets that support the view that patrolmen walk around, respond to service demands, or intervene in situations, with the provisions of the penal code in mind, matching what they see with some title or another, and deciding whether any particular apparent infraction is serious enough to warrant being referred for further process (1990: 245; see also Skolnick 1975: 147, 186).

The context of this comment was the identification of law as a resource, as discussed above (see Ch. 1). But the relevant point is much wider. Police learning, understanding, and use of law is a topic greatly in need of sociological and social psychological research. The need for study of 'to what degree the law is communicated to the police' was pointed out by LaFave long ago (1965: 525), but little research has been done in the area (cf. Wasby 1976).

More specifically, the way in which police are (or are not) informed about legal change also deserves study. A significant, but rarely mentioned, source of legal knowledge is police legal departments (cf. McGowan 1972: 667) or their privatized equivalents. As well as handling some prosecutions, they often advise on policy matters, respond to enquiries from operational officers about legal matters, and produce updating or other educational material. There have been some notable problems in the services provided. For example, the Legal and Training Section of the Queensland Police attracted scathing criticism from the Fitzgerald Commission: its lack of independence from 'the demands of operational policing' meant that 'legal skills and knowledge can be applied to pervert rather than uphold the course of justice'. Training lectures were found to be 'deficient and in some instances incorrect' and 'advice, including draft legislation, which has been given to Government . . . has been defective' because of its bias and self-interest (Fitzgerald 1989: 238–9). In England, attempts are being made to improve the quality of legal advice to officers (and to improve police–Crown Prosecution Service relations) by locating CPS personnel in police stations.[7]

Statutory changes are often complex: commitment to retraining may be lacking, as in the case of the much maligned training provided when PACE was introduced. A particular problem in Australia is the dual system by which different procedural rules apply to the processing of Commonwealth and state offences. However, judicial decisions seem to create particular problems of assimilation. In the forces studied in both England and Australia, such communication was often inadequate, with no regular system for translating such decisions into comprehensible guidance.[8] Not surprisingly, officers were more aware of the interpretive practices of the courts in which they appeared than of appellate courts (see also LaFave 1965: 429). As Caplan noted in the United States, a departmental order may be precise about such matters as 'the care of equipment, handling of stray dogs, [and] towing away of abandoned automobiles', but 'almost invariably yields to a looser, vaguer format' when communicating the effect of judicial decisions.

Often the instrument is a training bulletin or a legal memorandum that recites the facts of a particular case, notes the various arguments on both sides, states the holding of the case, and perhaps even notes the logic of the dissent—particularly if the minority's position supports the action taken by the police (1974: 58).

As Chapter 5 showed, the interpretation in New South Wales of the *Williams* case provides an example of police adopting the dissenting minority judgment as the law. More generally, police are often frustrated to find that their department's interpretation of a decision is contradicted by trial judges (Wilson and Alprin 1974: 47).

Even the officers actually involved in a case may not be aware of an appeal court's ruling: this was the case in the Australian case of *Foster*.[9] The investigating officers, who were strongly criticized for their treatment of a suspect, found out about the High Court proceedings and decision from a newspaper. Similarly, Caplan found in the United States,

[7] See CPS press release, 'First Pilot Scheme for CPS Lawyers in Police Stations', 26 Jan. 1996.
[8] An attempt is now made to do so via a quarterly journal, *Policing Issues and Practice*.
[9] N. 2 above; see Ch. 5, above.

There are no established mechanisms to communicate the results of judicial or prosecutorial decisions. . . . The system of departmental discipline, whatever its reach, runs along an entirely different track than the exclusionary rule process, and prosecutors and judges do not view it as their job to communicate to the department adverse decisions resulting from police misconduct (1974: 66; cf. McGowan 1972: 673).[10]

Judges may refer cases to senior officers or, if appropriate, to Royal Commissions, but are reluctant to be involved in discussion of the implications of a decision. In an example from England, Mitchell J did not consider it appropriate to discuss the *Heron* case (see Ch. 4, above) with officers inquiring into its implications for police practices and procedure (Northumbria Police 1994: 26). A broader conception of judicial responsibility would include involvement in a matter beyond the narrow confines of the court.[11] As Wasby comments in the only significant study of how judicial decisions affect (or rather do not affect) police, 'rules cannot be followed, much less internalized' if they are not communicated (1976: 6). The difficulty of the task must not be underestimated, as it so often is by those who equate mere provision of information with its communication (*ibid.* 227).

ii. The Legal Regulation of Policing

This section will discuss the relationship between policing and the 'rule of law', some implications of contemporary public law scholarship for the control of policing, and the prospects for the legal regulation of police practices.

(a) *Policing and the Rule of Law*

In discussions of the regulation of state agencies, the 'rule of law' has been a persistently problematic concept. As a rhetorical device, its plasticity has sometimes allowed it to act as a synonym for 'law and order'. Indeed, it can be argued that it 'has become meaningless thanks to ideological abuse and general over-use'.[12] In legal debates,

---

[10] The Royal Commission on Criminal Justice found similar problems in England and Wales, recommending that 'systematic arrangements' should be made to report a court's criticism to the chief officer of the force concerned (1993: 48).

[11] Obviously, there will be times when this is inappropriate, e.g., if an appeal is likely or possible. This was not the case in *Heron*, unrep., Leeds Crown Court, 1 Nov. 1993; see above, 172–3.

[12] Shklar (1987: 1) suggests, but dissociates herself from, this rejection.

the conventional beginning of discussions on the rule of law is Dicey's formulation in his *Introduction to the Study of the Law of the Constitution* (1927), a book which has had an enduring influence on English public law.[13] Dicey's 'unfortunate outburst of Anglo-Saxon parochialism' (Shklar 1987: 16) has caused much confusion and misunderstanding, not least because of its unsatisfactory resolution of the relationship between law and politics. Useful discussion of the rule of law requires concrete analysis and specification of concepts. In an attempt to assess the rule of law in the context of policing, Sanders and Young focus on 'two elements of the concept which seem most relevant to police powers: equality under the law, and the control of state officials' (1994b: 127). Their analysis provides a useful introduction to considering how the 'rule of law' relates to the legal regulation of policing.

(i) *Equality and Balance*

As regards equality, Dicey insisted that the 'ordinary law of the realm' should apply to state officials. By this he meant that state officials should be accountable to courts rather than to specialized tribunals: any such tribunals which existed merely added to, rather than replaced, 'the duties of an ordinary citizen' which were enforced by the courts (1927: 190). The inadequacy of his account has long been apparent. Profoundly affected by his opposition to the rise of 'collectivism', he misinterpreted contemporary developments. As Harlow and Rawlings suggest, his interpretation was 'inspired by an ardent belief in individualism, in laissez-faire economic policy and in the rectitude of lawyerly values' (1984: 19).[14]

Characteristically, Dicey was primarily concerned with remedies in this discussion of legal equality.[15] However, he is often interpreted as meaning that state officials should not have powers which set them

---

[13] While attacks on Dicey may have been 'completely devastating', Davis was wrong to suggest that, in the English context, 'his ideas were brushed aside' (1971: 31–2). They had a major influence which has been recognized in assessments of Dicey's work (e.g. Harlow and Rawlings 1984: ch. 1; Zellick (ed.) 1985: 583–723; McAuslan and McEldowney (eds.) 1985; Loughlin 1992: ch. 7). For a significant defence of Dicey, see Allan 1993.

[14] As W. A. Robson pointed out in 1928, a misunderstanding of French administrative law seems to have been responsible for Dicey's view here (Jowell 1994: 59). Davis (1971: 28–33) groups the Franks Committee, John Dickinson, and F. A. Hayek with Dicey as exponents of this 'extravagant version' of the rule of law.

[15] While 'Dicey's obsession with remedies made him oblivious to the importance of rights' (Barendt 1985: 607), this does not imply that remedies (or their absence) are not of great significance: see Bradley 1989: 188; Sanders and Young 1994a: 456–8.

apart from ordinary citizens (Sanders and Young 1994b: 127). Diceyan analysis was particularly misleading in the case of the police.[16] It clearly informed the Royal Commission on Police Powers and Procedure of 1928–9 which reported influentially that police were merely 'citizens in uniform' whose powers were essentially those of an ordinary member of the public (RCPPP 1929: 6; see Ch. 2, sect. i, above). This attempt to minimize the significance of the 'special powers' held by the police was a product of the Commission's insistence that policing depended fundamentally upon 'the goodwill of the public. . . . A proper and mutual understanding between the Police and the public is essential for the maintenance of law and order' (1929: 7). This approach can only properly be understood in its historical context: the Royal Commission was appointed at the end of a decade of popular scepticism towards and official concern about lack of confidence in the police (Dixon 1991: 241–8, 256–61). For present purposes, the Royal Commission's remarks are significant as having formed a central plank in the ideological presentation (and self-delusion) of the English police: the theme of 'citizens in uniform' was to inform and strengthen subsequent arguments for independence from political accountability in the later part of the century.[17] It was, of course, misleading in its failure to appreciate either the extent of police powers at the time or the trend towards their accumulation. In section iii below, the limits and possibilities of attempts within public law to transcend the restrictions inherited from Dicey will be discussed.

Discussion of equality raises the disjuncture between the formal and the substantive in its most familiar form: substantive inequality undermines the law's formal equality. (The classic reference is, of course, to France 1927: 106.) Sanders and Young are able to draw on overwhelming research evidence showing that police powers are applied 'unequally'. They argue convincingly that this is the product of the police mandate in an increasingly divided society and that this inevitably affects the impact of legal regulation (1994b; see also Brogden et al. 1988: ch. 6). A good example is the inefficacy of the (purported) attempt to inject substantive equality by legal regulation

---

[16] See the discussion of *Malone* v. *Metropolitan Police Commissioner* ([1979] Ch. 344) in Ch. 2, above.

[17] For example, this analysis of the place of law in policing and police–public relations was endorsed by the Royal Commission on the Police of 1960–2 (RCP 1962: 10–11).

of stop and search: as argued elsewhere, PACE Code C's provisions on stereotyping have been of largely presentational effect (Dixon *et al.* 1989). Whether legal regulation will inevitably skim over (or consolidate) substantive inequality is an empirical question, and will depend on contexts, methods, and subjects. It is suggested, for example, that the regulation of police use of firearms in the United States substantially reduced the racial imbalance in deaths resulting from police shootings (Walker 1993a: 26).

More complex issues are raised by other examples of attempts to equalize relations between state and citizen by balancing powers and rights: notably, the power to detain for investigative purposes is 'balanced' in England and Wales by the right to legal advice which (in a notable concession to the need to take account of substantive matters) is backed by legal aid and duty-solicitor services. The example shows the problems of attempts to 'balance'. Research evidence emphasizes the deficiencies of legal advice in police stations (McConville *et al.* 1994; Dixon *et al.* 1990a). Despite this, arguments are made that the balance has 'swung too far the other way' leading, notably, to the restriction of the right to silence (Jackson 1990; and see Ch. 6, above). As Sanders and Young (1994a: 460) suggest ironically, justifying crime control 'by reference to bits and pieces of due process' provides a new application for McBarnet's claim (1979: 39; see Ch. 1, above) that 'due process is for crime control'.

As Ashworth argues, the 'balance' metaphor has been the 'scourge of many debates about criminal justice policy' (1994: 292; cf. Jackson 1990). Despite repeated exposures of its deficiencies, the balance is usually said to be between the civil liberties of suspects and society's right to protect 'itself' by providing police powers. In cruder references, 'suspects' are replaced with offenders or criminals: by leaping to the conclusion which the justice process is intended to decide upon, this ends any useful discussion. In more sophisticated formulations, it may be acknowledged that there is a communal and not just an individual interest in the protection of rights. This is not merely a matter of principle—i.e. that a democratic society deserving the name should treat its citizens in a certain way. There is also the instrumental interest, which is a glaring but often ignored lesson of the miscarriage cases. If failure to provide suspects with substantial rights leads to a wrongful conviction, then those really guilty escape justice (usually forever, because the investigation has been misdirected for so long).[18] This failure to appreciate 'the double-sided nature of miscarriages of justice . . . serves to perpetuate a . . . misleading dichotomy between "soft" and "tough" measures, between effective crime control and civil liberties' (Hogg 1995: 314). It is necessary to see rights as expressing organizational and social, as well as individual, interests. In addition, as Braithwaite points out, empirical evidence belies claims that there is an inevitable 'trade-off between crime control and respect for civil liberties' and this should challenge the 'conceptualization of some sort of hydraulic relationship' between them (1989: 158–9). More specifically, the example of PACE shows that the complex relationship between police powers and suspects' rights is distorted by a simple metaphor of balance.

This discussion suggests that, seductive as it may be, the concept of balance is inherently problematic. Certainly, experience suggests that it provides an often irresistible temptation to degenerate into crude and unhelpful formulations. Its superficial utilitarianism trivializes important interests and inappropriately treats them as if they can be weighed off against each other. The inability to shift from metaphor to reality is exposed in the tendency of the Royal Commission on Criminal Justice to refer to 'the "balance" favouring one solution rather than another as if this were some ineffable mystery that requires no supporting explanation about how the conclusion was reached' (Ashworth 1994: 294). Ashworth calls for a fundamental reconsideration of the principles and fundamental purposes of criminal justice, a 'rights-based' approach (1994: 292–6; 1996; cf. Jackson 1990). But the concept of balance re-emerges in his own account. Arguing that this is an inevitable consequence of an internal perspective, Norrie suggests that it can only be avoided by starting

not from the internal values and practices of the system, but from the sociological context within which the system operates. Rather than the circular

---

[18] It bears emphasizing that cases like the Birmingham Six and the Hilton bombing (see Ch. 5, above) were miscarriages of justice not only for those who wrongfully spent years in jail, but also for the victims of appalling crimes, and for their families and society generally because of the failure to identify and punish the guilty. This is an aspect of victims' rights too often overlooked in attempts by law-and-order lobbyists to claim victims as their own. Public resistance to this by some victims' families was a notable feature of the 1995 NSW State election. Of course, in some miscarriage cases, there is no 'really guilty' person because there has been no crime: see e.g. the cases of the Ananda Marga (Carrington *et al.* (eds.) 1991) and Errol Madden (details of the latter are in R v. *Police Complaints Board, ex p. Madden* [1983] 2 All ER 353 at 365).

and ultimately unprofitable approach of applying the values within the system to it, we might get a better picture if we asked: (1) what are the social and historical conditions that make a criminal system of the kind we have possible?; and (2) what are the structural limits on, and historical dynamics of, change within such a system? (1995: 344).

(ii) *Control*

The most important directive of the 'rule of law' is that the activities of state officials should be legally authorized. The legal regulation of policing is not, if interpreted minimally, a particularly difficult or worthwhile objective. It is a jurisprudential cliché that the most tyrannical regime may operate legally by providing legal authority for its actions (for a recent example, see Brogden and Shearing 1993: 27–32, 60–7). Similarly, parliamentary supremacy can (in constitutional theory) authorize anything (Craig 1990: 36–9). The issue is what kind of rules are used to regulate policing, and what principles, contexts, and objectives inform their production: if procedural safeguards 'do function to protect citizens against state interventions of various kinds this is not because of their abstract, formal, universal nature. . . . Rather it depends on certain conditions—social, economic, institutional, etc.—governing the actual processes of justice in question and the context of their application' (Hogg 1991a: 23).

Sanders and Young have argued strongly that PACE provided a structure of rules, but did not control policing:

Police officers are rarely inhibited by 'due process' from doing what they want to do. They are not ruled by law even though their behaviour can usually be classified as lawful. This situation arises because either:

— the law is a product of state agencies (the police in particular); or
— the law is sufficiently flexible to accommodate what the police want to do . . .

The police are only governed by the rule of law to the extent that PACE requires them to follow certain routines. The content of those routines, and which routines are adopted, are becoming more and more a matter for the police alone. By this means the police conform to law without being controlled by it (1994b: 128–9, 131).

This account relies upon the foundation laid by *The Case for the Prosecution* (McConville *et al.* 1991a), in which it is argued that the nature of case construction is set by the police role in adversarial system, that '[l]egal "reform" is very often nothing more than the legitimation of police practice' (1991a: 177), and that managerial and supervisory controls will inevitably be rendered ineffective by police culture and the nature of the police organization. This account has been discussed above (see Chs. 1 and 4), and I have suggested some need for qualification in the presentation of the law's flexibility, in the determinant role ascribed to police culture, and in the distinction between procedure and substance. Rather than rehearse the debate over interpretation of the research evidence on PACE, it is more useful here to consider some conceptual and broader issues raised, directly or indirectly, by their analysis.

First, police influence over legislation is clearly an important issue. Of course, such influence varies over time and place. Some Australian police forces (and police unions) have enjoyed remarkable influence over law-making (Finnane 1994: 34–7, 48–51; Haldane 1995: 290–2). The NSW Detention After Arrest Bill of 1994 (see Ch. 5 above), had it passed, would have been almost a caricature of such laws. In England and Wales, police leaders have become increasingly active and more sophisticated since the 1960s in their attempts to influence public policy (Reiner 1992a: 91–6). Notably, Metropolitan Police Commissioners Mark and McNee argued that the law should be changed to authorize practices which their officers had unlawfully adopted, having determined that they were necessary for crime control. As Baxter and Koffman suggested it was 'indicative of the prestige and power of the police that an admission of such unconstitutional and lawless behaviour should be accepted with equanimity in a liberal democratic society' (1985: 1).

The complaisance of the Home Secretary of the day has been crucial to the success of police lobbying. The restriction of the right to silence in 1994 was, as argued in Chapter 6, a notable and regrettable example of the police getting what they wanted from Government. In both England and Wales and Australia, police seem devoted to the old cliché that attack is the best form of defence. While exposed to criticism for their contributions to, respectively, miscarriages of justice and corruption, there has been a brazenness in police calls for expansion of their powers and criticism of other sectors of the justice system which is sometimes hard to credit.[19] However, it would be wrong to treat PACE as an unproblematic capitulation to police demands. While police got most of the powers which they had

---

[19] See, e.g., Metropolitan Police Commissioner Condon's comments, reported in *Police Review* 17 Mar. 1995, 6.

requested (McNee 1983: 182–3), those powers were accompanied by safeguards and suspects' rights. It is this, of course, which accounts for the critical reception which PACE received from police and civil libertarians alike: both criticized aspects of the legislation which they disliked, while understating those which favoured their interests.

Secondly, Sanders and Young argue that cases of malpractice like the Cardiff Three are rare 'not because the police are usually reined in by the law. It is because they rarely have to go beyond the law to achieve their objective' (1994b: 152). When police stay within the law, it is because it suits them. This argument is flawed by its very uncontrovertibility: it defines out the possibility of police being 'reined in' by law. They argue that we 'need an explanation for patterns of conformity and breach if we are to assess the current effect of legal changes' (1994b: 129) and criticize the limitations of most of the research carried out for the Philips and Runciman Commissions which 'measured the extent of compliance with rules rather than the reasons for compliance and deviance' (Sanders and Young 1994b: 154). However, they assume that we already know these reasons, that compliance and deviance are unproblematic. On the contrary, I would suggest that these are complex matters of which our understanding is still limited.

Finally, there is an assumption that courts (with all their limitations: see Ch. 4, above) are central to legal regulation: the 'rule of law is necessarily legalistic. In other words it seeks to control behaviour by setting standards for specific encounters and establishing accountability in court settings for breach of those standards' (Sanders and Young 1994b: 131). As suggested in Chapter 2, judicial control of police powers has a significant history. Exponents of the rule of law tend to evoke that history while paying less attention to more recent shifts in judicial attitudes or to the practical inaccessibility of judicial remedies.[20] The histories of custodial interrogation in Chapters 4 and 5 did not find much evidence of modern judges enthusiastically protecting individual rights. On the contrary, the record in England and Australia has generally been of complicity with the informal growth of police powers. When there is some significant judicial activism (as in applications of PACE, sections 76 and 78, or in the High Court's

---

[20] e.g. Allan 1985. While he argues that 'a substantive role for the rule of law' is suggested by analysis of 'the collaborative and integral nature of the enactment of legislation and its subsequent application' (1985: 143), ironically, his analysis is flawed as a result of its narrow legalistic focus.

rulings on confessions), interventions tend to be unsystematic, episodic, and inconsistent (Dixon 1991d). However, there may be more to the rule of law than the rule of courts. As the discussion in section (e) will suggest, public law scholarship has substantially shifted attention away from courts in considering the legal regulation of state activity.

While these points suggest some qualification of Sanders and Young's approach, their central question deserves attention: does policing conform to the liberal conception of the rule of law? Specifically, does law protect freedom from arbitrary power in the way it provides police with legal authority? An excessive statutory delegation of discretion is, from a Diceyan perspective, as offensive as arbitrary power (Dicey 1927; Baxter 1985: 42). If discretion is limited by boundaries which are too wide and safeguards which are ineffective, then the requirements of the rule of law are not satisfied. From this perspective, the particular reason for failure is not important. For example, a power may be excessively broad because its use is not supervised or regulated (e.g. the power to stop and search under the NSW Crimes Act 1900, section 357E), or because it is closely but ineffectively regulated (stop and search under PACE, section 1), or because it is constructed out of legal loopholes and judicial connivance (detention for questioning in NSW), or because of a variety of legal and other factors (reception into custody under PACE, section 37). Police powers of these kinds offend the rule of law.

Further, as suggested in Chapter 2, police powers may be effectively (if not formally) extended by changes in substantive criminal law, as in broadening of public-order offences. The courts' usual stance has been to refuse to look beyond the alleged offence: they (and Dicey) treat the discretionary decision to proceed against a particular individual as irrelevant. This stance must be set in the context of judicial priorities which Glanville Williams stated bluntly: 'in criminal cases, the courts are anxious to facilitate the conviction of villains and they interpret the law whenever possible to secure this' (quoted Smith 1985: 610).

Can powers of the kind discussed here be brought within the rule of law? It is certainly the case that legal change can have some substantial effects: legal regulation of custodial interrogation in NSW could bring policing nearer to the rule of law. As regards offences, the decriminalization of some (Lacey 1995) and the reduction in available maximum penalties for others would be beneficial.[21] But the limits of legal regulation and change have to be acknowledged. As argued (in Ch. 2, sect. ix) above, legal regulation usually assumes that police powers are used for law enforcement. The reality (notably in the policing of public-order offences and use of stop/search powers) is that officers have other objectives which are at least as significant: pre-eminent among these are maintaining order and imposing authority. It is simply naïve to expect a traditional conception of the rule of law—closely defined legal authority supervised by the courts—to have sufficient purchase. The deficiencies of the rule of law are easy enough to point out: it is important but more difficult to go beyond the traditional conception to appreciate broader conceptions of the rule of law and to consider more active uses of legal regulation in combination with other methods of control.

(b) *The Rule of Law: Substance and Ideology*

This section is concerned with possible development of the 'rule of law' beyond its liberal attachments, and some broader issues which its consideration suggests. As noted above, a rule of law which merely provides freedom from interference by others or which is mere legal formalism is of little value or interest. The rule of law must have some positive ambition, such as provision of what Braithwaite and Pettit term 'dominion' (1990: 63, see also Cotterrell 1996: 466). Rules must not simply be made in the constitutionally prescribed manner, but must meet some standard, in the sense that they must be consistent with certain values and principles. It is this qualitative aspect which has tied the rule of law to the liberal and democratic political traditions.[22] However, to treat the rule of law as having relevance only within liberal-democratic theory would be a mistake.

The rule of law must provide rules which are substantial in their effect (New Zealand Law Commission 1992: 2). Such an effect may

[21] Reiner (1992a: 213) argues that imprisonment is an inappropriate and counterproductive sentence for some offences. A good example is the removal in 1993 of imprisonment as a potential sentence for offensive language under the Summary Offenses Act 1988 in NSW. Such amendments have to be supplemented by further action to ensure that those convicted do not go to jail nevertheless for non-payment of fines or non-completion of community service orders

[22] This is not to ignore earlier formulations of the rule of law, but to insist on the distinctiveness of the modern conception: see Loughlin 1992: 149–50. For discussion of how contemporary liberal jurisprudence on the nature of law relates to the rule of law, see Radin 1989.

well depend upon factors external to a specific rule. This developed notion of the rule of law was expressed by the Delhi Conference of the International Commission of Jurists which declared the rule of law to be a dynamic concept 'which should be employed not only to safeguard and advance the civil and political rights of the individual in a free society, but also to establish social, economic, educational and cultural conditions under which his [sic] legitimate aspirations and dignity may be realised' (quoted, Allan 1985; contrast Raz 1979: 210–11). In the context of policing, the need for rules to be made substantial by external action is exemplified by the right to legal advice: suspects may have such a 'right', but if no legal aid or duty solicitors are provided, the right is chimerical (Sanders and Young 1994b: 141). Appreciation of this was the spur to the US Supreme Court's decision in *Miranda* v. *Arizona*.[23] Defining the rule of law as including the action needed to make it substantial may be problematic. It can encourage legal imperialism, and it may dissipate the concept's force (Raz 1979: 211). However, positivist objections of this sort are unable to appreciate the qualitative dimension of the rule of law which historical and cultural studies can illuminate.

As well as material substance, the rule of law requires ideological substance: the concept that governmental action must be both legal and legitimate must have some meaning for both officials and citizens. There must be 'a widespread assumption within the society that law *matters* and should matter' (Krygier 1990: 646, original emphasis). If this is the case, 'public discussions and expectations of what is appropriate in public life' are quite different 'from a system where the very idea of subjecting the powerful to the law does not exist— either in principle or as a realistic possibility' (Krygier 1990: 643). The key text for analysis of this dimension of the rule of law remains Thompson's comments in *Whigs and Hunters*:

The essential precondition for the effectiveness of law, in its function as ideology, is that it shall display an independence from manipulation and shall seem to be just. It cannot seem to be so without upholding its own logic and criteria of equity; indeed, on occasion, by actually *being* just. And furthermore it is not often the case that a ruling ideology can be dismissed as mere hypocrisy; even rulers find a need to legitimize their power, to moralize their functions, to feel themselves to be useful and just (1977: 263, original emphasis; cf. Trubeck 1977: 558).

---

[23] 384 US 458 (1966).

The rulers of eighteenth-century England were:

the prisoners of their own rhetoric; they played the games of power according to rules which suited them, but they could not break those rules or the whole game would be thrown away. And . . . so far from the ruled shrugging off this rhetoric as a hypocrisy, some part of it at least was taken over as part of the rhetoric of the plebeian crowd, of the 'free-born Englishman' with his inviolable privacy, his habeas corpus, his equality before the law (1977: 263–4).

The deficiencies of Thompson's argument have been exposed in a number of valuable critiques (e.g. Horwitz 1977; Fine 1994). However, its continuing value lies in its insistence that the rule of law must be seen in terms of its reproduction of a mode of discourse in the process of historical friction and transmission between dominant and subordinate ideologies. The rule of law cannot be understood purely at the level of theories of ideology: it must be understood in the historical context of cultural construction in which symbols, discourse and rhetoric can play active, constitutive forces.[24] Unger made the point well:

In societies with a heavy commitment to the rule of law, people often act on the belief that the legal system does possess a relative generality and autonomy. To treat their understandings and values as mere shams is to assume that social relations can be described and explained without regard to the meanings the men [sic] who participate in those relations attribute to them. This . . . would be to blind oneself to what is specifically social about the subject matter and to violate a cardinal principle of method in social theory (1976: 56–7).

The promise of government limited by laws of a certain kind was one which affected popular cultures in complex and unexpected ways. The rule of law's power is well illustrated by Neal's study (1991) of the unlikely emergence and effect of claims based on it in the early convict settlement of New South Wales.

The relevance of this to understanding of law in policing is that attention must be paid to the discursive and ideological, as well as the instrumental, aspects of police law. Account must be taken of the desires, demands, and expectations which the legal form creates

[24] The classic study of such processes is Christopher Hill's essay on the potent myth of rights lost under the 'Norman yoke' (Hill 1954; see also *id.* 1996). For an invaluable collection of materials, see Hampton (ed.) 1984. For an account which situates Thompson's comments on the rule of law in the context of his broader historical and political work, see Palmer 1981.

among both officials and citizens (Tyler 1990; Allen 1996). The United States provides a useful comparison: while the 'due process revolution' may not have the instrumental effects on police practices which were anticipated or feared, Walker argues that there has been a significant effect on both police and popular attitudes to the justice system. The 'landmark Supreme Court cases of the 1960s . . . focused public attention on police decision making and its impact on individual liberty. This raised the level of public awareness of the constitutional aspects of police work to an extraordinarily high level' (1993a: 51; cf. Leo 1996a: 259). Even if information was communicated by means of antagonistic fictional representations such as *Dirty Harry* (Smith 1993: 90–107), public opinion and popular culture were influenced. The result was a 'climate of legality', a rising 'expectation of justice', and a 'shared awareness of the potential for redress' which affected police–public relations (Walker 1988: 20–2). Walker does not claim that his account is more than a sketch; but as this, it is of real interest. Taking it further in comparative studies would require cultural and geographical specification: Walker relates his thesis to the peculiarly legalistic nature of American society (1988: 3). He suggests the crucial ideological dialectic between public expectation and police culture. Specific instrumental changes stimulated by the Supreme Court such as 'wide-ranging reforms in the education, training, and supervision of police officers' have to be linked to a broader alteration in

the context of the working environment of policing. The principle of accountability—that there are limits on police powers, that those limits can be set down in writing (whether by a court decision or a departmental rule), and that officers should be routinely expected to answer for whether they comply with those rules—has been established, at least as an ideal. This principle is an established fact of life for a new generation of police officers (1993a: 51).

Walker's aside—'at least as an ideal'—suggests a weakness in his rather enthusiastic account: the difference between ideal and practice is crucial, and the latter is rarely the direct subject of the studies on which he relies. In addition, as argued in Chapter 5, police adherence to legality may be primarily instrumental rather than ideological, and may encourage new investigative tactics which raise new problems of morality and efficacy (Leo 1994; 1996a). A process by which legal change leads, not to unproblematic compliance, but to adaptation in which some elements are subverted while others are normalized is what should be expected in a more sophisticated account of reform processes (Brown 1987).

As Baxter suggests, 'if the policeman [*sic*] knows that he will not be able to rely on the passive ignorance of his suspect, then there is an improved chance that the policing function will operate in an atmosphere of mutual respect; where the citizen knows his rights, and where the policeman recognises the limits of his powers' (1985: 48). It is important here that Baxter stresses the need for change in the police: without this, educating young people about their rights would simply be to invite their characterization as 'smart-arses' or challengers to authority, as in the case discussed in Chapter 3, section ii, above. As suggested in Chapter 4, there is some evidence of new values and new attitudes to police work which are collectively described as a 'new professionalism'. Similarly, there may be change in suspects' attitudes, as demonstrated by the steady increase in rates of requests for legal advice (Brown 1997; Phillips and Brown 1997).

So it would be too easy to say that there is no practical difference between the systems of custodial interrogation in England and Australia which were discussed in Chapters 4 and 5. Differences must be appreciated not just at an instrumental level, but also in terms of ideology and of cultural attitudes to law and rights. Legal regulation is different from (not necessarily better than) a system which relies on consent, legal loopholes, and judicial complicity.

As noted above, Thompson's recuperation of the rule of law provoked vigorous criticism. His most significant critics emphasized the need to appreciate the contradictory nature of the rule of law as an ideological force. 'It undoubtedly restrains power, but it also prevents power's benevolent exercise. It creates formal equality—a not inconsiderable virtue—but it *promotes* substantive inequality by creating a consciousness that radically separates law from politics, means from ends, processes from outcomes' (Horwitz 1977: 566, original emphasis). Focusing on the inhibition of power distracts attention from law's other functions 'as instrument of domination, means of exchange, measure of right, source of punishment, framework of state, and so on' (Fine 1994: 205) and from the limitations of the legal form, particularly its individualism and its traditional reliance on judicial decision-making. As McConville *et al.* noted in their critique of McBarnet (see Ch. 1, above) the fundamental principles of criminal justice are constituted from crime control as well as due-process ideologies. The difficult but necessary task is to appreciate these multiple aspects of law without overemphasizing one.

Another significant objection to Thompson's approach to the rule of law could be that it, ironically, fails to take account of historical change. It can be argued that we no longer live in 'societies with a heavy commitment to the rule of law'.[25] As Gatrell suggests, changing relations between class, property, and the state in the nineteenth century produced a new conception of rights as concessions provided by the state, rather than as the property of citizens who have conceded power to the state (1990: 254–5). While there is obviously a danger here of slipping into rose-tinted nostalgia, notions of legality and justice seem to have lost strength in popular cultures. In England, account must be taken of both the shifts in popular attitudes to authority over the last century (in which the social effects of the World Wars and the rise and decline of corporatist social democracy were crucial). The process has accelerated since 1979, with the neo-conservative reshaping of culture and society. In societies deeply divided by race, gender, and class, it becomes increasingly hard to identify common cultural understandings of citizens' rights and officials' responsibilities. The slackening of communal sensibility, the socio-political and economic marginalization of sections of the working class, and the decline of liberal and democratic commitment are aspects of late-modern societies which directly affect the relationship between policing and law. Perceptive commentators suggest that fundamental changes are under way in the nature of criminal justice processes which threaten to make redundant traditional conceptions of rights and limits on authority (Ericson 1994a; Feeley and Simon 1994; Reiner 1992c).

If, as suggested above, the rule of law is a cultural construct, it should be expected that its English and Australian expressions will vary. In Australia, dominant cultural attitudes to law and authority have a distinctively dichotomized inflection. On one hand, there is a cynical, distrusting wariness of authority. However, against what is often the preferred self-image must be set a deep social conservatism (McQueen 1976). Attitudes to crime often present a stone-age lay criminology in which 'criminals' are distinguishable from respectable society, and the justice system should not be subject to pettifogging legal restraints in dealing with them. Cynicism has its place here too

[25] Of course, Unger's central theme was the challenge of 'bureaucratic-administrative' law to legal order.

in acceptance that officials may give ends priority over means. For example, this element of popular culture has constituted a serious obstacle to the reform process in Queensland in the very material shape of juries and magistrates refusing to convict police officers of palpable offences.[26] At the time of writing, New South Wales is being exposed to the consequences of such cynicism, as a Royal Commission demonstrates the pervasion of corruption through the police service. A related form of cynicism is politicians' shameless exploitation of the fear of crime. Fatuous mandatory life sentencing legislation and an unprincipled statute authorizing the detention of a named 'dangerous' individual without the necessity of criminal conviction exemplify a view of criminal justice, not as an important and complex area of public policy, but simply as the administration of a criminal class to be exploited in the scrabble for government.[27]

(c) Irony and Contradiction in Policing

Rather than ending in unmitigated post-modernist gloom, this discussion suggests a need to appreciate the complexity of modern policing, particularly the contradictions and irony which run through so many of its aspects. Irony pervades policing. Peter Manning's work traced this brilliantly in his analysis of sacred and profane aspects of police work (1977: 147 and *passim*). Relations between police and 'public' are profoundly ironic: officers serve and protect a social order about which they are cynical and resentful. They venerate 'the law', but deride laws, lawyers and courts: other similar dichotomies and contradictions in attitudes were discussed above in section i.

It is wrong to focus only on the 'negative' aspects of police powers as increasing power. The provision of powers may also be positive in defining what police may and may not do: law 'has the great virtue of limiting what it grants'.[28] The combination of empowering and restricting is a characteristic ambivalence of liberal governance (Barry *et al.* (eds.) 1996; McNay 1994: ch. 3). As Finnane suggests, regulation 'of any kind is a two-fold process: it not only constrains but

---

[26] See, e.g., 'Jury Acquits Detective on Drug Charge', *Courier Mail*, 15 Apr. 1994; 'Police Cleared of Abducting Black Children', *The Australian*, 25–6 Feb. 1995. For analysis of the context, see Bolen 1997.

[27] See Community Protection Act 1994 (NSW); Crimes Amendment (Mandatory Life Sentences) Act 1996 (NSW). In *Kable* v. *DPP*, unreported, 12 Sept. 1996, the High Court declared the latter to be constitutionally invalid.

[28] James Boyd White, quoted Krygier 1990: 640. Self-evidently, this depends on the breadth of those limits.

opens up a field of action' (1994: 90). If a police practice is recognized by legal authorization, there may also be recognition that rights of those subjected to powers need to be recognized and given substance. For example, if it is acknowledged that police detain suspects for questioning, then specified limits on detention and correlative rights (e.g. to legal advice) become significant issues. Whether the extension of powers is accompanied by positive rights in any particular instance is an empirical matter. The point for present purposes is that it is usually misleading to see power as working in a purely negative way: it may also have positive and unpredictable effects. The corollary also operates: reforms to criminal justice have characteristically 'enhanced rather than diminished the power of legal authorities' (Garland 1991: 13). This analysis is, of course, consistent with the reconceptualization of power in Foucault's work (e.g. 1975). From a very different perspective, it also fits with developments in public law which are discussed in subsection (d) below.

Another characteristically Foucauldian observation is that power is not monopolized by the state. An example from the PACE project indicates this, but also makes clear that it is not simply spread evenly across society. At 9.35 on a Friday night, I was discussing stop and search with a patrolling officer. On an industrial street, we passed a man carrying a canvas bag. The officer remarked that, if it were later at night, he would routinely stop and search a man walking with a bag in such an area. But at this time, a man carrying a bag is still not incongruous, and therefore not suspicious: he is probably going home from work. The officer knew that, if he stopped and attempted to search the man, strong objection would be likely. The construction and activation of his suspicion had to be understood as taking place in the context of relations and negotiations of power. The man would not have regarded himself as 'fair game' to be stopped and searched: the officer would have been acting out of order if he had done so. Of course, the perception that the police action is unjustified is not enough: the power of being a white, male, 'respectable' worker was necessary. The point was illustrated by the fact that, only a few minutes later, the officer did stop and question some 'suspects'—young people whose presence in that area at that time required explanation, particularly when they identified themselves as being from a 'notorious' council estate some distance away. More generally, young black people's experience of stop and search is, *inter alia*, that of a group without acknowledged resources of legitimate power (Singh 1994).

A pervasive characteristic of the criminal process is irony, expressed in contradiction and unintended consequences. Many examples could be provided. At a general level, in England and Wales 'many experienced police officers . . . feel somewhat frustrated at the paradox that public trust in them is at its lowest ebb precisely when professional standards are at an all-time high' (Reiner 1992c: 773). Without accepting this valuation of modern 'professionalism', there is considerable irony in the fact that the violence and malpractice of policing in the 1950s should be glorified as a 'golden age'.[29] Meanwhile, just as the New South Wales Police Service attracted attention as a leading example of the 'new policing' (Sparrow *et al.* 1990: 72–7), it was plunged into unprecedented scandals about corruption and misconduct. In the United States, Los Angeles provides an example of a police department apparently winning its fight against corruption, but at the cost of entrenching an authoritarian and militaristic police culture which brought its own problems: 'the accomplishments of police reform through the 1950s set the stage for the police–community-relations crisis of the 1960s' (Walker 1980: 212).

More specifically, PACE provides numerous examples of counter-productive measures. For example, the attempt to encourage due process by insisting that evidentially useful interrogation must be carried out in police stations has had the effect of subverting due process in arrest and detention practices: the policy of minimizing use of detention power has been gutted by the effect of limiting external questioning. A further irony is that restricting interrogation to stations has not had the desired effect: in-station regulation of questioning is weak; legal advice is often poor, even counter-productive from the suspect's viewpoint; and questioning in cells, in interview rooms when tapes are not turned on, and outside stations continues (Dixon *et al.* 1990a; McConville *et al.* 1994; Sanders and Young 1994b: 150).

Examples of technological change suggest that effects may not only be unforeseen, but also may have to be evaluated subjectively. Electronic recording of interviews may be interpreted as serving the interests of both suspect and police, even in the same case: research on video-recording in NSW suggests that quite incompatible interpretations of images may be made (Dixon and Travis 1997). In

---

[29] The shifts and uncertainty in Reiner's discussion of the golden age—was it real or a myth?—illustrate some of the issues here (1992a: ch. 2, 1994: 753; cf. Loader 1995).

respect of other technology, experience in NSW has shown how surveillance and money-tracing technologies developed by police can be used in the detection of corrupt police.[30] As Matza suggests, 'a key element of irony is latency—inherent qualities of phenomena that . . . culminate in outcomes that mock the expected result. . . . Latency occurs in overlap too, which stresses the good that may be obscured in evil, and the vice that lurks in virtue' (1969: 70).

These types of irony and contradiction are consistent with the discontinuities and inconsistencies which I have argued characterize the impact of PACE (see Ch. 4 above; Dixon 1992; 1995a). It is easy to caricature an approach such as this as lacking 'any theoretical position except indeterminacy' and implying that 'several factors jostle together with no sense of priority', thereby 'giving up the search for underlying explanations' (McConville and Sanders 1995: 202, 197). My argument is that contradiction and irony are fundamental features of social life. Relegating them to second-order phenomena misses the vital and often most interesting aspects. In seeking to generalize by looking for patterns, it is vital to appreciate that discontinuities and inconsistencies may be the pattern, and not to obscure that pattern by overlaying a neater, simpler, but less accurate representation.

This does not entail abandoning any concept of determination: patterns may be discontinuous and inconsistent without being random. Rather, it means taking seriously the complexity of 'patterning' or determination once concepts of culture and ideology are treated as being not mere theoretical devices, but as constructed and constructing features of a society's history and structure (Williams 1977: pt. 2). The resources for this project are unashamedly diffuse: use needs to be made of, for example, the sense of irony in the sociology of deviance, the understanding of culture and ideology in writers such as Williams and Thompson, and the sensitivity to complexity and contradiction in some post-structuralism. For me, reading social histories has been particularly important: the best of them require an attention to agency and contingency, to culture and discourse *as well as* to structure. Both empirical studies (e.g. Gatrell 1990; Hill 1954; Thompson 1977) and theoretical debates and controversies (contrast Dean 1994; Palmer 1990) provide a rich resource.

[30] A notable feature of the Royal Commission into the NSW Police Service established in 1994 was the use of sophisticated surveillance technology, followed by skilful use of resulting records in negotiations with informants and suspects.

(d) *Limits of Regulation*

An abiding problem in references to the 'rule of law' is the implicit Whiggish distrust of the state: the rule of law should protect freedom by insisting on the minimization of state intervention. In this respect, Dicey's rule of law fitted only a liberal ideal of a minimal state. If it is to have relevance for a society characterized by powerful and active institutions (e.g. in which the public police have wide powers and private police have an increasing role), the rule of law has to be developed to provide for the facilitation and regulation (and not merely the disapproval) of activity both by the state and by 'private' bodies carrying out 'public' functions.[31] Indeed, in this context, unspecific references to the 'rule of law' can obscure more than they illuminate.

English public law has been dominated by the Diceyan tradition, despite the evident incoherence resulting from attempts to maintain it in the face of massive changes in state activity (e.g. Wade 1988). There has been a long-standing 'dissenting' tradition which spawned significant challenges to the dominant tradition in the 1980s (Loughlin 1992). The contrast between dominant and subordinate traditions in public law is captured well by Loughlin's counterposition of two ideal types, 'normativism' and 'functionalism':

The normativist style in public law is rooted in a belief in the ideal of the separation of powers and in the need to subordinate government to law. This style highlights law's adjudicative and control functions and therefore its rule orientation and its conceptual nature. Normativism essentially reflects an ideal of the autonomy of law. The functionalist style in public law, by contrast, views law as part of the apparatus of government. Its focus is upon law's regulatory and facilitative functions and therefore adopts an instrumentalist social policy approach. Functionalism reflects an ideal of progressive evolutionary change. . . . For the normativist liberty might be identified with an absence of legal controls, whereas for the functionalist greater legal controls might mean more liberty (1992: 60, 61).

Similarly, Harlow and Rawlings (1984: chs. 1 and 2) contrast red-light theories (negatively centred on retrospective, judicial control of power in order to maximize individual freedom) and green-light

---

[31] See Ch. 3, above. The deconstruction of the public–private divide is a key issue in contemporary public law: see, e.g., the replacement of a formal by a functionalist approach in *R. v. Panel on Take-overs and Mergers ex p. Datafin PLC* [1987] QB 815.

theories (positively centred on prospective, internal control of power in order to encourage its best use in the communal interest).[32]

The relevance to policing of the new public law which has positive state regulation as its central project would seem to be clear. However, in England and Australia, there has been surprisingly little 'cross-over' between public-law and criminal justice: Lustgarten's *The Governance of Police* (1986) was a rare example of a discussion of policing from a public-law perspective. As Lacey suggests, many policing issues 'simply cannot be fitted (or distorted) into the conceptual straightjacket of trial-type process even by generous analogy', and have consequently been neglected in legal analysis (1992: 376). By contrast, in the United States, there has been a considerable body of work which exploits 'the promising potentialities of the simple idea that administrative law thinking can profitably be applied to criminal administration' (Davis 1974: 703; cf. Davis 1975: ch. 5). It is not appropriate to provide a full account here: attention will focus on merely the most prominent issue in the field, the use of rules.

If the American Bar Foundation study 'discovered' discretion in criminal justice (see Goldstein 1960; Ohlin and Remington (eds.) 1993; Walker 1992 and Ch. 1, above), it was K. C. Davis who set the terms of the debate about its control (Walker 1993b: 41). In *Discretionary Justice* (1971), a key text of the 'new' public law, Davis argued that discretion was inevitable and, in its proper place, beneficial,[33] that uncontrolled discretion was a major problem, and discretion should be controlled by confining, structuring, and checking. The primary tool was administrative rules, underlain by a broader commitment to open government (Davis 1971: 98). Davis was concerned with public administration in general; however, policing was a particular interest (Davis 1974; 1975) and provided many of the examples in *Discretionary Justice* (1971). He insisted that the police should be seen not just as an administrative agency, but as by far the largest, most active, and least regulated administrative agency in the modern state (1971: 222–3; 1974: 703). For Davis, police discretion implies the making of policy about law enforcement and order maintenance. The need for the development of rules to control discretion

---

[32] As both Loughlin and Harlow and Rawlings make clear, these are ideal types. They have long ancestries: as W. A. Robson pointed out, the opposition between what he termed the 'model of law' and the 'model of government' derives from the political conflicts of the seventeenth century (quoted, Harlow and Rawlings 1984: 35).

[33] While making this concession, Davis generally displayed a legalistic distrust of and lack of enthusiasm for discretion.

was widely accepted.[34] His work had widespread influence in the United States, while in England and Wales (and to a lesser extent Australia), it became a standard academic point of reference in public law.

Davis conveniently summarized his 'objectives of a good program for reform of police practices':

(1) to educate the public in the reality that the police make vital policy, (2) to induce legislative bodies to redefine crimes so that the statutory law will be practically enforceable, (3) to rewrite statutes to make clear what powers are granted to the police and what powers are withheld, and then to keep the police within the granted powers, (4) to close the gap between the pretenses of the police manuals and the actualities of police behaviour, (5) to transfer most of the policy-making power from patrolmen [*sic*] to the better qualified heads of departments, acting on the advice of appropriate specialists, (6) to bring policy-making out into the open for all to see, except where special need exists for confidentiality, (7) to improve the quality of police policies by inviting suggestions and criticism from interested parties, (8) to bring the procedures for policy determination into harmony with the democratic principle, instead of running counter to that principle, (9) to replace the present police policies based on guess-work with policies based on appropriate investigations and studies made by qualified personnel, and (10) to promote equal justice by moving from a system of ad hoc determination of policy by individual officers in particular cases to a system of central policy determination (1971: 90–1).

This list makes clear that Davis's ambition was a wholesale reform of policing and its legal context, rather than the (comparatively) narrow legal regulation of discretionary practices. This makes his insistence on the potential of administrative rule-making more surprising: he thought that '[a]ll ten objectives can be furthered and some can be fully accomplished through rule-making procedure, except that the second and third call for legislation' (1971: 91).[35] There is much to question in Davis's programme: for example, his assumptions about bureaucratic organization and efficiency, about the nature of policy and policy-making (contrast Grimshaw and Jefferson 1987), and about the commitment and quality of senior officers can all be challenged. He displays many of the characteristic of the legalistic-bureaucratic

---

[34] See Goldstein 1993: 214–18; R. J. Allen provided significant dissent, emphasizing the structural, functional, and political differences between police and administrative agencies to which rule-making could apply (1976; 1977; contrast Davis 1977).

[35] Some subsequent American writers have argued for legislative rather than administrative rules: see e.g. Berger 1990; Bradley 1990.

approach which was discussed in Chapter 1. As Walker comments, Davis had an 'almost uncritical' enthusiasm for administrative rule-making (Walker 1993a: 17). In his distrust of discretion (other than that exercised by judges), he shared more than he acknowledged with Dicey.

Most important is Davis's belief in the potency of legal regulation. More recent scholarship in public law and criminal justice has often been sceptical of enthusiasm for rules, and Davis's work is now more likely to find itself the subject of critique than praise.[36] This reaction chimes with the critique of rule-focused regulatory regimes by socio-legal scholars, as well as with more general theoretical challenges to legalism from the critical legal studies movement and elsewhere (Braithwaite and Braithwaite 1995: 336). Indeed, the critique of legal regulation has become widely accepted contemporary wisdom. Across a range of institutions, similar analyses are made and similar remedies are proposed. The force of the critiques will be acknowledged below. Thereafter, it is necessary to return to see what remains of value in regulation by rules and, in particular, to see how rules and other regulatory strategies can, indeed must, be combined.

Davis generally displays problematic characteristic of legalism: individualizing justice, exaggerating the success of rules, seeing decision-making as an event rather than a process, ignoring the patterning of behaviour by non-legal norms, favouring procedure over substance, and assuming that decision-makers are bureaucrats rather than professionals (Baldwin 1995: 19–33). Individualism is particularly problematic in criminal justice: as Reiss points out, Davis's concentration on individual applications of discretion blinds him to its patterning by race and class (1970: 790). Legalism breaks the subject-matter into legally digestible form—paradigmatically as decisions. The object of study or action is 'a discrete event or mental act which can be isolated, whereas "discretion" might often be thought to inhere in role-related conduct (such as the manner with which an official receives enquiries) and even in processes and situations (such as organizational structure), which cannot be analysed in those terms' (Lacey 1992: 380). This focus on decisions is the defining feature of the 'criminal justice paradigm' which has dominated understanding of the field since the 1950s (Walker 1992). It is only gradually being

---

[36] Problems of legal regulation in plea-bargaining, sentencing, and parole were influential here (Ohlin 1993). For a discussion of the relationship between contemporary criminal justice and the role of law, see Allen 1996.

challenged by more sociological paradigms which focus on process rather than decisions and on structure rather than system. In the case of policing, an excellent example of the limits of legalism is provided by the failure of the legal regulation of stop/search which was largely due to misunderstanding of the processual and contextual nature of street policing (Dixon *et al.* 1989). Take a very common instance: an officer stops and searches someone who is walking in a residential area late at night. A legalistic interpretation of PACE Code A would suggest that general suspicion would have to be supplemented by an additional factor, 'such as that a burglary has recently been committed in the area' (Stone 1986: 56). But what if the officer does not know about a specific burglary, but rather his or her experience instils belief that one or more burglaries will, almost certainly, be or have been committed in that area during his or her shift? Such cultural 'knowledge' based on patterns of crime may be valuable and, it can be argued, is enough legally to justify a stop/search (Leigh 1985: 162). But it is very different from the individually focused suspicion around which legal discussion usually takes place. A similar analysis could be made of arrest: as Lacey suggests, 'the project of subjecting this kind of discretion to the confining or structuring by standards which Davis advocated seems both unrealistic and misplaced' (1992: 385). Crucially, the potential for confining patrol officers' discretion is overstated: despite his interest in police research, he misunderstood the discretionary nature of policing.[37]

Rules can encourage an instrumentalism in which the unlikelihood of sanctions being applied overwhelms consideration of the rule's purpose. For instance, Davis himself provides excellent examples of the weak purchase of exclusionary rules: police officers who harassed a drug dealer in familiar displays of authority and order maintenance were not interested in trying to secure a conviction, and so were unconcerned about the unlawfulness of their actions (1975: 16–20). If procedural rules are seen as just being about what must be followed to get a conviction, policing practices which have other objectives are likely to be dominated by other determinants.

Attempts to regulate by precise rules may find that the innumerability of potential situations exhaust rule-making capacity. Unsuccessful attempts to control by rules encourage pragmatism and

[37] This should not be overstated: Davis appreciated that 'discretion is the essence of police work and is indispensable' (1975: 139). However, he was over-optimistic about the potential for its control by rules.

instrumentalism: '[d]etailed laws can provide a set of signposts to navigate around'. Some are more able to navigate (or hire navigators) than others: unequal distribution of wealth and power colours the effects of rules (Braithwaite and Braithwaite 1995: 336–7). Some 'regulatees' become particularly adept at soaking up rules without being constrained by them.[38] Some police officers express this with bravado, as in this detective's comment on the PACE requirement to record interrogations: 'I don't give a toss. I'll get round it. . . . Any rules they want me to work with, I work to find a way round them' (quoted, Dixon *et al.* 1990a: 133). It would be wrong to take this as evidence of some iron law of police deviance: whatever the law says, officers will try to get around it.[39] More interesting is the pragmatism of those who would probably identify themselves as 'new professionals', who have learnt that their work can be done within the rules, and who, specifically, have accepted the need to change questioning practices. They have no particular devotion to 'due process'. Rather, the key value is efficiency: the new professionals' critique of the 'dinosaurs' has been fuelled by a long series of prosecutions which have failed because officers have refused (or been unable) to change their investigative practices.[40] It might be desirable to have police officers who enthusiastically accepted due process, but the nature of policing makes this improbable (Smith 1995). 'New professionalism' is probably the best that can realistically be expected in present circumstances: enough has been said above to signal my limited favour for it. However, the impact of such a change should not be underestimated: as new working practices are established, so cultural shifts will occur. As will be discussed in more detail below, Samuel Walker argues strongly that this is one of the significant and under-appreciated effects of the 'due process' revolution in the United States (1988: 19–20).

A good example of the type of reform which Davis sought to encourage is provided by Wilson and Alprin's report (1974) on administrative rule-making by the Metropolitan Police Department of Washington D.C. This programme attempted to structure police decision-making by communicating effectively to officers the ratio of judicial decisions and the priorities of departmental policy. Examples were given relating to suspect identification procedures, vehicle

---

[38] This is the response to rules which McBarnet terms 'creative compliance': see Ch. 1, above; Baldwin 1995: 185–9.

[39] See comments on Baldwin and Kinsey in Ch. 1, above.

[40] See the comments on changes in US policing below and in Ch. 4, sect. vii above.

searches, and the use of deadly force. Guidelines were supervised by creating administrative arrangements to review cases when prosecutors decided not to proceed with a charge and incidents when a police officer's weapon was fired. Records were maintained of officer and unit performance so that 'patterns of misconduct or procedural error can be observed and corrected' (1974: 54). It was argued that these methods of control were much more effective than the traditional reliance on the exclusionary rule or disciplinary procedures.[41]

What has been the impact of such programmes? An important attempt to assess this is made by Samuel Walker, who follows Davis's 'preliminary inquiry' by providing 'an interim report on what works' in the legal regulation of discretion in the United States (1993a: 18). His focus is broad, including other sectors of criminal justice process as well as the police. His general conclusion is 'a moderately optimistic one. The control of discretion is possible. But . . . it is possible only as long as expectations are modest and the reforms carefully tailored and implemented' (1993a: 16). His major example of change in policing effected by rules is police shootings: the 'control of deadly force is arguably the great success story in the long effort to control police discretion' (1993a: 25; see *ibid*. 25–33; 1986: 363–4). Between the early 1970s and the late 1980s, the 'number of people shot and killed by the police was reduced by at least thirty per cent. . . . At the same time, the disparity between black and white citizens shot and killed was cut in half' (1993a: 26). He argues that internal rules and policies were responsible for this.[42]

Walker recognizes the problems of using police shootings as an example (although he is perhaps undercritical of the studies on which he relies). Use of a firearm is likely to be a discrete, public, critical event, and the combination of these characteristics makes it unlike other activities and practices (1986: 375–8; 1993b). Apart from this major but atypical case study, there are few examples of concerted attempts to control police discretion by rules which have been reliably assessed. The lack of research on such matters in the United States is surprising.[43] What comes in its place in the literature all too

[41] See also Krantz *et al*. 1979 and, for a strong argument in favour of rule making, Caplan 1974.

[42] According to Walker, the Supreme Court's ruling in *Tennessee* v. *Garner* 471 US 1 (1984) 'merely ratified (and then only inadequately) a national consensus that had already developed' (1993: 33).

[43] A rare example is Krantz *et al*.'s (1979) assessment of police policy- and rule-making in Boston, which reported limited success. Despite the extensive literature on

often is assertion and rhetoric: for example, the confident optimism of Wilson and Alprin about the malleability of discretion (see immediately above) is dismissed by Brown as 'myopic and unrealistic', a classic example of the legalistic-bureaucratic tendency to assume that changing rules will unproblematically change organizational practices, and which is likely to produce 'illusory controls' in the form of presentational rules (1988: 293). By contrast, Walker carefully picks the direct lessons and, more often, implications of the available research literature.[44] His conclusions are sensible and often of wider relevance. He argues that effective legal regulation is possible if the right targets and tools are chosen, and if 'techniques for monitoring compliance' are developed (1986: 372). He concludes that

First, it is not true that 'nothing works'. Reforms do not necessarily backfire and produce undesirable consequences. Nor are they always negated by covert resistance. Second, controls do not necessarily degenerate into empty formalism. . . . Third, discretion is not always displaced upstream or downstream. . . . Fourth, controls do not necessarily induce lying or other forms of improper evasion. . . . In short, some things work (1993a: 150).

While (perhaps partly because) Walker's evidence of effective rule change is so limited, he insists on the need to look at the indirect effects of rule changes and reform activity. Notably, the research evidence is clear that the heroic Supreme Court cases such as *Mapp*, *Miranda*, and *Escobedo* had relatively little direct effect on police practices (Leo 1996a: 287; Leo 1996c; Walker 1993a: 44–6). However, Walker and Leo argue, the indirect effects (which are still working through) have been significant.[45] The cases led police organizations to improve their training, supervisory practices, and general profes-

---

mandatory arrest for domestic violence, there are no studies of the long-term effects of such policies in non-experimental settings (Walker 1993a: 33–9; Manning 1993).

[44] See, e.g., his useful analysis of the comparative potential for regulation of police shootings, pursuits, and domestic violence interventions (1993a: ch. 2).

[45] As Leo complains, 'virtually all scholarship on American police interrogation is relegated to doctrinal analysis' (1996a: 262). The lack of empirical studies of the long-term response to *Miranda* has been surprising (Walker 1993a: 46). However, the decision's 30th anniversary saw publication of Cassell's important study which 'contends that the conventional academic wisdom about *Miranda*'s effects is simply wrong. As common sense suggests *Miranda* has significantly harmed law enforcement efforts' (1996a: 390; see also Cassell 1996b; Cassell and Hayman 1996). Cassell's account is challenged by Schulhofer (1996). Thomas argues that the evidence is inconclusive (1996a; 1996b). For the most sophisticated and empirically informed assessment, see Leo 1996c.

sionalism (Walker 1980: 229–32).[46] They encouraged a cultural shift towards the acceptance of accountability and legality: the significance of this was discussed in section ii, above. Skolnick writes of a 'legal archipelago . . . sets of islands of legal values . . . distributed throughout the broad experience of policing' (1993: 196). Unfortunately, the lack of research evidence is again a problem. Walker relies heavily on Orfield's report on Chicago narcotics officers[47] which found that the exclusionary rule 'had an enormous impact: educating officers about the law and legal principles, deterring misconduct, and stimulating long-term reforms' (Walker 1988: 19; see also 1993a: 49). While Orfield's work is valuable, the methodological limitations of relying on structured, questionnaire-based interviews have to be acknowledged. Apart from two limited studies in the 1960s (Wald *et al.* 1967; Milner 1971), the only observational research on interrogation in the United States is Leo's reports of his observations in 'Laconia',[48] supplemented by his analysis of videorecorded interrogations by two other police departments.[49] Leo argues that '*Miranda* has had a profound impact in at least four different ways: first, [it] has exercised a civilising influence on police interrogation behavior, and in so doing has professionalized police practices; second, [it] has transformed the culture and discourse of police detecting; third, [it] has increased popular awareness of constitutional rights; and fourth, [it] has inspired police to develop more specialized, more sophisticated and seemingly more effective interrogation techniques' (1996c: 668). Such developments (particularly the shift in interrogation from coercion to persuasion, manipulation, and deception) cannot be simplistically categorized as progress. Rather they must be seen as part of a more general reconstitution of techniques of power and processes of control (Leo 1994: 94–6; 1996a: 285; cf. Marx 1992).

Studies of regulation in this and other fields confirm the trite

---

[46] Walker (1989: 280) stresses the way in which legal change paved the way for such reforms: this is an important counter to the usual presentations of legal and other reforms as alternatives.

[47] Orfield 1987. Walker describes this as the only 'detailed study of how the exclusionary rule affects day-to-day detective work' (1993: 49). Also now available is Leo's research: see below.

[48] 'Laconia' is Leo's pseudonym for the large, urban Californian police department in which his main research was carried out: see Leo 1995.

[49] See Leo 1992; 1994; 1996a; 1996b; 1996c. While Leo's work is valuable and perceptive, it is not clear how representative are the departments and interrogations studied. At least in comparison with English and Australian officers, Leo's interrogators are unusually skilful and committed (cf. Baldwin 1993a).

observation that the best discipline is that which is internalized: the objective should be compliance rather than obedience (McGowan 1972: 672; Baldwin 1995: 302). It is commonplace to indicate the irony that criminologists who have accepted the limits of deterrence in controlling deviance should adopt it as the basis of police regulation (Reiner 1992a: 214). As Kagan argues 'the attempt to control regulatory enforcement primarily by external legal requirements is deeply troublesome in so far as it induces in both inspectors and the regulated an attitude of legal defensiveness, a concern for adequate documentation rather than substantive achievement, and a degree of rule-bound rigidity' (1984: 58). Regulatory strategies must aim to foster responsibility and competence, not mere rule-following.

How can this be achieved? The literature on regulation is too large and complex for detailed analysis here,[50] but some crucial lessons can be suggested, particularly from the work of John Braithwaite and his colleagues, which is distinguished not least by its positive and constructive emphasis. Sophisticated studies of business regulation have transcended the 'intellectual stalemate' produced by dogmatic dichotomies between co-operative and punitive regulatory strategies (Ayres and Braithwaite 1992: 3; cf. Fisse and Braithwaite 1993). Punishment and persuasion, coercion, and compliance are not exclusionary alternatives: 'compliance is optimized by regulation that is contingently cooperative, tough and forgiving' (Ayres and Braithwaite 1992: 51; cf. Braithwaite 1995: 55). The 'trick of successful regulation' is their 'synergy' (Ayres and Braithwaite 1992: 25; see ch. 2 *passim*; Ogus 1994: 94–7). In achieving this, understanding of specific structures and cultures of the subject of regulation is vital. But we should not assume too easily that 'we can pick which are the right cases for medicine and which for poison' (Braithwaite 1995: 55). Persuasion should be adopted first: thereafter, regulatory strategies must be adaptive, responding to the subject's mode of compliance or evasion (Ayres and Braithwaite 1992; Braithwaite 1995; Hawkins and Thomas (eds.) 1984).

There seems no good reason not to apply such insights to policing (Braithwaite 1992a; cf. Brogden and Shearing 1993). This should not be taken to suggest any complacency about the state of the police: this would be particularly peculiar in a critical observer of NSW policing in the mid-1990s. Rather, the driving-force is the need for

---

[50] For useful overviews, see Horwitz 1989: ch. 2; Ogus 1994.

change by effective police reform. Officers throughout police organizations should be consulted about the standards which they are expected to maintain, both procedural and ethical.[51] This approach is not 'soft': it would emphasize making disciplinary sanctions more effective: if other strategies fail or are inappropriate, punishment must be available in credible form. When police abuse their powers and position, the costs for individual citizens and groups can be high, and this must be reflected in public intolerance of police misconduct and official willingness to act decisively against it. Police disciplinary systems are deeply flawed, all too often ignoring procedural breaches,[52] while earning officers' disrespect for severely but unpredictably punishing less significant misconduct. However, such measures should go beyond individual or group punishment: the police organization should also, in appropriate circumstances, bear responsibility. This process could range from judges ensuring that notice is taken of particular cases (as suggested above in section i(c) to a programme of 'enforced self-investigation' and externally supervised reform (Braithwaite 1992a: 3; Fisse and Braithwaite 1993).

At another level, police should be encouraged to accept responsibility for ensuring that their activities are legal and ethical. The hostility amongst some British commentators (e.g. McConville *et al.* 1991a) to police self-regulation might be moderated by more familiarity with the literature on regulation outside criminal justice.[53] The policing literature provides no grounds to believe that externally controlled, punishment-oriented regimes are effective. As Walker suggests, 'one of the keys to long-term police reform is the development of the capacity for self-governance by law enforcement agencies' (1986: 384). This does not, of course, mean granting complete autonomy: self-governance must be developed along with procedures for external accountability (see subsect. (e) below). Confirmation of the potential for doing so can be found in the literature on regulatory

---

[51] This has been argued in various ways by e.g. Goldsmith 1991; Kleinig 1996; Mastrofski and Greene 1993: 82–3; Walker 1993b: 47; Wright and Burke 1995.

[52] The Royal Commission on Criminal Justice reported that 'there are hardly any formal disciplinary hearings for breaches of PACE' (RCCJ 1993: 48).

[53] If not, an argument for the exceptional nature of criminal justice needs to be made cogently. The disregard seems mutual: studies of regulation routinely overlook criminal justice. Indeed, Ogus defines it out of consideration, insisting that regulation is 'fundamentally a politico-economic concept and, as such, can best be understood by reference to different systems of economic organisation and the legal forms which maintain them' (1994: 1). This focus on economic activity unfortunately restricts discussion of issues such as regulatory failure and compliance (*ibid.*, ch. 16).

strategies for dealing with corruption and handling complaints: a 'double-track strategy' combining internal and external elements seems clearly desirable (Mollen 1994: 152; see also Dixon 1995a; Goldsmith 1991).

Nor does it mean simply that we must 'trust the police': trust is to be distinguished from the blind faith which has so often encouraged police misconduct. Rather, it means a police service must be constructed in which we can trust, and that trusting (i.e. requiring the acceptance of responsibility) will be an important part of that process. This provides insight into the crucial distinction between presentational, inhibitory, and working rules (Smith and Gray 1985: 440–2; see Ch. 1 above) and, most significantly for the study of law in policing, how rules can be more or less effective. As Braithwaite and Makkai suggest:

When we are trusted to do the right thing and then choose to do it, we convince ourselves that we did it because we believed it to be right; we internalize the conception of right that we are trusted to have. On the other hand, when we comply to secure extrinsic rewards or avoid the punishments of distrustful regulators, we convince ourselves that we did it for those extrinsic reasons rather than for the intrinsic virtue of doing right. . . . When, therefore our distrustful guardians cannot be around to put those rewards and punishments in our path, we do not bother with the extrinsically motivated behavior (1994: 2).

Just as 'knavery is returned in full measure' to police who treat people as knaves (Braithwaite 1995: 54), so treating police as knaves will be counter-productive: 'the trouble with institutions that assume that people will not be virtuous is that they destroy virtue' (Braithwaite 1995: 54). In contrast to the view that trust is inevitably abused and even inherently criminogenic, Braithwaite and Makkai insist that 'trust *nurtures* compliance' and 'engenders trustworthiness' (1994: 1, 2 original emphasis).

This resonates with another theme in Braithwaite's work: the uses and abuses of shame (Braithwaite 1989; Braithwaite and Mugford 1994). Police organizations react defensively to criticism, particularly if it comes in the adversarial context of a court case or judicial inquiry: they are left feeling 'more angry and scapegoated than sorry' (Braithwaite 1992a: 4). This is exemplified by the response of many New South Wales police officers to the Royal Commission into the NSW Police Service: complaints abound of low morale and victimization, while the integrity of the vast majority is stressed. An effective reform process requires organizations to accept responsibility, through a positive shaming process, both for problems and for their rectification. This might include attempts to develop 'restorative' justice which would reintegrate rather than ignore or exclude minor offenders. The reintegration must, of course, not be into traditional police cultures and practices. These must be reformed not just by legal regulation, but also by involving police officers in establishing and maintaining their own ethical standards.[54] It has been possible here only to indicate the potential relevance of the literature on regulation and associated fields, not to explore it or its limitations in depth. Enough has been said to suggest that there is much of relevance to policing.

(e) *Reforming and Regulating*

This analysis suggests that the question 'can law control policing?' must not be reduced to the traditional question 'can rules control discretion?' Rules may provide a 'framework and focus' (Braithwaite and Braithwaite 1995: 330), but are not enough. They are just one of the 'tools of government' (Baldwin 1995: 292, 304, citing Hood 1983). Rules are likely to have their place in any governmental strategy, but they must be used in thoughtful and original ways. Their objective must be clear, they must be designed and chosen carefully, they must be appropriate to the specific subject matter, their potential relationship with existing regulation by other normative systems (such as police cultures) must be appreciated, and supplements and alternatives to rules should be considered. Other methods of regulation— both legal and non-legal—must be considered: '[j]udging when to employ rules within government involves complex questions of design and strategy' (Baldwin 1995: 15; cf. Daintith 1994; Ayres and Braithwaite 1994: 101; Jowell 1975: 12–25). As Loughlin suggests, public law 'should adopt as its principal focus the examination of the manner in which the normative structures of law can contribute to the tasks of guidance, control, and evaluation in government' (1992: 264). In this context, the 'traditional rule of law ideal' is of marginal relevance, as 'continuities between the legal, the political and the social' are increasingly recognized (Lacey 1992: 386).

The need to consider alternatives to rules is emphasized further in

---

[54] See Dixon 1995b, Kleinig 1996, and, e.g. Neil Brewer's current research, 'Development of Ethical Behaviour in Junior Police Officers: A Test of Peer Modelling Effects' (NSW Police Advisory Council, 1996).

Lacey's critique of legal pretensions and particularly the 'intellectual and practical imperialism in which lawyers merely incorporate ever more inappropriate areas of activity into their own analytic and political framework' (Lacey 1992: 363). The crucial but difficult task is to use legal techniques and principles without slipping into a legal imperialism which denotes everything as 'legal', with all its implications of lawyers' claims to hegemony and its ignorance or dismissal of other disciplines. For example, if Davis's 'program for reform' is freed from its reliance on administrative rule-making, its potential grows: public education about policing, revision of substantive criminal law, clarification and definition of police powers, rewriting of police rule books, open policy-making, public consultation, and democratic accountability, and reliance on reliable research rather than 'common sense' are all desirable (Dixon 1995b). The relevance of open government for policing deserves emphasis: openness was a key theme of Davis's work, has featured strongly in the programmes of the new public law, and also is stressed (as 'transparency') in Brogden and Shearing's agenda for police reform (1993: 127–9).

The potential for development of legal remedies is a matter of controversy: strong arguments both for and against judicial review can be found among leading public lawyers (Richardson and Genn (eds.) 1994). This debate needs to be broadened beyond the public lawyers' circle. For example, D. J. Smith constructively suggested using the law more actively and creatively by legislatively encouraging the courts to subject policing policies to principles of fairness and justice by developing judicial review (1988: 440). Civil actions, so long dismissed as insignificant, are now to be taken seriously despite their acknowledged limitations (Clayton and Tomlinson 1992: 15). They might be taken more seriously if costs, rather than being absorbed by central funds, were (at least in part) allocated to the 'budget unit' responsible. Similarly, the other tools of public law—complaints procedures, ombudsmen, rights of consultation and participation, freedom of information—are all attracting renewed interest in England and Wales (particularly under the influence of the European Union: see Walker 1996a) and all have potentially great relevance to the control of policing.

Baldwin's and Lacey's work indicates the need to look beyond traditional legal regulation as a means of dealing with perceived problems in policing: this would include considering 'institutions of political accountability . . .; the structure and organization of areas in which discretionary power is exercised (encompassing questions about personnel, powers, and the relations between them); and substantive questions as to the institutional goals and assumptions of particular areas of administration' (Lacey 1992: 379). Of course, it is hardly original to argue for political accountability of police. For much of the later 1970s and 1980s, it became almost a cliché in English academic debate about policing. Its unreality was brought home with the abolition of the Greater London and metropolitan councils and subsequently the reformation of police authorities.[55] (Its parochialism is indicated by the disbelief in contemporary New South Wales which meets suggestions that local government should or could control policing.) In the mid-1990s, police accountability has attracted more politically astute and theoretically sophisticated attention (e.g. Jones et al. 1994; 1996; Loader 1996; Reiner and Spencer (eds.) 1993).

The experience of the 1980s in England also suggests the limits of proactive legal regulation. A good example is the Scarman-inspired attempt to structure police policy and discretion by legally requiring public consultation. The Police and Criminal Evidence Act, section 106, requires that '[a]rrangements shall be made in each police area for obtaining the views of people in that area about matters concerning the policing of that area and for obtaining their co-operation with the police in preventing crime in the area.' Researchers have been damning in their assessments of the resulting consultative committees: they have 'come to serve as little more than a forum for consensual impression management' (Weatheritt 1988: 172; see also Morgan 1992). Committees are unbalanced in their representation of the 'consumers' of police services: while local business will be represented, young black working-class males will almost certainly not be. Committees have been dependent on police for information and consequently reflect police definitions of problems and possible strategies. Police do not allow committees a significant role in policy formulation. Rather, influence is exerted by middle-management officers on committee members and, via them, on police authorities and senior management (Morgan 1992: 181). Such outcomes were predictable enough: unwillingness to transfer power routinely makes such consultative procedures frustrating and ineffective. It is an example of trying to make the system work in a different way

---

[55] For a useful review of these developments in the context of the history of police accountability in England and Wales, see Marshall and Loveday 1994.

without understanding the structural reasons for its current mode of operation (Hall 1982). This is a recurrent dilemma for attempts to use legal regulation positively.

It is necessary to emphasize the limits of legal regulation. Policing is conducted in a complex relationship with law, but is not consumed by it. For example, the general duties officer who comes across a sick drug user about to inject has to choose, *inter alia*, between arresting the person, ignoring the incident, and destroying the drugs. Her or his choice involves moral and ethical considerations, as well as, *inter alia*, profane matters such as departmental and local policies, and (official and personal) willingness to commit time to arresting and processing the user.

[P]olicing is for the most part *extralegal*, for while officers (often) work within the constraints of the law, they seldom invoke the law in performing police work; informal action, with or without coercive action, is commonplace, and hence the dimensions of police discretion are not delineated by officers' authority to apply legal sanctions (Worden 1989: 668).

There are four major dimensions of non-legal policing. First, policing may be conducted within the law, but be substantially unaffected by it: the arguments by Sanders and Young (1994b) were considered above. Secondly, as Chapter 3 above showed, 'policing by consent' is a crucial way of doing police work. Thirdly, while legal regulation focuses on controlling law enforcement, it is commonplace to point out that much police work includes social service and order maintenance as well as or rather than law enforcement. Fourthly, even when officers are dealing with suspected crime, legal influence may be compromised by other pervasive objectives (see sect. 2(i)(b) above). In achieving these, officers may use extra-legal or illegal means. Alternatively, they may use legal powers tactically, for example arresting and detaining suspects, even though there is no realistic prospect of bringing charges to court.[56] Finally, if, for one of the numerous reasons which produce guilty pleas, officers can be confident that a suspect will not contest the charge, legal supervision of law enforcement is likely to be minimal.

However, scepticism about rules must not be excessive, and must address not the simplicities of the legalistic-bureaucratic model (see Ch. 1, above), but a more sophisticated account in which both the lim-

---

[56] See, e.g., McConville *et al.*'s finding that no further action was taken against a quarter of their sample of arrested suspects (1991a: 104).

its and the possibilities of normative regulation are appreciated (Dixon 1995b). As Goldstein suggests, intelligent rule-making involves alerting 'officers to the alternatives available for dealing with a given situation, to the factors that should be considered in choosing from among available alternatives, and to the relative weight that should attach to each factor'.[57] Insistence on the need for structured discretion within new programmes of community- or problem-oriented policing (Moore 1992) are particularly important when a critique of legal regulation has been part of arguments that effective crime control, notably the 'war on drugs' (Skolnick 1994), requires that police should be allowed to slip the leash of legal restraint. In this context, the case for a 'new policing' based on professional use of discretion rather than rules (see Ch. 1, above) can be a stalking-horse for most undesirable developments in policing (Weisburd *et al.* 1993; Skolnick 1993).

Here as elsewhere, 'community' is Janus-faced: it excludes as it includes. The exclusion of those not defined as being of 'the community' is particularly problematic in its re-articulation of distinctions drawn by police cultures between the respectable and the unrespectable; between those who count, and those who do not (Matza 1969: 189; Reiner 1992a: 117–21). A NSW officer expressed the operational consequences: 'you treat good people as good and you treat shit as shit'. The brush is broad: another officer referred to 'the lower working class, the hoodlum element, the housing commission sort of families out west[58] who are brought up to hate coppers'. In acting and thinking in this way, police reproduce social divisions (Finnane 1994: 103). Ironically, 'good people' sometimes do not appreciate what the police do for them: the outcome is police cynicism. The dichotomies are particularly problematic for legal regulation if rights and safeguards are seen by police as being for 'decent people'.[59] In NSW, a history of cultural distinctions between 'criminals' and 'the community' creates particular difficulties in according full legal citizenship to the former. Such problems are exacerbated in Australia and elsewhere by deepening social and economic divisions,

[57] 1977: 111–12; cf. Davis's preference for rules as 'guides, not inexorable commands' (1977: 1171). Please note, however, Goldstein's later comments on the problem of getting police to treat written directions in this way (1993: 55).

[58] i.e. Sydney's western suburbs: see Powell 1993.

[59] See the quotation from an English officer in Ch. 3, sect. ii, above. Cf. Matza's argument that the 'dilemma of law and order' identified by Skolnick (1975) may be met by providing 'law' to one population and 'order' to another (1969: 188–95). The latter is not *necessarily* repressive: see, e.g., the police role in negotiating gambling law enforcement (Dixon 1991c: 266).

by racism, and by drug-related crime. A fundamental task of police reform must be to help police (and 'the community') to see, e.g., the Vietnamese heroin user, the westie 'hoodlum', or the Aboriginal suspect as part of, not an alien threat to, 'the community'. Another, as suggested in Ch. 1, is to take the 'ownership' of policing away from the police (Brogden and Shearing 1993: 170). Finally (as suggested in Chapter 5, sect. viii above), the political significance of policing needs to be understood by its practitioners: as Skolnick argued, their 'professionalism must rest on a set of values conveying the idea that police are as much an institution dedicated to the achievement of legality in society as they are an official social organization designed to control misconduct through the invocation of punitive sanctions. What must occur is a significant alteration in the ideology of police so that police "professionalization" rests on the values of a democratic legal order, rather than on technological proficiency' (1975: 238–9).

It should be clear that legal regulation must be combined with other processes and strategies if police reform is to be effected (Smith 1986: 94). Emerging as a key issue in considering the future of policing is the provision of positive direction to police officers (Krantz *et al.* 1979: 53). At one level, there is the need for 'reflection and public debate on the normative political issues of what the role of the police *should* be in a democratic society' (Lacey 1992: 385). An important contribution to this process has been made by John Braithwaite's identification of what a 'good police service' would look like (Braithwaite 1992b). Whether or not Braithwaite's republican theory is accepted, his work shows the benefits of connecting the study and practice of policing with broad social and political theory.

As Norris and Norris demonstrate, defining good policing is complex matter (1993; see also Bright 1995; Krantz *et al.* 1979: 55–6). Officers have to learn to recognize their own success other than in terms of traditional 'performance indicators' such as arrests. For example, as Homel suggests, police contributed to the remarkable effect of random breath-testing in reducing fatal car crashes in New South Wales. Yet 'it is astonishing how many constables in NSW are still not aware of the impact of RBT and their critical role in its ongoing success' (1994: 25). Police organizations must become as adept at identifying good practice and rewarding officers for carrying it out as they are at creating disciplinary rules and punishing officers for breaking them: 'a programme of "positive discipline" stressing and rewarding integrity is crucial' (Punch 1985: 196). This must involve both individual rewards and organizational recognition, e.g. by the communication of information about successes (Homel 1994: 25). Police organizations notoriously rely on negative discipline.[60] It is conventional to include them in Gouldner's category of 'punishment centred bureaucracies'. However, it is less often appreciated that the punishment in such bureaucracies is not just applied by management to workers, but also by workers to management (Gouldner 1954: chs. 11 and 12). Such 'punishment' was described by Punch in his study of corruption and reform efforts in Holland: 'informal resistance within the Amsterdam police was powerful enough to deflect investigations and to impede change' (1985: 199; see also Sherman 1974: 270). The difficulty of change should not be underestimated: Krantz *et al.* found that 'many of the problems associated with the use of negative sanctions also hampers the application of positive incentives' (1979: 61). To break away from this model, police organizations need to undergo fundamental cultural and normative change (Dixon 1995b).

Discussing the potential for change involves looking at the nature of policing, at the structural limits and possibilities of change, and the broader social, economic, and political forces which define those limits.[61] The experience of police reformers has been that police organizations are as manœuvrable as oiltankers. This is not just because of the bureaucratic problems which attract attention, such as staff unwillingness to change working practices, difficulties in communicating new policies, inadequate training, and poor human resources. Difficulties in achieving reform and legal regulation of policing are neither fortuitous nor haphazard. Rather they are products of fundamental elements in the practices and mandates of policing. But this should not justify slipping back into an excessively pessimistic determinism: police departments can be changed, have changed, and will continue to change.[62] The challenge is to identify the limits and possibilities of change, and the potential for legal regulation to facilitate, encourage, and contribute to such change (cf Chan 1997).

In conclusion, it is appropriate to reflect on some of the themes of this study. Complaints about our lack of knowledge of how law

---

[60] For a scathing critique of the negativity of Australian police forces, see McConkey *et al.* 1996: 51.

[61] Cf. the extensive critiques of community policing: e.g. McConville and Shepherd 1992; Klockars 1988.

[62] Their resistance should not be exaggerated: judges provide an example of other sectors of criminal justice which are even more resistant to change (Walker 1993a: 152).

affects policing (see preface) may now be seen in a rather different light. The now substantial literature (particularly on the impact of PACE) suggests that the issue is not lack of knowledge, but rather theoretical and political differences in its interpretation. This should, of course, surprise nobody except the straw empiricist. I have suggested my interpretation, one which stresses contingency: law's relationship with policing depends upon the nature of the law, the type of policing, and the social and political contexts. This is unfortunately, but again unsurprisingly, unhelpful to anyone seeking a formulaic resolution to the question of whether law can change policing.

From this perspective, law should be seen, not as having some fixed essence, but as an adaptable set of practices, discourses, techniques, and modes of regulation. It can provide both broad, discretionary, pragmatic adaptability and a clear rule-based regime. Its great strength as an ideology and as a mode of domination and accomplishment is that it can do both and can switch between them. Such an approach emphasizes the need for theoretically-based empirical work which explores the conjunctural circumstances in which law appears in particular forms.

Policing is similarly resistant to neat definition. It involves a wide range of practices, institutions, and cultures. Law's impact is modulated by various and varying combinations of these elements. Simple examples are provided by the contrast between activities on the street and in the station and by regional and national variations. Whatever its essential commonalities (Bittner 1990), policing in England and Australia is crucially different because of its cultural and political contexts: it is for this reason that, as Chapters 4 and 5 suggested, legal regulation of policing has diverged so markedly in these jurisdictions. As Chapter 3 argued, law does not subsume policing as a mode of governance: policing by consent provides a distinct but closely articulated mode. In addition, as noted above, the objectives of policing cannot be reduced to those of the legal process, charge, and conviction. As for studies of policing, the imperative must be breadth of vision, looking outwards to policing in other places and times and to theoretical work across the social sciences: the theoretical sophistication of a new generation of police research[63] suggests grounds for optimism about such developments.

---

[63] See references in Ch. 1, p. 48, above. For a review, see Dixon 1997.

Bibliography

ABRAHAMS, G. (1964), *Police Questioning and the Judges' Rules* (London: Oyez Publications).

ABRAMOVITCH, R., PETERSON-BADALI, M., and ROHAN, M. (1995), 'Young People's Understanding and Assertion of their Rights to Silence and Legal Counsel', *Canadian Journal of Criminology* 37: 1–18.

ADDISON, N. (1995), 'Beat the Defence', *Police Review*, 14 Apr. 1995, 20–1.

ADLER, J. S. (1989a), 'A Historical Analysis of the Law of Vagrancy', *Criminology* 27: 209–29.

—— (1989b), 'Rejoinder to Chambliss', *Criminology* 27: 239–50.

AINSWORTH, J. E. (1993), 'In a Different Register: The Pragmatics of Powerlessness in Police Interrogation', *Yale Law Journal* 103: 259–322.

ALLAN, T. R. S. (1985), 'Parliamentary Supremacy and the Rule of Law', *Cambridge Law Journal* 44: 111–43.

—— (1993), *Law, Liberty, and Justice* (Oxford: Clarendon).

ALLEN, F. A. (1996) *The Habits of Legality: Criminal Justice and the Rule of Law* (New York: Oxford University Press).

ALLEN, R. J. (1976), 'The Police and Substantive Rulemaking', *University of Pennsylvania Law Review* 125: 62–118.

—— (1977), 'The Police and Substantive Rulemaking: A Brief Rejoinder', *University of Pennsylvania Law Review* 125: 1172–81.

ALRC (1975), *Criminal Investigation: Interim Report*, Australian Law Reform Commission Report #2 (Canberra: Australian Government Publishing Service).

—— (1987), *Evidence*, Australian Law Reform Commission Report #38 (Canberra: Australian Government Publishing Service).

ALVESSON, M. (1993), *Cultural Perspectives on Organizations* (Cambridge: Cambridge University Press).

ANDERSON, D. M., and KILLINGRAY, D. (1991), 'Consent, Coercion and Colonial Control', in Anderson and Killingray (eds.), 1–15.

—— and —— (eds.) (1991), *Policing the Empire: Government, Authority and Control, 1830–1940* (Manchester: Manchester University Press).

ANDERSON, T. (1992), *Take Two: The Criminal Justice System Revisited* (Sydney: Bantam).

ARCHIBALD, W. F. A., GREENHALGH, J. H., and ROBERTS, J. (1901), *The Metropolitan Police Guide* (London: HMSO).

ARENELLA, P. (1983), 'Rethinking the Functions of Criminal Procedure', 72 *Georgetown Law Journal* 185–248.

ARONSON, M., and HUNTER, J. (1995), *Litigation* (5th edn., Sydney: Butterworths).

ASHWORTH, A. (1994), *The Criminal Process* (Oxford: Clarendon).

ASHWORTH, A. (1996), 'Crime, Community and Creeping Consequentialism' [1996] *Criminal Law Review* 220–30.

ATTORNEY GENERAL'S DEPARTMENT (1995), *Review of Part 1C of the Crimes Act 1914: Discussion Paper* (Canberra: Commonwealth Attorney General's Department).

AUGHTERSON, E. P. (1989), 'The Expansion of Police Powers in the Northern Territory', *Australian and New Zealand Journal of Criminology* 13: 103–16.

AYRES, I., and BRAITHWAITE, J. (1992), *Responsive Regulation: Transcending the Deregulation Debate* (New York: Oxford University Press).

BALDWIN, J. (1992a), *The Role of Legal Representatives at the Police Station*, Royal Commission on Criminal Justice Research Study #3 (London: HMSO).

—— (1992b), 'Suspect Interviews', *New Law Journal* 142: 1095–6.

—— (1992c), *Rethinking Police Interrogation in England and Wales*, Occasional paper #11 (New York Center for Research in Crime and Justice, New York: New York University School of Law).

—— (1993a), 'Police Interview Techniques', *British Journal of Criminology* 33: 325–53.

—— (1993b), 'Power and Police Interviews', *New Law Journal* 143: 1194–5, 1197.

—— (1994), 'Police Interrogation: What are the Rules of the Game?', in Morgan and Stephenson (eds.), 66–76.

—— and MCCONVILLE, M. (1977), *Negotiated Justice* (Oxford: Martin Robertson).

BALDWIN, R. (1981), Review of McBarnet 1983 (1st edn.), *British Journal of Law and Society* 8: 273–7.

—— (1985), 'Taking Rules to Excess', in C. Jones and M. Brenton (eds.), *The Yearbook of Social Policy in Britain 1984–5* (London: Routledge and Kegan Paul), 9–29.

—— (1989), 'Regulation and Policing by Code' in Weatheritt (ed.), 157–68.

—— (1990), 'Why Rules Don't Work', *Modern Law Review* 53: 321–37.

—— (1995), *Rules and Government* (Oxford: Clarendon).

—— and HOUGHTON, J. (1986), 'Circular Arguments: The Status and Legitimacy of Administrative Rules' [1986] *Public Law* 239–84.

—— and KINSEY, R. (1980), 'Behind the Politics of Police Powers', *British Journal of Law and Society* 7: 242–65.

—— and —— (1982), *Police Powers and Politics* (London: Quartet).

—— and —— (1985), 'Rules, Realism and the Police Act', *Critical Social Policy* 12: 89–102.

BANTON, M. (1964), *The Policeman in the Community* (London: Tavistock).

BARENDT, E. (1985), 'Dicey and Civil Liberties' [1985] *Public Law* 596–608.

BARRETT, E. L. (1962), 'Police Practices and the Law—From Arrest to Release or Charge', *California Law Review* 50: 11–55.

BARRY, A., OSBORNE, T., and ROSE, N. (eds.) (1996), *Foucault and Political Reason* (London: UCL Press).

BARTON, P. G. (1993a), 'Searches of Premises with Consent', *Criminal Law Quarterly* 35: 376–87.

—— (1993b), 'Consent by Others to Search your Place', *Criminal Law Quarterly* 35: 441–52.

BAXTER, J. (1985), 'Policing and the Rule of Law', in Baxter and Koffman (eds.), 38–61.

—— and KOFFMAN, L. (1985), 'Introduction', in Baxter and Koffman (eds.), 1–4.

—— and —— (1983), 'The Confait Inheritance', *Cambrian Law Review* 14: 11–33.

—— and —— (eds.) (1985), *Police: The Constitution and the Community* (Abingdon: Professional Books).

BAYLEY, D. (1994), *Police for the Future* (New York: Oxford University Press).

—— and SHEARING, C. D. (1996), 'The Future of Policing', *Law and Society Review* 30: 585–606.

BEACH, B. (1978), *Report of the Board of Inquiry into Allegations Against Members of the Victoria Police Force* (Melbourne: Government Printer).

BELSKY, M. H. (1984), 'Whither Miranda?', *Texas Law Review* 62: 1341–61.

BENNETT, W. L., and FELDMAN, M. S. (1981), *Reconstructing Reality in the Courtroom* (New Brunswick: Rutgers University Press).

BERGER, M. (1990), 'Legislating Confession Law in Great Britain', *University of Michigan Journal of Law Reform* 24: 1–64.

BEUN-CHOWN, J. (1991), 'Battle Looms over Police Reforms', *Illawarra Mercury*, 14 Sept.

BIRCH, D. J. (1989), 'The Pace Hots Up' [1989] *Criminal Law Review* 95–116.

—— (1990), 'Commentary on *Canale*' [1990] *Criminal Law Review* 329–30.

BITTNER, E. (1990), *Aspects of Police Work* (Boston, Mass.: Northeastern University Press).

BLAIR, I. (1985), *Investigating Rape* (London: Croom Helm).

BLOM-COOPER, L., and DREWRY, G. (1972), *Final Appeal* (Oxford: Clarendon).

BLUMBERG, A. S. (1967), 'The Practice of Law as Confidence Game', *Law and Society Review* 1: 15–39.

BOLEN, J. (1997), *The Whitrod Era in Queensland Policing: A Successful Strategy for Reform?* (Sydney: Institute of Criminology).

BORDUA, D. J. (ed.) (1967), *The Police* (New York: Wiley).

BOTTOMLEY, A. K., and COLEMAN, C. A. (1980), 'Police Effectiveness and the Public: The Limitations of Official Crime Rates', in R. V. G. Clarke and

J. M. Hough (eds.), *The Effectiveness of Policing* (Farnborough: Gower), 70–97.

BOTTOMLEY, A. K. and COLEMAN, C. A (1981), *Understanding Crime Rates* (Farnborough: Gower).

BOTTOMLEY, A. K., COLEMAN, C. A., DIXON, D., GILL, M., and WALL, D. (1991), *The Impact of PACE: Policing in a Northern Force* (Hull: Centre for Criminology and Criminal Justice).

BOTTOMS, A. E., and McCLEAN, J. D. (1976), *Defendants in the Criminal Process* (London: Routledge and Kegan Paul).

—— and STEVENSON, S. (1992), 'What Went Wrong? Criminal Justice Policy in England, 1945–70', in Downes (ed.), 1–45.

BOYLE, C. (1993), 'Guilt, Innocence and Truth', *Criminal Law Forum* 4: 573–80.

BOWMAN, C. (1992), 'The Arrest Experiments: A Feminist Critique', *Journal of Criminal Law and Criminology* 83: 201–8.

BRADLEY, C. (1989), 'Enforcing the Rules of Criminal Procedure', *Federal Law Review* 18: 188–211.

—— (1990), 'Criminal Procedure in the "Land of Oz": Lessons for America', *Journal of Criminal Law and Criminology* 81: 99–135.

—— (1993), *The Failure of the Criminal Procedure Revolution* (Philadelphia, Penn.: University of Pennsylvania Press).

BRADLEY, D., WALKER, N., and WILKIE, R. (1986), *Managing the Police* (Brighton: Wheatsheaf).

BRAITHWAITE, J. (1989), *Crime, Shame and Reintegration* (Cambridge: Cambridge University Press).

—— (1992a), 'Los Angeles and the Pathologies of Criminal Justice?', *Criminology Australia* (April/May), 2–5.

—— (1992b), 'Good and Bad Police Services and How to Pick Them', in P. Moir and H. Eijkman (eds.), *Policing Australia* (South Melbourne: Macmillan), 11–39.

—— (1995), 'Corporate Crime and Republican Criminological Praxis', in F. Pearce and I. Snider (eds.), *Corporate Crime* (Toronto: University of Toronto Press), 48–71.

—— and BRAITHWAITE, V. (1995), 'The Politics of Legalism', *Social and Legal Studies* 4: 307–41.

—— and MAKKAI, T. (1994), 'Trust and Compliance', *Policing and Society* 4: 1–12.

—— and MUGFORD, S. (1994), 'Conditions of Successful Reintegration Ceremonies', *British Journal of Criminology* 34: 139–71.

—— and PETTIT, P. (1990), *Not Just Deserts* (Oxford: Oxford University Press).

BRENNAN, F. (1983), *Too Much Order with Too Little Law* (St Lucia: University of Queensland Press).

BRIDGES, L., and BUNYAN, T. (1983), 'Britain's New Urban Policing Strategy—

The Police and Criminal Evidence Bill in Context', *Journal of Law and Society* 10: 85–107.

—— and HODGSON, J. (1995), 'Improving Custodial Legal Advice' [1995] *Criminal Law Review* 101–13.

BRIGHT, B. (1995), 'Good Practice Constables', *Policing* 11: 221–46.

BRITTAN, L. (1985), 'A Broad View' [1985] *Public Law* 389–93.

BROGDEN, M. (1981), ' "All Police is Conning Bastards"—Policing and the Problem of Consent', in B. Fryer *et al.* (eds.), *Law, State and Society* (London: Croom Helm), 202–28.

—— (1982), *The Police: Autonomy and Consent* (London: Academic Press).

—— (1987a), 'The Emergence of the Police—the Colonial Dimension', *British Journal of Criminology* 27: 3–14.

—— (1987b), 'An Act to Colonise the Internal Lands of the Island: Empire and the Origins of the Professional Police', *International Journal of the Sociology of Law* 15: 179–208.

—— (1991), *On the Mersey Beat: Policing Liverpool Between the Wars* (Oxford: Oxford University Press).

—— (1992), Review of Brake and Hale, *'Public Order and Private Lives'*, *International Journal of the Sociology of Law* 20: 185–7.

—— and BROGDEN, M. (1984), 'From Henry III to Liverpool 8: The Unity of Police Street Powers', *International Journal of the Sociology of Law* 12: 37–58.

——, JEFFERSON, T., and WALKLATE, S. (1988), *Introducing Policework* (London: Unwin Hyman).

—— and SHEARING, C. (1993), *Policing for a New South Africa* (London: Routledge).

BROWN, D. (1989), *Detention at the Police Station under the Police and Criminal Evidence Act 1984* (London: HMSO).

—— (1991), *Investigating Burglary: The Effects of PACE* (London: HMSO).

—— (1994), 'The Incidence of Right of Silence in Police Interviews: The Research Evidence Reviewed', *Home Office Research Bulletin* 35: 57–75.

—— (1997), *PACE Ten Years On: A Review of the Research* (London: HMSO).

——, ELLIS, T., and LARCOMBE, K. (1992), *Changing the Code: Police Detention under the Revised PACE Codes of Practice* (London: HMSO)

BROWN, D. B. (1984), Review of Sallmann and Willis (1984), *Legal Service Bulletin*, Aug., 186–90.

—— (1987), 'The Politics of Reform', in G. Zdenkowski, C. Ronalds, and M. Richardson (eds.), *The Criminal Injustice System* (Sydney: Pluto), 254–81.

—— and DUFFY, B. (1991), 'Privatising Police Verbal: The Growth Industry in Prison Informants', in Carrington *et al.* (eds.), 181–231.

——, FARRIER, D., and WEISBROT, D. (1996), *Criminal Laws* (Annandale, NSW: Federation Press).

BROWN, M. K. (1981), *Working the Street: Police Discretion and the Dilemmas of Reform* (2nd. edn., New York: Russell Sage Foundation).

BROWNLIE, I. (1960), 'Police Questioning, Custody and Caution' [1960] *Criminal Law Review* 298–324.

BURCHELL, G., GORDON, C., and MILLER, P. (eds.) (1991), *The Foucault Effect* (London: Harvester Wheatsheaf).

BURROWS, J., and TARLING, R. (1987), 'The Investigation of Crime in England and Wales', *British Journal of Criminology* 27: 229–51.

—— and —— (1982), *Clearing up Crime* (London: HMSO).

BURTON, F., and CARLEN, P. (1979), *Official Discourse* (London: Routledge).

BYRNE, P. J. (1993), *Criminal Law and Colonial Subject* (Cambridge: Cambridge University Press).

CAIDEN, G. E. (1977), *Police Revitalization* (Lexington, Mass.: Lexington Books).

CAIN, M. (1972), 'Police Professionalism', *Anglo-American Law Review* 1: 217–31.

—— (1973), *Society and the Policeman's Role* (London: Routledge and Kegan Paul).

—— (1993), 'Some go Backward, Some go Forward: Police Work in Comparative Perspective', *Contemporary Sociology* 22: 319–24.

CALLIGAN, S. (1988), *Points to Prove* (London: Police Review).

CAMERON, N. (1990), 'The Police and Crime Control: Effectiveness, Community Policing, and Legal Change', *Criminal Law Forum* 1: 477–512.

CAMPBELL, B. (1993), *Goliath* (London: Methuen).

CAPE, E. (1993), *Defending Suspects at Police Stations* (London: Legal Action Group).

CAPLAN, G. M. (1974), 'The Case for Rulemaking by Law Enforcement Agencies', in Weistart (ed.), 56–70.

CARLEN, P. (1976), *Magistrates' Justice* (Oxford: Martin Robertson).

CARRINGTON, K., DYER, M., HOGG, R., BARGEN, J., and LOHREY, A. (eds.) (1991), *Travesty: Miscarriages of Justice* (Sydney: Pluto).

CARTER, R. F. (1992), *Criminal Law of Queensland* (8th edn., Sydney: Butterworths).

CASSELL, P. G. (1996a), '*Miranda*'s Social Costs: An Empirical Reassessment', *Northwestern University Law Review* 90: 387–499.

—— (1996b), 'All Benefits, No Costs: The Grand Illusion of *Miranda*'s Defenders', *Northwestern University Law Review* 90: 1084–1124.

—— and HAYMAN, B. S. (1996), 'Police Interrogation in the 1990s: An Empirical Study of the Effects of *Miranda*', *University of California Law Review* 43: 839–931.

CHAMBLISS, W. J. (1964), 'A Sociological Analysis of the Law of Vagrancy', *Social Problems* 12: 67–77.

—— (1989), 'On Trashing Marxist Criminology', *Criminology* 27: 231–8.

CHAN, J. (1996), 'Changing Police Culture', *British Journal of Criminology* 36: 109–34.

—— (1997), *Changing Police Culture* (Melbourne: Cambridge University Press).

CHANDLER, R. (1959), *The Long Good-Bye* (Harmondsworth: Penguin).

CHAPPELL, D., and WILSON, P. R. (1969), *Police and the Public in Australia and New Zealand* (St Lucia: University of Queensland Press).

CHATTERTON, M. (1976), 'Police in Social Control', in J. F. S. King (ed.), *Control without Custody?* (Cambridge: Institute of Criminology), 104–22.

—— (1989), 'Managing Paperwork', in Weatheritt (ed.), 107–36.

CHESTERTON, R. (1996), 'Hyenas who Stripped their Prey Bare', *Daily Telegraph* (Sydney), 27 Sept.

CHRISTIAN, L. (1983), *Policing by Coercion* (London: Greater London Council).

CJC (1993a), *Report on a Review of Police Powers in Queensland: Volume I: An Overview* (Brisbane: Criminal Justice Commission).

—— (1993b), *Report on a Review of Police Powers in Queensland: Volume III: Arrest Without Warrant, Demand Name and Address and Move-On Powers* (Brisbane: Criminal Justice Commission).

—— (1994), *Report on a Review of Police Powers in Queensland: Volume IV: Suspects' Rights, Police Questioning and Pre-Charge Detention* (Brisbane: Criminal Justice Commission).

—— (1996), *Defendants' Perceptions of the Investigation and Arrest Process* (Brisbane: Criminal Justice Commission).

CLARKE, M. (1993), 'Oppressive Interview Rulings will Lead to Higher CID Standards', *Police Review*, 24 Dec. 1993, 7.

CLAYTON, H., and TOMLINSON, C. (1992), *Civil Actions against the Police* (London: Sweet and Maxwell).

CLELAND, F. H. (1949), 'Questioning Persons in Custody', *Australian Police Journal* 3: 15–37.

COHEN, P. (1979), 'Policing the Working-class City', in B. Fine, J. Lea, S. Picciotto, and J. Young (eds.), *Capitalism and the Rule of Law* (London: Hutchinson), 118–36.

COHEN, S. (1988), *Against Criminology* (New Brunswick: Transaction Books).

COLDREY J. (1986), *Section 460 of the Crimes Act 1958* (Report of the Consultative Committee on Police Powers of Investigation) (Melbourne: Government Printer).

—— (1989), *Body Samples and Examinations: Identification Tests and Procedures* (Report of the Consultative Committee on Police Powers of Investigation) (Melbourne: Government Printer).

COLEMAN, C., DIXON, D., and BOTTOMLEY, A. K. (1993), 'Police Investigative Procedures: Researching the Impact of PACE', in Walker and Starmer (eds.), 17–31.

COLEMAN, C., and MOYNIHAN, J. (1996), *Understanding Crime Data* (Buckingham: Open University Press).

COLLISON, M. (1995), *Police, Drugs and Community* (London: Free Association Books).

COLQUHOUN, P. (1800), *A Treatise on the Police of the Metropolis* (London: H. Baldwin).

—— (1803), *A Treatise on the Functions and Duties of A Constable* (London: W. Bulmer).

CONLEY, C. A. (1991), *The Unwritten Law: Criminal Justice in Victorian Kent* (New York: Oxford University Press).

CORDNER, G. W. (1989), 'Written Rules and Regulations: Are They Necessary?', *FBI Law Enforcement Bulletin* 58 (7), 17–21.

CORNISH, P., and TRUEMAN, T. (1989), 'Investigation and Interrogation in South Australia', paper presented to the conference of the Society for the Reform of the Criminal Law, Sydney.

COTTERELL, R. (1996) '*The Rule of Law in Transition*' Social & Legal; Studies 5: 451–70.

CRAIG, P. P. (1990), *Public Law and Democracy in the UK and the USA* (Oxford: Clarendon Press).

CRITCHLEY, T. A. (1978), *A History of Police in England and Wales* (2nd edn., London: Constable).

CROSS, A. R. N. (1970–1), 'The Right to Silence and the Presumption of Innocence', *Journal of the Society of Public Teachers of Law* 11: 66–75.

CUNNEEN, C. (1990), *Aboriginal–Police Relations in Redfern* (Sydney: Human Rights and Equal Opportunity Commission).

CURRAN, J. H., and CARNIE, J. K. (1986), *Detention or Voluntary Attendance? Police Use of Detention Under Section 2, Criminal Justice (Scotland) Act 1980* (Edinburgh: HMSO).

DAINTITH, T. (1994), 'The Techniques of Government', in Jowell and Oliver (eds.), 209–36.

DAVIES, T. Y. (1983), 'A Hard Look at What we Know (and Still Need to Know) about the "Costs" of the Exclusionary Rule' [1983] *American Bar Foundation Research Journal* 611–90.

DAVIS, G. (1992), Review of McConville *et al.* (1991a), *Policing and Society* 2: 322–4.

DAVIS, J. (1980), 'The London Garrotting Panic of 1862' in Gatrell *et al.* (eds.), 190–213.

DAVIS, K. C. (1971), *Discretionary Justice* (2nd edn., Urbana, Ill.: University of Illinois Press).

—— (1974), 'An Approach to Legal Control of Police', *Texas Law Review* 52: 703–25.

—— (1975), *Police Discretion* (St. Paul, Minn.: West Publishing).

—— (1977), 'Police Rulemaking on Selective Enforcement: A Reply', *University of Pennsylvania Law Review* 125: 1167–71.

DAVIS, M. (1990), *City of Quartz* (London: Verso).

DAWSON, J. B. (1982), 'The Exclusion of Unlawfully Obtained Evidence: A Comparative Study', *International and Comparative Law Quarterly* 31: 513–49.

DEAN, M. (1994), *Critical and Effective Histories* (London: Routledge).

DE GAMA, K. (1988), 'Police Powers and Public Prosecutions: Winning by Appearing to Lose?', *International Journal of the Sociology of Law* 16: 339–57.

DEMUTH, C (1978), *'Sus'*: *A Report on the Vagrancy Act 1824* (London: Runnymede Trust).

DENNING, A. (1949), *Freedom Under the Law* (London: Stevens).

DENNIS, I. (1993), 'Miscarriages of Justice and the Law of Confessions' [1993] *Public Law* 291–313.

—— (1995), 'Instrumental Protection, Human Right or Functional Necessity? Reassessing the Privilege against Self-incrimination', *Cambridge Law Journal* 54: 342–76.

—— (1996), 'Codification and Reform of Evidence Law in Australia' [1996] *Criminal Law Review* 477–89.

—— (ed.) (1987), *Criminal Law and Justice* (London: Sweet and Maxwell).

DEVLIN, P. (1960), *The Criminal Prosecution in England* (London: Oxford University Press).

—— (1967), 'The Police in a Changing Society', *Australian Police Journal* 21: 112–25.

DICEY, A. V. (1929), *The Law of the Constitution* (1st edn., 1885 London: Macmillan).

DIVER, C. S. (1980), 'A Theory of Regulatory Enforcement', *Public Policy* 28: 257–99.

DIXON, D. (1990), 'Juvenile Suspects and the Police and Criminal Evidence Act' in D. A. C. Freestone (ed.), *Children and the Law* (Hull: Hull University Press), 107–29.

—— (1991a), 'Common Sense, Legal Advice and the Right of Silence' [1991] *Public Law* 233–54.

—— (1991b), 'Politics, Research and Symbolism in Criminal Justice', *Anglo-American Law Review* 20: 27–50.

—— (1991c), *From Prohibition to Regulation* (Oxford: Clarendon Press).

—— (1991d), 'Interrogation, Corroboration, and the Limits of Judicial Activism', *Legal Service Bulletin* 16: 103–6.

—— (1992), 'Legal Regulation and Policing Practice', *Social and Legal Studies* 1: 515–41.

—— (1995a), *Issues in the Legal Regulation of Policing* (Sydney: Royal Commission into the NSW Police Service, unpublished).

DIXON, D. (1995b), *The Normative Structure of Policing* (Sydney: Royal Commission into the NSW Police Service, unpublished).

—— (1995c), 'New Left Pessimism', in Noaks *et al.* (eds.), 216–23.

—— (1996a), 'Reform of Policing by Legal Regulation', *Current Issues in Criminal Justice* 7: 287–301.

—— (1996b), 'History in Criminology', *Current Issues in Criminal Justice* 8: 77–81.

—— (1997), 'Criminal Law and Policing in Sociological Perspective', in R. Tomasic (ed.), *The Sociology of Law* (London: Sage).

—— (ed.) (1995), *Crime, Criminology and Public Policy*, supplement to the *Australian and New Zealand Journal of Criminology* (Sydney: Butterworths).

——, BOTTOMLEY, A. K., COLEMAN, C. A., GILL, M., and WALL, D. (1989), 'Reality and Rules in the Construction and Regulation of Police Suspicion', *International Journal of the Sociology of Law* 17: 185–206.

——, ——, ——, ——, and —— (1990a), 'Safeguarding the Rights of Suspects in Police Custody', *Policing and Society* 1: 115–40.

——, COLEMAN, C., and BOTTOMLEY, A. K. (1990b), 'Consent and the Legal Regulation of Policing', *Journal of Law and Society* 17: 345–62.

—— and TRAVIS, G. (1997), *The Impact of Electronic Recording of Police Questioning of Suspects on Criminal Justice in New South Wales*, Report to the Australian Research Council (Sydney: Faculty of Law, University of New South Wales, unpublished).

DOWNES, D. (ed.) (1992), *Unravelling Criminal Justice* (London: Macmillan).

DOYLE, J. F. (1992), 'Empowering and Restraining the Police', *Criminal Justice Ethics* 11: 52–7.

DREW, K. J. (1989), 'Criminal Investigation: The Police Perspective', *Current Issues in Criminal Justice* 1: 46–63.

DRIPPS, D. A. (1988), 'Against Police Interrogation and the Privilege against Self-incrimination', *Journal of Criminal Law and Criminology* 78: 699–734.

DWORKIN, R. (1977), *Taking Rights Seriously* (London: Duckworth).

EASTON, S. M. (1991), 'Bodily Samples and the Privilege against Self-incrimination' [1991] *Criminal Law Review* 18–29.

EDWARDS, A. (1993), 'The Right to Silence Improves Policing', *The Times*, 14 Dec., 33.

EGGER, S., and FINDLAY, M. (1988), 'The Politics of Police Discretion' in M. Findlay and R. Hogg (eds.), *Understanding Crime and Criminal Justice* (North Ryde, NSW: Law Book), 209–23.

EMSLEY, C. (1991), *The English Police: A Political and Social History* (Hemel Hempstead: Harvester).

ENGLISH, J. (1993), ' "Oppressive" or just firm?', *Police Review*, 10 Dec., 28–9.

ERICSON, R. (1981a), 'Rules for Police Deviance' in C. D. Shearing (ed.), *Organizational Police Deviance* (Toronto: Butterworths), 83–110.

—— (1981b), *Making Crime: A Study of Detective Work* (Toronto: Butterworths).

—— (1982), *Reproducing Order: A Study of Police Patrolwork* (Toronto: University of Toronto Press).

—— (1994a), 'The Royal Commission on Criminal Justice System Surveillance', in McConville and Bridges (eds.), 113–40.

—— (1994b), 'The Division of Expert Knowledge in Policing and Security', *British Journal of Sociology* 45: 149–75.

—— and Baranek, P. M. (1982), *The Ordering of Justice* (Toronto: University of Toronto Press).

—— and Haggerty, K. D. (1997), *Policing the Risk Society* (Toronto: University of Toronto Press).

Ewick, P., and Silbey, S. (1996), 'Subversive Stories and Hegemonic Tales: Towards a Sociology of Narrative', *Law & Society Review* 29: 197–226.

Ewing, K., and Gearty, C. A. (1990), *Freedom under Thatcher* (Oxford: Clarendon).

Feeley, M. (1979), *The Process is the Punishment* (New York: Russell Sage Foundation).

—— and Simon, J. (1994), 'Actuarial Justice', in D.Nelken (ed.), *The Futures of Criminology* (London: Sage), 173–201.

Feldman, D. (1986), *The Law Relating to Entry, Search and Seizure* (London: Butterworths).

—— (1990), 'Regulating Treatment of Suspects in Police Stations' [1990] *Criminal Law Review* 452–71.

Fenwick, H. (1995), 'Curtailing the Right to Silence, Access to Legal Advice and Section 78' [1995] *Criminal Law Review* 132–6.

Fielding, N. (1988a), *Joining Forces* (London: Routledge).

—— (1988b), 'Competence and Culture in the Police', *Sociology* 22: 45–64.

—— (1989), 'Police Culture and Police Practice', in Weatheritt (ed.), 77–87.

Fine, R. (1994), 'The Rule of Law and Muggletonian Marxism', *Journal of Law and Society* 21: 193–213.

Finnane, M. (1987), 'The Politics of Police Powers: The Making of the Police Offences Acts', in Finnane (ed.), 88–113.

—— (1989), 'Police Rules and the Organisation of Policing in Queensland', *Australian & New Zealand Journal of Criminology* 22: 95–108.

—— (1990), 'Police and Politics in Australia—the Case for Historical Revision', *Australian and New Zealand Journal of Criminology* 23: 218–28.

—— (1994), *Police and Government* (Melbourne: Oxford University Press).

—— and Garton, S. (1992), 'The Work of Policing: Social Relations and the Criminal Justice System in Queensland 1880–1914', *Labour History* 62: 52–70, 63:43–64.

—— (ed.) (1987), *Policing in Australia: Historical Perspectives* (Kensington: New South Wales University Press).

FISHER, H. (1977), *Report of an Inquiry by Sir Henry Fisher into the circumstances leading to the trial of three persons on charges arising out of the death of Maxwell Confait and the fire at 27 Doggett Road, London* (HC 90, 1977–8).

FISSE, B., and BRAITHWAITE, J. (1993), *Corporations, Crime and Accountability* (Cambridge: Cambridge University Press).

FITZGERALD, T. (1989), *Report of an Inquiry into Possible Illegal Activities and Associated Police Misconduct* (Brisbane: Government Printer).

FLETCHER, G. P. (1976), 'The Metamorphosis of Larceny', *Harvard Law Review* 89: 469–530.

FOSTER, J. (1989), 'Two Stations: An Ethnographic Study of Policing in the Inner City', in D. Downes (ed.), *Crime and the City* (London: Macmillan), 128–53.

FRANCE, A. (1927), 'Le lys rouge', in id. *Œuvres Complètes* (1st edn., 1894), (Paris: Calmann-Levy, 1–390), ix.

FOUCAULT, M. (1975), *Discipline and Punish* (Harmondsworth: Peregrine).

FRECKELTON, I. (1987), 'Criminal Investigation and the 6–hour Rule', *Law Institute Journal* (Mar.), 191–5.

FREEMAN, G. (1988), *George Freeman: An Autobiography* (Miranda, NSW: G. Freeman).

GAL, S. (1991), 'Between Speech and Silence', in M. di Leonardo (ed.), *Gender at the Crossroads of Knowledge: Feminist Anthropology in the Postmodern Era* (Berkeley, Cal.: University of California Press), 175–203.

GALLIGAN, D. J. (1987), 'Regulating Pre-trial Decisions' in Dennis (ed.), 177–202.

GARFINKEL, H. (1956), 'Conditions of Successful Degradation Ceremonies', *American Journal of Sociology* 61: 420–4.

GARLAND, D. (1990), *Punishment and Modern Society* (Oxford: Clarendon).

—— (1991), 'Designing Criminal Policy', *London Review of Books*, 10 Oct. 13–14.

GARTON, S. (1991), 'Pursuing Incorrigible Rogues: Patterns of Policing in NSW 1870–1930', *Journal of the Royal Australian Historical Society* 77: 16–29.

GATRELL, V. A. C. (1980), 'The Decline of Theft and Violence in Victorian and Edwardian England', in Gatrell *et al.* (eds.), 238–96.

—— (1990), 'Crime, Authority and the Policeman-State', in Thompson (ed.), 243–310.

——, LENMAN, B., and PARKER, G. (eds.) (1980), *Crime and the Law* (London: Europa).

GIBBS, H. (1987), 'The Powers of the Police to Question and Search', Sir Richard Blackburn Memorial Lecture, Australian Capital Territory Law Society.

—— (1988), 'Address at the Opening of the 2nd International Criminal Law Congress', *Australian Journal of Forensic Sciences* 20: 252–61.

—— (1989), *Detention Before Charge: Interim Report of the Commonwealth*

Review of Criminal Law (Canberra: Australian Government Publishing Service).

GOLDER, H. (1991), *High and Responsible Office: A History of the NSW Magistracy* (Sydney: Sydney University Press).

GOLDSMITH, A. (1990), 'Taking Police Culture Seriously', *Policing and Society* 1: 91–114.

—— (1991), 'External Review and Self-regulation', in A. J. Goldsmith (ed.), *Complaints Against Police: The Trend To External Review* (Oxford: Clarendon), 13–61.

GOLDSTEIN, H. (1977), *Policing a Free Society* (Cambridge: Ballinger).

—— (1990), *Problem-Oriented Policing* (Philadelphia, Penn.: Temple University Press).

—— (1993), 'Confronting the Complexity of the Policing Function', in Ohlin and Remington (eds.), 23–71.

GOLDSTEIN, J. (1960), 'Police Discretion not to Invoke the Criminal Process', *Yale Law Journal* 69: 543–94.

GOODERSON, R. N. (1970), 'The Interrogation of Suspects', *Canadian Bar Review* 48: 270–307.

GOULDNER, A. V. (1954), *Patterns of Industrial Bureaucracy* (New York: Free Press).

GRABOSKY, P. (1977), *Sydney in Ferment: Crime, Dissent and Official Reaction* (Canberra: Australian National University Press).

—— (1988), *Efficiency and Effectiveness in Australian Policing* (Canberra: Australian Institute of Criminology).

GREATER MANCHESTER POLICE (1988), *Solicitors and Interviews* (Manchester: GMP Development & Inspectorate Branch).

GREENE, J. R., and MASTROFSKI, S. D. (eds.) (1988), *Community Policing: Rhetoric or Reality* (New York: Praeger).

GREER, S. (1990), 'The Right to Silence: A Review of the Current Debate', *Modern Law Review* 53: 709–30.

GRIMSHAW, R., and JEFFERSON, T. (1987), *Interpreting Policework* (London: Allen and Unwin).

GUDJONSSON, G. (1992), *The Psychology of Interrogations, Confessions and Testimony* (Chichester: John Wiley).

HAILSHAM, L. (1981), *Halsbury's Laws of England* (4th edn., London: Butterworths), xxxvi.

HALDANE, R. (1995), *The People's Force: A History of the Victoria Police* (2nd edn., Carlton South: Melbourne University Press).

HALL, J. (1953), 'Police and Law in a Democratic Society', *Indiana Law Journal* 28: 133–77.

HALL, S. (1982), 'The Lessons of Lord Scarman', *Critical Social Policy* 2 (2): 66–72.

——, CRITCHER, C., JEFFERSON, J., CLARKE, J., and ROBERTS, B. (1978), *Policing the Crisis* (London: Macmillan).

HAMPTON, C. (ed.) (1984), *A Radical Reader: The Struggle for Change in England 1381–1914* (Harmondsworth: Penguin).

HANMER, J., RADFORD, J., and STANKO, E. A. (eds.) (1989), *Women, Policing and Male Violence* (London: Routledge).

HARLOW, C., and RAWLINGS, R. (1984), *Law and Administration* (London: Weidenfeld and Nicolson).

HARRIS, J. (1990), 'Society and the State in Twentieth-century Britain', in Thompson (ed.), 63–117.

HART, H. L. A. (1961), *The Concept of Law* (Oxford: Oxford University Press).

HAWKINS, K. (ed.) (1992), *The Uses of Discretion* (Oxford: Clarendon Press).

—— and THOMAS, J. M. (eds.) (1984), *Enforcing Regulation* (Dordrecht: Kluwer).

HAWKINS, R. (1991), 'The "Irish model" and the Empire', in Anderson and Killingray (eds.), 18–32.

HAY, D. (1975), 'Property, Authority and the Criminal Law', in D. Hay, P. Linebaugh, J. G. Rule, E. P. Thompson, and C. Winslow (eds.), *Albion's Fatal Tree* (Harmondsworth: Penguin), 17–63.

—— and SNYDER, F. (1989), 'Using the Criminal Law, 1750–1850', in D. Hay and F. Snyder (eds.), *Policing and Prosecution in Britain, 1750–1850* (Oxford: Clarendon), 3–52.

HEFFERNAN, W. C., and LOVELY, R. W. (1991), 'Evaluating the Fourth Amendment Exclusionary Rule: The Problem with Police Compliance with the Law', *University of Michigan Journal of Law Reform* 24: 311–69.

HENNING, T. (1994), 'A Little Knowledge is a Dangerous Thing, or When is an Arrest not an Arrest?', *Current Issues in Criminal Justice* 6: 90–106.

HIDDEN, P. (1993), 'Confessional Evidence', paper for 'Criminal Law Day' conference, 20 Mar.

HILL, C. (1954), 'The Norman Yoke', in J. Saville (ed.), *Democracy and the Labour Movement* (London: Lawrence and Wishart).

—— (1996), *Liberty Against the Law* (London: Allen Lane).

HILLIARD, B. (1988), 'High Spirits in West Mids', *Police Review*, 15 July 1988, 1489.

HILLYARD, P. (1987), 'The Normalization of Special Powers', in Scraton (ed.), 279–312.

—— (1993), *Suspect Community* (London: Pluto).

HIRST, P. Q. (1979), *On Law and Ideology* (London: Macmillan).

HOBBS, D. (1988), *Doing the Business: Entrepreneurship, the Working Class and Detective Work in the East End of London* (Oxford: Oxford University Press).

—— (1991), 'A Piece of Business: The Moral Economy of Detective Work in the East-End of London', *British Journal of Sociology* 42: 597–608.

HODGSON, J. (1992), 'Tipping the Scales of Justice: The Suspect's Right to Legal Advice' [1992] *Criminal Law Review* 854–62.

Hogg, R. (1983), 'Perspectives on the Criminal Justice System' in M. Findlay, S. J. Egger, and J. Sutton (eds.), *Issues in Criminal Justice Administration* (Sydney: George Allen and Unwin), 1–19.

—— (1991a), 'Policing and Penality', *Journal of Social Justice Studies* 4: 1–26.

—— (1991b), Identifying and Reforming the Problems of the Justice System', in Carrington *et al.* (eds.), 232–70.

—— (1995) 'Law and Order and the Fallibility of the Justice System' in Brown *et al.* 1996: 309–15.

—— and Golder, H. (1987), 'Policing Sydney in the Late Nineteenth Century', in Finnane (ed.), 59–73.

—— and Hawker, B. (1983), 'The Politics of Police Independence', *Legal Service Bulletin* 161–5, 221–4.

Holdaway, S. (1983), *Inside the British Police* (Oxford: Basil Blackwell).

—— (1989), 'Discovering Structure: Studies of the British Police Occupational Culture' in Weatheritt (ed.), 55–75.

Holland, D. C. (1967), 'Police Powers and the Citizen' [1967] *Current Legal Problems* 104–19.

Holstein, J., and Miller, G. (eds.) (1993), *Reconsidering Social Constructionism* (New York: Aldine de Gruyter).

Home Office (1989), *Report of the Working Group on the Right of Silence* (London: C4 Division, Home Office).

—— (1993), *Statistical Bulletin* 21/93 (London: Home Office).

—— (1994), *Statistical Bulletin* 15/94 (London: Home Office).

—— (1996), *Statistical Bulletin* 12/96 (London: Home Office).

Homel, R. (1994), 'Can Police Prevent Crime?', in K. Bryett and C. Lewis (eds.), *Un-Peeling Tradition: Contemporary Policing* (Brisbane: Centre for Australian Public Sector Management), 7–34.

Hood, C. (1973), *The Tools of Government* (London: Macmillan).

Horton, C., and Smith, D. J. (1990), *Evaluating Police Work* (London: Policy Studies Institute).

Horwitz, M. J. (1977), 'The Rule of Law: An Unqualified Human Good?', *Yale Law Journal* 86: 561–6.

Horwitz, R. B. (1989), *The Irony of Regulatory Reform* (New York: Oxford University Press).

Hough, J. M., and Clarke, R. V. G. (1980), 'Introduction', in R. V. G. Clarke and J. M. Hough (eds.), *The Effectiveness of Policing* (Farnborough: Gower), 1–16.

Howard, M. (1995), 'To Make the Punishment Fit the Organised Crime', *Weekly Telegraph*, 15 Nov. 1995.

HRA (1914), *Historical Records of Australia*: series 1: *Governors' Despatches to and from England* (Sydney: Library Committee of the Commonwealth Parliament), i.

—— (1916), *Historical Records of Australia*: series 1: *Governors' Despatches to and from England* (Sydney: Library Committee of the Commonwealth Parliament), vii.

HUNT, A. (1993), *Explorations in Law and Society* (New York: Routledge).

HUNTER, J. (1994), 'Unreliable Memoirs and the Accused', *Criminal Law Journal* 18: 8–28, 76–89.

—— and CRONIN, K. (1995), *Evidence, Advocacy and Ethical Practice*: A *Criminal Trial Commentary* (Sydney: Butterworths).

HUNTER, M. (1994), 'Judicial Discretion: Section 78 in Practice' [1994] *Criminal Law Review* 558–65.

HUTTON, N. (1987), 'The Sociological Analysis of Courtroom Interaction', *Australian & New Zealand Journal of Criminology* 20: 110–20.

IGNATIEFF, M. (1979), 'Police and People', *New Society*, 30 Aug., 443–5.

IMBERT, P. (1988), 'Policing London', *Police Journal* 61: 199–208.

IRVING, B. (1980), *Police Interrogation*, Royal Commission on Criminal Procedure Research Study #2 (London: HMSO).

—— and MCKENZIE, I. (1989a), 'Interrogating in a Legal Framework', in R. Morgan and D. J. Smith (eds.), *Coming to Terms with Policing* (London: Routledge), 153–73.

—— and —— (1989b), *Police Interrogation* (London: Police Foundation).

—— and DUNNIGHAN, C. (1993), *Human Factors in the Quality Control of CID Investigations*, Royal Commission on Criminal Justice Research Study #5 (HMSO: London).

JACKSON, G. (1991), 'Reform of Policing in New South Wales', *Anglo-American Law Review* 20: 15–26.

JACKSON, J. D. (1990), 'Getting Criminal Justice out of Balance', in S. Livingstone and J. Morison (eds.), *Law, Society and Change* (Aldershot: Dartmouth), 114–33.

—— (1991), 'Curtailing the Right of Silence: Lessons from Northern Ireland' [1991] *Criminal Law Review* 404–15.

—— (1995), 'Interpreting the Silence Provisions: The Northern Ireland Cases' [1995] *Criminal Law Review* 587–601.

JEFFERSON, T., and GRIMSHAW, R. (1982), 'Law, Democracy and Justice', in D. Cowell, T. Jones, and J. Young (eds.), *Policing the Riots* (London: Junction Books), 82–117.

—— and —— (1984), *Controlling the Constable* (London: Frederick Muller/The Cobden Trust).

——, WALKER, M., and SENEVIRATNE, M. (1992), 'Ethnic Minorities, Crime and Criminal Justice', in Downes (ed.) 138–64.

JOHNSON, S. L. (1991), 'Confessions, Criminals and Community', *Harvard Civil Rights-Civil Liberties Law Review* 26: 327–411.

JOHNSTON, L. (1992), *The Rebirth of Private Policing* (London: Routledge).

JONES, T., NEWBURN, T., and SMITH, D. J. (1994), *Democracy and Policing* (London: Policy Studies Institute).

——, ——, and —— (1996), 'Policing and the Idea of Democracy', *British Journal of Criminology* 36: 182–98.

JOWELL, J. (1975), *Law and Bureaucracy: Administrative Discretion and the Limits of Legal Action* (New York: Denellen).

—— (1994), 'The Rule of Law Today', in Jowell and Oliver (eds.), 57–78.

—— and OLIVER, D. (eds.) (1994), *The Changing Constitution* (3rd edn., Oxford: Clarendon Press).

JUSTICE (1979), *Pre-Trial Criminal Procedure* (London: Justice).

KABLE, J. (1989), 'Williams to Carr—Where Now?', *Current Issues in Criminal Justice* 1: 9–31.

KAGAN, R. A. (1984), 'On Regulatory Inspectorates and Police', in Hawkins and Thomas (eds.), 37–64.

KAYE, T. (1991), *Unsafe and Unsatisfactory? Report of the Independent Inquiry into the Working Practices of the West Midlands Serious Crimes Squad* (London: Civil Liberties Trust).

KEE, R. (1986), *Trial and Error* (London: Hamish Hamilton).

KEITH, M. (1993), *Race, Riots and Policing: Lore and Disorder in a Multi-Racist Society* (London: UCL Press).

KELLING, G. L. (1992), 'Towards New Images of Policing', *Law and Social Inquiry* 17: 539–59.

——, PATE, T., DICKERMAN, D., and BROWN, C. (1974), *The Kansas City Preventive Patrol Experiment* (Washington, DC: Police Foundation).

KEMP, C., NORRIS, C., and FIELDING, N. G. (1992), *Negotiating Nothing: Police Decision-Making in Disputes* (Aldershot: Avebury).

KENT, J. R. (1986), *The English Village Constable 1580–1642* (Oxford: Clarendon Press).

KIDSTON, R. R. (1960), 'Confessions to Police', *Australian Law Journal* 33: 369–72.

KILLMER, T., and CORNISH, P. (1989), 'The Reform of the Right to Silence: A South Australia Police Perspective', paper presented to the Society for the Reform of the Criminal Law Conference, Sydney, Mar.

KING, H. (1956), 'Some Aspects of Police Administration in New South Wales, 1825–1851', *Journal of the Royal Australian Historical Society* 42: 205–30.

KING, M. (1981), *The Framework of Criminal Justice* (London: Croom Helm).

KINSEY, R. (1982), 'Fair Cops?', *Modern Law Review* 45: 475–9.

—— and BALDWIN, G. R. (1982), 'New Rules—Old Game: Criminal Procedure and the Context of Reform in the UK', *International Journal of the Sociology of Law* 10: 303–16.

KIRBY, M. (1979), 'Controls over Investigation of Offences and Pre-trial Treatment of Suspects', *Australian Law Journal* 53: 626–47.

—— (1991), 'Miscarriages of Justice—Our Lamentable Failure?', Child &

Co. lecture: a public lecture delivered in London on 4 June 1991 (Sydney: M. Kirby).

KLEINIG, J. (1996), *The Ethics of Policing* (Cambridge: Cambridge University Press).

KLOCKARS, C. B. (1988), 'The Rhetoric of Community Policing', in Greene and Mastrofski (eds.), 239–58.

KRANTZ, S., GILMAN, B., BENDA, C., HALLSTROM, C. R., and NADWORNY, E. J. (1979), *Police Policymaking: The Boston Experience* (Lexington, Mass.: Lexington Books).

KRYGIER, M. (1990), 'Marxism and the Rule of Law: Reflections after the Fall of Communism', *Law and Social Inquiry* 15: 633–63.

LACEY, N. (1992), 'The Jurisprudence of Discretion: Escaping the Legal Paradigm', in Hawkins (ed.), 361–88.

—— (1995), 'Contingency and Criminalisation', in I. Loveland (ed.), *Frontiers of Criminality* (London: Sweet and Maxwell), 1–27.

LaFAVE, W. R. (1965), *Arrest* (Boston, Mass.: Little, Brown and Co.).

—— (1993), 'Police Rule Making and the Fourth Amendment', in Ohlin and Remington (eds.), 211–77.

LAMBARD, W. (1599), *The Dueties of Constables, Borsholders, Tythingman, and such other lowe and lay Ministers of the Peace* (London).

LAW COMMISSION (1995), *Consent in the Criminal Law*, Law Commission Consultation Paper #139 (London: HMSO).

LAW SOCIETY (1988), *Advising a Suspect in the Police Station* (2nd edn., London: Law Society).

LAWTON, F. (1987), 'How the Right to Silence has Blocked Convictions', *Independent*, 28 Aug.

LEE, J. (1981), 'Some Structural Aspects of Police Deviance in Relations with Minority Groups', in Shearing (ed.), 49–82.

LEE, J. A. (1990), *Report of the Royal Commission of Inquiry into the Arrest, Charging and Withdrawal of Charges Against Harold James Blackburn and Matters Associated Therewith* (Sydney: NSW Government).

LEE, S. (1987), 'Towards a Jurisprudence of Consent', in J. Eekelaar and J. Bell (eds.), *Oxford Essays in Jurisprudence: third series* (Oxford: Clarendon Press), 199–220.

LEIGH, L. H. (1975), *Police Powers in England and Wales* (London: Butterworths).

—— (1985), *Police Powers in England and Wales* (2nd edn., London: Butterworths).

—— (1986), 'Some Observations on the Parliamentary History of the PACE Act 1984', in C. Harlow (ed.), *Public Law and Politics* (London: Sweet and Maxwell), 91–117

LENG, R. (1993), *The Right to Silence in Police Interrogation*, Royal Commission on Criminal Justice Research Study #10 (London: HMSO).

—— (1994), 'The Right-to-silence Debate', in Morgan and Stephenson (eds.), 18–38.

—— (1995), 'Pessimism or Professionalism?', in Noaks *et al.* (eds.), 206–15.

——, McConville, M., and Sanders, A. (1992), 'Researching the Discretions to Charge and to Prosecute', in Downes (ed.), 119–37.

Lenman, B., and Parker, G. (1980), 'The State, the Community and the Criminal Law in Early Modern Europe', in Gatrell *et al.* (eds.), 11–48.

Leo, R. (1992), 'From Coercion to Deception: The Changing Nature of Police Interrogation in America', *Crime, Law and Social Change* 18: 35–59.

—— (1994), 'Police Interrogation and Social Control', *Social & Legal Studies* 3: 93–120.

—— (1995), 'Trials and Tribulations: Courts, Ethnography, and the Need for an Evidentiary Privilege for Academic Researchers', *The American Sociologist* 26: 113–34.

—— (1996a), '*Miranda*'s Revenge: Police Interrogation as a Confidence Game', *Law and Society Review* 30: 259–88.

—— (1996b), 'Inside the Interrogation Room', *Journal of Criminal Law and Criminology* 86: 266–303.

—— (1996c), 'The Impact of *Miranda* Revisited', *Journal of Criminal Law and Criminology* 86: 621–92.

Lidstone, K. W. (1978), 'A Maze in Law!' [1978] *Criminal Law Review* 332–42.

—— (1981), 'Investigative Powers and the Rights of the Citizen' [1981] *Criminal Law Review* 454–69.

—— (1984), 'Magistrates, the Police and Search Warrants' [1984] *Criminal Law Review* 449–58.

—— and Bevan, V. (nd), *Search and Seizure under the Police and Criminal Evidence Act 1984*, A report of research into the police use of search powers provided by the Police and Criminal Evidence Act 1984 funded by the Social Science Research Council (Sheffield: Faculty of Law, University of Sheffield).

—— and Early, T. L. (1982), 'Detention for Questioning in France, Scotland and England', *International & Comparative Law Quarterly* 31: 488–512.

Loader, I. (1995), 'Policing and the Social: Questions of Symbolic Power', paper presented to the British Criminology Conference, Loughborough.

—— (1996), *Youth, Policing and Democracy* (Basingstoke: Macmillan).

Loughlin, M. (1992), *Public Law and Political Theory* (Oxford: Clarendon Press).

LRCC (1983), *Police Powers—Search and Seizure in Criminal Law Enforcement*, Working Paper #30 (Ottawa: Law Reform Commission of Canada).

—— (1985), *Arrest*, Working Paper #41 (Ottawa: Law Reform Commission of Canada).

LRCC (1988), *Our Criminal Procedure*, Report #32 (Ottawa: Law Reform Commission of Canada).

—— (1991), *Recodifying Criminal Procedure* (Ottawa: Law Reform Commission of Canada), i.

LUCAS, G. A. G. (1977), *Report of the Committee of Inquiry into the Enforcement of Criminal Law in Queensland* (Brisbane: Government Printer).

LUSHER, E. A. (1981), *Report of the Commission to Inquire into New South Wales Police Administration* (Sydney: Government Printer).

LUSTGARTEN, L. (1985), 'Democratic Constitutionalism and Police Governance', in McAuslan and McEldowney (eds.), 128–50.

—— (1986), *The Governance of Police* (London: Sweet and Maxwell).

MACINNES, C. (1974), *Mr Love and Justice* (St Albans: Panther).

MACK, K., and ANLEU, S. (1996), *Pleading Guilty* (Melbourne: Australian Institute of Judicial Administration).

MACKAY, P. (1990), 'Changes in Custody Practice since the Introduction of the Police and Criminal Evidence Act 1984', *The Criminologist* 14: 63–82.

MACKENZIE, J. (1990), 'Silence in Hampshire', *New Law Journal* 140: 696.

MACLACHLAN, G., and REID, I. (1994), *Framing and Interpretation* (Carlton: Melbourne University Press).

MAGUIRE, M. (1994), 'The Wrong Message at the Wrong Time?', in Morgan and Stephenson (eds.), 39–49.

——, MORGAN, R., and REINER, R. (eds.) (1994), *The Oxford Handbook of Criminology* (Oxford: Clarendon Press).

—— and NORRIS, C. (1992), *The Conduct and Supervision of Criminal Investigations*, Royal Commission on Criminal Justice Research Study #5 (HMSO: London).

—— and —— (1994), 'Police Investigations: Practice and Malpractice', *Journal of Law and Society* 21: 72–84.

MAHER, L. (1997), *Sexed Work: Gender, Race and Resistance in a Brooklyn Drug Market* (Oxford: Clarendon Press).

MALLESON, K. (1993), *A Review of the Appeal Process*, Royal Commission on Criminal Justice Research Study #17 (London: HMSO).

MALOUF, D. (1990), *The Great World* (London: Chatto and Windus).

—— (1993), *Remembering Babylon* (London: Chatto and Windus).

MANN, M. (1970), 'The Social Cohesion of Liberal Democracy', *American Sociological Review* 35: 423–39.

MANNING, P. (1977), *Police Work* (Cambridge, Mass.: MIT Press).

—— (1980), *The Narcs' Game: Organizational and Informational Limits on Drug Law Enforcement* (Cambridge, Mass.: MIT Press).

—— (1989), 'Occupational Culture', in W. G. Bailey (ed.), *The Encyclopaedia of Police Science* (New York: Garland), 472–5.

—— (1992), ' "Big-bang" Decisions: Notes on a Naturalistic Approach', in Hawkins (ed.), 249–85.

—— (1993), 'The Preventive Conceit', *American Behavioral Scientist* 36: 639–50.

—— and HAWKINS, K. (1989), 'Police Decision-making', in Weatheritt (ed.), 139–56.

—— and —— (1990), 'Legal Decisions: A Frame Analytic Perspective', in S. Riggins (ed.), *Beyond Goffman* (Berlin: Aldine DeGruyter), 201–33.

MARENIN, O. (1985), 'Police Performance and State Rule' [1985] *Comparative Politics* 101–22.

—— (ed.) (1996), *Policing Change, Changing Police* (New York: Garland).

MARK, R. (1977), *Policing a Perplexed Society* (London: Allen and Unwin).

MARSHALL, G. (1965), *Police and Government* (London: Methuen).

—— and LOVEDAY, B. (1994), 'The Police: Independence and Accountability', in Jowell and Oliver (eds.), 295–322.

MARX, G. (1981), 'Ironies of Social Control', *Social Problems* 28: 221–46.

—— (1992), 'Commentary', *Crime, Law and Social Change* 18: 3–34.

MASTROFSKI, S. D., and GREENE, J. R. (1993), 'Community Policing and the Rule of Law', in Weisburd *et al.* (eds.), 80–102.

—— and —— (eds.) (1989), *Community Policing* (New York: Praeger).

—— and UCHIDA, C. D. (1993), 'Transforming the Police', *Journal of Research in Crime and Delinquency* 30: 330–58.

MATZA, D. (1969), *Becoming Deviant* (Englewood Cliffs, NJ: Prentice-Hall).

MAY, R. (1990), *Criminal Evidence* (London: Sweet and Maxwell).

MCAUSLAN, P., and MCELDOWNEY, J. F. (eds.) (1985), *Law, Legitimacy and the Constitution* (London: Sweet and Maxwell).

MCBARNET, D. J. (1976), 'Pre-trial Procedures and the Construction of Conviction', in P. Carlen (ed.), *The Sociology of Law*, Sociological Review Monograph 23: 172–201.

—— (1978a), 'False Dichotomies in Criminal Justice Research', in J. Baldwin and A. K. Bottomley (eds.), *Criminal Justice* (London: Martin Robertson), 23–34.

—— (1978b), 'The Fisher Report on the Confait Case', *Modern Law Review* 41: 455–63.

—— (1979), 'Arrest: The Legal Context of Policing', in S. Holdaway (ed.), *The British Police* (London: Edward Arnold), 24–40.

—— (1981a), 'The Royal Commission and the Judges' Rules', *British Journal of Law and Society* 8: 109–17.

—— (1981b), 'Balance and Clarity: Has the Royal Commission achieved Them?' [1981] *Criminal Law Review* 445–53.

—— (1982b), 'Legal Form and Legal Mystification', *International Journal of the Sociology of Law* 10: 409–17.

—— (1983), *Conviction* (2nd edn., London: Macmillan).

—— (1984), 'Law and Capital: The Role of Legal Form and Legal Actors', *International Journal of the Sociology of Law* 12: 231–38.

McBarnet, D. J. (1992), 'It's Not What You Do But the Way that You Do It: Tax Evasion, Tax Avoidance and the Boundaries of Deviance', in Downes (ed.), 247–68.

—— and Whelan, C. (1991), 'The Elusive Spirit of the Law: Formalism and the Struggle for Legal Control', *Modern Law Review* 54: 848–73.

McConkey, K. M., Huon, G. F., and Frank, M. G. (1996), *Practical Ethics in the Police Service* (Payneham, South Australia: National Police Research Unit).

McConville, M. (1989), 'Weaknesses in the British Judicial System', *Times Higher Education Supplement*, 3 Nov.

—— (1992), 'Videotaping Interrogations', *New Law Journal* 142: 960, 962.

—— and Baldwin, J. (1981), *Courts, Prosecution, and Conviction* (Oxford: Oxford University Press).

—— and —— (1982), 'Recent Developments in English Criminal Justice and the Royal Commission on Criminal Procedure', *International Journal of the Sociology of Law* 10: 287–302.

—— and Bridges, L. (eds.) (1994), *Criminal Justice in Crisis* (Aldershot: Edward Elgar).

—— and Hodgson, J. (1993), *Custodial Legal Advice and the Right to Silence*, Royal Commission on Criminal Justice Research Study #16 (London: HMSO).

——, ——, Bridges, L., and Pavlovic, A. (1994), *Standing Accused* (Oxford: Clarendon Press).

—— and Mirsky, C. (1986–7), 'Criminal Defense of the Poor in New York City', *New York University Review of Law and Social Change* 15: 581–941.

—— and Sanders, A. (1995), 'The Case for the Prosecution and Administrative Criminology', in Noaks et al. (eds.), 191–205.

——, ——, and Leng, R. (1991a), *The Case for the Prosecution: Police Suspects and the Construction of Criminality* (London: Routledge).

——, ——, and —— (1991b), 'Has PACE Changed the Rules', *Legal Action*, Oct., 9–10.

—— and Shepherd, D. (1992), *Watching Police, Watching Communities* (London: Routledge).

McCord, J. (1992), 'Deterrence of Domestic Violence', *Journal of Research in Crime and Delinquency* 29: 229–39.

McEniery, P. (1995), 'The Regulation of Custodial Interrogation in South Australia', unpublished LL.M. research paper, Faculty of Law, University of New South Wales.

McGowan, C. (1972), 'Rule-making and the Police', *Michigan Law Review* 70: 659–94.

McIntyre, D. M. (1967), *Law Enforcement in the Metropolis* (Chicago, Ill.: American Bar Foundation).

McKenzie, I. (1990a), 'Police Handcuffed in No Man's Land', *Independent*, 31 May.

—— (1990b), 'Regulating Custodial Interviews', Ph.D. thesis, University of Bath.

—— and Gallagher, G. P. (1989), *Behind the Uniform: Policing in Britain and America* (Hemel Hempstead: Harvester).

—— and Irving, B. (1988), 'The Right of Silence', *Policing* 4: 88–105.

——, Morgan, R., and Reiner, R. (1990), 'Helping the Police with their Inquiries' [1990] *Criminal Law Review* 22–33.

McNay, L. (1994), *Foucault* (London: Polity).

McQueen, H. (1976), *A New Brittania* (revised edn., Penguin: Ringwood).

Memon, A., Bull, R., and Smith, M. (1995), 'Improving the Quality of the Police Interview', *Policing and Society* 5: 53–68.

Miller, F. W. (1969), *Prosecution* (Boston, Mass.: Little, Brown and Co.).

——, Dawson, R. O., Dix, G. E., and Parnas, R. I. (1991), *The Police Function* (Westbury, NY: Foundation Press).

Milner, N. A. (1971), *The Court and Local Law Enforcement* (Newbury Park, Cal.: Sage).

—— (1974), 'Supreme Court Effectiveness and the Police Organization', in Weistart (ed.), 22–43.

Milte, K. L., and Weber, T. A. (1977), *Police in Australia* (Sydney: Butterworths).

Ministerial Council on the Administration of Justice (1993), *Directions in Australasian Policing* (Canberra: Ministerial Council).

Mitchell, B. (1983), 'Confessions and Police Interrogation of Suspects' [1983] *Criminal Law Review* 596–604.

Miyazawa, S. (1992), *Policing in Japan* (Albany, NY: SUNY Press).

Mollen, M. (1994), *Report of the Commission to Investigate Allegations of Police Corruption and the Anti-Corruption Procedures of the Police Department* (New York: Mollen Commission).

Moore, D. B. (1991), 'Origins of the Police Mandate—the Australian Case Reconsidered', *Police Studies* 4: 107–20.

—— and Wettenhall, R. (eds.), (1994), *Keeping the Peace: Police Accountability and Oversight* (Canberra: University of Canberra/Royal Institute of Public Administration Australia).

Moore, M. H. (1992), 'Problem-solving and Community Policing', in Tonry and Morris (eds.), 99–158.

—— and Stephens, D. W. (1991), *Beyond Command and Control* (Washington: Police Executive Research Forum).

Morgan, D., and Stephenson, G. (eds.) (1994), *Suspicion and Silence: The Right to Silence in Criminal Investigations* (London: Blackstone Press).

Morgan, R. (1989), 'Detention in the Police Station', paper presented to ESRC/Police Foundation conferences, Apr./May 1989.

MORGAN, R. (1992), 'Talking about Policing', in Downes (ed.) 165–83.

——, REINER, R., and MCKENZIE, I. (1990), *Police Powers and Policy: A Study of the Work of Custody Officers*, Report to the Economic and Social Research Council (Bristol: Faculty of Law, University of Bristol, unpublished).

MORTON, J. (1988), 'When Silence is Golden', *Police Review*, 4 Nov., 2300.

—— (1989), 'Coded Questions', *Police Review*, 17 Nov. 1989, 2326–7.

MOSTON, S., and ENGELBERG, T. (1993), 'Police Questioning Techniques in Tape Recorded Interviews with Criminal Suspects', *Policing and Society* 3: 223–37.

—— and STEPHENSON, G. M. (1993a), *The Questioning and Interviewing of Suspects Outside the Police Station*, Royal Commission on Criminal Justice Research Study #22 (London: HMSO).

—— and —— (1993b), 'The Changing Face of Police Interrogation', *Journal of Community and Applied Psychology* 3: 101–15.

——, ——, and WILLIAMSON, T. M. (1992), 'The Effects of Case Characteristics on Suspect Behaviour during Police Questioning', *British Journal of Criminology* 32: 23–40.

——, ——, and —— (1993), 'The Incidence, Antecedents and Consequences of the Use of the Right to Silence during Police Questioning', *Criminal Behaviour and Mental Health* 3: 30–47.

MUIR, W. K. (1977), *Police: Streetcorner Politicians* (Chicago, Ill.: University of Chicago Press).

MUNDAY, R. (1996), 'Inferences from Silence and European Human Rights Law' [1996] *Criminal Law Review* 370–85.

MURAKAMI, A., EDELMANN, R. J., and DAVIS, P. E. (1996), 'Interrogative Suggestibility in Opiate Users', *Addiction* 91: 1365–73.

MURPHY, K. (1990), 'Do the Police get a Fair Go?', *The Bulletin*, 28 Aug. 1990, 48–57.

NEAL, D. (1991), *The Rule of Law in a Penal Colony* (Cambridge: Cambridge University Press).

NELKEN, D. (1987), 'Criminal Law and Criminal Justice', in Dennis (ed.), 139–75.

NEW ZEALAND LAW COMMISSION (1992), *Criminal Evidence: Police Questioning*, Preliminary Paper #21 (Wellington: Law Commission).

—— (1994), *Police Questioning*, Report #31 (Wellington: Law Commission).

NOAKS, L., MAGUIRE, M., and LEVI, M. (eds.) (1995), *Contemporary Issues in Criminology* (Cardiff: University of Wales Press).

NORRIE, A. (1995), Review of Ashworth: *The Criminal Process* [1995] *Public Law* 342–4.

NORRIS, C., and NORRIS, N. (1993), 'Defining Good Policing', *Policing and Society* 3: 205–21.

NORTHUMBRIA POLICE (1990), 'Efficiency and Effectiveness', in Joint Consultative Committee, *Operational Policing Review* (Surbiton: JCC), 1–81.

—— (1994), *Report of an Enquiry into the Practices and Procedures adopted by Police Officers during Interviews with George Robert Thomas Heron following the murder of Nikki Davie Allan* (Ponteland: Northumbria Police, unpublished).

NOVEMBER, J. (1993), 'R. v. *Goodwin*: The Meaning of Arrest, Unlawful Arrest and Arbitrary Detention' [1993] *New Zealand Law Journal* 54–9.

NSW LRC (1987), *Police Powers of Arrest and Detention*, Discussion Paper #16 (Sydney: NSW Law Reform Commission).

—— (1990), *Police Powers of Detention and Investigation after Arrest*, LRC Report #66 (Sydney: NSW Law Reform Commission).

—— (1993), *People with an Intellectual Disability and the Criminal Justice System*, Research Report #3 (Sydney: NSW Law Reform Commission).

NSW OMBUDSMAN (1996), *The Foster Report* (Sydney: NSW Ombudsman).

NSW POLICE (1988a), Response by the Commissioner of Police to NSW LRC 1987 (unpublished, NSW Police).

—— (1988b), *NSW Police Service 1984 to 1988 to . . .* (Sydney: NSW Police).

—— (1994), *Australian Quality Award Application* (Sydney: NSW Police).

—— (1995), *Comprehensive Review of Criminal Investigation* (Sydney: NSW Police Service).

ODGERS, S. (1985), 'Police Interrogation and the Right to Silence', *Australian Law Journal* 50: 78–95.

—— (1990), 'Police Interrogation: A Decade of Legal Development', *Criminal Law Journal* 14: 220–48.

OGUS, A. (1994), *Regulation: Legal Form and Economic Theory* (Oxford: Clarendon).

OHLIN, L. E. (1993), 'Surveying Discretion by Criminal Justice Decision Makers', in Ohlin and REMINGTON (eds.), 1–22.

—— and REMINGTON, F. J. (eds.) (1993), *Discretion in Criminal Justice* (Albany, NY: State University of New York Press).

ORFIELD, M. (1987), 'The Exclusionary Rule and Deterrence: An Empirical Study of Chicago Narcotics Officers', *University of Chicago Law Review* 54: 1016–55.

PACKER, H. (1968), *The Limits of the Criminal Sanction* (Stanford, Cal.: Stanford University Press).

PARLIAMENTARY CRIMINAL JUSTICE COMMITTEE (1995), *Report on the Review of the Criminal Justice Commission's Report on a Review of Police Powers in Queensland*, Report #27, Legislative Assembly of Queensland.

PAG (PRISONERS ACTION GROUP) (1989), 'Will Video Stop Verbal?', *Current Issues in Criminal Justice* 1: 81–3.

PALEY, R. (1989), ' "An Imperfect, Inadequate and Wretched System?" Policing London before Peel', *Criminal Justice History* 10: 95–130.

PALMER, B. D. (1981), *The Making of E. P. Thompson* (Toronto: New Hogtown Press).

—— (1990), *Descent into Discourse* (Philadelphia, Penn.: Temple University Press).

PALMER, D. (1994), 'Magistrates, Police and Power in Port Phillip', in D. Philips and S. Davies (eds.), *A Nation of Rogues?* (Melbourne: Melbourne University Press), 73–96.

PALMER, M. J., and MURPHY, B. (1989), 'Investigatory Detention—a Need or a Want?', *Australian Police Journal* 43: 126–36.

PALMER, S. H. (1988), *Police and Protest in England and Ireland 1780–1850* (Cambridge: Cambridge University Press).

PARTINGTON, M. (1985), 'The Reform of Public Law in Britain', in McAuslan and McEldowney (eds.), 191–211.

PATTENDEN, R. (1991), 'Should Confessions be Corroborated?', *Law Quarterly Review* 107: 317–39.

—— (1992), 'Evidence of Previous Malpractice by Police Witnesses and *R* v. *Edwards*' [1992] *Criminal Law Review* 549–57.

PENNER, R. (1996), 'The Canadian Experience with the Charter of Rights' [1996] *Public Law* 104–25.

PENNINGS, H., and GRESOV, C. (1986), 'Techno-economic and Structural Correlates of Organizational Culture', *Organization Studies* 7: 317–34.

PHILIPS, D. (1980), ' "A New Engine of Power and Authority": The Institutionalisation of Law-enforcement in England 1780–1830', in Gatrell *et al.* (eds.), 155–89.

PHILLIPS, C., and BROWN, D. (1997), *Entry into the Criminal Justice System* (London: HMSO).

PHILLIPS, J. D. (1993), *The Right to Silence* (Canterbury: Kent County Constabulary, for Association of Chief Police Officers).

PICKOVER, D., and GREAVES, G. (1989), 'Hurd's Off-the-shelf Reply to Silence', *Police Review*, 28 Oct. 1989, 2238–9.

PIKE, M. S. (1985), *The Principles of Policing* (Basingstoke: Macmillan).

POLICE REVIEW (1988), ' "Enormous" Increase in Use of the Right to Silence', *Police Review*, 22 Apr.. 1988, 848.

POLLARD, C. (1996), 'Public Safety, Accountability and the Courts' [1996] *Criminal Law Review* 152–61.

POLYVIOU, P. G. (1982), *Search and Seizure* (London: Duckworths).

POWELL, D. (1993), *Out West: Perceptions of Sydney's Western Suburbs* (St. Leonards: Allen Unwin).

PROSSER, T. (1982), 'Towards a Critical Public Law', *Journal of Law and Society* 9: 1–19.

PUNCH, M. (1985), *Conduct Unbecoming: The Social Construction of Police Deviance and Control* (London: Tavistock).

—— (ed.) (1983), *Control in the Police Organization* (Cambridge, Mass.: MIT Press).

QUEENSLAND POLICE SERVICE (1992), 'Submission to the Office of the Minister for Police and Emergency Services and the Criminal Justice Commission in response to the Issues Paper: "Police Powers in Queensland" ' (Brisbane: Queensland Police Service, unpublished).

RADIN, M. J. (1989), 'Reconsidering the Rule of Law', *Boston University Law Review* 69: 781–819.

RADZINOWICZ, L. (1956), *A History of English Criminal Law and its Administration from 1750* (London: Stevens), iii.

RAFTER, N. H. (1990), 'The Social Construction of Crime and Crime Control', *Journal of Research in Crime and Delinquency* 27: 376–89.

RAZ, J. (1979) *The Authority of Law* (Oxford: Clarendon Press).

RCCJ (1993), *Report of the Royal Commission on Criminal Justice*, Cm. 2263 (London: HMSO).

RCCP (1981a), *The Investigation and Prosecution of Criminal Offences in England and Wales: the Law and Procedure*, Cmnd. 8092–1 (London: HMSO).

—— (1981b), *Report of the Royal Commission on Criminal Procedure*, Cmnd. 8092 (London: HMSO).

RCP (1962), *Report of the Royal Commission on the Police*, Cmnd. 1728 (London: HMSO).

RCPPP (1929), *Report of the Royal Commission on Police Powers and Procedure*, Cmd. 3297 (London: HMSO).

REINER, R. (1991), *Chief Constables* (Oxford: Oxford University Press).

—— (1992a), *The Politics of the Police* (Hemel Hempstead: Harvester Wheatsheaf).

—— (1992b), 'Police Research in the United Kingdom', in Tonry and Morris (eds.), 435–508.

—— (1992c), 'Policing a Postmodern Society', *Modern Law Review* 55: 761–81.

—— (1994), 'Policing and the Police', in Maguire, Morgan, and Reiner (eds.), 705–72.

—— and LEIGH, L. (1994), 'Police Power', in C. McCrudden and G. Chambers (eds.), *Individual Rights and the Law in Britain* (Oxford: Clarendon Press), 69–108.

—— and MORGAN, R. (eds.) (1995), 'Special Symposium in Honour of Professor Michael Banton', *Policing and Society* 5: 95–128.

—— and SPENCER, S. (eds.) (1993), *Accountable Policing* (London: Institute for Public Policy Research).

REISS, A. J. (1970), Review of Davis: 1971, *Michigan Law Review* 68: 789–96.

—— (1971), *The Police and the Public* (New Haven, Conn.: Yale University Press).

REISS, A. J., and BORDUA, D. J. (1967), 'Environment and Organisation', in Bordua (ed.), 25–55.

REMINGTON, F. J. (1965), 'Editor's Preface', in LaFave, 1965: xv–xix.

REUSS-IANNI, E. (1983), *Two Cultures of Policing: Street Cops and Management Cops* (New Brunswick: Transaction).

—— and IANNI, F. A. J. (1983), 'Street Cops and Management Cops: Two Cultures of Policing', in Punch (ed.), 251–74.

RICHARDSON, G., and GENN, H. (eds.) (1994), *Administrative Law and Government Action* (Oxford: Clarendon Press).

ROBINSON, C. D. (1979), 'Ideology as History: A Look at the Way Some English Police Historians Look at the Police', *Police Studies* 2: 35–49.

ROCK, P. (1994), 'Introduction', in *id.* (ed.), *History of Criminology* (Aldershot: Dartmouth), xi–xxix.

—— (1995), 'Sociology and the Stereotype of the Police', *Journal of Law and Society* 22: 17–25.

ROSE, D. (1992), *A Climate of Fear* (London: Bloomsbury).

—— (1996), *In the Name of the Law* (London: Jonathan Cape).

ROTHMAN, D. (1980), *Conscience and Convenience* (Boston, Mass.: Little, Brown).

RUBINSTEIN, J. (1973), *City Police* (New York: Ballantine).

RUSSELL, P. (1990), Speech to the Third International Criminal Law Congress, Hobart.

RYAN, C. L., and WILLIAMS, K. S. (1986), 'Police Discretion' [1986] *Public Law* 285–311.

SALLMANN, P., and WILLIS, J. (1984), *Criminal Justice in Australia* (Melbourne: Oxford University Press).

SANDERS, A. (1987a), 'Some Dangers of Policy Oriented Research', in Dennis (ed.), 203–19.

—— (1987b), 'Constructing the Case for the Prosecution', *Journal of Law and Society* 14: 229–53.

—— (1990), 'Judicial Creativity and Suspects' Rights', *Legal Action* (Jan.), 7–8.

—— (1991), 'The Ideology of "Safeguards" in Criminal Justice: The Case of the Custody Officer', paper presented to the British Criminology Conference, York, July 1991.

—— (1992), 'Reforming the Prosecution System', *Political Quarterly* 63: 25–36.

—— (1993), 'Controlling the Discretion of the Individual Officer', in Reiner and Spencer (eds.), 81–112.

—— (1994a), 'From Suspect to Trial', in Maguire *et al.* (eds.), 773–818.

—— (1994b), Book review, *Modern Law Review* 57: 675–9.

—— and BRIDGES, L. (1990), 'Access to Legal Advice and Police Malpractice' [1990] *Criminal Law Review* 494–509.

——, ——-, MULVANEY, A., and CROZIER, G. (1989), *Advice and Assistance at Police Stations and the 24 Hour Duty Solicitor Scheme* (London: Lord Chancellor's Department).

—— and YOUNG, R. (1994a), *Criminal Justice* (London: Butterworths).

—— and —— (1994b), 'The Rule of Law, Due Process and Pre-trial Criminal Justice', *Current Legal Problems* 47(2): 125–56.

SANDERS, W. (1977), *Detective Work* (New York: Free Press).

SANTOS, B. DE S. (1987), 'Law: A Map of Misreading', *Journal of Law and Society* 14: 279–302.

SARBIN, T. R., and KITSUSE, J. I. (1994), 'A Prologue', in T. R. Sarbin and J. I. Kitsuse (eds.), *Constructing the Social* (London: Sage), 1–18.

SARRE, R. (1994), 'The Legal Powers of Private Police and Security Providers', in P. Moyle (ed.), *Private Prisons and Police* (Leichhardt: Pluto), 259–80.

SAVILLE-TROIKE, M. (1985), 'The Place of Silence in an Integrated Theory of Communication', in D. Tannen and M. Saville-Troike (eds.), *Perspectives on Silence* (Norwood, NJ: Ablex), 1–19.

SCARMAN, L. (1981), *The Brixton Disorders*, Cmnd. 8427 (London: HMSO).

SCHULHOFER, S. J. (1996), '*Miranda*'s Practical Effect: Substantial Benefits and Vanishly Small Social Costs', *Northwestern University Law Review* 90: 500–63.

SCRATON, P. (1987a), 'Editor's Preface', in Scraton (ed.), vii–xi.

—— (1987b), 'Unreasonable Force', in Scraton (ed.), 145–89.

—— (ed.) (1987), *Law, Order and the Authoritarian State* (Milton Keynes: Open University Press).

SHARPE, J. (1983), 'Policing the Parish in Early Modern England', in Past and Present (ed.), *Police and Policing* (Oxford: Past and Present Society), 1–25.

SHEARING, C. D. (1992), 'The Relation Between Public and Private Policing', in Tonry and Morris (eds.), 399–434.

—— (1995), 'Transforming the Culture of Policing', in Dixon (ed.), 54–61.

—— (1996), 'Reinventing Policing: Policing as Governance', in Marenin (ed.), 286–307.

—— (ed.) (1981), *Organizational Police Deviance* (Toronto: Butterworth).

—— and ERICSON, R. V. (1991), 'Culture as Figurative Action', *British Journal of Sociology* 42:481–506.

—— and STENNING, P. C. (1982), *Private Security and Private Justice* (Quebec: Institute for Research on Public Policy).

—— and —— (eds.) (1987), *Private Policing* (Newbury Park, Cal.: Sage).

SHEPHERD, E., MORTIMER, A., and MOBASHERIS, R. (1995), 'The Police Caution', *Counsel*, Sept.–Oct.

—— (ed.) (1993), *Aspects of Police Interviewing*, Issues in Criminological and Legal Psychology #18 (Leicester: British Psychological Society).

Sherman, L. W. (1974), 'Explanation and Policy Recommendations', in L. W. Sherman (ed.), *Police Corruption: A Sociological Perspective* (New York: Anchor Books), 268–76.

—— (1978), *Scandal and Reform* (Berkeley, Cal.: University of California Press).

—— (1982), 'Learning Police Ethics', *Criminal Justice Ethics* 1: 10–19.

—— (1992a), 'Attacking Crime: Police and Crime Control', in Tonry and Morris (eds.), 159–230.

—— (1992b), *Policing Domestic Violence: Experiments and Dilemmas* (New York: Free Press).

—— (1993), 'Why Crime Control is not Reactionary', in Weisburd *et al.* (eds.), 171–89.

—— (1995), 'The Truly Conceited: *Ex Cathedra* Doctrine and the Policing of Crime', in Dixon (ed.), 45–51.

—— and Berk, R. A. (1984), 'The Specific Deterrent Effects of Arrest for Domestic Assault', *American Sociological Review* 49: 261–72.

Sieghart, P. (1985), 'Sanctions Against Abuse of Police Power' [1985] *Public Law* 440–7.

Simpson, H. B. (1895), 'The Office of Constable' *English Historical Review* 10: 625–41.

Singh, S. (1994), 'Understanding the Long-term Relationship between Police and Policed', in McConville and Bridges (eds.), 162–72.

Sitkin, S. M. and Bies, R. J. (eds.) (1994), *The Legalistic Organization* (Thousand Oaks, Cal.: Sage).

Shklar, J. N. (1987), 'Political Theory and the Rule of Law', in A. C. Hutchinson and P. Monahan (eds.), *The Rule of Law* (Toronto: Carswell), 1–16.

Skogan, W. G. (1990), *The Police and the Public in England and Wales: A British Crime Survey Report* (London: HMSO).

Skolnick, J. H. (1975), *Justice Without Trial* (2nd edn., New York: John Wiley).

—— (1982: 1983), Review of McBarnet, *Journal of Criminal Law and Criminology* 73: 1329–35.

—— (1993), 'Justice Without Trial Revisited', in Weisburd *et al.* (eds.), 190–205.

—— (1994), 'The Challenge of Crime in the 1990s', in *id. Justice Without Trial* (3rd edn., New York: Macmillan).

—— and Fyfe, J. J. (1993), *Above the Law* (New York: Free Press).

—— and Leo, R. A. (1992), 'The Ethics of Deceptive Interrogation', *Criminal Justice Ethics* 11: 3–12.

Skyrme, T. (1991), *History of the Justices of the Peace* (Chichester: Barry Rose), ii.

Smart, C. (1995), *Law, Crime and Sexuality* (London: Sage).

SMITH, A. T. H. (1985), 'Comment I' [1985] *Public Law* 608–11.

SMITH, D. J. (1986), 'The Framework of Law and Policing Practice', in J. Benyon and C. Bourne (eds.), *The Police* (Oxford: Pergamon), 85–94.

—— (1988), 'Mr Lustgarten and the Case of the Honest Copper', *Oxford Journal of Legal Studies* 8: 434–41.

—— (1995), 'Case Construction and the Goals of Criminal Process', paper presented to the British Criminology Conference, Loughborough, July 1995.

—— and GRAY, J. (1985), *Police and People in London* (London: Policy Studies Institute).

SMITH, J. C. (1959), 'Comment on R v. *Powell-Mantle*' [1959] *Criminal Law Review* 445–8.

—— (1964), 'The New Judges' Rules' [1964] *Criminal Law Review* 176–82.

SMITH, P. (1993), *Clint Eastwood: A Cultural Production* (Minneapolis, Minn.: University of Minnesota Press).

SOFTLEY, P. (1980), *Police Interrogation: An Observational Study of Four Stations*, Royal Commission on Criminal Procedure Research Study # 4 (London: HMSO).

SOUTH, N. (1989), 'Reconstructing Policing', in R. Matthews (ed.), *Privatizing Criminal Justice* (London: Sage), 76–104.

SPARROW, M. K., MOORE, M. H., and KENNEDY, D. M. (1990), *Beyond 911: A New Era for Policing* (New York: Basic Books).

STANKO, E. (1995), 'Policing Domestic Violence', in Dixon (ed.), 31–44.

STATEWATCH (1996), 'Policing the Streets: Stop and Search Powers in 1995', *Statewatch* 6(4): 13–15.

STEEDMAN, C. (1984), *Policing the Victorian Community* (London: Routledge and Kegan Paul).

STEER, D. (1980), *Uncovering Crime: The Police Role*, Royal Commission on Criminal Procedure Research Study #7 (London: HMSO).

STEVENSON, J. (1979), *Popular Disturbances in England 1700–1870* (London: Longman).

STREET, H. (1963), *Freedom, the Individual and the Law* (3rd edn., Harmondsworth: Penguin).

STURMA, M. (1983), *Vice in a Vicious Society: Crime and Convicts in Mid-Nineteenth Century New South Wales* (St Lucia: University of Queensland Press).

STYLES, J. (1987), 'The Emergence of the Police', *British Journal of Criminology* 27: 15–22.

SUTTON, P. (1986), 'The Fourth Amendment in Action: An Empirical View of the Search Warrant Process', *Criminal Law Bulletin* 22: 405–29.

TAPPER, C. (1990), *Cross on Evidence* (7th edn., London: Butterworths).

TEH, G. L. (1973), 'Detention for Interrogation', *Melbourne University Law Review* 9: 11–41.

TENDLER, S. (1988), 'Nothing You Want to Know about Everything', *Police Review*, 15 July 1988, 1488.

THOMAS, G. C. (1996a), 'Is *Miranda* a Real-world Failure?', *University of California Law Review* 43: 821–37.

—— (1996b), 'Plain Talk about the *Miranda* Empirical Debate', *University of California Law Review* 43: 933–59.

THOMPSON, E. P. (1963), *The Making of the English Working Class* (Harmondsworth: Penguin).

—— (1977), *Whigs and Hunters* (Harmondsworth: Peregrine).

—— (1980), *Writing by Candlelight* (London: Merlin).

—— (1993), *Customs in Common* (Harmondsworth: Penguin).

—— (1995), 'Agenda for Radical History', *Critical Inquiry* 21: 299–304.

THOMPSON, F. M. L. (ed.) (1990), *The Cambridge Social History of Britain 1750–1950* (Cambridge: Cambridge University Press), iii.

TIFFANY, L. P., McINTYRE, D. M., and ROTENBERG, D. L. (1967), *Detection of Crime* (Boston, Mass.: Little, Brown and Co.).

TOMASIC, R., and BOTTOMLEY, S. (1993), *Directing the Top 500* (St Leonards, NSW: Allen and Unwin).

TONRY, M., and MORRIS, N. (eds.) (1992), *Modern Policing* (Chicago, Ill.: University of Chicago Press).

TRUBECK, D. M. (1977), 'Complexity and Contradiction in the Legal Order', *Law and Society Review* 11: 529–69.

TWINING, W. (1973), 'The Way of the Baffled Medic: Prescribe First; Diagnose Later—If at All', *Journal of the Society of Public Teachers of Law* 12: 348–55.

TYLER, T. R. (1990), *Why People Obey the Law* (New Haven, Conn.: Yale University Press).

UNGER, R. M. (1976), *Law in Modern Society* (New York: The Free Press).

VAN DUIZEND, R., SUTTON, L. P., and CARTER, C. A. (1985), *The Search Warrant Process: Preconceptions, Perceptions, Practices* (Washington: National Center for State Courts).

VAN MAANEN, J. (1974), 'Working the Street: A Developmental View of Police Behaviour', in H. Jacob (ed.), *The Potential for Reform of Criminal Justice* (Beverley Hills, Cal.: Sage), 83–130.

—— (1978), 'On Watching the Watchers', in P. Manning and J. Van Maanen (eds.), *Policing* (Santa Monica, Cal.: Goodyear), 309–49.

—— and PENTLAND, P. T. (1994), 'Cops and Auditors: The Rhetoric of Records', in Sitkin and Bies (eds.), 53–90.

VEGA, J. (1988), 'Coercion and Consent: Classic Liberal Concepts in Texts on Sexual Violence', *International Journal of the Sociology of Law* 16: 75–89.

VENNARD, J. (1984), 'Disputes Within Trials over the Admissibility and Accuracy of Incriminating Statements'[1984] *Criminal Law Review* 15–24.

VINCENT, C. L. (1990), *Police Officer* (Ottawa: Carlton University Press).

WADE, H. W. R. (1988), *Administrative Law* (Oxford: Clarendon Press).

WAIGHT, P. K., and WILLIAMS, C. R. (1985), *Cases and Materials on the Law of Evidence* (Sydney: The Law Book Company).

WALD, M. R., AYRES, D., HESS, D. W., SCHANTZ, M., and WHITEBREAD, C. H. (1967), 'Interrogations in New Haven', *Yale Law Journal* 76: 1519–1648.

WALDRON, J. (1990), *The Law* (London: Routledge).

WALKER, C., and STARMER, K. (eds.) (1993), *Justice in Error* (London: Blackstone Press).

WALKER, N. (1996a), 'Defining Core Police Tasks: The Neglect of the Symbolic Dimension?', *Policing and Society* 6: 53–71.

—— (1996b), 'Policing the European Union', in Marenin (ed.), 251–77.

WALKER, R. (1984), 'The New South Wales Police Force, 1862–1900', *Journal of Australian Studies* 15: 25–38.

WALKER, S. (1977), *A Critical History of Police Reform* (Lexington, Mass.: Lexington Books).

—— (1980), *Popular Justice: A History of American Criminal Justice* (New York: Oxford University Press).

—— (1986), 'Controlling the Cops: A Legislative Approach to Police Rulemaking', *University of Detroit Law Review* 63: 361–91.

—— (1988), *The Rule Revolution: Reflections on the Transformation of American Criminal Justice, 1950–1988* (Madison, Wisc.: Institute for Legal Studies).

—— (1989), 'Conclusion: Paths to Police Reform—Reflections on 25 Years of Change', in D. J. Kenney (ed.), *Police and Policing* (New York: Praeger), 271–84.

—— (1992), 'Origins of the Contemporary Criminal Justice Paradigm: the American Bar Foundation Survey, 1953–1969', *Justice Quarterly* 9: 47–76.

—— (1993a), *Taming the System: The Control of Discretion in Criminal Justice 1950–1990* (New York: Oxford University Press).

—— (1993b), 'Historical Roots of the Legal Control of Police Behaviour', in Weisburd *et al.* (eds.), 32–55.

WALKLEY, J. (1987), *Police Interrogation* (London: Police Review).

WAMBAUGH, J. (1976), *The Choir Boys* (London: Weidenfeld and Nicolson).

WASBY, S. L. (1976), *Small Town Police and the Supreme Court: Hearing the Word* (Lexington, Mass.: Lexington Books).

WASIK, M., and TAYLOR, R. D. (1995), *Blackstone's Guide to the Criminal Justice and Public Order Act 1994* (London: Blackstone Press).

WEATHERBURN, D., MATKA, E., and LIND, B. (1996), *Crime Perception and Reality: Public Perceptions of the Risk of Criminal Victimisation in Australia* (Sydney: Bureau of Crime Statistics and Research).

WEATHERITT, M. (1986), *Innovations in Policing* (London: Croom Helm).

WEATHERITT, M. (1988), 'Community Policing: Rhetoric or Reality', in Mastrofski and Greene (eds.), 153–75.

—— (ed.) (1989), *Police Research* (Aldershot: Avebury).

WEBSDALE, N. (1991), 'Disciplining the Non-disciplinary Spaces', *Policing and Society* 2: 89–115.

WEINBERGER, B. (1991), 'Are the Police Professional? An Historical Account of the British Police Institution', in C. Emsley and B. Weinberger (eds.), *Policing Western Europe* (Westport, Conn.: Greenwood Press), 74–89.

WEISBURD, D., and UCHIDA, C., with GREEN, L. (1993), 'Raising Questions of Law and Order', in Weisburd *et al.* (eds.), 3–9.

—— and ——, with —— (eds.) (1993), *Police Innovation and Control of the Police* (New York: Springer-Verlag).

WEISTART, J. C. (ed.) (1974), *Police Practices* (Dobbs Ferry, NY: Oceana Publications).

WERTHEIMER, A. (1987), *Coercion* (Princeton, NJ: Princeton University Press).

WHITE, S. O. (1972), 'A Perspective on Police Professionalization', *Law and Society Review* 72: 61–85.

WILLIAMS, G. (1960), 'Questioning by the Police' [1960] *Criminal Law Review* 325–46.

—— (1962), 'England', in C. R. Sowle (ed.), *Police Power and Individual Freedom* (Chicago, Ill.: Aldine Publishing), 41–8, 185–93.

—— (1987), 'The Tactic of Silence', *New Law Journal* 137: 1107.

WILLIAMS, G. H. (1984), *The Law and Politics of Police Discretion* (Westport, Conn.: Greenwood Press).

WILLIAMS, J. (1993), *Bloody Valentine: A Killing in Cardiff* (London: Harper Collins).

WILLIAMS, R. (1977), *Marxism and Literature* (Oxford: Oxford University Press).

WILLIAMSON, T. (1990a), 'Are Nice Cops Winning? Trends in Police Questioning', paper presented to the British Psychological Society.

—— (1990b), 'Strategic Changes in Police Interrogation', Ph.D. thesis, University of Kent.

—— (1993), 'From Interrogation to Investigative Interviewing', *Journal of Community and Applied Psychology* 3: 89–99.

—— (1994), 'Reflections on Current Police Practice', in Morgan and Stephenson (eds.), 107–16.

WILLIS, C. (1983), *The Use, Effectiveness and Impact of Police Stop and Search Powers*, Home Office Research and Planning Unit paper #15 (London: HMSO).

——, MACLEOD, J., and NAISH, P. (1988), *The Tape Recording of Police Interviews with Suspects* (London: HMSO).

WILLIS, J., and SALLMANN, P. (1985), 'The Debate about Section 460 of the

Victorian Crimes Act', *Australian and New Zealand Journal of Criminology* 18: 215–37.

WILSON, J. Q. (1968), *Varieties of Police Behaviour* (Cambridge, Mass.: Harvard University Press).

WILSON, J. V., and ALPRIN, G. M. (1974), 'Controlling Police Conduct: Alternatives to the Exclusionary Rule', in Weistart (ed.), 44–55.

WOLCHOVER, D., and HEATON-ARMSTRONG, A. (1996), *Wolchover and Heaton-Armstrong on Confession Evidence* (London: Sweet & Maxwell).

WOOD, J. R. T (1996a), *Interim Report of the Royal Commission into the NSW Police Service* (Sydney: Royal Commission).

—— (1996b), *Immediate Measures for the Reform of the Police Service of New South Wales*, Interim Report of the Royal Commission into the NSW Police Service (Sydney: Royal Commission).

WOOTTEN, J. H. (1991), *Report of the Inquiry into the Death of David John Gundy*, Royal Commission into Aboriginal Deaths in Custody.

WORDEN, R. E. (1989), 'Situational and Attitudinal Explanations of Police Behaviour', *Law and Society Review* 23: 668–711.

WORRALL, A. (1990), *Offending Women* (London: Routledge).

WRIGHT, A., and BURKE, M. (1995), 'The Greater Manchester Blue Book', *Policing* 4: 331–41.

WRIGHTSON, K. (1980), 'Two Concepts of Order: Justices, Constables and Jurymen in Seventeenth Century England', in J. Brewer and J. Styles (eds.), *An Ungovernable People* (London: Hutchinson), 21–46.

WRONG, D. (1961), 'The Oversocialized Conception of Man in Modern Sociology', *American Sociological Review* 26: 183–93.

YEAGER, D. (1990), 'Rethinking Custodial Interrogation', *American Criminal Law Review* 28: 1–71.

YOUNG, J. (1994a), 'Incessant Chatter: Recent Paradigms in Criminology', in Maguire *et al.* (eds.), 69–124.

—— (1994b), *Policing the Streets: Stops and Search in North London* (Enfield: Centre for Criminology, Middlesex University).

YOUNG, M. (1991), *An Inside Job: Policing and Police Culture in Britain* (Oxford: Clarendon).

—— (1993), *In the Sticks: Cultural Identity in a Rural Police Force* (Oxford: Clarendon).

YOUNG, N. H. (1989), *Justice Regained* (Annandale: Federation Press).

YOUNG, P. W. (1986), *The Law of Consent* (Sydney: The Law Book Company).

ZANDER, M. (1977), 'When is an Arrest Not an Arrest?', *New Law Journal* 127: 352–4, 379–82.

—— (1979), 'The Investigation of Crime' [1979] *Criminal Law Review* 203–19.

—— (1988), *A Matter of Justice* (London: Taurus).

ZANDER, M. (1994), 'Abolition of the Right to Silence, 1972–1994', in Morgan and Stephenson (eds.), 141–55.

—— (1995), *The Police and Criminal Evidence Act 1984* (London: Sweet and Maxwell).

—— and HENDERSON, P. (1993), *The Crown Court Study*, Royal Commission on Criminal Justice Research Study # 19 (London: HMSO).

ZDENDOWSKI, G., and BROWN, D. (1982), *The Prison Struggle* (Ringwood: Penguin).

ZELLICK, G. J. (ed.) (1985), 'All Souls—*Public Law* Seminar: Dicey and the Constitution' [1985] *Public Law* 583–723.

ZUCKERMAN, A. (1989), 'Trial by Unfair Means' [1989] *Criminal Law Review* 855–65.

—— (1991), 'Miscarriage of Justice and Judicial Responsibility' [1991] *Criminal Law Review* 492–500.

Index